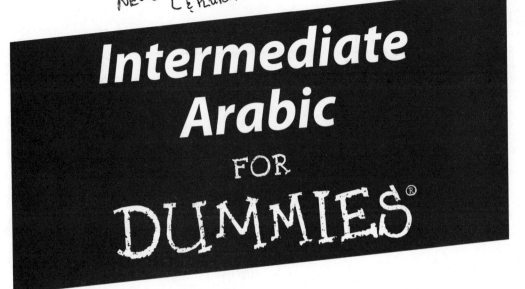

Intermediate Arabic
FOR
DUMMIES®

by Keith Massey, PhD

WILEY

Wiley Publishing, Inc.

Intermediate Arabic For Dummies®

Published by
Wiley Publishing, Inc.
111 River St.
Hoboken, NJ 07030-5774
www.wiley.com

WILEY

Intermediate Arabic For Dummies®

The Arabic Letters

The following tables show the Arabic and English transliteration characters used to represent Arabic letters in this book. I separate the consonants and vowels into two tables. The consonants are in the traditional order of the Arabic alphabet, which you need to know in order to look things up in the Arabic-English dictionary at the back of this book or in any larger dictionary you might buy. In parentheses after the transliteration, you can find out whether the consonant is a Sun Letter (SL) or a Moon Letter (ML). A discussion of the Sun and Moon Letters can be found in Chapter 2. A full lesson on writing is in Chapter 3.

The Arabic Consonants

Arabic Script	English Transliteration	Arabic Script	English Transliteration
ء	' (ML)	ض	D (SL)
ب	b (ML)	ط	T (SL)
ت	t (SL)	ظ	DH (ML)
ث	th (SL)	ع	3 (SL)
ج	j (ML)	غ	gh (ML)
ح	H (ML)	ف	f (ML)
خ	kh (ML)	ق	q (ML)
د	d (SL)	ك	k (ML)
ذ	dh (SL)	ل	l (SL)
ر	r (SL)	م	m (ML)
ز	z (SL)	ن	n (SL)
س	s (SL)	ه	h (ML)
ش	sh (SL)	و	w (ML)
ص	S (SL)	ي	y (ML)

The Arabic Vowels

Arabic Script	English Transliteration
َ	a
ِ	i
ُ	u
ا	aa
ي	ii
و	uu

Intermediate Arabic For Dummies®

Forming the Past Tense Verb

The past tense is produced with a system of suffixes. You use the same suffixes regardless of which of the ten verb forms you're using. (To examine the ten verb forms, you can consult either Chapter 9 or Appendix A.) Here's a table showing the past tense of a typical Form I verb so you can spot the suffixes in a pinch.

Past tense conjugation for شَرِبَ (shariba; *to drink*)	
شَرِبْتُ ('anaa sharibtu; *I drank*)	شَرِبْنا (naHnu sharibnaa; *we drank*)
شَرِبْتَ ('anta sharibta; *you drank*) شَرِبْتِ ('anti sharibti; *you drank*)	شَرِبْتُمْ ('antum sharibtum; *you drank*) شَرِبْتُنَّ ('antunna sharibtunna; *you drank*)
شَرِبَ (huwa shariba; *he drank*) شَرِبَتْ (hiya sharibat; *she drank*)	شَرِبوا (hum sharibuu; *they drank*) شَرِبْنَ (hunna sharibna; *they drank*)
شَرِبَتْ كُلَّ القَهْوَةِ مِنْ جَديد. (sharibat kulla-I-qahwati min jadiid. *She drank all the coffee again.*)	

Forming the Present Tense Verb

The system of prefixes and suffixes that make up the present tense are the same in all of the ten verb forms. You use these all the time. Remember that you can form the future tense just by adding the prefix سَ (sa-) to the beginning of these verbs. The following table shows the present tense of the verb شَرِبَ (shariba; *to drink*).

Present tense conjugation for شَرِبَ (shariba; *to drink*)	
أَشْرَبُ ('anaa 'ashrabu; *I drink*)	نَشْرَبُ (naHnu nashrabu; *we drink*)
تَشْرَبُ ('anta tashrabu; *you drink*) تَشْرَبِينَ ('anti tashrabiina; *you drink*)	تَشْرَبُونَ ('antum tashrabuuna; *you drink*) تَشْرَبْنَ ('antunna tashrabna; *you drink*)
يَشْرَبُ (huwa yashrabu; *he drinks*) تَشْرَبُ (hiya tashrabu; *she drinks*)	يَشْرَبُونَ (hum yashrabuuna; *they drink*) يَشْرَبْنَ (hunna yashrabna; *they drink*)
هَلْ تَشْرَبِينَ شاي أَمْ قَهْوة؟ (hal tashrabiina shaay 'am qahwa? *Do you drink tea or coffee?*)	

For Dummies: Bestselling Book Series for Beginners

About the Author

Keith Massey has been studying languages his whole life, starting with high school Latin and continuing to a PhD in Biblical Hebrew and Arabic at the University of Wisconsin-Madison. After 9/11, he went to work at the Top Secret National Security Agency as an Arabic linguist, where he served for more than four years. He now teaches Latin and Arabic in New Jersey, summering with his wife in her native Romania. An avid traveler, Keith has visited 15 different countries, 5 of which have been Arabic-speaking countries.

Dedication

To my father Bill and my late mother Nancy, who taught me the value of hard work.

And to Dustin Cowell, my first Arabic instructor. May this book further the mutual understanding between cultures to which you have devoted your life.

Author's Acknowledgments

First and foremost, I want to thank my wife, Adriana, for her support as I wrote this book.

Thanks to my agent, Barb Doyen, for her encouragement throughout this process. And to all the people at Wiley Publishing, especially to project editor Stephen Clark and copy editor Jessica Smith for their extraordinary patience and enormous talent in this project. Thanks also goes to acquisitions editor Michael Lewis, senior copy editors Sarah Faulkner and Danielle Voirol, and technical editor Dr. Haitham M. Alkhateeb.

Last but not least, thanks to my former colleagues David, Jennifer, Michael, and Ron for their friendship at the Fort and beyond as well as to my students Arielle Shahid and Sherron Tynan for their helpful suggestions on the manuscript.

Publisher's Acknowledgments

We're proud of this book; please send us your comments through our Dummies online registration form located at www.dummies.com/register/.

Some of the people who helped bring this book to market include the following:

Acquisitions, Editorial, and Media Development

Project Editor: Stephen R. Clark

Acquisitions Editor: Michael Lewis

Copy Editor: Jessica Smith

Editorial Program Coordinator:
Erin Calligan Mooney

Technical Editor: Haitham M. Alkhateeb

Editorial Manager: Christine Meloy Beck

Editorial Assistants: Joe Niesen, David Lutton

Cartoons: Rich Tennant (www.the5thwave.com)

Composition Services

Project Coordinator: Katie Key

Layout and Graphics: Carl Byers, Carrie A. Cesavice

Proofreaders: Jessica Kramer, Shannon Ramsey

Indexer: Carol A. Burbo

Special Help: Sarah Faulkner and Danielle Voirol

Publishing and Editorial for Consumer Dummies

Diane Graves Steele, Vice President and Publisher, Consumer Dummies

Joyce Pepple, Acquisitions Director, Consumer Dummies

Kristin A. Cocks, Product Development Director, Consumer Dummies

Michael Spring, Vice President and Publisher, Travel

Kelly Regan, Editorial Director, Travel

Publishing for Technology Dummies

Andy Cummings, Vice President and Publisher, Dummies Technology/General User

Composition Services

Gerry Fahey, Vice President of Production Services

Debbie Stailey, Director of Composition Services

Contents at a Glance

Table of Contents

Introduction

*I*f you've picked up this book, you've likely succeeded in learning the beginning level of Modern Standard Arabic. مَبْروك! (**mabruuk!** *Congratulations!*) What you've accomplished is no easy feat. Unlike the Romance languages, such as French and Spanish, your English didn't really help you at all with Arabic. Instead, you were learning a language with completely different ways of expressing everything.

Now you're ready to take your Arabic to the next level and improve your writing skills. You may be a student in an Arabic course looking for something to supplement your course materials and help you get a higher grade. Or perhaps you plan to visit an Arabic-speaking country sometime soon. Or maybe you're conducting business with Arabic speakers and know that being able to write an official letter in Arabic will give you an edge (and it will). Whatever your reason, *Intermediate Arabic For Dummies* can help you achieve your particular needs. You'll even have some fun along the way.

About This Book

Intermediate Arabic For Dummies is primarily a workbook for people who have a basic to beginning knowledge of Arabic and are ready to move to the next level of ability by improving their writing skills. That's why it's important that you not just read this book, but you use it as well! Write notes to yourself in the margin, and highlight things you want to concentrate on.

More importantly, however, you should complete each exercise in your own handwriting in the spaces provided. Then you can easily compare your answers with the correct answers provided in the key at the end of each chapter. You may even want to reinforce each exercise by then writing out the answer again to correct any mistakes you made. Believe it or not, you'll remember things you see in your own handwriting much more efficiently than you would by just looking at the type-written answers.

Each chapter of this book gives you exercises that let you practice your Arabic writing in the topic that's being focused on. I include many different types of exercises. Some are fill-in-the-blanks. Others are more involved, giving you the chance to edit or compose different types of communications, such as business letters and e-mails. This book can help you learn everything you need to confidently compose and read higher-level communications.

Remember that this book is a reference tool that doesn't have to be read from cover to cover. Instead, you can just review the topics that you need to know about — when you need to know about them. Check out the Table of Contents or the Index to find the topic you're interested in. Feel free to bounce around the book and skip any of the chapters that don't pertain to you (such as the chapter on the alphabet if you already know how to read and write it). The beauty of this book is that each chapter is a self-contained unit that doesn't assume knowledge of the others.

Conventions Used in This Book

To help you easily digest the information that you see in this book, I use the following conventions:

- ✔ All Arabic words and examples are presented in both Arabic script and English transliteration. The English transliteration is in **bold.**

- ✔ English translations of Arabic examples, both individual words and sentences, are *italicized*.

- ✔ Arabic doesn't have capital letters like English does. Because the transliteration method makes use of some capital letters to distinguish among Arabic sounds, the transliteration also won't be automatically capitalized.

- ✔ Answer Keys are provided at the end of each chapter. That way you don't lose time searching in the back of the book for specific exercises.

- ✔ I use several abbreviations throughout the book. Most of them are pretty intuitive:
  - F (feminine)
  - M (masculine)
  - S (singular)
  - P (plural)

- ✔ To reduce clutter in the writing, I follow the common convention of not writing redundant vowels in my Arabic. Because there's always a ˊ (**fatHa**) preceding a ة (**taa' marbuuTa**), I don't write out the ˊ (**fatHa**). I also don't write the ˊ (**fatHa**) or ˚ (**sukuun**) of the definite article الـ (**'alif laam**). After all, those sounds can always be assumed. I do, however, always write a ّ (**shadda**) over a sun letter following the الـ (**'alif laam**). (To discover more about the vowels, see Chapter 3. For an exploration of the الـ (**'alif laam**), go to Chapter 2.)

- ✔ I don't always include the formal and final vowels on nouns in the examples and exercises in this book because they usually aren't pronounced in formal media sources. Chapters that focus on learning the formal and final vowels will, of course, comprehensively include them.

Foolish Assumptions

As someone interested in learning an intermediate level of Arabic, I assume that your basic or beginning knowledge includes the following:

- ✔ You have personal motivations for advancing to the next level in your Arabic.

- ✔ You don't want a book that's just a grammar textbook. You know where to find those. You're after something that introduces a few important topics in each chapter and then covers them fully.

✔ You have experience with the fundamentals of Arabic grammar. This includes knowing the present, future, and past tenses of the verb. You understand the rules for making a noun definite and for constructing simple **'iDaafas.** You're also familiar with the more common prepositions and particles of Arabic. If you're a bit rusty on any of these topics, don't worry — Chapters 1 and 2 give you the chance to review those things.

However, I don't assume that you know how to read and write in the Arabic alphabet. In fact, if you learned your beginning Arabic from *Arabic For Dummies* by Amine Bouchentouf (Wiley), you know that the alphabet wasn't included there. Not including this information allowed you to concentrate instead on speaking ability. But if you haven't studied the Arabic alphabet yet, you need to master it before you can consider yourself at the intermediate level. In Chapter 3, I help you learn it in a thorough and engaging way. In the meantime, all exercises and lessons include Arabic script and English transliteration for you to get started improving your Arabic right away.

How This Book Is Organized

Intermediate Arabic For Dummies is divided into six parts. The parts begin with the basics of the language and the alphabet and continue through exploration of the nouns, verbs, and particles. Each part has at least two chapters where you can discover the topic of that part in depth. Here's how the various parts break down.

Part I: Polishing Your Arabic Skills

In this part, you review the alphabet, the numbers, and other words necessary to express things like dates and time in Arabic. I also provide you with a grammar review in case it has been a while since you studied to your basic level. I also show you how to use both the dictionaries included in this book as well as the larger ones you may acquire. Finally, I include a chapter on reading and writing the Arabic alphabet.

Part II: Becoming a Master at Using Nouns

The chapters in this part present several topics necessary for an intermediate level command of nouns. You learn the three cases of the noun, and you meet the mystifying types of broken plurals. You also get the info you need to confidently coordinate complicated **'iDaafa** strings and add in adjectives. I round out this part with a chapter that helps you become a master at adding pronouns and relative clauses to your writing.

Part III: Staying Active: Forming Arabic Verbs

In Part III, you discover how to write with every imaginable type of verb. First I introduce all ten forms of the Arabic verb and show you how to produce them when you throw in the irregular stems. Then you discover how to create commands and put objects on your verbs. The final chapter in this part introduces the various moods of the verb and demonstrates their uses in complicated constructions.

Part IV: Enlivening Your Writing with Particles

If you're looking to make your writing even more sophisticated, this is the part for you. It equips you to use any of the dozens of particles in Arabic to join clauses, form conditional sentences, and enliven your writing with the use of the verbal noun and participles. This part also explains how to negate your sentences.

Part V: The Part of Tens

The chapters in this part give you further hints and help you improve your ability to write in the Arabic language. I show you ten common mistakes to steer clear of, and I provide ten tips to polish your Arabic writing.

Part VI: Appendixes

The last part of this book provides you with valuable references. You get a full chart that shows you how to produce all forms of the Arabic verb. You also get English-Arabic and Arabic-English dictionaries to use in completing the exercises throughout the book.

Icons Used in This Book

To help you navigate the chapters in this book, I use tiny pictures, called icons, in the margins. These icons help you spot particularly important or potentially troublesome concepts. The following icons appear in this book:

I use this icon whenever I introduce something that you should keep in mind while practicing your Arabic.

This icon highlights information that can provide you with another angle when trying to understand a particular point. These tips can save you time and frustration.

This icon points to differences between English and Arabic. The information highlighted with this icon can help you learn, because it lets you compare how your native language is similar to or different from Arabic. Comparing languages can be a powerful way to enhance your memory.

When you see this icon, it means that there's a common error to be found nearby. Trust me, I've made them all. Hopefully, I've made them (and kept track of them) so you won't have to.

This icon highlights the practice exercises, which help to reinforce the text I cover. These exercises are a good opportunity to improve your Arabic. I've even tried to make them fun.

Where to Go from Here

From here on out, dig in and follow your instincts! If you start a chapter and find that it just isn't what you want to concentrate on, skip to something else. In my own language studies, I've had days when I just didn't want to concentrate on verb forms. Instead, I was hungry for some grammatical information. A week later, I couldn't get enough of verbs. I'm giving you a wide variety of things to master. Whatever you do, I urge you to never rush your studies. Working regularly for a little while is better than cramming in hours of study in one sitting once a month.

If I can, I'd like to give you a little advice: Complete all the exercises! There's nothing like committing yourself to putting down an answer on paper to force you to see where you need more study. Don't be afraid of making errors. You've probably already seen that native speakers of Arabic are ever appreciative of your efforts. As you advance to the use of more intermediate concepts, errors are unavoidable, but the rewards are great. ‏حَظّاً سَعيداً!‏ (**HaDHDHan sa3iidan!** *Good luck!*)

Part I
Polishing Your Arabic Skills

The 5th Wave   By Rich Tennant

ADULT ED
Writing in ARABIC
INSTRUCTOR
Mr. Alkhateeb

" My wife and I are taking the course together.
I figure I only have to learn half as much, since
she finishes all of my sentences anyway."

In this part . . .

The chapters in Part I help you refresh your basic knowledge of Arabic and boost your confidence as you work to improve your writing skills. I offer you a quick review of the cardinal and ordinal numbers and how they're used to tell time and express dates. I also give you a quick refresher on the basic Arabic grammatical issues, such as nouns, pronouns, possessive suffixes, verbs, and the main types of Arabic sentences. Also in this part is a chapter on how to read and write the Arabic alphabet. This is essential knowledge if you don't already have it. With the information in this part, you'll be bravely treading into the more advanced parts of the book in no time.

Chapter 1

Looking at Numbers, Times, and Dates

In This Chapter

▶ Mastering the Arabic cardinal and ordinal numbers

▶ Telling time using two methods

▶ Expressing dates in Arabic

Catullus said, "Give me a thousand kisses." And Elizabeth Barrett Browning declared, "How do I love thee? Let me count the ways." Obviously, even the language of love can't get by without numbers! In fact, numbers and all the ways you need to use them are so important that they deserve to start off this brief review of basic Arabic. Besides telling that special someone when you'd like to see them again (for example, at 3 o'clock tomorrow or on Tuesday, March 4th, at 5:17 p.m.), people use numbers in commerce and for making appointments in all matters formal and mundane.

This chapter reviews the basics surrounding numbers and their use in making appointments and telling time. By the end of this chapter, you'll be using numbers comfortably and confidently. I can't promise that you'll be able to avoid setting a lunch date with that boring office mate, but at least you'll know how much your half of the bill is!

Focusing on Arabic Numbers

Numbers come in two forms in almost every language. The most common form is called the *cardinal* number. You use cardinal numbers when you look at a price tag or do your taxes. In other words, you use these types of numbers for any type of counting. The second type of number is called the *ordinal* number, which allows you to rank something. For example, you may want to tell a client that you work on the fourth floor.

In the following sections, I give you the lowdown on both cardinal and ordinal numbers. I also introduce you to Arabic numerals, which are important because, as in English, you use them as a handy way to refer to numbers without writing out the whole word. I mean, after all, we call it the "War of 1812," not the "War of Eighteen Twelve."

Cardinal numbers: The digits you count with

Cardinal numbers are the ones that you use constantly in life, so they deserve to be considered ahead of the ordinals. If you haven't yet mastered the basic forms of cardinal numbers, now would be a great time to do so. In Table 1-1, I show you many of the Arabic cardinal numbers.

Many Arabic numbers have both a masculine and a feminine form (which I discuss later in this section), so I list both forms where necessary in the table. In this chart, I display the words in Arabic and English transliteration without any of the case endings (see Chapter 4 for more on the forms of the cases), with the exception of the numbers 11–19, which invariably have a (**fatHa**) ending.

Table 1-1	The Arabic Cardinal Numbers	
Masculine	*Feminine*	*Translation*
صِفْر (Sifr)		0
واحِد (waaHid)	واحِدة (waaHida)	1
إِثْنان (´ithnaani)	إِثْنَتان (´ithnataani)	2
ثَلاثَة (thalaatha)	ثَلاث (thalaath)	3
أَرْبَعة (´arba3a)	أَرْبَع (´arba3)	4
خَمْسة (khamsa)	خَمْس (khams)	5
سِتّة (sitta)	سِتّ (sitt)	6
سَبْعة (sab3a)	سَبْع (sab3)	7
ثَمانية (thamaaniya)	ثَماني (thamaanii)	8
تِسْعة (tis3a)	تِسْع (tis3)	9
عَشَرة (3ashara)	عَشْر (3ashr)	10
أَحَد عَشَر (´aHada 3ashara)	إِحْدى عَشْرَة (´iHdaa 3ashrata)	11
إِثْنا عَشَر (´ithnaa 3ashara)	إِثْنَتا عَشْرَة (´ithnataa 3ashrata)	12
ثَلاثَة عَشَر (thalaathata 3ashara)	ثَلاث عَشْرَة (thalaatha 3ashrata)	13
أَرْبَعة عَشَر (´arba3ata 3ashara)	أَرْبَع عَشْرَة (´arba3a 3ashrata)	14
خَمْسة عَشَر (khamsata 3ashara)	خَمْس عَشْرَة (khamsa 3ashrata)	15
سِتّة عَشَر (sittata 3ashara)	سِتّ عَشْرَة (sitta 3ashrata)	16
سَبْعة عَشَر (sab3ata 3ashara)	سَبْع عَشْرَة (sab3a 3ashrata)	17
ثَمانية عَشَر (thamaaniyata 3ashara)	ثَماني عَشْرَة (thamaani 3ashrata)	18

Masculine	Feminine	Translation
تِسْعَةَ عَشَرَ (tis3ata 3ashara)	تِسْعَ عَشْرَةَ (tis3a 3ashrata)	19
عِشْرونَ (3ishruuna)		20
واحِد وَعِشْرونَ (waaHid wa-3ishruuna)		21
إِثْنان وَعِشْرونَ (ʼithnaani wa-3ishruuna)		22
ثَلاثَة وَعِشْرونَ (thalaatha wa-3ishruuna)		23
أَرْبَعة وَعِشْرونَ (ʼarba3a wa-3ishruuna)		24
خَمْسة وَعِشْرونَ (khamsa wa3-ishruuna)		25
سِتّة وَعِشْرونَ (sitta wa-3ishruuna)		26
سَبْعة وَعِشْرونَ (sab3a wa-3ishruuna)		27
ثَمانِية وَعِشْرونَ (thamaaniya wa3-ishruuna)		28
تِسْعة وَعِشْرونَ (tis3a wa-3ishruuna)		29
ثَلاثونَ (thalaathuuna)		30
أَرْبَعونَ (ʼarba3uuna)		40
خَمْسونَ (khamsuuna)		50
سِتّونَ (sittuuna)		60
سَبْعونَ (sab3uuna)		70
ثَمانونَ (thamaanuuna)		80
تِسْعونَ (tis3uuna)		90
مِئة (mi'a)		100
مِئة وَواحِد (mi'a wa-waaHid)		101
مِئتان (mi'ataani)		200
ثَلاثُمِئة (thalaathumi'a)		300
ثَلاثُمِئة وَخَمْسة وَسِتّونَ (thalaathumi'a wa-khamsa wa-sittuun)		365
خَمْسُمِئة (khamsumi'a)		500
سَبْعُمِئة (sab3umi'a)		700
أَلْف (ʼalf)		1,000
أَلْفان (ʼalfaani)		2,000
مِئة أَلْف (mi'at ʼalf)		100,000
مِلْيون (milyuun)		1,000,000

Dealing with gender in cardinal numbers

English has one gender-neutral form for each of the cardinal numbers. Arabic, however, has masculine and feminine forms (refer to Chapter 2 for more on gender of nouns). One of the maddening aspects of Arabic numbers is the strange practice of *reverse gender agreement*. In other words, the numbers that look similar to feminine nouns or adjectives are the ones you use with masculine nouns (and vice versa). Here are two examples of plural nouns with reverse gender agreement:

ثَلاث سَيّارات (**thalaath sayyaaraat**; *three cars*)

خَمْسـة رجـال (**khamsa rijaal**; *five men*)

As you can see, سَيّارات (**sayyaaraat**; *cars*) is feminine, but it takes the masculine-appearing form of the number. Similarly, رجـال (**rijaal**; *men*) is masculine but it takes the feminine-appearing form. So you need to know the gender of the noun you want to count. Then all you have to do is select the appropriate number from the list I provide you.

Putting two-digit numbers in the correct order

Another difference between English and Arabic is the order of two-digit numbers. After 20, English puts the second digit after the first, joining them with a hyphen. For example, you would write *twenty-three*. Arabic, on the other hand, puts the second digit first and joins the two numbers with the word و (**wa**; *and*). Here's an example: ثَلاثة وَعِشْـرونَ (**thalaatha wa-3ishruuna**), which translates to *twenty-three*.

Writing about one of something

To say there's one of something, such as one house or one woman, the number must follow the noun and agree in gender and case (see Chapter 2 for more on gender and Chapter 4 for more on case). *Note:* In this section and the others that follow, I underline the numbers themselves to help you explore the examples. The following example shows you a masculine and a feminine noun accompanied by the number one in Arabic:

بَيْت واحِد (**baytun <u>waaHidun</u>**; <u>*one*</u> *house*)

إمْرَأة واحِدة ('**imra'atun <u>waaHidatun</u>**; <u>*one*</u> *woman*)

Writing about two of something

If you want to talk about two of something in Arabic (two pens or two letters, perhaps), you have two options. The first option is to use the dual form of the noun. (Chapter 4 explains the dual form.) If you use the dual form of the noun, you won't even be using a separate word for *two*. The ending of the noun itself will indicate that there are two of whatever you're talking about. Here are a masculine and a feminine noun with the dual endings underlined:

قَلَمان (**qalam<u>aani</u>**; <u>*two*</u> *pens*)

رسـالَتان (**risaalat<u>aani</u>**; <u>*two*</u> *letters*)

Your other option is to use the dual form with the number two following (agreeing in gender and case, of course). You would use this option if you were trying to emphasize the fact that you're talking about two of something. You might need to emphasize the number to dispel a misunderstanding. If someone thought there were three books on the table, you could correct them, saying:

لا. هُناكَ كِتابان إثنان عَلى الطّاوِلَةِ.

(**laa. hunaaka kitaabaani 'ithnaani 3alaa-T-Taawilati.** *No. There are two books on the table.*)

Take a look at these two nouns that have the number two in Arabic added for emphasis:

بَيْتان إثْنان (**baytaani 'ithnataani;** *two houses*)

طاوِلَتان إثْنَتان (**Taawilataani 'ithnataani;** *two tables*)

Writing about three to ten of something

When you're speaking about three to ten of something, you first write the number using the form that appears to be the opposite gender of the noun that you want to count. (When most folks speak Modern Standard Arabic — and even when they write it — they don't usually use the formal final vowels that can appear with the counted nouns.) Then you write the noun in its indefinite genitive plural form (refer to Chapter 4 for more on this form). Look closely at these examples of genitive plural nouns following numbers:

أَرْبَعة رِجال (**'arba3at rijaalin;** *four men*)

سَبْعَ مَجَلّاتٍ (**sab3a majallaatin;** *seven magazines*)

Throughout this section, I tell you what the formal ending after the numbers is. I even show you the formal final vowels in my examples so you can become accustomed to them. But if you drop them from your speech and writing, you'll still be correct. So that you can see what the same examples would be without the formal final vowels, here they are:

أَرْبَعة رِجال (**'arba3at rijaal;** *four men*)

سَبْعَ مَجَلّات (**sab3a majallaat;** *seven magazines*)

Writing about eleven to ninety-nine of something

To count things between eleven and ninety-nine, you have to put the noun that's following the number in the indefinite accusative singular form (see Chapter 4). Here are some examples of indefinite accusative singular nouns following their numbers:

تِسْعَ عَشَرة جَريدَةً (**tis3a 3asharat jariidatan;** *nineteen newspapers*)

أَرْبَعونَ يَوْماً (**'arba3uuna yawman;** *forty days*)

Writing about hundreds or thousands of something

When you talk about things occurring in even multitudes of hundreds or thousands, you write your number and use the indefinite genitive singular noun after it (see Chapter 4). Check out these examples:

أَلْف دولار (**'alf** duulaarin; *a thousand dollars*)

ثَلاثُمِئَةٍ رَجُل مِن إِسْبارْطة (**thalaathumi'ati** rajulin min 'isbaarTa; *three hundred men from Sparta*)

Writing about even multiples of ten

The multitudes of ten have two different forms, depending on whether the number is being used in the nominative or accusative/genitive cases. You can learn more about the cases and when you use them in Chapter 4. To produce the accusative/genitive form of the multiples of ten, you just have to change the ون (**-uuna**) ending into an ين (**-iina**) ending. Here are the nominative and accusative/genitive forms of twenty in Arabic:

عِشْرونَ (**3ishruuna**; *twenty;* nom.)

عِشْرينَ (**3ishriina**; *twenty;* acc./gen.)

Writing numbers with three or more digits

In Arabic, when stating numbers that have three or more digits, you write the highest digit first and work your way down, adding the word *and* between number sets. Take a look at the following two multiple-digit numbers. This is how the number 5,678 would be rendered in English according to Arabic style: Five thousand, and six hundred, and eight and seventy. As you can see, with the exception of the way Arabic expresses seventy-eight, this is how we state large numbers in English as well.

Here are a few more examples:

ثَلاثُمِئة وَخَمْسة وَسِتّونَ (**thalaathumi'a wa-khamsa wa-sittuuna**; *365*)

ثَلاثة آلاف وَخَمْسُمِئة وَسِتّة وَتِسْعونَ (**thalaathat 'aalaaf wa-khamsumi'a wa-sitta wa-tis3uuna**; *3,596*)

Sometimes you need to write about a counted number in the definite state. For instance, you may need to discuss the set of five questions your boss asked you to answer. To do this in Arabic, just put the number after the noun and add the definite article to both. Reverse gender agreement still applies in this case. Here are two examples for you:

فَكَّرْتُ بِالأسْئِلة الخَمْسة.

(**fakkartu bil-'as'ila al-khamsa.** *I thought about the five questions.*)

مَرَّت الأيّامُ المِئَةُ سَريعاً.

(**marrat al-'ayyaamu al-mi'atu sarii3an.** *The hundred days passed quickly.*)

Ordinal numbers: The numbers you rank things with

Ordinal numbers aren't quite as common in ordinary use (forgive the pun). But you need to use them whenever you express things that occur in an order or series. In a hotel, for instance, you may discover that your room is on the fifth floor. Or you may be considered first in your class. Table 1-2 shows you the ordinal numbers (through 12) in Arabic. I explain what to do with numbers above 12 later in the section.

Table 1-2	Arabic Ordinal Numbers	
Masculine	*Feminine*	*Translation*
أوّل ('awwal)	أُولى ('oola)	1st
ثاني (thaani)	ثانية (thaaniya)	2nd
ثالِث (thaalith)	ثالِثة (thaalitha)	3rd
رابِع (raabi3)	رابِعة (raabi3a)	4th
خامِس (khaamis)	خامِسة (khaamisa)	5th
سادِس (saadis)	سادِسة (saadisa)	6th
سابِع (saabi3)	سابِعة (saabi3a)	7th
ثامِن (thaamin)	ثامِنة (thaamina)	8th
تاسِع (taasi3)	تاسِعة (taasi3a)	9th
عاشِر (3aashir)	عاشِرة (3aashira)	10th
حادي عَشَر (Haadi 3ashara)	حادية عَشَرة (Haadiya 3ashara)	11th
ثاني عَشَر (thaani 3ashara)	ثانية عَشَر (thaaniya 3ashara)	12th

To properly use ordinals in Arabic, remember that ordinal numbers are adjectives. You have to choose the form that matches the gender of the noun it modifies. The following examples show both masculine and feminine nouns:

الرَّجُل العاشِر (ar-rajul al-3ashir; *the* <u>tenth</u> *man*)

السّاعة التّاسِعة (as-saa3a at-taasi3a; *the* <u>ninth</u> *hour [9 o'clock]*)

No abbreviation exists in Arabic to turn a cardinal into an ordinal like in English, when you write 1st and 3rd.

In Arabic, for any ordinal above 12, all you have to do is use the cardinal form. Take a look at the following example, which is a big number without a separate ordinal form:

المَرّة المِلْيون (al-marra al-milyuun; *the* <u>millionth</u> *time*)

Suppose that you're reading an Arabic newspaper, and you come across a food critic's ratings of some local eating establishments. She lists them in her order of preference, like this:

مَطْعَم لولو (**maT3am luuluu**)

جَوْهَر لُبْنانَ (**jawhar lubnaan**)

بَيْت الكَباب (**bayt al-kabaab**)

نَجْمة سـوريّة (**najmat suuriya**)

فَلافِل مَرْوان (**falaafil marwaan**)

ذِكْرَيات المَغْرب (**dhikrayaat al-maghrib**)

As a friend asks you in English how his favorite places fared, you need to find them in the list and write the ranking in ordinal numbers on the line provided.

Q. Memories of Morocco

A. سـادس (**saadis**; *sixth*)

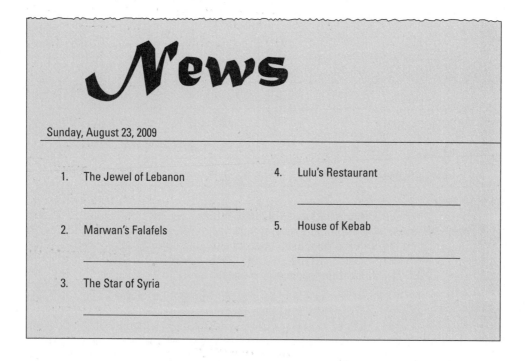

News

Sunday, August 23, 2009

1. The Jewel of Lebanon

    _____

2. Marwan's Falafels

    _____

3. The Star of Syria

    _____

4. Lulu's Restaurant

    _____

5. House of Kebab

    _____

Arabic numerals: The symbols you write numbers with

In addition to the Arabic cardinal and ordinal numbers themselves (which I discuss earlier in this chapter), you also need to know the forms of the *Arabic numerals* (the symbols used to depict numbers). They're called Arabic numerals because the Europeans borrowed them from the Arabs and acknowledged their source. The Arabs, however, actually borrowed them originally from India. Here are zero through nine in Arabic numerals (notice that a couple of them do resemble their Western counterparts; others, not so much):

✔ · *(0)*

✔ ١ *(1)*

✔ ٢ *(2)*

✔ ٣ *(3)*

✔ ٤ *(4)*

✔ ٥ *(5)*

✔ ٦ *(6)*

✔ ٧ *(7)*

✔ ٨ *(8)*

✔ ٩ *(9)*

For numbers ten and higher, just combine the Arabic numerals from the chart above and use the same order you would for English. Here you can see a few larger numbers:

١٩٤٢ *(1942)*

٢٠٠٨ *(2008)*

Arabic uses a comma where English uses a decimal point. And Arabic doesn't usually separate large numbers the way English does with the comma. Consider these examples:

١٠٠٠٠٠٠ *(1,000,000)*

٣,٥ *(3.5)*

As financial officer for your company, you need to fill out checks for several purchases. The amounts are in دينار (**dinaars**) — the unit of currency used in many Arab countries, such as Bahrain and Iraq — but they have been given to you as English numerals. To do your job properly, first convert them into Arabic numerals and then write the Arabic numeral and the number itself, in Arabic. For the purpose of the exercise, use the masculine forms of the numbers.

Q. 952

A. ٩٥٢ / تِسْعُمِئَة وَإِثْنانِ وَخَمْسُونَ (**tis3umi'a wa-'ithnaani wa-khamsuuna**)

6. 460

_____

7. 356

_____

8. 748

_____

9. 1,754

_____

10. 4,238

_____

Discovering How to Tell Time the Arabic Way

Time flies when you're having fun. It drags when you're looking forward to something later. And like money, it seems we never have quite enough of it. Because telling time is such a major part of our lives, knowing how to tell time and write it correctly is another one of those necessary skills in life.

In English you ask, "What time is it?" Someone asking you the time in Arabic will say كَم السّاعة (**kam as-saa3a**). Literally, this translates as "How much is the hour?" Arabic has two methods of telling time, one of which shows a better command of language. I explain both in this section.

Before you can tell time, however, here are a few words that you need to know:

اَلسّاعة (**as-saa3a**; _the hour [o'clock]_)

دَقيقة (**daqiiqa**; _minute_) 1:00

دَقائِق (**daqaa'iq**; _minutes_)

نِصْف (**niSf**; _half [to indicate 30 minutes]_) 0.5 $\frac{1}{2}$

رُبْع (**rub3**; _a quarter [to indicate 15 minutes]_) 0.25 $\frac{1}{4}$

ثُلُث (**thulth**; _a third [to indicate 20 minutes]_) 0.33 $\frac{1}{3}$

صَباحاً (**SabaaHan**; _in the morning_)

مَساءً (**masaa'an**; _in the evening_)

لَيْلاً (**laylan;** *at night*)

ظُهْراً (**dhuhran;** *afternoon*)

To tell time in Arabic, you replace the cardinal number with the correct ordinal form. Because ٱلسَّاعة (**as-saa3a**), the Arabic word for *hour,* is a feminine noun, you select the feminine forms of the ordinal. The only exception is that you use the feminine form of the cardinal واحِدة (**waaHida**) for 1:00.

To express the number of minutes on the hour up to the 30-minute mark, you add وَ (**wa**), followed by the number of minutes in cardinal form. وَ (**wa**) translates to *and* in English. You can use رُبْع (**rub3**) for a quarter hour (15 minutes), ثلُث (**thulth**) for 20 minutes, and نِصْف (**niSf**) for the half hour (30 minutes). The following examples show you how to use these fractions to tell time:

4:30 translates to ٱلسَّاعة ٱلرَّابِعة وَٱلنِّصْف (**as-saa3a ar-raabi3a wa-n-niSf;** literally *the hour the fourth and the half*)

2:15 translates to ٱلسَّاعة ٱلثَّانِية وَٱلرُّبْع (**as-saa3a ath-thaaniya wa-r-rub3;** literally *the hour the second and the quarter*)

To state more complex times, you write the hour, followed by more specific minutes. For one or two minutes, you can just use the singular and dual forms of the word *minute,* دَقِيقة (**daqiiqa**) and دَقيقَتان (**daqiiqataani**). For more than two minutes, you use the cardinal number, followed by the plural form of *minute,* دَقائِق (**daqaa'iq**). Here are examples of one, two, and seven minutes past an hour:

9:01 translates to ٱلسَّاعة ٱلتَّاسِعة وَدَقِيقة (**as-saa3a at-taasi3a wa-daqiiqa;** literally *the hour the ninth and a minute*)

7:02 translates to ٱلسَّاعة ٱلسَّابِعة وَدَقيقَتان (**as-saa3a as-saabi3a wa-daqiiqataani;** literally *the hour the seventh and two minutes*)

3:07 translates to ٱلسَّاعة ٱلثَّالِثة وَسَبْع دَقائِق (**as-saa3a ath-thaalitha wa-sab3 daqaa'iq;** literally *the hour the third and seven minutes*)

If the time you want to write is after the half hour, you can write that it's half past an hour, and then just add another number as necessary. For example, the time *6:35* translates to ٱلسَّاعة ٱلسَّادِسة وَٱلنِّصْف وَخَمْسَ دَقائِق (**as-saa3a as-saadisa wa-n-niSf wa-khamsa daqaa'iq;** literally *the hour the sixth and a half and five minutes*).

There comes a point, however, when it becomes easier to talk about how many minutes there are until the next hour. The times *3:55* and *2:45* are both close enough to the next hour that it's convenient to use إِلَّا (**'illaa**), which in English is *except* (but here it's the equivalent of *to* in the sense of "a quarter to four"). After إِلَّا (**'illaa**), you use the accusative form of the noun or number. Consider the following examples:

3:55 translates to ٱلسَّاعة ٱلرَّابِعة إِلَّا خَمْسَ دَقائِق (**as-saa3a ar-raabi3a 'illaa khamsa daqaa'iq;** literally *the hour the fourth except five minutes*)

2:45 translates to ٱلسَّاعة ٱلثَّالِثة إِلَّا رُبعاً (**as-saa3a ath-thaalitha 'illaa rub3an;** literally, *the hour the third except a quarter*)

Now it's time for some practice. Read the time given in English, and then write it in Arabic in the space provided.

Q. 4:15

A. اَلسّـاعـة الرّابـعـة وَالـرُّبـع (**as-saa3a ar-raabi3a wa-r-rub3**)

11. 3:20

_____

12. 10:13

_____

13. 7:50

_____

14. 2:45

_____

15. 12:30

_____

Making Dates: Getting to Know the Arabic Days and Months

Whether they're dreaded deadlines or anniversaries that you don't want to forget, knowing dates is a critical skill in any language. In this section, I prepare you for writing out some dates in Arabic by presenting some important categories of words: days of the week and months in a year.

Before you begin, however, check out some useful words for talking about dates:

يَوْم (**yawm**; *day*)

أُسْـبـوع (**'usbuu3**; *week*)

شَـهْـر (**shahr**; *month*)

سَنة (**sana**; *year*)

اليَوْم (**al-yawm**; *today*)

أَمْس ('**amsi**; *yesterday*)

غَداً (**ghadan**; *tomorrow*)

Exploring the days of the week

The days of the week in Arabic are easy to remember because most of them are based on numbers, with Sunday being number one (it's the first day of the week, after all). When you get to the end, the word for Friday means "Gathering Day," because it's the main prayer day for Muslims. Saturday preserves the Hebrew word "Sabbath."

Here are the days of the week in Arabic:

يَوْم الأَحَد (**yawm al-'aHad**; *Sunday*)

يَوْم الإِثْنَيْن (**yawm al-'ithnayni**; *Monday*)

يَوْم الثُّلاثاء (**yawm ath-thulathaa'**; *Tuesday*)

يَوْم الأَرْبَعاء (**yawm al-'arba3aa'**; *Wednesday*)

يَوْم الخَميس (**yawm al-khamiis**; *Thursday*)

يَوْم الجُمْعة (**yawm al-jum3a**; *Friday*)

يَوْم السَبْت (**yawm as-sabt**; *Saturday*)

Whether you're speaking or writing, it isn't uncommon to save time by dropping off the word يَوْم (**yawm**) and just state the second element. In other words, الخَميس (**al-khamiis**) can mean Thursday all on its own.

Remembering the months of the year

Most of the Arab world today uses the Gregorian calendar with names for the months borrowed from the Western world. An ancient Semitic system of names, which dates back more than 3,000 years, has also been preserved. In many Arabic language newspapers, you see the Western month, followed by the ancient Semitic months in parentheses. In Table 1-3, I provide you with the Western months in Arabic along with their ancient Semitic equivalents and Western translations.

Table 1-3	The Western Months in Arabic with Their Semitic Equivalents	
Western Months in Arabic	**Semitic Months in Arabic**	**Western Translation**
يَنـايِر (yanaayir)	كـانون الثّـاني (kaanuun ath-thaani)	*January*
فِبْـرايِر (fibraayir)	شُـبـاط (shubaaT)	*February*
مـارِس (maaris)	آذار (’aadhaar)	*March*
أَبْـريل (’abriil)	نيسـان (niisaan)	*April*
مايـو (maayu)	أيّـار/ مايِس (’ayyaar/maayis)	*May*
يونْـيو (yuunyuu)	حَـزيران (Haziiraan)	*June*
يولْـيو (yuulyuu)	تَمّـوز (tammuuz)	*July*
أَغُسْـطُس (’aghustus)	آب (’aab)	*August*
سِـبْـتِمْـبَر (sibtimbar)	أَيْـلـول (’ayluul)	*September*
أُكْـتوبَر (uktuubar)	تِشْـرين الأوّل (tishriin al-’awwal)	*October*
نوفيمْـبَر (nufiimbar)	تِشْـرين الثّـاني (tishriin ath-thaani)	*November*
ديسَـمْبِر (diisambir)	كـانون الأوّل (kaanuun al-’awwal)	*December*

Writing full dates with the day, month, and year

To find out the date in Arabic, you can ask someone, ما التّاريخ (**maa at-taariikh?** *What's the date?*). The response, as in English, can be in either cardinal or ordinal numbers. Here are examples of a date with a cardinal number and one with an ordinal:

العِشْـرونَ مِن أبْريل (**al-3ishruuna min ’abriil;** *April 20*)

الأوّل مِن يَناير (**al-’awwal min yanaayir;** *January 1st*)

To write a date in Arabic, you reverse the order of the month and day that you use in English. For example, January 14, 2008, in English becomes 14 January, 2008, in Arabic.

Here's where your knowledge of the Arabic numerals is going to come in handy. To write a date in Arabic numerals, you can do one of two things: You can put the whole thing in numerals and separate them with back slashes, or you can write out the month in Arabic (with the rest in numerals). The following examples show you how to write January 15, 2008, using both options:

١٥ يَناير ٢٠٠٨ (**yanaayir**) / ٢٠٠٨/١/١٥

Convert the following dates into both of the two Arabic options.

0. April 10, 2006

A. ١٠ أَبْريل ٢٠٠٦ ('**abriil**)

٢٠٠٦/٤/١٠

16. September 18, 2004

_____

17. July 4, 1776

_____

18. February 14, 1963

_____

19. June 26, 2008

_____

20. March 15, 1923

_____

21. December 9, 1985

_____

22. October 3, 1939

_____

Answer Key

Sunday, August 23, 2009

1. ثاني (**thaanii;** *second*)

2. خامس (**khaamis;** *fifth*)

3. رابع (**raabi3;** *fourth*)

4. أوّل (**'awwal;** *first*)

5. ثالث (**thaalith;** *third*)

---

6 أَرْبَعُمِئة وَسِتّونَ / ٤٦٠ (**'arba3umi'a wa-sittuuna**)

7 ثَلاثُمِئة وَسِتّة وَخَمْسونَ / ٣٥٦ (**thalaathumi'a wa-sitta wa-khamsuuna**)

8 سَبْعُمِئة وَثمانية وَأَرْبَعونَ / ٧٤٨ (**sab3umi'a wa-thamaaniya wa-'arba3uuna**)

9 أَلْف وَسَبْعُمِئة وَأَرْبَعة وَخَمْسونَ / ١٧٥٤ (**'alf wa-sab3umi'a wa 'arba3a wa-khamsuuna**)

10 أَرْبَعة آلاف وَمِئَتان وَثمانية وَثَلاثون / ٤٢٣٨ (**'arba3at 'aalaaf wa-mi'ataani wa-thamaaniya wa-thalaathuuna**)

11 اَلسّاعة الثّالِثة وَالثُّلُث (**as-saa3a ath-thaalitha wa-th-thulth**)

12 اَلسّاعة العاشِرة وَثَلاثَ عَشْرةَ دَقيقةً (**as-saa3a al-3aashira wa-thalaatha 3ashrata daqiiqatan**)

13 اَلسّاعة الثّامِنة إلّا 3ashara daqaa'iq عَشَرَ دَقائِق (**as-saa3a ath-thaamina 'illaa 3ashara daqaa'iq**)

14 اَلسّاعة الثّالِثة إلا رُبعاً (**as-saa3a ath-thaalitha 'illaa rub3an**)

15 اَلسّاعة الثّانية عَشَرَ وَالنِّصْف (as-saa3a ath-thaaniya 'ashara wa-n-niSf)

16 ١٨ سِبْتِمْبَر (sibtimbar)؛ ٢٠٠٤ /٩/١٨

17 ٤ يولْيو (yuulyuu)؛ ١٧٧٦/٧/٤

18 ١٤ فِبْرايِر (fibraayir)؛ ١٩٦٣/٢/١٤

19 ٢٦ يونْيو (yuunyuu)؛ ٢٠٠٨/٦/٢٦

20 ١٥ مارس (maaris)؛ ١٩٢٣/٣/١٥

21 ٩ ديسَمْبِر (diisambir)؛ ١٩٨٥ /١٢/٩

22 ٣ أُكْتوبَر ١٩٣٩ (uktuubir)؛ ١٩٣٩/١٠/٣

Chapter 2

Arabic 101 Refresher

. . . .

. . . .

I love languages and have studied a good number of them. No matter how familiar I become with a language, however, I still find it valuable to go back and **review the basics** every now and then. In so doing, sometimes I discover new and better ways to remember things that have long plagued me. So, no matter how recently you completed your basic studies in Arabic (and I'm assuming you have already completed at least a year's worth of studies and are about to take or are currently in an intermediate level course), a refresher will help you as you move on.

If you're a bit rusty, this chapter can **reinvigorate** your knowledge of some things I don't cover elsewhere in this book. In the remaining chapters, I go beyond the material reviewed here, which is the reason you picked up *Intermediate Arabic For Dummies* in the first place.

In this chapter, you encounter a description of what the Arabic **triliteral root** is and how it works. You experience the many ways that nouns can function in your sentence. This chapter also acquaints you with how to add the Arabic definite article, the equivalent of English *the,* to your nouns. You see how to describe possession in Arabic, and you have the chance to review past, present, and future tense verbs. Finally, you discover the two main types of Arabic sentences.

This is a lot to cover, but gaining the skills from the material in this chapter provides you with a sound foundation. And this foundation will help you become proficient at the intermediate level.

Understanding How the Arabic Triliteral Root System Impacts Nouns

As you likely learned in the first semester of your first year of Arabic studies, the vast majority of Arabic words are derived from a root that's made of three consonants. Each of these three-consonant roots are referred to as a *triliteral root*. (This name comes from the Latin for, you guessed it, *three letters*.) Thousands of different triliteral roots exist in Arabic. It's important to know about these triliteral roots because Arabic uses them in stable word patterns to form almost every noun and verb in the language.

A triliteral root has an inherent meaning. For example, consider the triliteral root كتب (**k-t-b**). This root means *to write*. Arabic uses the three consonants of the root **k-t-b** in different word patterns, each of which (because of the root meaning) will have something to do with the concept of *writing*.

Grammarians model word patterns in Arabic with a sort of "dummy" root, فعل (**f-3-l**). The root **f-3-l** means *to do,* but when it's used to model word patterns, don't think about its meaning at all. Instead, view the use of **f-3-l** to show patterns as a sort of blueprint. The three consonants of the root **f-3-l** show you where the three consonants of any triliteral root will go when you use the word pattern in question.

In the following example, I demonstrate how you use the root فعل (**f-3-l**) as the model for word patterns. These are the word patterns:

> فَعَلَ (**fa3ala;** *to do something*)
>
> مَفْعَلٌ (**maf3alun;** *the place to do that something*)
>
> فاعِلٌ (**faa3ilun;** *one who does that something*)

Here are the same word patterns from the previous list with the triliteral root كتب (**k-t-b**), which means *to write:*

> كَتَبَ (**kataba;** *to write*)
>
> مَكْتَبٌ (**maktabun;** *office,* or *place of writing*)
>
> كاتِبٌ (**kaatibun;** *writer*)

As you make your way through this book and advance in your Arabic studies, you'll become familiar with many productive word patterns that have stable meanings no matter what root you insert. Notice, for instance, how the words on the pattern **faa3ilun** mean *one who does something.* The words on the pattern **maf3alun** mean *place* [where the verb happens].

Now's your chance to practice replacing the consonants of the dummy root **f-3-l** with another root. For each of the items below, I give you a word pattern using **f-3-l** and a new triliteral root. Your job is to substitute the consonants of **f-3-l** with the consonants of the new root. This exercise gives you a little practice writing in Arabic (if you're rusty on that important skill). You can also guess at the meaning of the word you create, based on the root meaning and the word pattern.

Q. Pattern: فاعِلٌ (**faa3ilun**); practice root: ركب (**r-k-b**; *to ride*)

A. راكِبٌ (**raakibun**; *rider*)

1. Pattern: فاعِلٌ (**faa3ilun**); practice root: سمع (**s-m-3**; *to hear*)

_____

2. Pattern: مَفْعَلٌ (**maf3alun**); practice root: طبخ (**T-b-kh**; *to cook*)

_____

3. Pattern: فاعِلٌ (**faa3ilun**); practice root: حكم (**H-k-m**; *to pass judgment*)

_____

4. Pattern: مَفْعَلٌ (**maf3alun**); practice root: خرج (**kh-r-j**; *to exit*)

_____

Naming People, Places, and Things: Nouns 101

As you know, a *noun* is the part of speech in a language that names people, places, things, or even more abstract concepts, such as qualities and actions. This section offers a brief refresher on noun basics. I present the various types of nouns you find within a sentence and explain what they are. I also discuss how the topic of gender fits with nouns in the Arabic language. (To read about the noun cases, visit Chapter 4.)

Exploring the types of Arabic nouns

As in English, nouns fall into several different categories. Here are the categories in which a noun can appear in Arabic:

- **Animate:** Included in this category are humans, real or imaginary, and animals (and some might add aliens!). Here's an example:

  ذلكَ الرَّجُلُ وَسيمٌ.

  (**dhaalikaa-r-rajulu wasiimun.** *That* <u>man</u> *is handsome.*)

- **Thing:** Here you have any inanimate object that you can see, touch, taste, or somehow feel. For example:

  أكَلْتُ الطَّعامَ سَريعاً.

  (**'akaltu aT-Ta3aama sarii3an.** *I ate the* <u>food</u> *quickly.*)

✔ **Proper noun:** Whether it's a person's name or a place like New Jersey, a proper noun refers to something ordinarily capitalized in English (but Arabic has no capital letters). Check out this example:

زارَتْ القاهِرَةَ.

(**zaarat al-qaahirata.** *She visited* <u>*Cairo*</u>.)

✔ **Abstract quality or concept:** This broad category basically covers anything that doesn't fit in the previous three categories. Some items that fall into this category include feelings, concepts, and even actions. Consider this example:

السُّكوت مِن الذَّهَب.

(**as-sukuut** min adh-dhahab. <u>*Silence*</u> *is golden.*)

Engendering differences

An important feature of Arabic nouns is their gender. So in this section, I show you ways to recognize the gender of an Arabic noun.

English nouns may describe males and females, but there's no grammatical gender for inanimate nouns or abstract concepts. So, John may be referred to as *he* and Mary as *she,* but the table is referred to as *it.* In Arabic, the pronoun *it* doesn't exist. Instead, every noun is either masculine or feminine. When the noun is masculine, it takes masculine adjectives. When it's feminine, feminine adjectives are the correct choice. (See Chapter 6 for more information on how adjectives and genders interact.)

Working with masculine nouns

In Arabic, two clues can tell you whether a noun is masculine. For instance, an Arabic noun is masculine if:

✔ The noun describes something intuitively masculine, such as a man, brother, or uncle.

✔ The noun doesn't have the ة (**taa' marbuuTa**), which is the ordinary ending for a feminine noun.

As an example of the first rule, here are a couple of masculine nouns describing males:

رَجُل (**rajul;** *man*)

جَدّ (**jadd;** *grandfather*)

Unfortunately, Arabic has no masculine ending (as, for instance, you have with the Spanish word **carro,** meaning *car*). There's nothing about a typical masculine noun that tells you it's masculine except the fact that it doesn't have the ة (**taa' marbuuTa**). Here are a few examples of masculine nouns that aren't intuitively masculine:

كَأْس (**ka's**; *glass*)

هاتِف (**haatif**; *telephone*)

نِظام (**niDHaam**; *system*)

Getting girly with feminine nouns

In Arabic, two factors help you determine whether a noun is feminine. For instance, a noun is feminine if it:

- Describes something understood as feminine, such as a woman, an aunt, or a grandmother
- Ends with the regular feminine ending, the ة (**taa' marbuuTa**)

The following are examples of the first rule. These feminine nouns describe females in Arabic:

اِمْرَأَة (**imra'a**; *woman*)

بِنْت (**bint**; *girl, daughter*)

And now here are examples of the second rule. These nouns that describe gender-neutral objects are still feminine nouns in Arabic. You can guess that they're feminine because of the ة (**taa' marbuuTa**) ending.

سَيّارة (**sayyaara**; *car*)

جَريدة (**jariida**; *newspaper*)

There are always exceptions to the rule, of course. There are a handful of nouns with ة (**taa' marbuuTa**) that are masculine. There are some nouns without it that are feminine. And there's no rhyme or reason to the few violations of the expected rules. So you have to look up words that you aren't familiar with. Note that most comprehensive dictionaries on the market only tell you the gender of nouns that violate the expected gender. I don't use any of these rare irregular nouns in this book, but be on the lookout for them elsewhere.

In this practice set, I give you the chance to recognize the probable gender of a noun and add the appropriate form of the adjective. For each item, I give you the noun and a masculine adjective. Put the adjective after the noun. I don't throw any curve balls at you in this exercise. The gender will be what you can and should safely assume.

Q. قَرْية (**qarya**; *village*); صَغير (**Saghiir**; *small*)

A. قَرْية صَغيرة (**qarya Saghiira**; *small village*)

5. شُبّاك (**shubbaak**; *window*); مَفْتوح (**maftuuH**; *open*)

6. دَرّاجة (**darraaja;** *bicycle*); سَريع (**sarii3;** *fast*)

   _____

7. عُلْبة (**3ulba;** *box*); ثَقيل (**thaqiil;** *heavy*)

   _____

8. شارع (**shaari3;** *road*); طَويل (**Tawiil;** *long*)

   _____

Being Specific with the Definite State

The *definite state* is the form of a noun that refers to a specific example of that noun — not just any theoretical case. In other words, when you say that you saw *the* movie, you're referring to a specific, or definite, movie. But if you ask someone whether they saw *a* movie on Friday night, you aren't asking about a specific movie. Grammarians use the term definite state to refer to a noun that's given some equivalent to the English word *the,* which is considered a definite article. A noun in English with the word *the* in front of it is considered to be in the definite state. By contrast, if you use the indefinite article *a/an,* you're describing the indefinite state.

Arabic creates the definite state by adding the prefix اَل (**al-**) to a noun. Even though **al-** is a prefix on the word — not a separate word like *the* — grammarians still generally call **al-** the definite article. Because the definite article in Arabic is made up of just the two consonants اَ (**'alif**) and ل (**laam**), Arab speakers and writers frequently refer to making a noun definite as "adding the **'alif laam.**"

The following are two nouns that I make definite by adding the **'alif laam.** In each case, I first show you the noun by itself and then the noun with the prefixed definite article:

كِتاب (**kitaab;** *a book*)

الكِتاب (**al-kitaab;** *the book*)

سَيّارة (**sayyaara;** *a car*)

السَّيّارة (**as-sayyaara;** *the car*)

Notice that in the Arabic script, I have indeed added the **'alif laam** to each noun. But with سَيّارة (**sayyaara**), the definite version has no ل (**laam**) at all. Instead, you find a double *s* sound. This is because about half of the consonants in Arabic absorb the *l* sound of the **laam** and turn into a doubled consonant.

In the following sections, you discover how each consonant behaves when you add the **'alif laam** to it. The Arabic consonants are classified as sun letters or moon letters depending on what they do to the **laam** in the definite state.

The sun letters

Consonants that assimilate the **laam** of the **'alif laam** are called *sun letters*. The reason they're called this is because the first letter of the word for *sun* in Arabic, شَـمْـسٌ (**shamsun**), is a sun letter itself.

The assimilation of the **laam** to produce a doubled consonant is primarily a matter of pronunciation. In writing, you use the usual **'alif laam** as the prefix to create the definite state. If, however, the first consonant of the word is one of the sun letters, you acknowledge the assimilation of the **laam** by writing a ˝ (**shadda**), which is the symbol for a doubled consonant, above the sun letter itself. (If you're uncertain about the **shadda,** you can review Arabic writing rules in Chapter 3.) What's great about this in Arabic is that there's a convenient way to visually recognize that a noun is definite, even if the pronunciation doesn't have a **laam** with sun letters.

Table 2-1 displays each of the sun letters, along with a noun that begins with each.

Table 2-1	The Arabic Sun Letters
Arabic Sun Letter	*Example Word Beginning with the Sun Letter*
ت (taa')	التّين (**at-tiin**; *the fig*)
ث (thaa')	الثَّلْج (**ath-thalj**; *the snow*)
د (daal)	الدَّمّ (**ad-damm**; *the blood*)
ذ (dhaal)	الذّئْب (**adh-dhi'b**; *the wolf*)
ر (raa')	الرَّئيس (**ar-ra'iis**; *the president*)
ز (zaay)	الزّيْت (**az-zayt**; *the oil*)
س (siin)	السَّبَب (**as-sabab**; *the reason*)
ش (shiin)	الشّـمْس (**ash-shams**; *the sun*)
ص (Saad)	الصَّديق (**aS-Sadiiq**; *the friend*)
ض (Daad)	الضّمير (**aD-Damiir**; *the conscience*)
ط (Taa')	الطّبيب (**aT-Tabiib**; *the physician*)
ظ (DHaa')	الظِّلّ (**aDH-DHill**; *the shadow*)
ل (laam)	اللَّوْن (**al-lawn**; *the color*)
ن (nuun)	النّاس (**an-naas**; *the people*)

The moon letters

The *moon letters* are those consonants that don't assimilate the **laam**. Instead, with the moon letters, the **'alif laam** goes onto the word as a simple prefix pronounced **al-**. The reason they're named as they are is that the first letter of the word for *moon* in Arabic, قَمَرٌ (**qamrun**), is a moon letter itself.

Table 2-2 displays each of the moon letters along with examples of words beginning with each of the moon letters.

Table 2-2	The Arabic Moon Letters
Arabic Moon Letter	*Example Word Beginning with the Moon Letter*
ء (hamza)	الأكْل (**al-'akl**; *the food*)
ب (baa')	البَيْت (**al-bayt**; *the house*)
ج (jiim)	الجار (**al-jaar**; *the neighbor*)
ح (Haa')	الحُبّ (**al-Hubb**; *the love*)
خ (khaa')	الخال (**al-khaal**; *the maternal uncle*)
ع (3ayn)	العمّة (**al-3amma**; *the paternal aunt*)
غ (ghayn)	الغَنَم (**al-ghanam**; *the sheep*)
ف (faa')	الفول (**al-fuul**; *the beans*)
ق (qaaf)	القَمْر (**al-qamr**; *the moon*)
ك (kaaf)	الكَلِمة (**al-kalima**; *the word*)
م (miim)	الماء (**al-maa'**; *the water*)
ه (haa')	الهَدِية (**al-hadiya**; *the present*)
و (waaw)	الوَلَد (**al-walad**; *the boy*)
ي (yaa')	اليَد (**al-yad**; *the hand*)

It's your turn to put your newfound knowledge of the **'alif laam** into practice. For each of the words I give you, add the **'alif laam**.

Q. صَوْم (**Sawm**; *fasting*)

A. الصَّوْم (**aS-Sawm**; *the fasting*)

9. مَتْحَف (**matHaf**; *museum*) _____

10. سوق (**suuq**; *market*) _____

11. كَتْف (**katf**; *shoulder*) _____

12. ثَمَن (**thaman**; *price*) _____

13. تَأْمِين (**ta'miin**; *insurance*) _____

14. رَقَم (**raqam**; *number*) _____

15. حَرِير (**Hariir**; *silk*) _____

16. دَرّاجة (**darraaja**; *bicycle*) _____

17. جامِع (**jaami3**; *mosque*) _____

18. أُمّ ('**umm**; *mother*) _____

Working with Pronouns and Pronoun Suffixes

Pronouns are words that can take the place of nouns. For instance, in English, you can say, "I saw my <u>friend</u> at the party and went with <u>him</u> to the buffet table. <u>He</u> ate all the breadsticks!" Instead of repeating the word *friend,* you can use pronouns to be more concise. In this example, you can see how English has separate pronouns for both subjects (*he*) and objects (*him*) of verbs.

English also has possessive pronouns. With possessive pronouns, you're able to say "I attended <u>his</u> wedding" and "I know <u>their</u> secret." While English has separate words for pronouns and possessive pronouns, Arabic only has separate, or independent, pronouns for the subjects of verbs. When you need to express a pronoun as the object of a verb or to express a possessive pronoun, you use pronoun suffixes on the nouns and verbs.

Discovering the independent forms of Arabic pronouns

An independent (or stand-alone) form of the Arabic pronoun is used when the pronoun is the subject of a verb or the main topic of an equational sentence. However, in a sentence with a verb, the pronouns aren't strictly necessary, because the verb form itself also tells you who's performing the action. But you can add the independent forms of the Arabic pronoun to provide emphasis about who's doing the action. (For example, you may want to make it very clear that "*You* need to take out the garbage, not *me*.")

In Arabic, when you're talking to or about a group that has mixed gender, you use the masculine plural forms. You only use the feminine plural forms when talking to or about a group that's composed of three or more female people.

Table 2-3 shows the independent forms of the Arabic pronoun.

Table 2-3	The Independent Forms of the Arabic Pronoun
Arabic Pronoun	*Translation*
أَنَا ('ana)	I
أَنْتَ ('anta)	you (M)
أَنْتِ ('anti)	you (F)
هُوَ (huwa)	he
هِيَ (hiya)	she
نَحْنُ (naHnu)	we
أَنْتُمْ ('antum)	you (MP)
أَنْتُنَّ ('antunna)	you (FP)
هُمْ (hum)	they (MP)
هُنَّ (hunna)	they (FP)

Tacking on the possessive pronoun suffixes to Arabic nouns

Unlike English, Arabic doesn't have separate possessive pronouns such as *his*, *our*, and *their*. Instead, Arabic has possessive pronouns that you attach as suffixes to the noun. (When you want to express possession of one full noun over another noun, you use the **'iDaafa** construction covered later in this chapter.)

To form the possessive, you attach the proper possessive pronoun suffix to the noun without adding the **'alif laam** to make it definite. After all, if I tell you that I like his car, I'm referring to a specific, or definite, car. You attach your pronouns to the noun after the case ending with only one exception — the suffix ي (**-ii**), which is used to express *my*.

In Table 2-4, I use the nominative case, but these possessive pronoun suffixes go on a noun in the accusative or genitive as well. (To see the cases covered in detail, you can go to Chapter 4 of this book.) In the table, you see the possessive suffixes added to the nouns after the normal *u* vowel of the nominative. In the exception, you remove the nominative ending *u* and add the suffix ي (**-ii**) directly to the noun. I show you how to apply the suffixes using the example noun كِتاب (**kitaab;** *book*).

Table 2-4		Possessive Pronoun Suffixes
Arabic Possessive Pronoun Suffix	**Translation**	**Example Forms Using the Noun** كِتاب (*kitaab; book*)
ي (-ii)	*my*	كِتابي (**kitaab<u>ii</u>**; my book)
كَ (-ka)	*your* (MS)	كِتابُكَ (**kitaabuka**; your [MS] book)
كِ (-ki)	*your* (FS)	كِتابُكِ (**kitaabuki**; your [FS] book)
ﻪ (-hu)	*his*	كِتابُهُ (**kitaabu<u>hu</u>**; his book)
ها (-haa)	*her*	كِتابُها (**kitaabuhaa**; her book)
نا (-naa)	*our*	كِتابُنا (**kitaabu<u>naa</u>**; our book)
كُم (-kum)	*your*	كِتابُكُم (**kitaabu<u>kum</u>**; your book)
كُنّ (-kunna)	*your* (FP)	كِتابُكُنّ (**kitaabukunna**; your [FP] book)
هُم (-hum)	*their*	كِتابُهُم (**kitaabu<u>hum</u>**; their book)
هُنّ (-hunna)	*their* (FP)	كِتابُهُنّ (**kitaabu<u>hunna</u>**; their [FP] book)

When you put the possessive suffixes on a noun with the ة (**taa' marbuuTa**) — the Arabic feminine ending that's described earlier in the chapter — you change the **taa' marbuuTa** into a ت (**taa'**). Then you add the usual endings. Consider the feminine noun إجابة (**'ijaaba**; *answer*). Here's what it looks like with the possessive pronoun suffixes added:

إجابَتي (**'ijaabatii**; *my answer*)

إجابَتُها (**'ijaabatuhaa**; *her answer*)

For each of the supplied English nouns and pronouns, add the possessive suffix in Arabic.

Q. his house

A. بَيتُهُ (**baytuhu**; *his house*)

19. my job _____

20. his name _____

21. our hope _____

22. her university _____

23. your (MP) president _____

24. their (FP) idea _____

25. your (MS) food _____

26. your (FS) pen _____

Getting Active with Arabic Verbs

Verbs are the words in a language that really make life exciting because they express action. One interesting thing you may have discovered is that Arabic manages to get by without using a verb that means *to be* in the present tense. So, instead of saying "I am happy," you just say "I happy." (You can explore sentences without the verb *to be* in the present tense in the later section "Adding up equational sentences." But, don't worry. Arabic has a rich inventory of ways to describe the other actions that spice up your life.

In Chapter 9, I introduce you to the ten forms of the Arabic verb. And Chapter 10 helps you sort out the irregular verbs that can sometimes be troublesome. In this section, however, you can review the formation of the past, present, and future tenses of simple and regular verbs.

Writing the past tense verb

I start with the past tense because Arabic dictionaries use the past tense form as the base word to show you any verb. Another good reason to start with it is because it's easier than the present — you only have to add suffixes to form the past tense. (The present requires both prefixes and suffixes.) So I start you out easy with the past tense.

Simply put, the *past tense* describes actions or conditions that happened in the past. In Arabic, you express past tense by adding one of the many past tense personal pronoun suffixes to the verb. All verbs in Arabic use the same endings to produce the past tense. Table 2-5 shows the different personal pronoun suffixes that you use.

Table 2-5	Personal Pronoun Suffixes for Verbs in the Past Tense	
Arabic Pronoun	*Translation*	*Suffix*
أَنَا ('anaa)	I/me	تُ (-tu)
أَنْتَ ('anta)	you (MS)	تَ (-ta)
أَنْتِ ('anti)	you (FS)	تِ (-ti)
هُوَ (huwa)	he	ـَ (-a)
هِيَ (hiya)	she	تْ (-at)
نَحْنُ (naHnu)	we	نا (-naa)
أَنْتُم ('antum)	you (MP)	تُمْ (-tum)
أَنْتَنَّ ('antunna)	you (FP)	تُنَّ (-tunna)
هُمْ (hum)	they (MP)	و (-uu)
هُنَّ (hunna)	they (FP)	نَ (-na)

As an example, the following table shows all the forms of the verb, شَرِبَ (**shariba;** *to drink*), in the past tense.

Past tense of شَرِبَ (shariba; *to drink*)	
شَرِبْتُ ('anaa sharibtu)	شَرِبْنا (naHnu sharibnaa)
شَرِبْتَ ('anta sharibta) شَرِبْتِ ('anti sharibti)	شَرِبْتُم ('antum sharibtum) شَرِبْتُنَّ ('antunna sharibtunna)
شَرِبَ (huwa shariba) شَرِبَتْ (hiya sharibat)	شَرِبوا (hum sharibuu) شَرِبْنَ (hunna sharibna)
شَرِبْتُ الماء سَريعاً لأَنّي كُنْتُ عَطْشان جِدّاً. (sharibtu al-maa' sarii3an li'annii kuntu 3aTshaan jiddan. *I drank the water quickly, because I was very thirsty*)	

You don't necessarily need to use the separate pronouns in addition to the verb since the suffixes of the past tense tell you who's performing the action. Use the pronouns only if you want to emphasize who's performing the action.

Creating the present tense verb

The *present tense* expresses action occurring in the present time. In Arabic, forming the present tense is a bit more complicated than forming the past tense. The main reason is because every verb in the present tense receives a prefix, but some also get a suffix. I explain the rules a little later in this section.

Before you can properly form the present tense of a verb, you need to look in the dictionary to determine the vowel that goes over the second consonant of the verb. You can read more about these vowels in Chapter 3. You don't have to worry about which vowel to choose, however; it's predetermined. You just need to find out which one is correct in the dictionary. (And you'll be able to find it easily since I give you the past and present tense of each verb. Whatever vowel you find following the second consonant of the triliteral root in the present tense is the vowel you use for all the forms of the present.) Each verb uses only one of the three possible vowels: **Damma, kasra,** and **fatHa.** Table 2-6 shows examples of verbs using each of the three vowels.

Table 2-6	Examples of Verbs Using the Three Vowels	
Arabic Vowel	***Arabic Verb***	***Translation***
فَتْحة (fatHa; *a*)	يَشْرَبُ (yashrabu)	*he drinks*
كَسْرة (kasra; *i*)	نَجْلِسُ (najlisu)	*we sit*
ضَمّة (Damma; *u*)	تَشْكُرُ (tashkuru)	*she thanks*

Before I show you all the forms of the present tense, I need to describe the steps for generating the present tense verb. Here they are:

1. **Attach the necessary prefix for each person of the verb to the first consonant.**

   The first consonant won't be followed by a vowel (you write a consonant without a vowel in Arabic by placing the ˚ [**sukuun**] symbol over the consonant).

2. **After the second consonant, add the vowel that the particular verb uses in the present tense.**

   You can discover the correct vowel in your dictionary.

3. **Add a Damma to the third consonant of the root.**

   The following are exceptions to this rule:

   - *You* (FS) takes the suffix يـنَ (**-iina**).
   - *You* (MP) and *they* (MP) take the suffix ونَ (**-uuna**).
   - *You* (FP) and *they* (FP) take the suffix نَ (**-na**).

Table 2-7 shows the prefixes and suffixes that you must add to create the present tense.

Table 2-7	**Personal Pronoun Prefixes and Suffixes for Verbs in the Present Tense**		
Arabic Pronoun	*Translation*	*Prefix*	*Suffix*
أنَا ('anaa)	I/me	أ ('a-)	˚ (-u)
أنْتَ ('anta)	you (MS)	تَ (ta-)	˚ (-u)
أنْتِ ('anti)	you (FS)	تَ (ta-)	يـنَ (-iina)
هُوَ (huwa)	he	يَ (ya-)	˚ (-u)
هِيَ (hiya)	she	تَ (ta-)	˚ (-u)
نَحْنُ (naHnu)	we	نَ (na-)	˚ (-u)
أنْتُم ('antum)	you (MP)	تَ (ta-)	ونَ (-unna)
أنْتُنَّ ('antunna)	you (FP)	تَ (ta-)	نَ (-na)
هُم (hum)	they (MP)	يَ (ya-)	ونَ (-uuna)
هُنَّ (hunna)	they (FP)	يَ (ya-)	نَ (-na)

As an example, the following table shows all the forms of the verb, شَرِبَ (**shariba;** *to drink*), in the present tense.

Present tense of شَرِبَ (shariba; *to drink*)	
أَشْرَبُ ('anaa 'ashrabu)	نَشْرَبُ (naHnu nashrabu)
تَشْرَبُ ('anta tashrabu) تَشْرَبِينَ ('anti tashrabiina)	تَشْرَبُونَ ('antum tashrabuuna) تَشْرَبْنَ ('antunna tashrabna)
يَشْرَبُ (huwa yashrabu) تَشْرَبُ (hiya tashrabu)	يَشْرَبُونَ (hum yashrabuuna) يَشْرَبْنَ (hunna yashrabna)
نَشْرَبُ عَصير تُفّاح كُلّ يَوْم. (nashrabu 3aSiir tuffaaH kull yawm. *We drink apple juice every day.*)	

Forming the future tense verb

If there were an Olympic event for the easiest way to form the future tense in a language, Arabic would likely take the gold medal. All you have to do to write a verb in the future tense is add سَـ (**sa**) to the present tense form. How easy is that?

Following are the future tense forms of the verb, شَرِبَ (**shariba**; *to drink*). Notice that the forms here are identical to the present tense forms except for the addition of the prefix سَـ (**sa**).

شَرِبَ (shariba; *to drink*)	
سَأَشْرَبُ ('anaa sa'ashrabu)	سَنَشْرَبُ (naHnu sanashrabu)
سَتَشْرَبُ ('anta satashrabu) سَتَشْرَبِينَ ('anti satashrabiina)	سَتَشْرَبُونَ ('antum satashrabuuna) سَتَشْرَبْنَ ('antunna satashrabna)
سَيَشْرَبُ (huwa sayashrabu) سَتَشْرَبُ (hiya satashrabu)	سَيَشْرَبُونَ (hum sayashrabuuna) سَيَشْرَبْنَ (hunna sayashrabna)
سَنَشْرَبُ القَهْوة مَعاً عِنْدَما يَصِلُ أَحْمَد إِنْ شاءَ الله. (sanashrabu al-qahwa ma3an 3indamaa yaSilu 'aHmad, 'in shaa'a allah. *We will drink coffee together when Ahmad arrives, God willing.*)	

Producing the proper form of the verb is an important skill to master as you move on to the various forms and irregular verbs in the rest of the book. So be sure to take a run through this exercise before you begin. In the following sentences, each blank needs a verb. For clues, you get the root and vowel of the verb you need. To keep you from having to go to the dictionary, I give you the present tense vowel of each verb in parentheses. For the sake of the exercise, use past tense for anything in the past, present for anything today, and future for tomorrow.

Q. [أَكَلَ 'akala (u) to eat]. أنا وَأَصْدِقائي ____ في المَطْعَم أمس ('anaa wa-'aSdiqaa'ii ____ fii-l-maT3am 'amsi. *My friends and I ____ at the restaurant yesterday.*)

A. أنا وَأَصْدِقائي أَكَلْنا في المَطْعَم أمس ('anaa wa-'aSdiqaa'ii 'akalnaa fii-l-maT3am 'amsi. *My friends and I ate at the restaurant yesterday.*)

27.	[كَتَبَ **kataba** (u) to write] كَريم رِسالةً اليَوْم ____ (____ kariim risaalatan al-yawm. *Karim ____ a letter today.*)
28.	[لَعَبَ **la3aba** (a) to play] الوَلَد كُرة القَدَم غَداً ____ (____ al-walad kurat al-qadam ghadan. *The boy ____ soccer tomorrow.*)
29.	[ذَهَبَ **dhahaba** (a) to go] فاطمة إلى لُبْنان الأُسْبوع الماضي ____ (____ faaTima 'ilaa lubnaan al-'usbuu3 al-maaDii. *Fatima ____ to Lebanon last week.*)
30.	[شَكَرَ **shakara** (u) to thank] مَرْوان أُسْتاذَهُ أمس ____ (____ marwaan 'ustaadhahu 'amsi. *Marwan ____ his professor yesterday.*)
31.	[حَضَرَ **HaDara** (u) to come] أنْتِ ____ إلى الحَفْلة غَداً ('anti ____ 'ilaa-l-Hafla ghadan. *Tomorrow you ____ to the party.*)
32.	[قَرَأ **qara'a** (a) to read] النِّساء الكُتُب اليَوْم ____ (____ an-nisaa' al-kutub al-yawm. *The women ____ the books today.*)
33.	[بَدَأ **bada'a** (a) to begin] أنا ____ واجباتي أمس ('anaa ____ waajibaatii 'amsi. *I ____ my homework yesterday.*)
34.	[نَزَلَ **nazala** (i) to disembark] صَديقي مِنّ الطّائرة غَداً ____ (____ Sadiiqii mina-T-Taa'ira ghadan. *My friend ____ from the plane tomorrow.*)

Grasping Arabic Grammar Essentials

As you know, nouns are the things and verbs are the actions. Knowing how to put these items together is where you enter that often feared area of grammar. To compare language to baking a cake, nouns and verbs alike are the ingredients you use. But grammar is the recipe that tells you the specific ways to combine those ingredients so you can produce something good. Grammar lets writers produce a work in a way that's understandable (and hopefully enjoyable) to all.

In terms of their grammar, there are two main types of languages. One type relies on word suffixes or prefixes to determine what every part of speech is doing in the sentence. We call these *inflected languages*. Latin is one of them; it has different endings for every possible function of the words. Another type of language is what's called a *word order language*. English is a member of this class. In English, the subject comes before the verb and the object comes after.

Modern Standard Arabic is an inflected language that has developed into a word order language. What do I mean by that? Well, Arabic has case endings (which you can read about in Chapter 4) that tell you whether a noun is the subject or the object. However, because word order also tells you the subject and object, you can drop those endings out of your pronunciation without causing any loss of understanding. It isn't surprising that all the modern dialects have abandoned the case endings.

In this section, I give you a brief overview of a few important grammatical issues in Arabic, including a description of the two types of sentences (equational and verbal) and an explanation of the **'iDaafa** structure. Familiarity with these concepts equips you to expand your use of Arabic into the more complicated grammatical constructions that are covered in Part IV of this book.

Adding up equational sentences

The most basic sentence in Arabic is one in which you write *A* [*is*] *B*. This type of sentence is known as an *equational sentence*. In Arabic, there's no verb meaning *to be* in the present tense. Instead, it's understood from the context. To give you an idea of how this works, I put the word *to be* in brackets in the English translation of the examples to remind you that this word is missing in the Arabic.

In the following examples, I show you the possible types of equational sentences. What they have in common is the lack of a present tense verb *to be* as well as the existence of two parts. The first part (*A*) is the *subject*. The subject could be a name, pronoun, or proper noun. The second part (*B*) is called the *predicate*. The predicate is the additional information your equational sentence imparts about the subject. That information could be in the form of an adjective (if you're describing an attribute of the subject) or a proper noun or name.

Here's an example of an equational sentence in which *A* could be a proper name and *B* could be another noun:

مُحَمَّد مُهَنْدِس.

(**Muhammad muhandis.** *Muhammad* [*is*] *an engineer.*)

A could also be a noun and *B* could be a proper name, like this:

اِسْمِي أَحْمَد.

(**ismii 'aHmad.** *My name* [*is*] *Ahmad.*)

And, finally, *A* could be a pronoun and *B* could be an adjective, as in this example (which also adds a temporal adverb):

أَنا تَعْبان اليَوْم.

(**'anaa ta3baan al-yawm.** *I [am] tired today.*)

You can add the interrogative particle هَل (**hal**) to an equational sentence to make it a question. There's no direct English equivalent for **hal**; it just introduces a question. Consider this example:

هَل أَنْتَ مُتَأَكِّد مِن ذلِكَ؟

(**hal 'anta muta'akkid min dhaalika?** *[Are] you sure about that?*)

Creating action with verbal sentences

A *verbal sentence* contains a verb in the predicate. In a verbal sentence, the fact that a particular action took place or is taking place is an integral part of the information being conveyed. It may also be true that the verbal sentence tells you who's doing the action or to whom the action is being done. Here's an example of a verbal sentence:

نامَ الكَلْب كُلّ اليَوّم.

(**naama al-kalb kulla-l-yawm.** *The dog slept all day.*)

Here the word *dog* is the subject and *slept* is the verb. This sentence displays the normal word order you use in Arabic. The first word of the sentence is your verb. Immediately following your verb comes your subject. There's no object to the verb. However, if your sentence requires you to add an object, you express the object immediately after the subject. For example, here's a sentence with a subject, a verb, and an object:

أَكَلَتْ القِطّة الفَأْر.

(**'akalat al-qiTTa al-fa'r.** *The cat ate the mouse.*)

Here the word *cat* is the subject, *ate* is the verb, and, well, the *mouse* is the unfortunate object.

Expressing possession with the 'iDaafa structure

An **'iDaafa** is the grammatical construction used in Arabic to express possession of one noun over another. To form an **'iDaafa**, you put two nouns next to each other, with the second noun possessing the first. Refer to Chapter 7 for help on perfecting your use of complicated and long **'iDaafas**. For now, I keep it simple and just go over the two-word **'iDaafa.**

In English, you have two ways to express possession of one noun over another. You can use the word *of,* as in the phrase, *the house of Ahmad.* You can also use the possessive suffix *'s,* as in *Ahmad's house.* In Arabic, you express either one of these two English phrases with an **'iDaafa** in which you put together the two words, بَيْت أَحْمَد (**bayt 'aHmad;** literally, *house Ahmad*).

One inviolable rule about the Arabic **'iDaafa** is that the first word in the **'iDaafa** can never take the ال (**'alif laam**). If the second word is definite — it's either a proper name like Ahmad or it's a noun with the **'alif laam** — the whole **'iDaafa** is translated as if both members are definite. Here's an example of an **'iDaafa** with a noun in the definite state coming second. Notice that the translation renders both definite:

مُساعِد الرَّئيس

(**musaa3id ar-ra'iis;** *the assistant of the president* or, *the president's assistant*)

You see in the final example that when the first word in an **'iDaafa** ends with the **taa' marbuuTa,** you pronounce the word as if there's a final *t.* In Arabic writing, however, there's no difference in spelling.

The only way to master the **'iDaafa** construction is by practicing extensively. So in the following exercise, I provide you with several English possessive phrases. Produce the indicated **'iDaafas** in Arabic based on those English phrases.

0. the tree's leaves

A. أوْراق الشَّجَرة (**'awraaq ash-shajara**)

35. the man's shirt _____

36. a friend's pen _____

37. the girl's school _____

38. a cup of coffee _____

39. the friend's car _____

40. the college stadium _____

41. a man's daughter _____

42. the professor's address _____

Navigating Arabic Bilingual Dictionaries

Have you ever forgotten a word even in English? In that moment, you may tell a friend that there's a word you need, and it's right on the tip of your tongue. You use so many words every day that you're bound to have difficulties even in your native language. However, how much more frustrating it is to find yourself needing a word that you've never even learned! That's where bilingual dictionaries come in.

Consider the following common Arabic saying: العَرَبيّة مُحيط. (**al-3arabiyya muHiiT.** *Arabic is an Ocean.*). Arabic contains the largest number of native words of all other languages on the planet. (English has more words overall, but a majority of English words are borrowed from other languages.) So obviously, you need to know your way around a dictionary, whether it's one in the back of this book or a separate Arabic-English dictionary.

Using the dictionaries in the appendixes of this book

As you go through this book, you may need to consult the dictionaries in the appendixes to complete the exercises. So to help you do that most efficiently, you need a little guidance on how to use them. When you need to find the Arabic equivalent to an English word, look it up in the English-Arabic dictionary. You look it up alphabetically (according to the English word).

To help you distinguish between nouns and verbs, a verb is always given in the form of an infinitive (*to* + a verb). Compare the following two entries; the first one is a verb and the second a noun:

to answer: أجابَ (**'ajaaba**) / يُجيبُ (**yujiibu**)

answer: جَواب (**jawaab**) / أجُوبة (**'ajwiba**)

For the Arabic-English dictionary, I include all forms alphabetically by the order of the Arabic alphabet — as opposed to listing words under their triliteral roots (which is how many other dictionaries are organized). If you're unsure of the order of the Arabic alphabet, it's included in the Cheat Sheet at the front of the book. This organization should help you more quickly locate the forms you need. When I give you a verb, I supply the present tense in parentheses along with the past tense. For nouns and adjectives, I give you the plural form in parentheses.

Finding your way through a regular Arabic-English dictionary

The main difference between the dictionaries you encounter in this book and many of the full dictionaries on the market is that many follow the convention of organizing by root rather than presenting each word alphabetically. In this book's Arabic-English dictionary, you find the word مَكْتَب (**maktab;** *office*) on the same page as مَصْنَع (**maSna3;** *factory*) because both start with *m*. In other full dictionaries, however, you would find مَكْتَب (**maktab;** *office*) on the same page as كاتِب (**kaatib;** *writer*) because all the words formed from the root كتب (**k-t-b;** *to write*) are put together.

For a good alphabetical dictionary that's organized the same way as the dictionaries in this book, try *Al Mawrid* (English-Arabic/Arabic-English dictionary) by Mounir Baalbaki. A good dictionary that's organized by triliteral root is *The Hans Wehr Dictionary of Modern Written Arabic.*

Answer Key

1 سامِعٌ (**saami3un**; *hearer*)

2 مَطْبَخٌ (**maTbakhun**; *kitchen*)

3 حاكِم (**Haakim**; *judge*)

4 مَخْرَجٌ (**makhrajun**; *exit*)

5 شُبّاك مَفْتوح (**shubbaak maftuuH**; *open window*)

6 دَرّاجة سَريعة (**darraaja sarii3a**; *fast bicycle*)

7 عُلْبة ثَقيلة (**3ulba thaqiila**; *heavy box*)

8 شارِع طَويل (**shaari3 Tawiil**; *long road*)

9 المَتْحَف (**al-matHaf**; *the museum*)

10 السّوق (**as-suuq**; *the market*)

11 الكَتْف (**al-katf**; *the shoulder*)

12 الثَّمَن (**ath-thaman**; *the price*)

13 التَّأْمين (**at-ta'miin**; *the insurance*)

14 الرَّقَم (**ar-raqam**; *the number*)

15 الحَرير (**al-Hariir**; *the silk*)

16 الدَّراجة (**ad-darraaja**; *the bicycle*)

17 الجامِع (**al-jaami3**; *the mosque*)

18 الأُمّ (**al-'umm**; *the mother*)

19 وَظيفَتي (**waDHiifatii**; *my job*)

20 اسمُهُ (**ismuhu**; *his name*)

21 أَمَلُنا (**'amalunaa**; *our hope*)

22 جامِعَتُها (**jaami3atuhaa**; *her university*)

23 رَئيسُكُم (**ra'iisukum**; *your president*)

24 فِكْرَتُهُنَّ (**fikratuhunna**; *their idea*)

25 طَعامُكَ (**Ta3aamuka**; *your food*)

26 قَلَمُكِ (**qalamuki**; *your pen*)

27.	يَكْتُبُ كَريم رِسالةً البَوْم. (**yaktubu** kariim risaalatan al-yawm. *Karim <u>writes</u> a letter today.*)
28.	<u>سَيَلْعَبُ</u> الوَلَد كُرة القَدَم غَداً. (**sa-yal3abu** al-walad kurat al-qadam ghadan. *The boy <u>will play</u> soccer tomorrow.*)
29.	<u>ذَهَبَتْ</u> فاطِمة إلى لُبنان الأُسْبوع الماضي. (**dhahabat** faaTima 'ilaa lubnaan al-'usbuu3 al-maaDii. *Fatima <u>went</u> to Lebanon last week.*)
30.	<u>شَكَرَ</u> مَرْوان أُستاذَهُ أَمْسِ. (**shakara** marwaan 'ustaadhahu 'amsi. *Marwan <u>thanked</u> his professor yesterday.*)
31.	أَنتِ <u>سَتَحْضُرينَ</u> إلى الحَفْلة غَداً. ('anti **sa-taHDuriina** 'ilaa-l-Hafla ghadan. *Tomorrow you <u>will come</u> to the party.*)
32.	<u>تَقْرَأُ</u> النِّساء الكُتُب البَوْم. (**tagra'u** an-nisaa' al-kutub al-yawm. *The women <u>read</u> the books today.*)
33.	أَنا <u>بَدَأتُ</u> واجِباتي أَمْسِ. ('anaa **bada'tu** waajibaatii 'amsi. *I <u>started</u> my homework yesterday.*)
34.	<u>سَيَنْزِلُ</u> صَديقي مِنَ الطّائِرة غَداً. (**sa-yanzilu** Sadiiqii mina-T-Taa'ira ghadan. *My friend <u>will disembark</u> from the plane tomorrow.*)

35 قَميص الرَّجُل (**qamiiS ar-rajul**)

36 قَلَم صَديق (**qalam Sadiiq**)

37 مَدْرَسة البِنْت (**madrasat al-bint**)

38 فِنْجان قَهوة (finjaan qahwa)

39 سَيّارة الصَّديق (sayyaarat aS-Sadiiq)

40 مَلْعَب الكُلِّية (mal3ab al-kulliya)

41 بِنْت رَجُل (bint rajul)

42 عُنْوان الأُسْتاذ (3unwaan al-'ustaadh)

Chapter 3

The Write Stuff: How to Read and Write the Arabic Alphabet

In This Chapter

▶ Discovering Arabic letters that connect in only one direction

▶ Producing Arabic letters that connect in two directions

▶ Writing the vowels and special characters in Arabic

Many times, when native speakers of Arabic discover that I know how to speak their language, they ask me if I also know how to read and write it. When I tell them I do, they're ordinarily more impressed (and even astounded) with the fact that I know the Arabic alphabet than with the fact that I know how to speak the language itself! This is because, for good or bad, the Arabic alphabet is a difficult matter.

If you have no background yet in how to read and write the Arabic script that you find in this book, you can still get started learning some intermediate level Arabic. This is because as an extra feature of this book, I include English transliteration for everything. But learning the alphabet still is essential for you if you intend to gain any depth in the language.

The purpose of this chapter is to provide a straightforward presentation of each Arabic letter. I show you how to recognize and write each letter. I also explore how each consonant is pronounced and how to add vowels to your consonants.

Understanding the Basics of Writing Arabic Script

Arabic, as you probably know, is written from right to left. Arabic letters that can be connected only to letters on their own right side are called *non-connectors*. This name is conventionally used even though it's a bit of a misnomer, since the so-called non-connectors can indeed connect to letters that precede them in a word. But they can't ever connect to letters that follow them. Other letters can connect to letters that both precede and follow them. These letters are called *connectors*.

When I present each of the letters to you, I give you the name of the letter in Arabic, which is a dummy word that starts with that letter (like how we, in English, pronounce the letter *b* as *bee*.) In this chapter, I use consistent names for the potential shapes of both the non-connectors and the connectors from the start. Here's a description of the potential letters:

- **Independent (I):** The form of the letter that stands alone and not connected to any other letter.

- **Initial Connected (In.C.):** The form of the letter that's not connected to any letter on its own right side but is connected to a following letter on its left side.

- **Medial (Med.):** The form of the letter that's connected to other letters on both its right and left sides.

- **Final Connected (F.C.):** The form of the letter that's connected to another letter on its own right side but is also the final letter of a word.

One of the benefits of a *For Dummies* book is the modular organization. In other words, topics are self-contained in the book for you to explore however and whenever you see fit. Indeed, the rest of this book is organized that way. My advice to you, however, is that if you're currently making your first foray into the alphabet, you should work through this particular chapter from start to finish. Because the Arabic letters connect with one another in a cursive script, they really need to be explored from start to finish so you can build on what you learn.

Exploring the Non-Connectors

Letters that can connect only on their own right side are called *non-connectors.* Because they can never connect to letters that follow them, they won't have a form for the Initial Connected and Medial letters. They also, by definition, can never connect to one another. I show you each of the non-connectors in the following sections.

أَلِف ('alif)

The أَلِف (**'alif**) as a letter by itself represents the long *a* vowel (transliterated in this book as **aa.** You write the Independent أَلِف (**'alif**) as a single line downward. The Final Connected أَلِف (**'alif**) goes upward from the letter that it's connected to. Table 3-1 shows the two shapes of the أَلِف (**'alif**) as you will see them in the book and written by hand.

Table 3-1		Shapes of the أَلِف ('alif)	
Location	*Font*	*Handwritten*	*Example*
I	ا	ا	دار (**daar**; *house*)
F.C.	ـا	ـا	كانَ (**kaana**; *he was*)

واو (waaw)

The واو (**waaw**), which is transliterated as **w** in this book, can represent two sounds. It can be a consonant equal to the English *w* in *wish*. It also can stand for the long *u* vowel (transliterated in this book as **uu**) as in the English word *food.* There are two ways to know when the واو (**waaw**) is being used as a consonant. If there's a vowel symbol above or below the واو (**waaw**), it represents the consonantal sound *w*. (You can explore vowels in the final section of this chapter.) Also, if the واو (**waaw**) is followed by a long vowel, written with an أَلِف ('**alif**), يَاء (**yaa'**), or واو (**waaw**), it's being used as a consonant. If the واو (**waaw**) doesn't have a vowel, it's being used to represent a long *u* vowel on whatever consonant it's following.

You write the Independent واو (**waaw**) like a large comma with a space inside. The Final Connected واو (**waaw**) forms the same shape. Table 3-2 shows the two shapes of the واو (**waaw**) as you will see them in the book and written by hand.

Table 3-2		Shapes of the واو (waaw)	
Location	*Font*	*Handwritten*	*Example*
I	و	9	يَزورُ (**yazuuru**; *he visits*)
F.C.	ـو	ـو	نور (**nuur**; *light*)

دال (daal) and ذال (dhaal)

The دال (**daal**) and ذال (**dhaal**) are formed with the same shape. The only difference is that the ذال (**dhaal**) has a dot drawn above the letter and the دال (**daal**) doesn't. The form is written like a 45-degree angle pointing left.

دال (daal)

The دال (**daal**), which is transliterated in this book as **d,** represents the same sound as the English *d* as in *door.* See Table 3-3 for the two shapes of the دال (**daal**) as you will see them in the book and written by hand.

Table 3-3		Shapes of the دال (daal)	
Location	*Font*	*Handwritten*	*Example*
I	د	ل	دار (**daar**; *house*)
F.C.	ـد	ـلـ	عَبـد (**3abd**; *servant*)

ذال (dhaal)

The ذال (**dhaal**), which is transliterated in this book as **dh,** represents the same sound as the English *th* as in *this.* Table 3-4 shows the two shapes of the ذال (**dhaal**) as you will see them in the book and written by hand.

Table 3-4		Shapes of the ذال (dhaal)	
Location	*Font*	*Handwritten*	*Example*
I	ذ	ذ	دَوْق (**dhawq;** *taste*)
F.C.	ـذ	ـذ	لَذيـذ (**ladhiidh;** *tasty*)

راء (raa') and زاي (zaay)

The راء (**raa'**) and زاي (**zaay**) are written with the same shape. The one difference is that the زاي (**zaay**) has a dot placed above it, and the راء (**raa'**) doesn't. The form is drawn as a curved line pointing to the left and dropping a bit below the line of writing.

راء (raa')

The راء (**raa'**) represents a trilled *r* sound (like Spanish **perro,** meaning *dog*). راء (**raa'**) is transliterated as **r** in this book. Refer to Table 3-5 for the two shapes of the letter as you will see them in the book and written by hand.

Table 3-5		Shapes of the راء (raa')	
Location	*Font*	*Handwritten*	*Example*
I	ر	ر	راتِب (**raatiib;** *salary*)
F.C.	ـر	ـر	مُرّ (**murr;** *bitter*)

زاي (zaay)

The زاي (**zaay**) represents the *z* sound as in the English word *zebra.* زاي (**zaay**) is transliterated in this book as **z.** See Table 3-6 for the two shapes of the زاي (**zaay**) as you will see them in the book and written by hand.

Table 3-6		Shapes of the زاي (zaay)	
Location	Font	Handwritten	Example
I	ز	ز	زَارَ (zaara; he visited)
F.C.	ـز	ـز	أُرزّ ('aruzz; rice)

تاء مَرْبوطَة (taa' marbuuTa)

The تاء مَرْبوطَة (taa' marbuuTa) is a form that occurs only as the last letter of words, which are almost always feminine. You pronounce it as a final *a*. It's transliterated in this book as **a**. As an Independent letter, the تاء مَرْبوطَة (taa' marbuuTa) is written as a small circle with two dots directly above it. In the Final Connected form, it looks like a small raised oval shape with two dots directly above it. See Table 3-7 for the two shapes of the تاء مَرْبوطَة (taa' marbuuTa) as you will see them in the book and written by hand.

Table 3-7		Shapes of the تاء مَرْبوطَة (taa' marbuuTa)	
Location	Font	Handwritten	Example
I	ة	ة	كُرَة (kura; ball)
F.C.	ـة	ـة	كَلِمَة (kalima; word)

ألِف مَكْسورَة ('alif maksuura)

The ألِف مَكْسورَة ('alif maksuura) is a form that occurs only as the last letter of a word. You pronounce it as a final **a**. It's written like an *s* shape, and it's transliterated in this book as **aa**. Refer to Table 3-8 to see the two shapes of the ألِف مَكْسورَة ('alif maksuura) as you will see them in the book and written by hand.

Table 3-8		Shapes of the ألِف مَكْسورَة ('alif maksuura)	
Location	Font	Handwritten	Example
I	ى	ى	لَدى (ladaa; at)
F.C.	ـى	ـى	مَعْنى (ma3naa; meaning)

Taking a Look at Connectors

The majority of Arabic letters can connect on both their right and left sides. These are called *connectors*. They have four different shapes depending on their positions relative to other letters.

باء (baa'), تاء (taa'), ثاء (thaa'), نون (nuun), and ياء (yaa')

The letters باء (**baa'**), تاء (**taa'**), ثاء (**thaa'**), نون (**nuun**), and ياء (**yaa'**) are written with the same shapes. The only differences are that باء (**baa'**) is written with a single dot under the shape, تاء (**taa'**) is written with two dots above, ثاء (**thaa'**) is written with three dots above, نون (**nuun**) is written with a single dot above, and ياء (**yaa'**) rounds out the series with two dots below.

You write the Independent form like a bowl. The Initial Connected form is like a small comma that connects to the next letter. The Medial form is like a single wave between the letters on each side of the letter. The Final Connected form is like the Independent form, just connected with the letter preceding it.

باء (baa')

The باء (**baa'**), which is transliterated in this book as **b,** represents the *b* as in the English word *bakery*.

Table 3-9 shows the four shapes of the باء (**baa'**) as you will see them in the book and written by hand.

Table 3-9		Shapes of باء (baa')	
Location	*Font*	*Handwritten*	*Example*
I	ب	ب	كِتاب (kitaab; *book*)
In.C.	بـ	بـ	باب (baab; *door*)
Med.	ـبـ	ـبـ	قَبْلَ (qabla; *before*)
F.C.	ـب	ـب	كَتَبَ (kataba; *he wrote*)

تاء (taa')

The تاء (**taa'**) represents the *t* as in the English word *toast*. تاء (**taa'**) is transliterated in this book as **t.** In Table 3-10 you can see the four shapes of the تاء (**taa'**) as you will see them in the book and written by hand.

Table 3-10 Shapes of تاء (taa')

Location	*Font*	*Handwritten*	*Example*
I	ت	ت	ماتَ (**maata;** *he died*)
In.C.	تـ	تـ	تَسْكُنُ (**taskunu;** *she lives*)
Med.	ـتـ	ـتـ	كَتَبَتْ (**katabat;** *she wrote*)
F.C.	ـت	ـت	أَكَلَتْ (**'akalat;** *she ate*)

ثاء *(thaa')*

The **ثاء** (**thaa'**), which is transliterated in this book as **th,** represents the *th* as in the English word *thin.* Table 3-11 shows the four shapes of the **ثاء** (**thaa'**) as you will see them in the book and written by hand.

Table 3-11 Shapes of ثاء (thaa')

Location	*Font*	*Handwritten*	*Example*
I	ث	ث	مُلَوَّث (**mulawwath;** *polluted*)
In.C.	ثـ	ثـ	ثُمَّ (**thumma;** *then*)
Med.	ـثـ	ـثـ	مِثْلَ (**mithla;** *like*)
F.C.	ـث	ـث	حَديث (**Hadiith;** *recent*)

نون *(nuun)*

The **نون** (**nuun**), which is transliterated in this book as **n,** represents the *n* as in the English word *new.* You write the Independent and Final Connected **نون** (**nuun**) like a bowl — but a bit deeper in shape than the **باء** (**baa'**), **تاء** (**taa'**), and **ثاء** (**thaa'**). Refer to Table 3-12 for the four shapes of the **نون** (**nuun**) as you will see them in the book and written by hand.

Table 3-12		Shapes of نون (nuun)	
Location	*Font*	*Handwritten*	*Example*
I	ن	ن	كـانَ (**kaana**; *he was*)
In.C.	ﻧ	ن	نار (**naar**; *fire*)
Med.	ﻨ	ـنـ	لَنـا (**lanaa**; *to us*)
F.C.	ن	ـن	أَعْلَنَ (**'a3lana**; *he announced*)

ياء (*yaa'*)

The ياء (**yaa'**), which is transliterated in this book as **y**, can represent two sounds in Arabic. As a consonant, it's the same as the *y* in the English word *yes*. However, it also can be used to signify the long *i* vowel (transliterated in this book as **ii**). There are two ways to know when the ياء (**yaa'**) is being used as a consonant. If you see a vowel symbol above or below the ياء (**yaa'**), it represents the consonantal sound *y*. (You can explore vowels in the final section of this chapter.) If the ياء (**yaa'**) is followed by a long vowel — written with an أَلِف (**'alif**), ياء (**yaa'**), or واو (**waaw**) — it's also being used as a consonant. If the ياء (**yaa'**) doesn't have a vowel, it's being used to represent a long *i* vowel on whatever consonant it's following.

You write the Independent ياء (**yaa'**) like an *s* shape, which is identical in form to the أَلِف مَكْسورَة (**'alif maksuura**). The Initial Connected and Medial forms are identical in shape to the other letters in this section, except that the ياء (**yaa'**) has two dots below the letter. The Final Connected form of the ياء (**yaa'**) is like the Independent form. Table 3-13 shows the four shapes of the ياء (**yaa'**) as you will see them in the book and written by hand.

Table 3-13		Shapes of ياء (yaa')	
Location	*Font*	*Handwritten*	*Example*
I	ي	ى	جاري (**jaarii**; *my neighbor*)
In.C.	ﻳ	ـيـ	يَتيم (**yatiim**; *orphan*)
Med.	ﻴ	ـيـ	فيل (**fiil**; *elephant*)
F.C.	ي	ـى	مِنّي (**minnii**; *from me*)

جيم (jiim), حاء (Haa), and خاء (khaa')

The جيم (**jiim**), حاء (**Haa'**), and خاء (**khaa'**) are written with the same form. The only differences are that the جيم (**jiim**) has one dot below, the حاء (**Haa'**) has no dot at all, and the خاء (**khaa'**) has one dot above.

You write the Independent form like a sharp angle with a hook below. The Initial Connected and Medial forms have the same sharp angle, but no hook. The Final Connected form is like the Independent form, but it's connected to the letter preceding it.

جيم (jiim)

The جيم (**jiim**), transliterated in this book as **j,** represents the same sound as *j* in the English word *jam.* Check out Table 3-14 for the four shapes of the جيم (**jiim**) as you will see them in the book and written by hand.

Table 3-14		Shapes of جيم (jiim)	
Location	*Font*	*Handwritten*	*Example*
I	ج	جـ	حاجّ (**Haajj**; *pilgrim*)
In.C.	جـ	جـ	جَميلَة (**jamiila**; *beautiful*)
Med.	ـجـ	ـجـ	لَجْنَة (**lajna**; *committee*)
F.C.	ـج	ـج	ثَلْج (**thalj**; *snow*)

حاء (Haa')

The حاء (**Haa'**) represents a strong *h* sound that doesn't occur in English. It's pronounced somewhere in between the English *h* and the خاء (**khaa'**), which you can read about in the next section. The حاء (**Haa'**) is transliterated in this book as **H.** Refer to Table 3-15 for the four shapes of the حاء (**Haa'**) as you will see them in the book and written by hand.

Table 3-15		Shapes of حاء (Haa')	
Location	*Font*	*Handwritten*	*Example*
I	ح	حـ	سِلاح (**silaaH**; *weapon*)
In.C.	حـ	حـ	حِصان (**HiSaan**; *horse*)
Med.	ـحـ	ـحـ	بَحْر (**baHr**; *sea*)
F.C.	ـح	ـح	قَبيح (**qabiiH**; *ugly*)

خاء (khaa')

The خاء (**khaa'**), which is transliterated in this book as **kh,** represents the same sound as *ch* in the Scottish *loch.* Table 3-16 shows the four shapes of the خاء (**khaa'**) as you will see them in the book and written by hand.

Table 3-16		Shapes of خاء (khaa')	
Location	*Font*	*Handwritten*	*Example*
I	خ	خ	طَبّاخ (**Tabbaakh;** *cook*)
In.C.	خ	حـ	خَلّ (**khall;** *vinegar*)
Med.	خ	ـحـ	شَخْص (**shakhS;** *person*)
F.C.	خ	ـح	مَطْبَخ (**maTbakh;** *kitchen*)

سين (siin) and شين (shiin)

سين (**siin**) and شين (**shiin**) are written with the same shape. The only difference is that شين (**shiin**) has three dots above it, and سين (**siin**) has none. The Independent form is written with two small hooks, followed by a larger hook. The Initial Connected form keeps the two small hooks and connects to the following letter. The Medial form has the two hooks connected on both sides. The Final Connected form is like the Independent form except that it's connected to the preceding letter.

سين (siin)

The سين (**siin**), which is transliterated in this book as **s,** is the same sound as the *s* in the English word *soup.* See Table 3-17 for the four shapes of the سين (**siin**) as you will see them in the book and written by hand.

Table 3-17		Shapes of سين (siin)	
Location	*Font*	*Handwritten*	*Example*
I	س	سل	ناس (**naas;** *people*)
In.C.	سـ	للـ	سَيّارَة (**sayyaara;** *car*)
Med.	ـسـ	ـلللـ	نَسْر (**nasr;** *eagle*)
F.C.	س	ـلل	شَمْس (**shams;** *sun*)

شين (*shiin*)

The شين (**shiin**), which is transliterated in this book as **sh**, is the same sound as the *sh* in the English word *should*. Table 3-18 shows the four shapes of the شين (**shiin**) as you will see them in the book and written by hand.

Table 3-18		Shapes of شين (shiin)	
Location	*Font*	*Handwritten*	*Example*
I	ش	ﺵ	فِراش (**firaash**; *mattress*)
In.C.	شـ	ﺸ	شارع (**shaari3**; *street*)
Med.	ـشـ	ـﺸـ	فِشار (**fishaar**; *popcorn*)
F.C.	ـش	ـﺶ	قَشّ (**qashsh**; *straw*)

صاد (*Saad*) and ضاد (*Daad*)

صاد (**Saad**) and ضاد (**Daad**) are written with the same shape. The only difference is that ضاد (**Daad**) has one dot above it and صاد (**Saad**) has none. The Independent form is written like a deflated balloon, followed by a large hook. The Initial Connected form keeps the deflated balloon and connects to the following letter. The Medial form has the deflated balloon connected on both sides. The Final Connected form is like the Independent form except that it's connected to the preceding letter.

صاد (*Saad*)

The صاد (**Saad**), which is transliterated in this book as **S**, is a rich and dark *s* sound, such as you hear in the English word *sauce*. Refer to Table 3-19 for the four shapes of the صاد (**Saad**) as you will see them in the book and written by hand.

Table 3-19		Shapes of صاد (Saad)	
Location	*Font*	*Handwritten*	*Example*
I	ص	ﺹ	فُرَص (**furaS**; *opportunities*)
In.C.	صـ	ﺻ	صَوْم (**Sawm**; *fasting*)
Med.	ـصـ	ـﺼـ	قِصّة (**qiSSa**; *story*)
F.C.	ـص	ـﺺ	لِصّ (**liSS**; *thief*)

ضاد (Daad)

The ضاد (**Daad**) is a rich and dark *d* sound, with no correspondence in English. It's pronounced like the English *d,* but with the Arabic sound your tongue touches the roof of your mouth more broadly. The letter is transliterated in this book as **D**. Table 3-20 shows the four shapes of the ضاد (**Daad**) as you will see them in the book and written by hand.

Table 3-20		Shapes of ضاد (Daad)	
Location	*Font*	*Handwritten*	*Example*
I	ض	ض	أَمْراض (**'amraaD**; *diseases*)
In.C.	ضـ	ضـ	ضَمير (**Damiir**; *conscience*)
Med.	ـضـ	ـضـ	فِضّة (**fiDDa**; *silver*)
F.C.	ـض	ـض	بَيْض (**bayD**; *eggs*)

طاء (Taa') and ظاء (DHaa')

طاء (**Taa'**) and ظاء (**DHaa'**) are written with the same shape. The only difference is that ظاء (**DHaa'**) has one dot above it, and طاء (**Taa'**) has none. The Independent form is written like a deflated balloon, with a straight line coming down to touch the base on the left side. The Initial Connected form is the same as the Independent form except that it connects to the following letter. The Medial form is the same form as well, but it's connected on both sides. The Final Connected form is also like the Independent, but it's connected to the preceding letter.

طاء (Taa')

The طاء (**Taa'**) is a rich and dark *t* sound, with no correspondence in English. It's pronounced like the English *t,* but your tongue touches the roof of your mouth more broadly. This letter is transliterated in this book as **T**. Review Table 3-21 to see the four shapes of the طاء (**Taa'**) as you will see them in the book and written by hand.

Table 3-21		Shapes of طاء (Taa')	
Location	*Font*	*Handwritten*	*Example*
I	ط	ط	خُطوط (**khuTuuT**; *lines*)
In.C.	ط	ط	طائرَة (**Taa'ira**; *airplane*)
Med.	ـط	ـط	قِطّة (**qiTTa**; *cat*)
F.C.	ـط	ـط	حَطّ (**HaTTa**; *he put*)

ظَاء (DHaa')

The ظَاء (**DHaa'**) is a rich and dark *th* sound, with no correspondence in English. It's pronounced like the English *th* in *this*, but your tongue touches the roof of your mouth more broadly. This letter is transliterated in this book as **DH**. Table 3-22 shows the four shapes of the ظَاء (**DHaa'**) as you will see them in the book and written by hand.

Table 3-22		Shapes of ظَاء (DHaa')	
Location	*Font*	*Handwritten*	*Example*
I	ظ	ظ	غِلاظ (**ghilaaDH**; *rude people*)
In.C.	ظ	ظـ	ظِفُر (**DHifr**; *fingernail*)
Med.	ظ	ظـ	عَظِيم (**3aDHiim**; *great*)
F.C.	ظ	ظـ	حَظّ (**HaDHDH**; *luck*)

عَيْن (3ayn) and غَيْن (ghayn)

عَيْن (**3ayn**) and غَيْن (**ghayn**) are written with the same shape. The only difference is that غَيْن (**ghayn**) has one dot above it, and عَيْن (**3ayn**) has none. The Independent form is written like the English letter *c*, with a hook. The Initial Connected form is the same as the Independent form except that it doesn't have the hook, and it connects to the following letter. The Medial form is like an inverted filled-in triangle, connected on both sides. The Final Connected form is written like the Medial form except that it has a final hook.

عَيْن (3ayn)

The عَيْن (**3ayn**) has no correspondence in English. It's produced by tightening the back of the throat and then speaking a vowel through it. This letter is transliterated in this book as **3**. To see the four shapes of the عَيْن (**3ayn**) as you will see them in the book and written by hand, check out Table 3-23.

Table 3-23		Shapes of عَيْن (3ayn)	
Location	*Font*	*Handwritten*	*Example*
I	ع	ع	مَوْضُوع (**mawDuu3**; *issue*)
In.C.	عـ	عـ	عَميق (**3aamiiq**; *deep*)
Med.	ع	عـ	مَلْعَب (**mal3ab**; *stadium*)
F.C.	ع	ع	قِطَع (**qiTa3**; *pieces*)

غَيْن (ghayn)

The غَيْن (ghayn) has no correspondence in English. It's like a *g* sound, but it's *fricatized*, meaning that it's raspy in the back of your throat. The letter is transliterated in this book as **gh.** Table 3-24 shows the four shapes of the غَيْن (ghayn) as you will see them in the book and written by hand.

Table 3-24		Shapes of غَيْن (ghayn)	
Location	*Font*	*Handwritten*	*Example*
I	غ	غ	دِماغ (**dimaagh;** *brain*)
In.C.	غ	غـ	غَرْب (**gharb;** *west*)
Med.	غ	ـغـ	لُغَة (**lugha;** *language*)
F.C.	غ	ـغ	مَبْلَغ (**mablagh;** *sum [of money]*)

فاء (faa') and قاف (qaaf)

فاء (**faa'**) and قاف (**qaaf**) are written with the same shape. The only difference is that فاء (**faa'**) has one dot above it, and قاف (**qaaf**) has two. The Independent form is a small circle (written clockwise) with a hook. The Initial Connected form is the same as the Independent form except that it doesn't have the hook, and it connects to the following letter. The Medial form is written as a clockwise circle, connected on both sides. The Final Connected form is a circle with a final hook. The hook of the فاء (**faa'**) stays on the line of writing, but the hook of the قاف (**qaaf**) drops below.

فاء (faa')

The فاء (**faa'**), which is transliterated in this book as **f,** is the same sound as the *f* in the English word *fortune*. To see the four shapes of the فاء (**faa'**) as you will see them in the book and written by hand, refer to Table 3-25.

Table 3-25		Shapes of فاء (faa')	
Location	*Font*	*Handwritten*	*Example*
I	ف	ف	جافّ (**jaaff;** *dry*)
In.C.	ف	فـ	فُرْصَة (**furSa;** *opportunity*)
Med.	ف	ـفـ	حَفْلَة (**Hafla;** *party*)
F.C.	ف	ـف	كَتِف (**katf;** *shoulder*)

قاف (qaaf)

The قاف (**qaaf**) has no correspondence in English. It's like a *k* sound, but it's pronounced at the back of the throat, as if you were cawing like a crow. The letter is transliterated in this book as **q.** Table 3-26 shows the four shapes of the قاف (**qaaf**) as you will see them in the book and written by hand.

Table 3-26		Shapes of قاف (qaaf)	
Location	*Font*	*Handwritten*	*Example*
I	ق	ق	سـوق (**suuq**; *market*)
In.C.	ق	ڧ	قَلْب (**qalb**; *heart*)
Med.	ـقـ	ـڧـ	بَقَرة (**baqara**; *cow*)
F.C.	ـق	ـق	شَـرْق (**sharq**; *east*)

كاف (kaaf)

The كاف (**kaaf**), which is transliterated in this book as **k,** is the same sound as the English *k* in *kind.* The كاف (**kaaf**) has distinctly different shapes depending on its position. As an Independent letter, it's a right angle facing left with a symbol like an *s* written alongside it. As an Initial Connected or Medial letter, it's like a sharp angle facing rightward. The Final Connected form is like the Independent form except that it's connected to the preceding letter. See Table 3-27 for the four shapes of the كاف (**kaaf**) as you will see them in the book and written by hand.

Table 3-27		Shapes of كاف (kaaf)	
Location	*Font*	*Handwritten*	*Example*
I	ك	ك	مُلوك (**muluuk**; *kings*)
In.C.	كـ	كـ	كِتاب (**kitaab**; *book*)
Med.	ـكـ	ـكـ	مُمْكِن (**mumkin**; *maybe*)
F.C.	ـك	ـك	سِلْك (**silk**; *wire*)

لام (laam)

The لام (laam) is the same sound as the *l* in the English word *loaf.* The letter is transliterated as **l**.

Be careful not to mix the لام (laam) up with the ألِف ('alif); both are written as a straight vertical line, so it's easy to do. The way to distinguish the ألِف ('alif) from the لام (laam) is to remember that the لام (laam) is a connector. So, if you see a straight line that connects with the next letter, it's a لام (laam). If it doesn't connect with the next letter, you know it's an ألِف ('alif). Additionally, the لام (laam) has a hook on the Independent form and the Final Connected form.

To see the four shapes of the لام (laam) as you will see them in the book and written by hand, refer to Table 3-28.

Table 3-28		Shapes of لام (laam)	
Location	*Font*	*Handwritten*	*Example*
I	ل	ل	شِـمـال (shimaal; *north*)
In.C.	لـ	لـ	لُغَة (lugha; *language*)
Med.	ـلـ	ـلـ	مَمْلَكَة (mamlaka; *kingdom*)
F.C.	ـل	ـل	رَجُل (rajul; *man*)

ميم (miim)

The ميم (miim) is the same sound as the *m* in the English word *meat.* It's transliterated in this book as **m**.

Be careful not to mix the ميم (miim) up with the فاء (faa') and قاف (qaaf), since they're all essentially small circles. There are two ways to distinguish the ميم (miim) from the فاء (faa') and the قاف (qaaf). Most importantly, the ميم (miim) has no dots, and the others each have some. Also, the ميم (miim) is written counterclockwise. The Independent and Final Connected forms of the ميم (miim) have tails that drop below the line of writing.

Table 3-29 shows the four shapes of the ميم (miim) as you will see them in the book and written by hand.

Table 3-29		Shapes of ميم (miim)	
Location	*Font*	*Handwritten*	*Example*
I	م	ρ	أمامَ (**'amaama;** *in front of*)
In.C.	ـمـ	ـ⌒o	مَشـى (**mashaa;** *he walked*)
Med.	ـمـ	─o─	جُمْلَة (**jumla;** *sentence*)
F.C.	ـم	ρ~	حَكـيـم (**Hakiim;** *wise*)

The ألِف (**'alif**), لام (**laam**), هاء (**haa'**), حاء (**Haa'**), خاء (**khaa'**), جيم (**jiim**), and ميم (**miim**) can join together in peculiar ways. When these letters connect to certain others, they take on slightly different shapes than when they connect with any other letter. The technical name for these atypically connected forms is *ligature.* For instance, you'll notice that the ألِف (**'alif**) leans more to the left than normal when following a لام (**laam**). Here's an example: ﻻ (**laa;** *no/not*).

Similarly, when the preposition ل (**li-**) is followed by a noun with the ال (**'alif laam**), you don't write the ألِف (**'alif**). This allows you to avoid writing three straight lines in a row. Here's an example:

ل الرَّجُل (**li ar-rajul**) becomes لِلرَّجُـل (**li-r-rajuli;** *to the man*)

In some Arabic fonts, when a ميم (**miim**) follows a لام (**laam**), the ميم (**miim**) may be written so that it's sticking a bit to the right of the لام (**laam**).

Finally, in some Arabic fonts, when a هاء (**haa'**), حاء (**Haa'**), خاء (**khaa'**), or جيم (**jiim**) follows a لام (**laam**), the لام (**laam**) may be written sticking out of the middle of the following letter.

هاء *(haa')*

The هاء (**haa'**), which is transliterated in this book as **h,** is the same sound as the *h* in the English word *hot dog.* The هاء (**haa'**) has distinct shapes depending on its position. For example, the Independent form is a small circle. The Initial Connected form is a larger circle with the smaller circle inside it, which is then connected to the following letter. The Medial form is written as a figure eight above and below the line of writing. The Final Connected form is like a raised oval connected to the preceding letter. Refer to Table 3-30 for the four shapes of the هاء (**haa'**) as you will see them in the book and written by hand.

Table 3-30		Shapes of هاء (haa')	
Location	**Font**	**Handwritten**	**Example**
I	ه	○	إشْـتِباه (**ishtibaah**; *similarity*)
In.C.	ﻬ	ﻬ	هُم (**hum**; *they*)
Med.	ﻬ	8	شَـهادَة (**shahaada**; *testimony*)
F.C.	ﻪ	ﻪ	كِتابُهُ (**kitaabuhu**; *his book*)

ء (hamza)

The ء (**hamza**), which is transliterated in this book as **'**, represents the glottal stop. The *glottal stop* is that slight catch of air before actually releasing a vowel. For instance, think of how some people pronounce the word *Latin* (sort of like *La'in*). In Arabic, the ء (**hamza**) is written as a tiny symbol like a backwards *z*.

The ء (**hamza**) can be written above or below three letters: the أَلِف (**'alif**), the واو (**waaw**), or the ياء (**yaa'**). These letters are called the *seats* of the ء (**hamza**). It may also, in some cases, be written all on its own without one of the seats.

There's a complicated set of rules governing where you place the ء (**hamza**). Instead of memorizing the dozens of rules for it, you'll instead intuitively pick up the rules by practicing your Arabic reading. The beauty of having full transliteration in this book is that you can always see how the Arabic is pronounced.

Here are several examples showing you the possible ways you may see the ء (**hamza**):

أَكْلة (**'akla**; *food*)

أُمّ (**'umm**; *mother*)

إمْرَأة (**'imra'a**; *woman*)

أَسْئِلَة (**'as'ila**; *questions*)

سُؤال (**su'aal**; *question*)

أَصْدِقاء (**'aSdiqaa'**; *friends*)

Examining Vowels and Special Characters

Arabic was originally a purely consonantal alphabet. In other words, there were no vowels at all. As time went on, especially as people were learning Arabic as a second language, it was necessary to invent a system for telling readers what vowels a word had and when a consonant had no vowels or was doubled. Because this secondary system was invented later, it was tacked onto the alphabet as a system of symbols that you write above and below the existing letters. In this section, I introduce you to these important symbols.

ˊ (fatHa)

The ˊ (**fatHa**) represents a short *a* vowel. It's written as a short dash above the letter. In other words, if you write a ˊ (**fatHa**) above a تاء (**taa'**), the combination is written تَ (**ta-**). And if you write a ˊ (**fatHa**) above a كاف (**kaaf**), you produce كَ (**ka-**).

Here are examples of words with only ˊ (**fatHa**) to help you spot how they produce the short *a* vowel within the words. In each word, you see a ˊ (**fatHa**) written above the first consonant:

كَلْب (**kalb**; *dog*)

رَبّ (**rabb**; *Lord*)

دَمّ (**damm**; *blood*)

ˎ (kasra)

The ˎ (**kasra**) represents a short *i* vowel. It's usually written as a short dash below the letter. See the section on the ˝ (**shadda**) for an exception to this rule. In other words, if you write a ˎ (**kasra**) below a تاء (**taa'**), the combination is written تِ (**ti-**). If you write a ˎ (**kasra**) below a كاف (**kaaf**), you produce كِ (**ki-**).

Here are examples of words with only ˎ (**kasra**) to help you spot how they produce the short *i* vowel within the words. In each word, you see a ˎ (**kasra**) written below the first consonant:

حِلْم (**Hilm**; *dream*)

مِصْر (**miSr**; *Egypt*)

طِفْل (**Tifl**; *child*)

ˊ (Damma)

The ˊ (**Damma**) represents a short *u* vowel. It's a tiny واو (**waaw**) above the letter. If you write a ˊ (**Damma**) above a تاء (**taa'**), the combination is written تُ (**tu-**). If you write a ˊ (**Damma**) above a كاف (**kaaf**), you produce كُ (**ku-**).

Here are examples of words with only ´ (**Damma**) to help you spot how they produce the short *u* vowel within the words. In each word, you see a ´ (**Damma**) written below the first consonant:

قُرْب (**qurb**; *near*)

فُرْن (**furn**; *oven*)

أُمّ ('**umm**; *mother*)

° (sukuun)

The ° (**sukuun**) represents the absence of a vowel. It's a tiny circle written above the letter. Notice how in the following examples, the first consonant is followed by a vowel, but the second consonant isn't. In each case, you spot a ° (**sukuun**) written above the second consonant. This tells you that the second consonant isn't followed by a vowel and closes the syllable with the first consonant and the vowel between them:

جُمْلَة (**jumla**; *sentence*)

مَكْتَب (**maktab**; *office*)

دَرْس (**dars**; *lesson*)

ّ (shadda)

The ّ (**shadda**) represents the doubling of a consonant. It's a symbol similar to a tiny *w* written above the letter. You can then write a vowel over the ّ (**shadda**) to indicate that the doubled consonant has a vowel that follows it.

Notice how in the following examples, the first consonant has a vowel, but the second consonant has a ّ (**shadda**) and a vowel. In each case, you spot a ّ (**shadda**) and a vowel written above the second consonant:

مَكَّة (**makka**; *Mecca*)

حَتَّى (**Hattaa**; *until*)

قِصَّة (**qiSSa**; *story*)

When the ّ (**shadda**) is followed by the vowel ِ (**kasra**), people usually write the ِ (**kasra**) below the ّ (**shadda**) but over the consonant itself (even though in every other situation, the ِ (**kasra**) is below the consonant). In other words, a short dash *above* a ّ (**shadda**) represents the vowel ´ (**fatHa**). A short dash *below* the ّ (**shadda**) but *above* the consonant represents the vowel ِ (**kasra**). The font in this book universally represents the ِ (**kasra**) between the ّ (**shadda**) and the consonant. Note how in these examples, the ِ (**kasra**) is above the consonant but below the ّ (**shadda**):

يُدَرِّسُ (**yudarrisu**; *he teaches*)

تُقَبِّلِينَ (**tuqabbiliina**; *you kiss*)

آ (madda)

Arabic doesn't permit the writing of two أَلِف ('alifs) side by side. Something about too many long lines in a row just wasn't seen as attractive. Whenever circumstances of the language produce two أَلِف ('alifs) at the beginning of a word, you instead write a single أَلِف ('alif) with a آ (madda) over it. A آ (madda) is a wavy line you write over an أَلِف ('alif) to indicate the sound **'aa** — that is, an initial glottal stop followed by a long *a* vowel.

Here are some examples of words with the آ (madda):

آلَة ('aala; *tool*)

آسِف ('aasif; *sorry*)

أ (waSla)

The أ (waSla) is an elongated oval written over an أَلِف ('alif) to indicate that the أَلِف ('alif) has lost its vowel. The short *a* vowel over the أَلِف ('alif) in the ال ('alif laam) ordinarily disappears whenever there's a preceding vowel. Because this vowel disappearance is expected, people don't bother writing the أ (waSla) at all. I don't use the أ (waSla) in this book. But just so you know what it is, here's an example of a sentence with a أ (waSla):

ذَهَبَ الرَّجُلُ إلى دُبَيَّ.

(**dhahaba-r-rajulu 'ilaa dubayya.** *The man went to Dubai.*)

Part II
Becoming a Master at Using Nouns

The 5th Wave   By Rich Tennant

"If you're having trouble with the irregular plural of Arabic nouns, try using flash cards and taking more fiber."

In this part . . .

This is the part where you encounter the three cases of the Arabic noun. This is crucial information as you move officially into intermediate territory. But wait, there's more — literally more as you discover the ways Arabic takes the noun and describes the plural of it. In this part, you also experience the adjectives necessary to liven things up a bit. Then I introduce you to the ways to compare things — and label one as the best.

Finding out how to make one noun possess another puts you in the territory of the infamous **'iDaafa** construction. In this part, the **'iDaafa** becomes your best friend. Finally, in this part, I explain how to add relative clauses to your writing.

Chapter 4

Making Your Case with the Three Cases of the Arabic Noun

In This Chapter

▶ Discovering the use of nominative case for subjects

▶ Forming the accusative case for direct objects

▶ Using the genitive case after prepositions and in an **'iDaafa**

*I*f you're like most people, you've never had to worry about case endings before — even in English. English nouns are the same whether they're the subject, the object, or the word after a preposition. But English pronouns do preserve cases in some instances. "Him" can't be a subject and "She" can't be an object, after all. Unlike English, Arabic relies fairly heavily on cases.

The good news for you is that the situation isn't nearly as bad as it could be. Latin has five cases, and depending on which of the five declensions of nouns they go on, there are dozens of different endings.

Arabic has only three cases (nominative, accusative, and genitive), and with very few exceptions, the ending is the same regardless of the gender and number of the noun. In this chapter, I show you the three case endings and how to produce them for the different nouns in an Arabic sentence.

Getting to the Point with the Nominative Case

The term *nominative* refers to nouns that are the subject of a sentence. In English grammar, there are several pronouns that have a separate nominative form. For example, in these sentences, "I" and "She" are nominative:

I study Arabic.

She is a fine doctor.

Any other form of the pronoun would create a grammatically incorrect sentence, such as this one (my apologies to Tarzan):

Me study Arabic.

Unlike English, Arabic has separate nominative forms of all nouns, not just pronouns.

The primary use of the nominative is as the subject of a sentence. Nominative is used in *equational sentences*, where the verb *to be* will be unstated. The nominative case is also used in verbal sentences. (See Chapter 2 for more on equational and verbal sentences.) Here's an example of an equational sentence and a verbal sentence with subjects in the nominative case:

الطّباخُ في المَطْبَخِ.

(**aT-Tabbaakhu fii-l-maTbakhi.** *The cook is in the kitchen.*)

قَرَأَ الـمُدَرِّسُ الإمْتِحاناتِ.

(**qara'a al-mudarrisu al-'imtiHaanaati.** *The teacher read the tests.*)

In the following sections, I show you the simple nominative and the indefinite nominative forms.

Keeping it simple: Simple nominative form

The *simple nominative* form is the form that's used with definite nouns. To produce the simple nominative form, you simply place a ´ (**Damma**) on the last consonant of the noun. The ´ (**Damma**) is the tiny واو (**waaw**) shaped symbol that indicates a short *u* vowel. If you're uncertain about the writing of a ´ (**Damma**), you may want to review Chapter 3, where I cover all the consonants and vowels in written Arabic. Here are examples of a few definite nouns with a ´ (**Damma**) added to the last consonant:

البَيْتُ (**al-baytu;** *the house*)

الرِّجالُ (**ar-rijaalu;** *the men*)

الطّاولاتُ (**aT-Taawilaatu;** *the tables*)

Ordinarily, the ة (**taa' marbuuTa**) is pronounced as the vowel *a* at the end of a word. But when you put the simple nominative ending *u* on the ة (**taa' marbuuTa**), you pronounce the ة (**taa' marbuuTa**) like a **taa'** (a *t* sound). Here's an example of a noun with ة (**taa' marbuuTa**) without the simple nominative, followed by the same word with the additional ´ (**Damma**). Note how the *t* sound is inserted:

الأُسْتاذة (**al-'ustaadha;** *the professor*)

الأُسْتاذةُ (**al-'ustaadhatu;** *the professor*)

Adding an n for the indefinite nominative form

When a noun is indefinite, you still express the nominative case with a ´ (**Damma**), but you add a final *n* in the pronunciation. However, this particular sound isn't represented with the letter نون (**nuun**). Instead, it's represented with a special form of the vowel. The Arabic name for such a final vowel closed with an *n* is تَنوين (**tanwiin**). Western grammarians have coined the term *nunation* to refer to this addition of a final *n* sound to the indefinite forms in Arabic. To write the indefinite nominative ending, you use a unique shape, which resembles a **Damma** with a hook on it: ٌ. Here's an example of that indefinite nominative ending in action: كِتابٌ (**kitaabun**; *a book*).

In handwritten forms, sometimes you may see two **Dammas** simply drawn next to each other or inverted beside each other. No matter which form you see, these **Dammas** have the rather descriptive name **Dammatayn** (which literally means "two **Dammas**"). The **Dammatayn** looks like this: ٌ.

When you write equational sentences with all the vowels expressed, you use the nominative for both parts of the sentence. The subject can be definite, but the predicate is indefinite. Here are two equational sentences with indefinite predicates:

السَّيّارةُ جَديدةٌ.

(**as-sayyaaratu jadiidatun.** *The car is new.*)

الرَّئيسُ مَسرورٌ.

(**ar-ra'iisu masruurun.** *The president is happy.*)

An indefinite noun also can be the subject in a verbal sentence. Here's an example:

سَيُشرِفُ مُديرٌ عَلى هذا القِسْم.

(**sayushrifu mudiirun 3alaa-haadha-l-qismi.** *A director will oversee this department.*)

In this practice set, I give you a number of Arabic sentences. Rewrite the sentence (for further writing practice) but add to the sentence the proper form of the nominative (**Damma** or the **Dammatayn**) wherever it should be found. Note that nominal sentences require you to fill in two nominatives.

Q. الصَّديقة لَطيفة. (**aS-Sadiiqa laTiifa.**)

A. الصَّديقةُ لَطيفةٌ. (**aS-Sasiiqatu laTiifatun.** *The girlfriend is nice.*)

1. الكِتاب مُهمّ. (**al-kitaab muhimm.**)

_____

2. أَرسَلَ العامِل الصُّنْدوقَ إلى الشّاحِنة. ('**arsala al-3aamil aS-Sunduuqa 'ilaa-sh-shaaHinati.**)

_____

3. ‏مَكْتَبة الجامعةِ كَبيرة.‏ (**maktaba al-jaami3ati kabiira.**)

_____

4. ‏ذلكَ الوَلَد مُضْحِك.‏ (**dhaalika-l-walad muDHiq.**)

_____

5. ‏أَحْضَرَ الطّالِب الطّعامَ هُنا.‏ ('**aHDara aT-Taalib aT-Ta3aama hunaa.**)

_____

6. ‏المُحَرِّر مَشْغول غَداً.‏ (**al-muHarrir mashghuul ghadan.**)

_____

7. ‏رَجَعَ السَّفير مِن الرِّحْلَةِ.‏ (**raja3a as-safiir mina-r-riHlati.**)

_____

8. ‏المُؤَلِّف رائِع.‏ (**al-mu'allif raa'i3.**)

_____

9. ‏فازَتْ المُغَنِّية بِجائِزَةٍ.‏ (**faazat al-mughanniya bi-jaa'izatin.**)

_____

10. ‏زَوْجَتي جَميلة.‏ (**zawjatii jamiila.**)

_____

Making a Statement with the Accusative Case

The _accusative case_ is the most poorly named of the cases because it sounds like it committed a crime or something. Actually, though, it's not criminal at all. It's mostly used to indicate the direct object in a sentence. Whoever said this case was difficult was falsely accusing it.

The English language preserves a few separate accusative forms for pronouns. Consider these examples:

> _I love her._

> _She hates him._

In Arabic, however, separate pronouns are all nominative. When you need to put a pronoun in a different case, it will always be a suffix on either a verb or a preposition.

In this section, I show you the simple accusative, indefinite accusative, and accusative as predicate forms.

Forming the simple accusative form with fatHa

In Arabic, the *simple accusative* is used with definite nouns. This case is formed by adding a ˉ (**fatHa**) to the final consonant of a word. Here are three definite nouns with the ˉ (**fatHa**) indicating the simple accusative case:

البَيْتَ (**al-bayta**; *the house*)

الأُسْتاذَةَ (**al-'ustaadhata**; *the professor*)

الرِّجالَ (**ar-rijaala**; *the men*)

Nouns with a feminine sound plural ending, however, form their accusative with a ˏ (**kasra**). For example, consider this feminine plural noun: الطّاولاتِ (**aT-Taawilaati**; *the tables*).

Using the indefinite accusative

The *indefinite accusative* ending is used to express the accusative case of an indefinite noun. Like the nominative, the indefinite accusative adds a final نون (**nuun**) sound after the ˉ (**fatHa**). This is indicated with a doubled **fatHa,** which is called **fatHatayn.** The **fatHatayn** looks like this: ˝.

When the **fatHatayn** is added to a singular feminine noun, there's no other change in spelling. You can see in these examples that the **fatHatayn** symbol is placed directly above the ة (**taa' marbuuTa**):

حَديقةً (**Hadiiqatan**; *a park*)

زيارةً (**ziyaaratan**; *a visit*)

Because masculine nouns don't have distinct and recognizable endings like the feminine nouns, Arabic uses the convention of putting the indefinite accusative ending on a masculine noun after first adding a dummy أَلِف (**'alif**) to carry the symbol. Here are two masculine nouns in the indefinite accusative:

كِتاباً (**kitaaban**; *a book*)

ناراً (**naaran**; *a fire*)

Dealing with the accusative as predicate

As you probably know, an equational sentence in the present uses two nominatives. (See the earlier section "Getting to the Point with the Nominative Case" for more details.) But a special class of verbs that requires an accusative predicate exists in Arabic. Here's an example of an equational sentence:

الجَوُّ لَطيفٌ اليَوْمَ.

(**al-jawwu laTiifun al-yawma.** _The weather is nice today._)

Remember that you don't have to state the verb _to be_ in Arabic. It's just understood.

You can use the verb كانَ (**kaana**; _was_) to create a subject-predicate sentence refer-ring to the past tense. But كانَ (**kaana**) requires a predicate in the accusative case. Notice in the following example how the subject of كانَ (**kaana**) is in the nominative, but the predicate is in accusative:

كانَ الجَوُّ لَطيفاً أَمْس أَيْضاً.

(**kaana-l-jawwu laTiifan 'amsi 'ayDan.** _Yesterday the weather was also nice._)

The predicate can also be another noun, as in this example:

كانَ الرَّجُلُ طَبّاخاً جَيِّداً.

(**kaana ar-rajulu Tabbaakhan jayyidan.** _The man was a good cook._)

The class of verbs that takes the accusative predicate is known by the quaint name, كانَ وَأَخَواتُها (**kaana wa'akhawaatuhaa**; _kaana and her sisters_). Some words in this group of verbs occur quite rarely. Here are examples of the most important ones that you (as an intermediate student) should know:

- ✔ لَيْسَ (**laysa**; _[there is] not_)
- ✔ أَصْبَح (**aSbaHa**; _to become_)
- ✔ ما يَزالُ (**maa yazaalu**; _yet, still_)
- ✔ لا يَعودُ (**laa ya3uudu**; _no longer, anymore_)

Here are a few important points to remember about some of these verbs:

- ✔ لَيْسَ (**laysa**) allows you to negate a nominal sentence in the present. (To see all the forms of **laysa**, check out Chapter 17 of this book.) Here are a few examples:

  لَسْتُ جائِعاً الآنَ. (**lastu jaa'i3an al-'aana.** _I'm not hungry now._)

  لَيْسَ مُسْتَعِدّاً لِلإمْتِحان. (**laysa musta3iddan lil'imtiHaani.** _He isn't ready for the test._)

- ✔ You can use ما يَزالُ (**maa yazaalu**) by itself to complement an equational sen-tence. Check out this example:

  ما تَزالُ حَزينةً عَلى المُشْكِلة. (**maa tazaalu Haziinatan 3alaa-l-mushkila.** _She's still sad about the problem._)

  ما يَزالُ (**maa yazaalu**) can also be used as an auxiliary to give the meaning _still_ to a following verb. Consider this example:

  ما يَزالُ يَذْهَبُ إلى الحَفْلةِ؟ (**maa yazaalu yadh-habu 'ilaa-l-Haflati?** _Is he still going to the party?_)

In the following exercise, I give you a number of Arabic sentences that require, depending on the verb, a nominative or accusative indefinite as the predicate adjective or noun. In brackets is the English equivalent of the Arabic word you need (which you can find in the dictionary). Write in the blank the correct form of the Arabic word or words.

0. [sure]. عَن رَأيِكَ. _____ كُنْتُ (kuntu _____ 3an ra'yika.)

A. كُنْتُ مُتَأكِّداً عَن رَأيِكَ. (kuntu <u>muta'akkidan</u> 3an ra'yika.)

11. [happy] جِدّاً هُناكَ. _____ كانَتْ (kaanat _____ jiddan hunaaka.)

12. [optimistic] _____ لَيْسَ إنْساناً (laysa 'insaanan _____)

13. [a cheap restaurant] _____ ما يَزالُ (maa yazaalu _____)

14. [preferable]. لِلرَّئيس _____ هَذا المُرَشَّح (haadhaa-l-murashshakhu _____ l-ir-ra'iisi.)

Writing All the Rest with the Genitive Case

The genitive case is generally used everywhere the nominative and accusative cases aren't used. In this section, I show you the simple and indefinite forms of the genitive and offer several examples of how to use the genitive.

Working with simple genitive form

The *simple genitive* form is used whenever a definite noun follows a preposition or follows the first member of an **'iDaafa** (Refer to Chapter 7 for more on **'iDaafas.**) You form this case in Arabic by adding a ِ (**kasra**) — the short *i* vowel — to the final consonant of the noun. Like the nominative and accusative cases, you use the same ending regardless of gender and number. The following are two definite nouns in the genitive:

الكِتاب (**al-kitaabi;** *the book*)

الرَّجُل (**ar-rajuli;** *the man*)

Understanding indefinite genitive

The *indefinite genitive* ending is used to express the genitive case of an indefinite noun. Like the nominative and accusative, the indefinite genitive adds a final نون

(**nuun**) sound after the ِ (**kasra**). This is indicated with a doubled **kasra** (called **kasratayn**). The **kasratayn** looks like this: ٍ. Take a look at a few examples:

كِتابٍ (**kitaabin;** *a book*)

رَجُلٍ (**rajulin;** *a man*)

Discovering the uses of the genitive case

You use the genitive case in two important situations: following the head of an **'iDaafa** and following a preposition. I explain each situation in the following sections.

Following the head of an 'iDaafa

You use the genitive case for all the words that follow the head of an **'iDaafa** — no matter how many there are. In the following two examples, you see how the second and third words in an **'iDaafa** are in the genitive case:

سَيّارةُ الرَّجُلِ (**sayyaaratu ar-rajuli;** *the man's car*)

سَيّارةُ صَديقِ الرَّجُلِ (**sayyaaratu Sadiiqi-r-rajuli;** *the man's friend's car*)

Following a preposition

You use the genitive whenever a noun directly follows a preposition. Here are examples with several different prepositions. Notice the use of the genitive after each one:

مَعَ الرَّجُلِ (**ma3a-r-rajuli;** *with the man*)

إلى الحَديقةِ (**ilaa-l-Hadiiqati;** *to the park*)

مِنَ البَيْتِ (**mina-l-bayti;** *from the house*)

لِصَديقٍ (**liSadiiqin;** *for a friend*)

A noun can follow a preposition but also can be the head of an **'iDaafa.** In the following example, I underline a word governed by a preposition and that starts out a long **'iDaafa:**

وَجَدتُ آلَتي التَّصْويرِ تَحْتَ مَقْعَدِ سَيّارةِ بِنْتِ خالَتي.

(**wajattu 'aalatii-t-taSwiiri tahta maq3adi sayyaarati binti khaalatii.** *I found my camera under the seat of my cousin's car.*)

When a noun in the genitive has possessive pronoun suffixes, the suffixes هُ (**hu**) and هُم (**hum**) change their vowels to *i* (written with a ِ [**kasra**]) to match the vowel of the genitive ending. Linguists call this a *euphonic change* (meaning it just sounds better). Here are a few examples of nouns in the genitive with euphonically changed possessive pronoun suffixes:

مَعَ أُمِّهِ (**ma3a ummihi;** *with this mother*)

في بَيْتِهِم (**fii baytihim;** *in their house*)

Your friend is about to send this follow-up to a phone interview, but his potential employer won't be very impressed if he spots a bunch of grammatical errors! Help your friend out by underlining the words that are incorrect. Then write the proper form in the spaces provided. *Note:* Your friend has made eight mistakes. (So he obviously really needs your help!)

New Message

| Send | Cut | Copy | Paste | Undo | abc✔ Check |

السَّيِّد براون.

أَشْكُرُكُمْ عَلى المُقابَلَةِ بِالهاتِفِ اليَوْمَ. أَنا مَسْرورٌ لِلفُرْصةِ. لَسْتُ مُتَأَكِّدٌ إِذا أَرْسَلْتُ لَكُمْ عُنْوانُ مَكْتَبِي الجَديد. الأُسْبوع الماضي أَصْبَحْتُ مُديرٌ في قِسْمَ آخَر في الشَّرِكةِ وَتَغَيَّرَ مَكانَ مَكْتَبِي. فَهُوَ:

١٢ شارِع المَطار

الدوحة. قَطَر

مِنْ جَديد أَشْكُرُكُمْ عَلى اِهْتِمامُكُم بي.

ويلْيَم سميث

---

15. _____

16. _____

17. _____

18. _____

19. _____

20. _____

21. _____

22. _____

Answer Key

1 الكِتابُ مُهِمٌّ. (al-kitaabu muhimmun. *The book is interesting.*)

2 أَرْسَلَ العامِلُ الصُّنْدوقَ إلى الشّاحِنةِ. ('arsala al-3aamilu aS-Sunduqa 'ilaa-sh-shaaHinati. *The worker sent the box to the truck.*)

3 مَكْتَبةُ الجامِعةِ كَبيرةٌ. (maktabatu al-jaami3ati kabiiratun. *The university library is big.*)

4 ذلِكَ الوَلَدُ مُضْحِكٌ. (dhaalikaa-l-waladu muDHikun. *That boy is funny.*)

5 أَحْضَرَ الطّالِبُ الطّعامَ هُنا. ('aHDara aT-Taalibu aT-Ta3aama hunaa. *The student brought the food here.*)

6 المُحَرِّرُ مَشْغولٌ غَداً. (al-muHarriru mashghuulun ghadan. *The editor is busy tomorrow.*)

7 رَجَعَ السَّفيرُ مِن الرِّحْلةِ. (raja3a as-safiiru mina-r-riHlati. *The ambassador returned from the trip.*)

8 المُؤَلِّفُ رائِعٌ. (al-mu'allifu raa'i3un. *The composer is outstanding.*)

9 فازَتْ المُغَنِّيةُ بِجائِزةٍ. (faazat al-mughanniyatu bi-jaa'izatin. *The singer won an award.*)

10 زَوْجَتي جَميلةٌ. (zawjatii jamiilatun. *My wife is beautiful.*)

11 مَسْرورةً (masruuratan)

12 مُتَفائِلاً (mutafaa'ilan)

13 مَطْعَماً رَخيصاً (maT3aman rakhiiSan)

14 مُفَضَّلٌ (mufaDDalun)

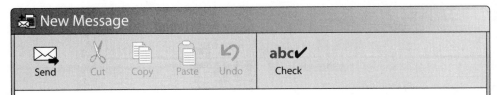

السَّيِّد براون،

أَشْكُرُكُم عَلَى المُقابَلَةِ بِالهاتِفِ اليَوْمَ. أَنا مَسْرورٌ لِلفُرْصِة. لَسْتُ مُتَأَكِّد إذا أَرْسَلْتُ لَكُم عُنوانُ مَكْتَبِي الجَدِيد. الأُسْبوع الماضِي أَصْبَحْتُ

مُدِيِّر فِي قِسْمَ آخَر فِي الشَّرِكِة وَتَغَيَّرَ مَكانَ مَكْتَبِي. فَهُوَ:

١٢ شارِع المَطار

الدوحة. قَطَر

مِنْ جَدِيد أَشْكُرُكُم عَلى إهْتِمامُكُم بِي.

وِيليَم سميث

(as-sayyid brawn,

'ashkurukum 3alaa-l-<u>muqaabalta</u> bil'haatifi al-yawma. 'anaa <u>masruuru</u> lil-furSati. lastu <u>muta'akkidun</u> 'idhaa 'arsaltu lakum <u>3unwaanu</u> maktabii al-jadiidi. al-'usbuu3a al-maaDii 'aSbaHtu <u>mudiirun</u> fii <u>qisma</u> 'aakhar fii-sh-sharikati wa-taghayyara <u>makaana</u> maktabii. fa-huwa:

12 shaari3 al-maTaar
ad-dawHa qaTar

min jadiid 'ashkurukum 3alaa <u>'ihtimaamukum</u> bii.

William Smith)

(Mr. Brown,

I thank you for the phone <u>interview</u> today. I am <u>happy</u> for the opportunity. I wasn't <u>sure</u> if I sent you the <u>address</u> of my new office. Last week I became a <u>director</u> in another <u>department</u> in the company and my office <u>location</u> changed. Here it is :

12 Airport St.
Doha, Qatar

Again, I thank you for your <u>interest</u> in me.

William Smith)

15 الْمُقَابَلَةِ (**al-muqaabalati;** *interview*)

Because this word follows the preposition, it should have been genitive.

16 مَسْرُورٌ (**masruurun;** *happy*)

As the indefinite predicate, this word should have had a **Dammatayn.**

17 مُتَأَكِّداً (**muta'akkidan;** *sure*)

When this word is used with **laysa,** it should be in the accusative.

18 عُنْوانَ (**3unwaana;** *address*)

Because this is the object, it should have been in the accusative.

19 مُديراً (**mudiiran;** *director*)

When this word is used with **'aSbaHa,** it should be in the accusative.

20 مَكانُ (**makaanu;** *location*)

Because this is the subject of the verb, it should be nominative.

21 قِسْمٍ (**qismin;** *department*)

Because this word follows a preposition, it should be genitive.

22 إهْتِمامِكُم (**'ihtimaamikum;** *your interest*)

Because this word follows a preposition, it should be genitive.

Chapter 5

Forming the Plural in Arabic

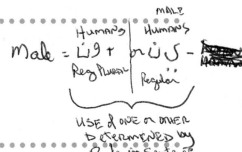

In This Chapter

▶ Forming the plural of regular feminine nouns

▶ Using broken plural patterns to form the masculine plural

▶ Recognizing and working with irregular plurals

▶ Putting nouns in the dual

Most languages have relatively simple ways of creating the plural. English, for instance, puts an *s* on the end of almost every noun. Sure, English has a handful of nouns like *child/children* and *goose/geese* that dance to their own tune. But 99 percent of English nouns just add *s* to form the plural. In Arabic, however, well over half of the total nouns form their plural in a way that's similar to the *goose/geese* situation in English.

Let's face it: Among world languages, Arabic may have the most irregular and difficult-to-master system when it comes to talking about more than one thing. This system is called the *broken plural*. At times over the years, the system has made me feel like a broken man! One grammarian lists 29 different patterns in use in Classical Arabic; and half of these patterns are still used in Modern Standard Arabic today. Don't worry, though. In this chapter, I do everything I can to help you see how Arabic plurals work.

You have two options for grasping the forms of the plural in Arabic. I recommend that you pursue both of them at once. First, remember this one key bit of information: You just have to bite the bullet and memorize both the singular and plural of any new vocabulary item you want to acquire. If you make vocabulary cards, it's a good idea to put both the singular and the plural on the cards. Any good dictionary will give you both forms.

Your second method of attack to grasp plurals in Arabic is what I cover in this chapter. I show you that, in the end, Arabic does have some tendencies of regularity in this otherwise bewildering system. By the end of this chapter, you still won't be able to take any new noun and infallibly produce the plural. But that's not your fault. The language just isn't fully regular. However, what you will be able to do is predict with a high degree of accuracy the plural of several common patterns of nouns. In addition, you'll discover the more regular system of forming the dual.

English has a single plural ending for almost all nouns, regardless of gender. Arabic has different plural endings for the different genders. So in this chapter, I explain the ins and outs of making both feminine and masculine nouns plural. (If you need a refresher on masculine and feminine nouns, spend some time with Chapter 2.)

Working with Feminine Plural Nouns

The best way to discover the wonderful world of plurals is with the more or less regular class of nouns: feminine nouns. Feminine nouns frequently have the recognizable ة (**taa' marbuuTa**) endings. The masculine noun, by contrast, doesn't have a recognizable ending and will also not have a regular way to form the plural.

Many feminine nouns form the plural easily and regularly. All you have to do to form the regular feminine plural is to take off the ة (**taa' marbuuTa**) ending and replace it with a different ending. But in other cases, unfortunately, the plural form will be unpredictable. So when it comes to making feminine nouns plural, you have two different situations: regular plurals and broken plurals. I explain what each of these two methods is and how to form both in the following sections.

Regular plural endings with ة (taa' marbuuTa)

There are nouns that form their plural by just adding a regular plural ending to the noun or by replacing a singular ending with a plural ending. Arabic grammarians call this regular category the *sound plurals*. They're called this because grammarians consider them safe and sound. A more descriptive name for the sound plurals may be to call them *suffixed plurals*. In the case of feminine nouns, the sound plural is formed by removing the ة (**taa' marbuuTa**) and replacing it with the following sound plural ending: ات (**aat**).

Here are a few examples of how to form the plural of a regular feminine noun with the ة (**taa' marbuuTa**) ending:

سَيّارة (**sayyaara;** *car*) becomes سَيّارات (**sayyaraat;** *cars*)

طاولة (**Taawila;** *table*) becomes طاولات (**Taawilaat;** *tables*)

ساعة (**saa3a;** *hour*) becomes ساعات (**saa3aat;** *hours*)

Regular broken plurals with ة (taa' marbuuTa)

I wish I could tell you that whenever you see the ة (**taa' marbuuTa**) ending, you just replace it with ات (**aat**) to form the plural of a feminine noun. But, as you probably can guess, it's a bit more complicated than that. For reasons that no one really knows, early Arabic speakers developed a system of forming plurals in which you don't add an ending. Instead, you just change the vowels in the word.

Arab grammarians call this phenomenon the *broken plural*. It's analogous to English plural formations such as *mouse/mice* and *foot/feet*. Languages closely related to Arabic, such as Hebrew and Aramaic, don't have broken plurals, so it's something early Arabic speakers developed all on their own. The term *broken plural* is just a translation of the term that's used to describe them in Arabic: جَمْع تَكسير (**jam3 taksiir**). Perhaps an Arab grammarian coined this term because they "broke" the regular pattern.

Luckily, there's a rule of sorts that you can use to predict the plural of certain feminine nouns. When a feminine noun with the ة (taa' marbuuTa) ending has a long *i* vowel — written with ياء (yaa') — after the second letter of the root, it usually has a plural on a specific pattern.

However, before I show you that pattern, I need to explain what Arab grammarians mean when they use the term *pattern*. Because almost every Arabic word has three root consonants in it, grammarians long ago began using the Arabic root فَعَلَ (fa3ala; *to do*) as a convenient model to describe any word pattern. Here's an example: The noun كَلِمة (kalima) means *word*. But that noun also has a shape to it. It has the vowel *a* after the first consonant, the vowel *i* after the second, and the ة (taa' marbuuTa) after the third. By inserting the shape of the word **kalima** into the root فَعَل (fa3ala), you produce the nonexistent word فَعِلة (fa3ila). You can then say that كَلِمة (kalima) is a noun on the *pattern* of فَعِلة (fa3ila).

This is a convenient way to reference the various plural forms you see in this book. When I say, for instance, that a certain noun forms its plural on a specific pattern, all you have to do is insert that noun's three consonants into that pattern. For example, كِتاب (kitaab; *book*) forms its plural on the pattern of فُعُل (fu3ul). So to produce the word *books* in Arabic, you replace the consonants in order to produce the word كُتُب (kutub).

Getting back to feminine nouns with ة (taa' marbuuta) and a long *i* vowel after the second consonant, they almost always form their plural on the pattern فَعائل (fa3aa'il). For example:

جَريدة (jariida; *newspaper*) becomes جَرائد (jaraa'id; *newspapers*)

حَقيبة (Haqiiba; *suitcase*) becomes حَقائب (Haqaa'ib; *suitcases*)

The type of plural any given noun has isn't a matter of choice or style. Each noun has a set plural you should learn at the same time that you learn the singular. You can discover the correct plural for a noun in the dictionary if you're uncertain of it.

Some nouns that don't have the ة (taa' marbuuTa) ending also take the feminine sound plural ending. Check out the following examples:

طَلَب (Talab; *request*) becomes طَلَبات (Talabaat; *requests*)

خِطاب (khiTaab; *speech*) becomes خِطابات (khiTaabaat; *speeches*)

In this exercise, I have listed the singular forms of some important feminine nouns. Put them in the correct plural form using the rules I explain in this section. In other words, if you see a long vowel in ياء (yaa') after the second consonant of the root, you know you should form the plural using the same pattern as جَريدة (jariida; *newspaper*), which is shown earlier in the chapter. Otherwise, you can be sure that you just need to use the regular plural ending of ات (aat). *Note:* There are, of course, always exceptions in any language. But to help you build confidence, I include only nouns that aren't exceptions to the rule.

Q. كَلِمة (**kalima**; *word*)

A. كَلِمات (**kalimaat**; *words*)

1. جَزيرة (**jaziira**; *island*) _____

2. شاحِنة (**shaaHina**; *truck*) _____

3. كَنيسة (**kaniisa**; *church*) _____

4. عادة (**3aada**; *custom*) _____

5. كُلِّية (**kulliya**; *college*) _____

6. وَظيفة (**waDHiifa**; *job*) _____

7. صَفْحة (**SafHa**; *page*) _____

8. طَبيعة (**Tabii3a**; *character*) _____

9. حَفْلة (**Hafla**; *party*) _____

10. قَصيدة (**qaSiida**; *ode*) _____

Memorizing Masculine Plural Nouns

Here's some potentially bad news: The more common and basic a masculine noun is, the more unpredictable its plural will be. There's simply no way, based solely on the shape of the singular form, to predict that the plural of رَجُل (**rajul**; *man*) would be رجال (**rijaal**; *men*). Because of this irregularity, you just have to memorize the plural forms. A dictionary can help you determine the plural forms of the words you intend to put to memory.

The broken plural system in Arabic follows tendencies, but no rules work 100 percent of the time. When I tell you that a given word pattern frequently takes a certain plural pattern, there will always be exceptions. Also keep in mind that the particular plural pattern a noun uses is already determined. You can't choose which of the patterns you want to use. Instead, your task is just to learn what pattern it does follow.

However, do note that a few patterns are somewhat predictable. So, in this section, I show you ten common plural patterns and give you examples of important and useful words that follow each of them. In some cases, you can see that certain forms of singulars have a tendency to follow a given pattern. After you've seen the potential patterns of plurals, you'll have a better chance of correctly guessing that something you run across in Arabic is a plural. And recognizing plurals allows you to succeed in finding the correct singular in a dictionary.

There are other plural patterns than the ten I focus on here. But they're used for a smaller number of nouns. You quickly reach a point of diminishing returns when you try to learn every possible plural pattern that Arabic uses. The ten you master in this chapter can equip you to recognize and produce the plurals of the vast majority of Arabic nouns.

To form the plural, you need to know two things. You need to know the three consonants that make up the triliteral root for that word. You also need to know the word pattern that particular noun uses to form its plural. After you know those two things, all you have to do is substitute the consonants in the dummy root of the word pattern (we use the root فعل [**f-3-l**; *to make, do*] traditionally) with the three consonants of the word you want to turn into the plural. If you're unsure of how to do that, I discuss the triliteral root in depth and show you how to find the three consonants in Chapter 2.

Plural Pattern 1: فُعّال *(fu33aal)*

فُعّال (**fu33aal**) is a regular plural pattern for any noun derived from a Form I participle, which follows the word pattern فاعِل (**faa3il**). An example of a noun that falls into this category is the word كاتِب (**kaatib;** *writer*). As a participle, this word means [*someone*] *writing,* and would take the sound plural endings. (A full discussion of the sound plural endings for participles is found in Chapter 18.) But the participle has also transitioned into a noun that means *one who writes* (that is, a *writer*). When this word is used as a noun, it doesn't take the sound plural endings. Instead it forms its plural with Plural Pattern 1. The following are two common examples of plurals made with Pattern 1:

كاتِب (**kaatib;** *writer*) becomes كُتّاب (**kuttaab;** *writers*)

عامِل (**3aamil;** *worker*) becomes عُمّال (**3 ummaal;** *workers*)

Plural Pattern 2: أَفْعال *('af3aal)*

Nouns formed on the pattern فَعَل (**fa3al**) frequently follow Pattern 2, أَفْعال (**'af3aal**). Here are a few common examples:

وَلَد (**walad;** *child*) becomes أَوْلاد (**'awlaad;** *children*)

مَثَل (**mathal;** *proverb*) becomes أَمْثال (**'amthaal;** *proverbs*)

Plural Pattern 3: فُعول *(fu3uul)*

Many nouns formed on the patterns فِعْل (**fi3l**), فَعْل (**fa3l**), and فُعْل (**fu3l**) form the plural with Pattern 3, فُعول (**fu3uul**). Here are some common examples:

بَنْك (**bank;** *bank*) becomes بُنوك (**bunuuk;** *banks*)

فَصْل (**faSl;** *semester*) becomes فُصول (**fuSuul;** *semesters*)

Pattern 3 is also sometimes used for nouns with the patterns فَعَل (**fa3al**) and فَعِل (**fa3il**), such as مَلِك (**malik**; *king*), which becomes مُلوك (**muluuk**; *kings*).

Note that because this plural pattern separates the second and third consonants of the triliteral root, nouns with a doubled final consonant split them up if it takes the pattern that صَفّ (**Saff**; *class*) takes. It becomes صُفوف (**Sufuuf**; *classes*).

Plural Pattern 4: فُعَل (fu3al)

You'll see Pattern 4 — فُعَل (**fu3al**) — mostly with nouns of the patterns فُعْلة (**fu3la**) and فَعْلة (**fa3la**). The following are some important nouns that use Pattern 4:

غُرْفة (**ghurfa**; *room*) becomes غُرَف (**ghuraf**; *rooms*)

دَوْلة (**dawla**; *state*) becomes دُوَل (**duwal**; *states*)

Plural Pattern 5: فِعال (fi3aal)

Unfortunately, many different patterns of nouns use Pattern 5, فِعال (**fi3aal**). But it's a common enough plural pattern that you need to be ready for it. Some important nouns that use Pattern 5 include the following:

رَجُل (**rajul**; *man*) becomes رجال (**rijaal**; *men*)

بَلَد (**balad**; *country*) becomes بلاد (**bilaad**; *countries*)

To reinforce your mastery of the first five broken plural patterns, in this exercise I give you several singular nouns along with their plural pattern in brackets. Substitute the consonants of the singular into the pattern, and you'll successfully convert the noun into the plural.

Q. عُقْدة (**3uqda**; *knot*) [فُعَل; **fu3al**]

A. عُقَد (**3uqad**; *knots*)

11. فُرْصة (**furSa**; *opportunity*) [فُعَل; **fu3al**] _____

12. بَيْت (**bayt**; *house*) [فُعول; **fu3uul**] _____

13. صَنْف (**Sanf**; *kind*) [أَفْعال; **'af3aal**] _____

14. حَقّ (**Haqq**; *law*) [فُعول; **fu3uul**] _____

15. كَلْب (**kalb**; *dog*) [فِعال; **fi3aal**] _____

16. راكِب (**raakib**; *rider*) [فُعّال; **fu33aal**] _____

17. قَلْب (**qalb**; *heart*) [فُعول; **fu3uul**] _____

18. قِسم (**qism**; *division*) [أفْعال; **'af3aal**] _____

19. نُقْطة (**nuqTa**; *point*) [فُعَل; **fu3al**] _____

Plural Pattern 6: فَواعِل *(fawaa3il)*

Nouns of the form فاعِل (**faa3il**) that don't refer to humans can take a plural according to Pattern 6, فَواعِل (**fawaa3il**). Here are a few common examples:

طابِع (**Taabi3**; *printer*) becomes طَوابِع (**Tawaabi3**; *printers*)

شارِع (**shaari3**; *street*) becomes شَوارِع (**shawaari3**; *streets*)

خاتِم (**khaatim**; *ring*) becomes خَواتِم (**khawaatim**; *rings*)

Plural Pattern 7: مَفاعِل *(mafaa3il)*

Nouns referring to places, such as museums, schools, factories, and so on, that have the pattern of either مَفْعَل (**maf3al**) or مَفْعَلة (**maf3ala**) take Pattern 7 — مَفاعِل (**mafaa3il**) — almost exclusively. The following are some common examples:

مَصْنَع (**maSna3**; *factory*) becomes مَصانِع (**maSaani3**; *factories*)

مَكْتَب (**maktab**; *office*) becomes مَكاتِب (**makaatib**; *offices*)

Note that the expected plural of the noun مَكْتَبة (**maktaba**; *library*) would be identical to the plural of مَكْتَب (**maktab**; *office*). To avoid this potential problem, you'll usually see a sound plural for this word instead: مَكْتَبات (**maktabaat**; *libraries*).

Plural Pattern 8: أفْعِلاء *(af3ilaa')*

Nouns of the form فَعيل (**fa3iil**) usually use plural Pattern 8, أفْعِلاء (**af3ilaa'**). (Sometimes these nouns use Pattern 9, however. So refer to the next section for details on that pattern.) Here are some examples of nouns that use Pattern 8 to form the plural:

صَديق (**Sadiiq**; *friend*) becomes أصْدِقاء (**'aSdiqaa'**; *friends*)

غَنيّ (**ghanii**; *rich person*) becomes أغْنِياء (**'aghniyaa'**; *rich people*)

Plural Pattern 9: فُعَلاء (fu3alaa')

Nouns of the form فَعيل (fa3iil) frequently use Pattern 9 — فُعَلاء (fu3alaa') — to form the plural. (Do note that nouns of this form may occasionally use Pattern 8, which is discussed in the previous section.) The following are common examples of nouns that use Pattern 9 to form the plural:

زَميل (**zamiil**; *colleague*) becomes زُمَلاء (**zumalaa'**; *colleagues*)

رَئيس (**ra'iis**; *president*) becomes رُؤَساء (**ru'asaa'**; *presidents*)

Plural Pattern 10: فُعُل (fu3ul)

Pattern 10 — فُعُل (fu3ul) — is another frustratingly random pattern that happens to be used with many words you need to know to be proficient in Arabic. The following are some examples of nouns that use Pattern 10 to form the plural:

كِتاب (**kitaab**; *book*) becomes كُتُب (**kutub**; *books*)

مَدينة (**madiina**; *city*) becomes مُدُن (**mudun**; *cities*)

To help you remember the way Patterns 6–10 work, in this exercise I give you several singular nouns along with their plural pattern in brackets. Substitute the consonants of the singular form into the pattern to convert the noun into the plural form.

Q. مَصْدَر (**maSdar**; *source*) [مَفاعِل; **mafaa3il**]

A. مَصادِر (**maSaadir**; *sources*)

20. وَزير (**waziir**; *minister*) [فُعَلاء; **fu3alaa'**] _____

21. مَسْجِد (**masjid**; *mosque*) [مَفاعِل; **mafaa3il**] _____

22. جَبَل (**jabal**; *mountain*) [فِعال; **fi3aal**] _____

23. عاصِمة (**3aaSima**; *capital*) [فَواعِل; **fawaa3il**] _____

24. مَخْبَز (**makhbaz**; *bakery*) [مَفاعِل; **mafaa3il**] _____

25. زَعيم (**za3iim**; *leader*) [فُعَلاء; **fu3alaa'**] _____

26. فِراش (**firaash**; *bed*) [فُعُل; **fu3ul**] _____

27. قَريب (**qariib**; *relative*) [أَفْعِلاء; **'af3ilaa'**] _____

28. مَرْكَز (**markaz**; *center*) [مَفاعِل; **mafaa3il**] _____

Discovering Nouns with Irregular Plurals

Several important nouns have irregular plurals, or they use patterns that aren't common enough to treat separately. There's no way to predict that any of these nouns should have the plural form that they have. And because these are some important and common nouns, you should just commit the singular and the plural forms to memory:

أب (**'ab;** *father*) becomes آباء (**'aabaa';** *fathers*)

أُمّ (**'umm;** *mother*) becomes أُمَّهات (**'ummahaat;** *mothers*)

أَخ (**'akh;** *brother*) becomes إِخْوة (**'ikhwa;** *brothers*)

أُخْت (**'ukht;** *sister*) becomes أَخَوات (**'akhawaat;** *sisters*)

إِمْرَأة (**'imra'a;** *woman*) becomes نِساء (**nisaa';** *women*)

يَوْم (**yawm;** *day*) becomes آيَّام (**'ayyaam;** *days*)

سَنة (**sana;** *year*) becomes سَنَوات (**sanawaat;** *years*)

أَرْض (**'arD;** *land*) becomes أراضٍ / الأراضي (**'araaDin/al-'araaDii;** *lands*)

كُرْسِي (**kursii;** *chair*) becomes كَراسٍ / الكَراسي (**karaasin/al-karaasii;** *chairs*)

Seeing Double: Forming the Dual

You've heard that two's company and three's a crowd. Anytime you have exactly two of something, you can call it a pair, a couple, or, grammatically, a dual. (That's why two people fighting is called a *duel.*) The broken plural patterns covered in preceding sections are challenging to learn. But the formation of dual nouns, covered in this section, is a little easier to take. In Arabic you use a special ending, referred to as *the dual* ending, whenever you refer to only two of something (rather than three or more of something). Compared to the broken plural, mastering the dual will be a breeze.

To form the dual in Arabic, all you have to do is take the singular form and add the ending ان (**aani**) for the nominative and يْن (**ayni**) for the accusative and genitive. (Check out Chapter 4 if you need a refresher on working with these cases.) Masculine and feminine nouns both take the same endings, but remember that the ة (**taa' marbuuTa**) is secretly a **taa'** and will turn back into a **taa'** whenever you add an ending to it.

The dual of masculine nouns

In this section, I include some examples of how to form the dual when working with masculine nouns. Consider the following masculine singular noun: كتاب (**kitaab;** *book*).

Here's how to form the dual of *two books* in all three cases:

> **Nominative:** كِتابان (**kitaabaani**)
>
> **Accusative and genitive:** كِتابَيْن (**kitaabayni**)

When a dual noun appears as the first word of an **'iDaafa,** the final letter ن (**nuun**) will disappear. (For more on the **'iDaafa** construction, check out Chapter 7.) Here's an example of what I mean:

> بَيْتا الرَّجُل جَديدان جِدّاً.
>
> (**baytaa-r-rajuli jadiidaani jiddan.** *The man's two houses are very new.*)

The dual of feminine nouns

As noted earlier, the dual of feminine nouns uses the same endings as the masculine nouns. Consider this singular feminine noun: سَيّارة (**sayyaara;** *car*).

Here's how to form the dual of *two cars* in each of the three cases:

> **Nominative:** سَيّارَتان (**sayyaarataani**)
>
> **Accusative and genitive:** سَيّارَتَيْن (**sayyaaratayni**)

Suppose you're throwing a dinner party, and just as you're about to go shopping, you find out that a few more good friends will be coming. That means you need to double your supplies. Examine your shopping list, and then convert every item into the dual form. You can just produce the dual of the Arabic word provided, but do produce both the nominative and accusative forms. وَجْبة طَيِّبة (**wajba Tayyiba**). In other words, *Bon Appetit!*

Q. One item on your grocery list is a block of cheese جُبْنة (**jubna**). Convert this to the dual form, or two blocks of cheese.

A. جُبْنَتان / جُبْنَتَيْن (**jubnataani/jubnatayni;** *two blocks of cheese*)

29.	A bottle (of milk), زُجاجة (**zujaaja**)
	Two bottles (of milk):_____
30.	A bag (of potatoes), كيس (**kiis**)
	Two bags (of potatoes):_____
31.	A whole chicken, دَجاجة (**dajaaja**)
	Two whole chickens:_____
32.	A loaf of bread, رَغيف (**raghiif**)
	Two loaves of bread:_____

Answer Key

1. جَزائِر (**jazaa'ir**; *islands*)

2. شَاحِنات (**shaaHinaat**; *trucks*)

3. كَنائِس (**kanaa'is**; *churches*)

4. عادات (**3aadaat**; *customs*)

5. كُلِّيات (**kulliyaat**; *colleges*)

6. وَظائِف (**waDHaa'if**; *jobs*)

7. صَفُحات (**SafHaat**; *pages*)

8. طَبائِع (**Tabaa'i3**; *characters*)

9. حَفُلات (**Haflaat**; *parties*)

10. قَصائِد (**qaSaa'id**; *odes*)

11. فُرَص (**furaS**; *opportunities*)

12. بُيوت (**buyuut**; *houses*)

13. أَصُناف (**'aSnaaf**; *kinds*)

14. حُقوق (**Huquuq**; *laws*)

15. كِلاب (**kilaab**; *dogs*)

16. رُكّاب (**rukkaab**; *riders*)

17. قُلوب (**quluub**; *hearts*)

18. أَقُسام (**'aqsaam**; *divisions*)

19. نُقَط (**nuqaT**; *points*)

20. وَزَراء (**wuzaraa'**; *ministers*)

21. مَساجِد (**masaajid**; *mosques*)

22. جبال (**jibaal**; *mountains*)

23. عَواصِم (**3awaaSim**; *capitals*)

24. مَخايِز (**makhaabiz**; *bakeries*)

25. زُعَماء (**zu3amaa'**; *leaders*)

26. فُرُش (**furush**; *beds*)

27. أَقُرباء (**'aqribaa'**; *relatives*)

28. مَراكِز (**maraakiz**; *centers*)

29.	زُجاجَتَيْن / زُجاجَتان (**zujaajataani/zujaajatayni**; *two bottles [of milk]*)
30.	كيسَيْن / كيسان (**kiisaani/kiisaayni**; *two bags [of potatoes]*)
31.	دَجاجَتَيْن / دَجاجَتان (**dajaajataani/dajaajatayni**; *two chickens*)
32.	رغيفَيْن / رَغيفان (**raghiifaani/raghiifayni**; *two loaves of bread*)

Chapter 6

Bringing Your Sentences to Life with Adjectives and Adverbs

*1*f nouns and verbs are the meat and potatoes of language, adjectives and adverbs are certainly the spices that make the meal interesting. Being able to incorporate these important words expertly into your writing brings your prose to life — even if it's just a simple business memo.

You may have noticed that an adjective or adverb has found its way into every sentence of this chapter opening. So being hesitant with them can have a paralyzing effect on what you want to say. Mastering adjectives and adverbs is a win-win for you.

In this chapter, I show you the forms of the Arabic adjectives and the rules for how to use them within your sentences. This information will come in handy on a variety of occasions, such as when you want to compliment your boss about that *nice* tie. In this chapter, you also explore how to make a comparative adjective in Arabic. This information will equip you to tell your old friend that she looks *younger* than the last time you saw her. You also see how to jazz up your description of actions with Arabic adverbs. You'll need them if you want to include on your resume how *well* you perform your duties. This chapter is a great way to make your Arabic writing even better!

Describing People and Things with Adjectives

To use adjectives in Arabic, you need to know how to properly form them and also how and where to add them to your sentence. The simple explanation is that an adjective must agree grammatically with the word it describes and come immediately after that word, as in the following example. I underline the adjective so you can spot it:

تُعْجِبُكِ سَيّارَتي الجَديدة؟

(**tu3jibuki sayyaaratii al-jadiida?** *Do you like my <u>new</u> car?*)

Recognizing adjective patterns

To recognize an adjective in Arabic, you must become familiar with the different word patterns that adjectives can follow. There are a handful of word patterns that are frequently adjectives, but a strong majority of adjectives in Arabic use the word pattern فَعيل (**fa3iil**). To give you an idea of how two very different adjectives can each have the same word pattern, compare these antonyms:

كَبير (**kabiir;** *big*)

صَغير (**Saghiir;** *small*)

These words mean the exact opposite, but what they do have in common is the exact same shape. They each have the vowel *a* after the first consonant and the long *i* after the second consonant.

Because the فَعيل (**fa3iil**) word pattern is so common, it's the best adjective type to master first. Here are several common adjectives that follow this word pattern:

جَديد (**jadiid;** *new*)

قَديم (**qadiim;** *old*)

جَميل (**jamiil;** *beautiful/handsome*)

قَبيح (**qabiiH;** *ugly*)

To read about some of the other adjective forms, check out the following section.

Wrestling with Arabic forms of the adjective

In your basic studies of Arabic nouns, you became acquainted with the masculine and feminine gender as well as the singular and plural. (To review these concepts, visit Chapters 2 and 5.) In the later section, "Keeping adjectives in agreement," you discover that you have to use adjective forms that match your noun in gender and in number. The good news is that three of the four potential adjective endings are formed regularly.

The only tricky thing about adjectives in Arabic is that the masculine plural forms are unpredictably irregular. They're irregular in the sense that their shapes can't be predicted from the most basic form of the adjective — the masculine singular. As a result, you have to simply memorize the masculine plural (unless you want to reach for this book or your dictionary every time you want to write one).

The following sections introduce you to the shapes of the irregular masculine plurals as well as the (thankfully) fully regular masculine singular and feminine singular and plural forms.

Looking at irregular masculine plurals

In this section, I show you the forms of some common adjectives so you see the various shapes that the masculine plural can take. Every adjective forms the feminine singular regularly by adding the suffix ة (**a**) and the plural by adding the suffix ات (**aat**). But the pesky masculine plural turns out different in all three of the common adjectives shown in Table 6-1. Because the masculine singular is the most basic form (it doesn't have suffixes like the feminine forms), the masculine singular is the word that will double as the dictionary entry for every adjective.

Table 6-1	The Forms for Some Common Adjectives			
Masc. Singular	*Fem. Singular*	*Masc. Plural*	*Fem. Plural*	*English*
كَبير (kabiir)	كَبيرة (kabiira)	كِبار (kibaar)	كَبيرات (kabiiraat)	*big*
جَديد (jadiid)	جَديدة (jadiida)	جُدُد (judud)	جَديدات (jadiidaat)	*new*
مَريض (mariiD)	مَريضة (mariiDa)	مَرْضى (marDaa)	مَريضات (mariiDaat)	*sick*

A majority of adjectives form the masculine plural on the word pattern فِعال (**fi3aal**), such as كِبار (**kibaar**; *big*) in the previous table. So if you're ever in a bind, don't have access to a dictionary, and need to take a wild guess at forming a masculine plural adjective, go ahead and put it in the فِعال (**fi3aal**) word pattern. Even if you're wrong, people will understand what you mean to say. And most of the time you'll be right anyway.

Adjectives can appear in several other word patterns as well. The word pattern فَعيل (**fa3iil**) (which you discover in the previous section) is so pervasive in the Arabic language that it deserves to be learned as a type. The other potential word patterns an adjective can take, however, are numerous and not individually common. Table 6-2 shows you four other word patterns for adjectives. The feminine will be regular, but be ready for the masculine plurals to be irregular.

Table 6-2	Four Adjective Word Patterns		
Arabic Word Pattern	*Masc. Singular*	*Masc. Plural*	*English*
فَعِّل (fa33il)	جَيِّد (jayyid)	جِياد (jiyaad)	*good*
فَعَل (fa3al)	حَسَن (Hasan)	حِسان (Hisaan)	*nice, good*
فَعْل (fa3l)	صَعْب (Sa3b)	صِعاب (Si3aab)	*difficult*
فُعْل (fu3l)	مُرّ (murr)	أَمْرار ('amraar)	*bitter*

Seeing patterns in feminine adjectives

Because feminine adjectives are always regular, the only thing worth mentioning that's specific to feminine forms is a feature of adjectives on the word pattern فَعْلان (fa3lan). In Classical Arabic, these adjectives had a different feminine singular than what I show you in Table 6-3. That feminine singular was formed on the word pattern فَعْلى (fa3laa). You may see this obsolete feminine form in older books, but in Modern Standard Arabic it has been replaced by the more regular forms that I show you in Table 6-3.

Table 6-3	Adjectives That Use the فَعْلان (fa3lan) Form	
Masc. Singular	*Fem. Singular*	*English*
عَطْشان (3aTshaan)	عَطْشانة (3aTshaana)	thirsty
غَضْبان (ghaDbaan)	غَضْبانة (ghaDbaana)	angry
كَسْلان (kaslaan)	كَسْلانة (kaslaana)	lazy

Adjectives like عَطْشان (3aTshaan; *thirsty*) are *diptotes*, meaning that they have only two case endings (the normal nominative *u* and the accusative *a* for both accusative and genitive). They also don't take *nunation* (the additional *n* sound after the vowel to make it indefinite).

Using participles as adjectives

A number of adjectives in Arabic are actually participles. To understand what I mean, think about it from the standpoint of English: When you say something is *exciting*, you're using the word as an adjective to describe that thing. But because of that *-ing* ending, *exciting* is a present participle. (A detailed description of participle formation is available to you in Chapter 18.)

The good news for you is that all the adjectives derived from participles take the regular masculine and feminine singular and plural sound endings. Table 6-4 shows three participles that have adjectival meanings.

Table 6-4	Participles with Adjectival Meanings				
Participle Word Pattern	*Masc. Singular*	*Fem. Singular*	*Masc. Plural*	*Fem. Plural*	*English*
مَفْعول (maf3uul)	مَشْغول (mash-ghuul)	مَشْغولة (mash-ghuula)	مَشْغولونَ (mashghu-luuna)	مَشْغولات (mashghuu-laat)	busy
فاعِل (faa3il)	جائِع (jaa'i3)	جائِعة (jaa'i3a)	جائِعونَ (jaa'i3uuna)	جائِعات (jaa'i3aat)	hungry
مُتَفَعِّل (mutafa33il)	مُتَأَخِّر (muta'akhkhir)	مُتَأَخِّرة (muta'akhkhira)	مُتَأَخِّرونَ (muta'akhkhiruuna)	مُتَأَخِّرات (muta'akhkhiraat)	late

Forming adjectives when naming places

I'm from Wisconsin originally. People there call themselves "Wisconsonites" (that is, they did until the label "Cheesehead" came along). Similarly, people from New York are called "New Yorkers." And somebody from America is considered an "American." In English, we have plenty of different endings to turn a place name into an adjective. It all depends on the ending of the word and, well, just what sounds the best. And then there's Indiana with its Hoosiers — who knows what that's all about!

Arabic, on the other hand, has a more regular way to form an adjective from a place name. You can add a doubled يّ (**yaa'**) to almost every country (and even city) to create an adjective that describes a person from that place. It's known as the نِسْبة (**nisba**) ending because **nisba** in Arabic means *relationship*. With the place name مِصْر (**miSr**; *Egypt*), you just add the نِسْبة (**nisba**) ending to the end to produce the following: مِصْريّ (**miSrii**; *Egyptian*).

To form the feminine and the plurals with نِسْبة (**nisba**), keep in mind that the ending is actually a doubled يّ (**yaa'**). Notice in the following examples the doubled يّ (**yaa'**) in the feminine singular (FS) forms and the masculine and feminine plural forms (MP and FP):

مِصْريّة (**miSriyya**; *Egyptian*; FS)

مِصْريّون (**miSriyyuuna**; *Egyptians*; MP)

مِصْريّات (**miSriyyaat**; *Egyptians*; FP)

أُرْدُن ('**urdun**; *Jordan*)

أُرْدُنيّ ('**urdunii**; *Jordanians*; MS)

أُرْدُنيّة ('**urduniyya**; *Jordanian*; FS)

أُرْدُنيّون ('**urduniyyuuna**; *Jordanians*; MP)

أُرْدُنيّات ('**urduniyyaat**; *Jordanians*; FP)

When you put the نِسْبة (**nisba**) ending on a word with a final consonant, the word doesn't undergo any further change. When you put the نِسْبة (**nisba**) on a word with a final vowel or ة (**taa' marbuuTa**), you drop the final syllable and add the نِسْبة (**nisba**) ending. (See Chapters 1 and 2 for more on the **taa' marbuuTa**.) Here are a few examples:

أَمْريكا ('**amriika**; *America*) becomes أَمْريكيّ ('**amriikii**; *American*)

ليبْيا (**liibyaa**; *Libya*) becomes ليبيّ (**liibii**; *Libyan*)

مَكّة (**makka**; *Mecca*) becomes مَكّيّ (**makkii**; *Meccan*)

Some country names have an ال (**'alif laam**), the Arabic definite article. The country we call Kuwait in English is literally called الكُوَيْت (**al-kuwayt;** *The Kuwait*) in Arabic. For country names that have the ال (**'alif laam**), you have to remove it and then add the نِسْبة (**nisba**) ending. Take a look at two examples:

العِراق (**al-3iraaq;** *Iraq*) becomes عِراقيّ (**3iraqii;** *Iraqi*)

القاهِرة (**al-qaahira;** *Cairo*) becomes قاهِريّ (**qaahirii;** *Cairene*)

Labeling abstract concepts with adjectives

In English, we have adjectives that are formed from more abstract concepts than place names. Think, for instance, about how you can form the adjective *melodic* from the word *melody* and *responsive* from *response*.

In Arabic, you can create such abstract adjectives by putting the نِسْبة (**nisba**) ending on virtually any noun. Notice in the following examples how a noun generates a **nisba** adjective:

عائِلة (**3aa'ila;** *family*) becomes عائِليّ (**3aa'ilii;** *familial/domestic*)

مال (**maal;** *money*) becomes ماليّ (**maalii;** *monetary*)

Some adjectives are formed by putting the نِسْبة (**nisba**) ending on a historical root that you couldn't have predicted. (A *historical root* is a root that was used thousands of years ago but changed over time.) Obsolete consonants from the historical root reappear when you put on the نِسْبة (**nisba**) ending. Here are several examples of **nisba** adjectives formed on roots that are slightly different than the nouns they come from:

لُغة (**lugha;** *language*) becomes لُغَويّ (**lughawii;** *linguistic*)

أب ('**ab;** *father*) becomes أَبَويّ ('**abawii;** *paternal/fatherly*)

أخ ('**akh;** *brother*) becomes أَخَويّ ('**akhawii;** *fraternal/brotherly*)

It's time for you to take your نِسْبة (**nisba**) adjective formation quiz! For each of the following place names and nouns, create a **nisba** adjective. If you can also correctly write the English translation of your newly created adjective, you get extra credit. Two of the questions prompt you to produce feminine singular. All the rest should be masculine singular. Good luck!

Q. روسيا (**ruusiyaa;** *Russia*)

A. روسيّ (**rusii;** *Russian*)

1.	لُبْنان (**lubnaan**; *Lebanon*)
2.	فَرَنْسا (**faransaa**; *France*)
3.	تونس (**tuunis**; *Tunisia*)
4.	فِلِسْطين (**filisTiin**; *Palestine* [FS])
5.	السّودان (**as-suudaan**; *Sudan*)
6.	عِلْم (**3ilm**; *knowledge, science*)
7.	سِرّ (**sirr**; *secret* [FS])
8.	تَجْرِبة (**tajriiba**; *experiment*)

Adding colors to your writing

Most of the adjectives describing color in Arabic are formed on the same word pattern as the comparative form: أَفْعَل (**'af3al**). This pattern is discussed later in the chapter. You can see in Table 6-5 that the masculine forms are of the same pattern as the comparative adjective, but there are feminine singular forms as well (unlike the comparative adjective, which doesn't have a feminine singular form).

Table 6-5	Adjectives Describing Color	
Masculine	*Feminine*	*English*
أَحْمَر ('**aHmar**)	حَمْراء (**Hamraa'**)	red
أَخْضَر ('**akhDar**)	خَضْراء (**khaDraa'**)	green
أَزْرَق ('**azraq**)	زَرْقاء (**zarqaa'**)	blue
أَبْيَض ('**abyaD**)	بَيْضاء (**bayDaa'**)	white
أَسْوَد ('**aswad**)	سَوْداء (**sawdaa'**)	black
أَصْفَر ('**aSfar**)	صَفْراء (**Safraa'**)	yellow
أَسْمَر ('**asmar**)	سَمْراء (**samraa'**)	brown

When you get beyond the basic color wheel, however, you run into words formed with the نِسْبة (**nisba**) ending on nouns. Here are a few examples of how the نِسْبة (**nisba**) ending produces a color from a noun:

> ذَهَب (**dhahab;** *gold* [the metal]) becomes ذَهَبِيّ (**dhahabii;** *golden* [the color])

> بُرْتُقال (**burtuqaal;** *orange* [the fruit] becomes بُرْتُقالِيّ (**burtuqaalii;** *orange* [the color])

Keeping adjectives in agreement

In Arabic, when you're using an adjective as a predicate, it must agree with the subject in gender and number. Here's an assortment of examples using all the genders and numbers of Arabic:

> الرَّجُل تَعبان.

> (**ar-rajul ta3baan.** *The man is tired.*)

> البِنْت ذَكِيّة.

> (**al-bint dhakiyya.** *The girl is intelligent.*)

> النِّساء مَشْهورات.

> (**an-nisaa' mashhuuraat.** *The women are famous.*)

> المِصْريّونَ لِطاف.

> (**al-maSriyyuuna liTaaf.** *The Egyptians are nice.*)

Unlike English, adjectives in Arabic always follow the nouns they describe. For example, in English you write *the white house.* In Arabic, this same phrase would literally be *the house the white.* Look at these two examples:

> البَيْت الأَبْيَض (**al-bayt al-'abyaD;** *the white house*)
> مَوْضوع مُهِمّ (**mawDu3 muhimm;** *an important issue*)

In the previous two examples, I use what's called the *attributive adjective.* An attributive adjective is so named because it attributes a description to the noun. In other words, it's an attributive adjective when you describe a noun in your sentence with the adjective placed before it in English, such as *blue cheese, sour cream,* and *the greasy spoon.* When an adjective is attributive in Arabic, it always has to agree with the noun in gender (masculine or feminine), number (singular or plural), or state of definiteness (whether it has *the* or *a/an*). (See Chapter 2 for more on the definite state.)

Notice how the adjectives in the following two sentences match their nouns' definite or indefinite state:

> رَأَيْتُ شَيْئاً غَريباً هُناكَ.

> (**ra'aytu shay'an ghariiban hunaaka.** *I saw a strange thing there.*)

البِناية الطَّويلة على اليَسار هِيَ السِّفارة.

(**al-binaaya aT-Tawiila 3ala-l-yasaar hiya as-sifaara.** *The tall building on the left is the embassy.*)

In other words, when you state an indefinite noun such as شَيئاً (**shay'an;** *a thing*), the adjective following the word will also be indefinite (as in the first example). But after a definite noun, such as *the building* (**al-binaaya**) in the second example, the adjective describing the noun also has to have the ال ('**alif laam**).

The only exception to adjectives following nouns comes with the *demonstrative adjectives*. These are the adjectives that *demonstrate* who or what you're talking about, for example *this car* or *that girl*. The Arabic demonstrative adjectives come immediately before the nouns they go with, but they still agree in gender. As a rule, they only go before nouns with the ال ('**alif laam**). Here are the masculine and feminine forms of *this* and *that* in Arabic with examples:

هذا البَيْت (**haadha-l-bayt;** *this* house) MS

هذِهِ السَّيّارة (**haadhihi-s-sayyaara;** *this car*) FS

ذلِكَ الرَّجُل (**dhaalika-r-rajul;** *that man*) MS

تِلْكَ الشَّقّة (**tilka-sh-shaqqa;** *that* apartment) FS

In addition to using adjectives to describe *the nice girl,* you can also use an adjective in a sentence such as *The girl is nice.* This is known as the *predicate adjective*. It's simple to form in Arabic because you just put it after the noun and don't add the ال ('**alif laam**) to the adjective. Here are two examples:

البِنْت لَطيفة. (**al-bint laTiifa.** *The girl is nice.*)

البِناية جَميلة. (**al-binaaya jamiila.** *The building is beautiful.*)

A possessive pronoun suffix, such as *my* or *her,* also makes its noun definite. Because of that, if the noun in your sentence has one of the possessive pronoun suffixes, you have to make your adjective definite to match. (You can review possessive pronoun suffixes in Chapter 2.) You don't put the same possessive pronoun suffix on the adjective. Instead, you just add the ال ('**alif laam**) to the adjective. This is the equivalent of saying, as in the following example, *my idea the new.* Take a look at how adjectives describing nouns with possessive pronoun suffixes have the ال ('**alif laam**):

فِكْرَتي الجَديدة (**fikratii al-jadiida;** *my new idea*)

مِهْنَتُها الصَّعْبة (**mihnatuhaa aS-Sa3ba;** *her difficult occupation*)

Handling feminine singular for inanimate plurals

A curious grammatical rule in Arabic is that only humans are counted as plurals when it comes to adjective agreement. So the plural forms explored in the earlier section, "Wrestling with Arabic forms of the adjective," are used to describe men, women, children, and even animals.

But never will you see plural adjectives used for houses, cars, or balloons. Instead, whenever an inanimate object is plural, you use feminine singular adjectives. Here are some examples of inanimate plurals with their feminine singular adjectives:

القِصَص مُضْحِكة.

(**al-qiSas muDHika.** *The stories are funny.*)

الإجابات صَحيحة.

(**al-'ijaabat SaHiiHa.** *The answers are correct.*)

هذِهِ الأَحْلام حُلْوَة.

(**haadhihi-l-'aHlaam Hulwa.** *These dreams are sweet.*)

In this exercise, I list several phrases in English, each one containing a noun and an adjective. Using the dictionary in the back of this book, look up any words you don't know, and then write the phrase in Arabic.

0. my tall friend

A. صَديقي الطَّويل (**Sadiiqii aT-Tawiil**)

9. a small problem _____

10. the clean plates _____

11. The pen is blue. _____

12. The house is big. _____

13. the happy students (mixed group) _____

14. the good doctors (FP) _____

15. The books are useful. _____

16. The cat (FS) is black. _____

17. a scared dog _____

18. the nice director (MS) _____

19. My grandmother is famous. _____

20. our favorite restaurant _____

21. their only opportunity _____

22. your (FS) final choices _____

Describing Verbs with Adverbs

G.K. Chesterton said, "If a thing is worth doing, it's worth doing badly." An *adverb* describes the manner with which a verb is performed (badly or otherwise). Adverbs are easily formed in English. Most every adjective you know can get *-ly* tacked onto the end; at that point, you've made yourself an adverb. Perhaps someone can cook *beautifully* so their guests can eat *greedily*. And English has just one irregular adverb, "well" (which may explain why so many people don't use it when they should!).

Arabic creates adverbs regularly as well. You can take any adjective, put it in the masculine singular accusative indefinite form, and then use it as an adverb. (For a review of the accusative singular, see Chapter 4.) You put your adverb after the verb, as in English. Here are three adjectives turned into adverbs in the accusative indefinite:

جَميل (**jamiil;** *beautiful*)

هِيَ تُغَنّي جَميلاً (**hiya tughanni jamiilan.** *She sings beautifully.*)

بَطيء (**baTii';** *slow*)

تَكَلَّم بَطيئاً مِن فَضْلِكَ. (**takallam baTii'an, min faDlika.** *Please speak slowly.*)

جَيّد (**jayyid;** *good*)

كَتَبَت جَيّداً (**katabat jayyidan.** *She wrote well.*)

In English, you can use a noun plus a preposition to create an adverbial phrase. For example, in the sentence, *Walk <u>carefully</u> on that ice,* the adverb is *carefully.* Now consider the sentence, *Handle this package <u>with care</u>.* It showcases an adverbial phrase — *with care.*

Arabic also uses some prepositional phrases adverbially. You can add the prefixed preposition **bi-** to abstract nouns, and they take on an adverbial sense. Here are three common examples:

بِضَبْط (**biDabT;** *with exactitude/exactly*)

بِسَهولة (**bisahuula;** *with ease/easily*)

بِصَعوبة (**biSa3uuba;** *with difficulty*)

Each of the following sentences has a blank and an Arabic word in brackets. Your challenge is to put the bracketed word into the form of an adverb.

Q. دَرَسْتُ العَرَبيّة _____ أمْس. (**darastu al-3arabiyya _____ 'amsi.**) [قَليل; **qaliil**]

A. قَليلاً; **qaliilan** / *I studied Arabic a little yesterday.*

23. _____ يُعْجِبُهُ السَّفَر فَسافَرَ (**yu3jibuhu as-safar fa-saafara _____**)
    [واسِع; **waasii3**]

24. _____ ما كانَتْ غَضْبانة بَلْ تَكَلَّمَتْ (**maa kaanat ghaDbaana bal takallamat _____**)
    [هُدوء; **huduu'**]

25. ـــــــــ كَتَبَ رَأْيَهُ ـــــــــ فِي مَقالَتِهِ. (kataba ra'yahu _____ fii maqaalatihi.) [واضِح; waaDiH]

26. ـــــــــ ذَهَبـوا ـــــــــ لِأَنَّهُم كانوا مُتَأَخِّرِينَ. (dhahabuu _____ li'annahum kaanuu mutaa.) [سـريع; sarii3]

This Is Better than That: Making Comparisons

Earlier in this chapter, I show you how to use adjectives and adverbs, so now you can probably describe someone as beautiful or tell her that she sings beautifully. Another important skill is knowing how to tell someone that she's *more* beautiful than another person. (Maybe I should caution you that whether you're doing it in English or Arabic, you should be careful about the kinds of comparisons you make!).

To form the comparative in English, you can just add the suffix *-er* to most adjectives. For example:

> *big* becomes *bigger*
>
> *small* becomes *smaller*

As always, there are exceptions to this rule. For instance, you wouldn't say "beautifuller." If you did call someone "beautifuller," she would understand that you intend a compliment, but she wouldn't exactly be impressed with your language ability! Instead, you need to say someone is *more beautiful,* or you can switch to *prettier.*

Arabic, on the other hand, forms the comparative in several different ways depending on the words you're using. I explain everything you need to know in the following sections.

Forming the comparative from the triliteral root

Like English, Arabic has a regular way to form the comparative. You take the three consonants of the adjective's *triliteral root* (the three consonants any word contains), and you put them in the word pattern أَفْعَل ('af3al).

In the following list, you see how several adjectives turn into the comparative form when you put their roots into the word pattern. To put the root into the comparative form, you add the prefix أ ('a-) and use the a vowel, which is written with the ˊ (fatHa), over the second consonant of your root. Here are some examples:

صَغير (Saghiir; *small*) becomes أَصْغَر ('aSghar; *smaller*)

حَسَـن (Hasan; *good*) becomes أَحْسَـن ('aHsan; *better*)

صَعْب (Sa3b; *difficult*) becomes أَصْعَب ('aS3ab; *more difficult*)

Dealing with geminate roots

If an adjective has *geminate roots,* meaning it has the same second and third consonant, the two consonants are doubled in the comparative form, and you put the accent on the second syllable. Here are some examples of geminate roots becoming comparative adjectives:

حارّ (**Harr;** *warm*) becomes أَحَرّ ('**aHarr;** *warmer*)

قَليل (**qaliil;** *little/few*) becomes أَقَلّ ('**aqall;** *fewer*)

خَفيف (**khafiif;** *light*) becomes أَخَفّ ('**akhaff;** *lighter*)

Encountering waaw or yaa' as a third consonant

If an adjective has a واو (**waaw**) or a ياء (**yaa'**) as its third consonant, the comparative form is written with the أَلِف مَكْسورة ('**alif maksuura**) in place of the final consonant. (See Chapter 3 for information on the '**alif maksuura.**) Take a look at a few examples:

غَني (**ghanii;** *rich*) becomes أَغْنى ('**aghnaa;** *richer*)

عال (**3aalin;** *high*) becomes أَعْلى ('**a3laa;** *higher*)

حُلْو (**Hulw;** *sweet*) becomes أَحْلى ('**aHlaa;** *sweeter*)

ذَكي (**dhakii;** *intelligent*) becomes أَذْكى ('**adhkaa;** *more intelligent*)

When you use the comparative as a predicate, the preposition مِن (**min**) functions like English *than.* Just as you put the English word *than* directly in front of the word you want to compare, so also you put **min** directly in front of the noun you want to compare in Arabic. **Min** ordinarily means *from.* So in Arabic you're saying something like, *John is taller from Steve.* But when you use **min** in a comparative sentence, always translate it as *than.* The following sentences show you some examples:

هُوَ أَطْوَل مِن أَخي.

(**huwa 'aTwal min 'akhii.** *He is taller than my brother.*)

هِيَ أَذْكى مِنّي.

(**hiya 'adhkaa minnii.** *She is smarter than I.*)

The comparative can function as an attributive adjective, as well. However, to do so correctly, the adjective must match its noun in definiteness, as in these examples:

بِعْتُ السَّيّارَةَ الأَغْلى.

(**bi3tu as-sayyaarata al-'aghlaa.** *I sold the more expensive car.*)

لَبِسَ القَميص الأَرْخَص.

(**labisa al-qamiiS al-'arkhaS.** *He wore the cheaper shirt.*)

For each of the following items, I give you a simple English sentence with something being compared to something else. Translate these into Arabic, observing the rules you have discovered in this section.

0. Ahmad is taller than Latiif.

A. أَحْمَد أَطْوَل مِنْ لَطيف. (**'aHmad 'aTwal min laTiif.**)

27. My car is faster than your car. _____

28. This house is newer than that apartment. _____

29. She is nicer than her sister. _____

30. The student is smarter than the teacher! _____

Being Super with the Superlative

The superlative takes your writing beyond saying something is merely good or even better. With the superlative, the object you're talking about is really great. It may even be stupendous! It's sort of like when two kids go back and forth saying, "My dad's better than your dad!" Then a third kid walks up and ends the argument by stating in the superlative, "Well, my dad's the best of all!"

To produce the superlative in English, you usually add *-est* to the regular adjective. Arabic doesn't have a separate form for the superlative. Instead, you use the comparative form in any of three constructions to produce a superlative idea. In the following sections, I explain each of the constructions.

Comparative plus ال ('alif laam)

You can add the ال (**'alif lam**) to a comparative adjective used as a predicate, and it will pick up a superlative sense. If you're rusty on adding the ال (**'alif laam**), see Chapter 2. Here are two examples:

هذا الكِتاب الأَقْصَر.

(**haadha-l-kitaab al-'aqSar.** *That book is shortest.*)

أُسْتاذي الأَجَدّ هُنا.

(**'ustaadhii al-'ajadd hunaa.** *My professor is the newest one here.*)

Comparative plus the indefinite singular

An indefinite noun following the comparative form can provide a superlative sense. (See Chapter 4 for more on creating indefinite nouns.) Take a look at two cases of this option:

هـٰذِهِ أَفْضَل فِكْرة سَمِعْتُها.

(**haadhihi afDal fikra sami3tuha.** *That's the best idea I've heard.*)

هُوَ أَفْقَر رَجُل فـي القَرْية.

(**huwa 'afqar rajul fii-l-qarya.** *He's the poorest man in the town.*)

Comparative plus an 'iDaafa

A comparative in an **'iDaafa** construction with a definite plural noun produces a superlative in Arabic. (To discover more about the **'iDaafa**, refer to Chapters 2 and 7.) Here are two examples of this superlative expression:

هُوَ أَصْغَر الطُّلّاب فـي الصَّفّ.

(**huwa 'aSghar aT-Tullab fii-S-Saff.** *He's the youngest student in the class.*)

كـانَ عيد ميلادي فـي أَحَرّ الأَيّام فـي السَّنة.

(**kaana 3iid miilaadii fii aHarr al-'ayyaam fii-s-sana.** *My birthday was on the warmest day of the year.*)

In this exercise, I give you a few English sentences using superlatives. Each one is accompanied by three Arabic versions, only one of which expresses the English correctly. Remember that one of the Arabic sentences does match the English sentence provided, so dig in and find the one that follows the rules you discovered in this section.

Q. This test was the hardest.

    a) كـانَ هـذا الإمْتِحان الأَصْعَب. (kaana haadhaa-l-imtiHaan al-'aS3ab.)

    b) كـانَ هـذا الإمْتِحان أَصْعَب. (kaana haadhaa-l-'imtiHaan 'aS3ab.)

    c) كـانَ هـذا الإمْتِحان أَسْهَل. (kaana haadhaa-l-'imtiHaan 'as-hal.)

A. a; كـانَ هـذا الإمْتِحان الأَصْعَب. (kaana haadhaa-l-imtiHaan al-'aS3ab.)

31. He discussed the most interesting issue with his friends.

    a) ناقَشَ المَوْضوع الأَهَمّ مَعَ أَصْدِقائِه. (naaqasha al-mawDuu3 al-'ahamm ma3a 'aSdiqaa'ihi.)

    b) ناقَشَ أَهَمّ المَواضِع مَعَ أَصْدِقائِه. (naaqasha 'ahamm al-mawaaDi3 ma3a 'aSdiqaa'ihi.)

    c) ناقَشَ المَوْضوع المُهِمّ مَعَ أَصْدِقائِه. (naaqasha al-mawDuu3 al-muhimm ma3a 'aSdiqaa'ihi.)

32. I preferred the newest kind.

a) فَضَّلْتُ الصِّنْف الأَجَدّ. (**faDDaltu aS-Sanf al-'ajadd.**)

b) فَضَّلْتُ الصِّنْف الأَجْدَد. (**faDDaltu aS-Sanf al-'ajdad.**)

c) فَضَّلْتُ أَجَدّ الأَصْناف. (**faDDaltu 'ajadd al-'aSnaaf.**)

33. Use the sharpest knife.

a) إِسْتَعْمِلْ سَكِينة حادّة. (**ista3mil sakiina Haadda.**)

b) إِسْتَعْمِلْ السَكِينة الأَحَدّ. (**ista3mil as-sakiina al'aHadd.**)

c) إِسْتَعْمِلْ أَحَدّ سَكِينة. (**ista3mil 'aHadd sakiina.**)

34. He is the dumbest man in the office.

a) هُوَ رَجُل غَبِيّ في المَكْتَب. (**huwa rajul ghabii fii-l-maktab.**)

b) هُوَ أَغْبى رَجُل في المَكْتَب. (**huwa 'aghbaa rajul fii-l-maktab.**)

c) هُوَ أَغَبّ رَجُل في المَكْتَب. (**huwa 'aghabb rajul fii-l-maktab.**)

Answer Key

1.	لُبْنانيّ (**lubnaanii**; *Lebanese*)
2.	فَرَنْسيّ (**faransii**; *French*)
3.	تونسيّ (**tuunisii**; *Tunisian*)
4.	فِلَسْطينيّة (**filisTiiniiya**; *Palestinian*)
5.	سـودانيّ (**suudaanii**; *Sudanese*)
6.	عِلْميّ (**3ilmii**; *learned/scientific*)
7.	سِرّيّة (**sirriyya**; *secret*)
8.	تَجْريبيّ (**tajriibii**; *experimental*)

9 مُشْكِلة صَغيرة (mushkila Saghiira)

10 الصُّحون النَّظيفة (aS-SuHuun an-naDHiifa)

11 القَلَم أَزْرَق. (al-qalam 'azraq.)

12 البَيْت كَبير. (al-bayt kabiir.)

13 الطُّلّاب المَسْروروَن (aT-Tullaab al-masruuruuna)

14 الطَّبيبات الجَيِّدات (aT-Tabiibaat al-jayyidaat)

15 الكُتُب مُفيدة. (al-kutub mufiida.)

16 القِطّة سـوداء. (al-qiTTa sawdaa'.)

17 كَلْب خائِف (kalb khaa'if)

18 مُدير لَطيف (mudiir laTiif)

19 جَدَّتي مَشْهورة. (jaddatii mash-huura.)

20 مَطْعَمُنا المُفَضَّل (mat3amunaa al-mufaDDal)

21 فُرْصَتُهُم الوَحيدة (furSatuhum al-waHiida)

22 إخْتِياراتُكِ الأخيرة ('ikhtiyaaraatuki al-'akhiira)

23 واسِعـاً; waasi3an / He likes travel, so he's traveled widely.

24 بِهُدوء; bihuduu' / She wasn't angry, rather she spoke calmly.

25 واضِحـاً; waaDiHan / He wrote his opinion clearly in his article.

26 سَريعـاً; sarii3an / They went quickly because they were late.

27 سَيّارَتي أسْرَع مِن سَيّارَتِكَ. (sayyaaratii 'asra3 min sayyaaratika.)

28 هذا البَيْت أجَدّ مِن تِلكَ الشَّقّة. (haadhaa-l-bayt 'ajadd min tilka-sh-shaqqa.)

29 هيَ ألْطَف مِن أُخْتِها. (hiya 'alTaf min 'ukhtihaa.)

30 الطّالِب أذْكى مِن المُدَرِّس! (aT-Taalib 'adhkaa min al-mudarris!)

31 ناقَشَ أهَمّ المَواضِع مَعَ أصْدِقائِه. b; (naaqasha 'ahamm al-mawaaDi3 ma3a 'aSdiqaa'ihi.)

32 فَضّلْتُ أجَدّ الأصْناف. c; (faDDaltu 'ajadd al-'aSnaaf.)

33 إسْتَعْمِلْ أحَدّ سَكينة. c; (ista3mil 'aHadd sakiina.)

34 هُوَ أغْبى رَجُل في المَكْتَب. b; (huwa 'aghbaa rajul fii-l-maktab.)

Chapter 7

Making Connections: Mastering the 'iDaafa Construction

In This Chapter

▶ Creating **'iDaafas** in Arabic

▶ Using adjectives to modify words in a complex **'iDaafa**

*T*he goal of the lesson of this chapter is . . . Wait, let me try to write that more clearly: This chapter's lesson's goal . . . Huh, that still doesn't sound quite right. How about, the goal of this chapter's lesson? Oh bother! What I'm *trying* to write requires the **'iDaafa** in Arabic. The **'iDaafa** is the way that Arabic expresses possession of one noun over another. So you need it to state things like *this lesson's goal* or *the goal of this chapter.*

You've seen simple two-word **'iDaafas** in your beginning Arabic studies. (I provide you with a review of the **'iDaafa** and practice with the two-word **'iDaafa** in Chapter 2.) Intermediate level Arabic, however, permits **'iDaafas** of several items. You can also describe one or more of the words in the **'iDaafa** with adjectives. Keeping track of the genders and numbers through it all can be a real feat. But mastering the complex **'iDaafa** allows you to write much more concisely and correctly. This chapter familiarizes you with the rules of the **'iDaafa** of the Arabic language. Oh, *there* it is! This chapter's goal is to present Arabic's **'iDaafa** rules!

Showing Possession and Relationship with 'iDaafas

In English, you describe possession or relationship using apostrophes; you use either 's or s'. Or you can use the preposition *of.* For example, the phrase *the man's office* means the same thing as *the office of the man.*

In Arabic, however, possession is indicated a bit differently. You use the **'iDaafa** construction to express how one noun either possesses another or is in some kind of relationship with another. You describe possession or relationship by putting the two words next to each other with no words in between them. Here's an example: مَكْتَب الرَّجُل (**maktab ar-rajul**), which means *the man's office* (or literally, *office the man*).

If you're *vowelling* your text fully (meaning you add the formal final vowels that indicate the noun's case), the second member of the **'iDaafa** chain will be in the genitive, like this: مَكْتَب الرَّجُل (**maktab ar-rajuli;** *the man's office*). **Note:** I'm not going to include all the formal final vowels in this chapter because the main lesson to take away here is the order of the words and agreement of the words in gender and state of definiteness. If you want to master the case endings, consult Chapter 4.

Tracking multiple words in an 'iDaafa

Adding multiple members to your **'iDaafa** is just a matter of, well, piling them on. But keep in mind that every time you add a new word to the **'iDaafa,** you're indicating that the added word is somehow connected to the one before it. However, if there are three words in the **'iDaafa,** you aren't saying that all three are necessarily related to one another; you're just saying that each is related to the word on either side of it.

Arabists sometimes call the first word in an **'iDaafa** the *head* of the **'iDaafa.** It's really the topic being discussed in the sentence. One inviolable rule about the Arabic **'iDaafa** is that the first word can never take the ال (**'alif laam**). If the second word is definite, either being a noun with the ال (**'alif laam**), a proper name, or a noun with a possessive pronoun suffix, the whole **'iDaafa** is translated as if both members are definite.

To help you grasp the **'iDaafa** concept, I start by showing you two-word **'iDaafas,** and then I build from there. You'll frequently need to create even longer **'iDaafas** than those with two words, such as to render the phrase *Arabic's 'iDaafa rules*. But you need to be comfortable with two-word **'iDaafas** before moving on to three (or four or five).

Two-word 'iDaafas

A two-word **'iDaafa** expresses possession of one noun over just one other noun. Here's a two-word **'iDaafa** that expresses actual ownership:

بَيْت الرَّجُل (**bayt ar-rajuli;** *the house of the man* or *the man's house*)

Even though the **'iDaafa** expresses possession, you can also use it to describe relationships of one person with another. We do the same thing in English. Here are examples of two-word **'iDaafas** describing relationships:

زَوْجة الرَّجُل (**zawjat ar-rajuli;** *the wife of the man* or *the man's wife*)

مُديرة الرَّجُل (**mudiirat ar-rajuli;** *the boss of the man* or *the man's boss*)

Three-word 'iDaafas

Adding a third word to an **'iDaafa** doesn't imply that the first and third words have anything to do with each other (apart from the fact that each is somehow connected to the second word). Each item is only in charge, so to speak, of the item in front of it. Check out this three-word **'iDaafa** as an example:

سَيّارة مُدير صَديقي (**sayyarat mudiir Sadiiqii;** *my friend's boss's car*)

You may go further to write, for instance, *My friend's boss's car is red.* In the course of the **'iDaafa,** you discover who owns the car — namely, the boss. You also understand something about the man who owns the car — that he's my friend's boss.

'iDaafas with more than three words

If you're writing complex sentences in Arabic, you may need to write an **'iDaafa** that has more than three words. Pushing the envelope just a bit further, here's an example to show you how to make an **'iDaafa** grow to impressive lengths:

وَجَدتُّ آلة التَّصْوير تَحْت مَقْعَد سَيّارةِ اِبْن خالـي

(**wajadtu 'aalat a-taSwiir taHt maq3adi sayyaarati ibni khaalii.** *I found the camera under the seat of my cousin's car.*)

There's no separate word in Arabic for the English *cousin.* Instead, you write *son/daughter of uncle/aunt.* So the word *cousin* is already starting out as an **'iDaafa.** When you put the possessive suffix on a word, that possessive suffix is in an **'iDaafa** with the noun it owns. (If you're rusty on the use of the possessive suffixes, you can find a review of them in Chapter 2.) Add all this together and the previous sentence contains a whopping five-word **'iDaafa:**

مَقْعَد سَيّارةِ اِبْن خـالـي (**maq3adi sayyaarati ibni khaalii;** *seat – car – son – uncle – my*)

Keeping these levels of ownership straight is difficult for English speakers. And because Arabic sentences frequently include **'iDaafas** longer than three members, mastering what relationships an **'iDaafa** does and doesn't imply is crucial to effective reading and writing in Arabic.

Now it's your turn to create some **'iDaafas.** Each of the following English phrases requires an **'iDaafa** to express it in Arabic. Put these **'iDaafas** in the correct order (in Arabic). The sample practice question shows you a three-word **'iDaafa,** but in the exercise I start you out slow with a few two-word **'iDaafas** before moving on to the more difficult ones.

Q. the color of her company's building

A. لَوْن بِناية شَرِكَتِها (**lawn binaayat sharikatihaa**)

1. my wife's job _____

2. the book's author _____

3. his friend's house _____

4. the door of the doctor's office _____

5. his mother's friend's phone _____

6. the university library's director _____

7. the city's transportation system _____

8. the radio program's announcer _____

9. the beauty of the summer season _____

10. the importance of my father's opinion _____

Crafting complex 'iDaafas using the different noun cases

'iDaafas aren't just isolated phrases telling you how nouns possess each other. An **'iDaafa** can be the subject of a verb. It can be the direct object. An **'iDaafa** can even follow a preposition. When an **'iDaafa** appears in one of these grammatical positions, it will only be the head of the **'iDaafa** that changes its grammatical case. (I discuss the grammatical cases of nouns in Chapter 4.) In this section, I show you some multiple member **'iDaafas** in the nominative, accusative, and genitive cases.

No matter how long your **'iDaafa** is, every word that follows the head of it will be in the genitive case. But if the head of the **'iDaafa** is the subject of a verb or is the subject of an equational sentence, it should be in the nominative case. (See Chapter 2 for more on equational sentences.) To help you visualize how the case of the head of the **'iDaafa** changes, I underline the head of the **'iDaafa** in all my examples.

Here are two **'iDaafas** in nominative case. The first example is an equational sentence. The second is a verbal sentence:

كِتابُ أُمّي طَويلٌ جِدّاً.

(**kitaabu** 'ummi Tawiilun jiddan. *My mother's book is too long.*)

ذَهَبَتْ بِنْتُ خالةِ زَوْجتِكَ إلى أوروبا.

(dhahabat **bintu** khaalati zawjatika 'ilaa 'uuruubaa. *Your wife's cousin went to Europe.*)

Similarly, when the head of an **'iDaafa** is the object of a verb, it's in the accusative case, and all the other members that follow it are in the genitive. Take a look at this example, which shows an accusative as the first word in an **'iDaafa:**

قَرَأتُ مَجْموعةَ مَقالاتِ مُدَرِّسي.

(qara'tu **majmuu3ata** maqaalaati mudarrisii. *I read my teacher's essay collection.*)

The only way the head of an **'iDaafa** can itself be genitive is when the **'iDaafa** is governed by a preposition. Here's an example with the **'iDaafa** head underlined:

أتى المُديرُ إلى حَفْلِ تَقاعُدِ المُوَظَّفِ.

('ataa al-mudiiru 'ilaa **Hafli** taqaa3udi al-muwaDHDHafi. *The director came to the employee's retirement party.*)

There are just five nouns that have irregular forms for their three cases when they appear in an **'iDaafa.** For your reference, Table 7-1 shows those five nouns and their forms.

Table 7-1	Common Nouns Having Irregular Forms in an 'iDaafa		
	Nominative	*Accusative*	*Genitive*
father	أَبو (**'abuu**)	أَبا (**'abaa**)	أَبي (**'abii**)
brother	أَخو (**'akhuu**)	أَخا (**'akhaa**)	أَخي (**'akhii**)
father-in-law	حَمو (**Hamuu**)	حَما (**Hamaa**)	حَمي (**Hamii**)
owner of	ذو (**dhuu**)	ذا (**dhaa**)	ذي (**dhii**)
mouth	فو (**fuu**)	فا (**faa**)	في (**fii**)

When a noun with a masculine sound plural ending is at the head of an **'iDaafa,** you drop off the final ن (**nuun**) of the suffix. (To study all the sound plural endings, see Chapter 18.) Here are two examples:

كانَ مُراسِلو الجَريدة مَشْغولينَ اليَوْم.

(**kaana muraasiluu al-jariida mashghuuliina al-yawm.** *The newspaper correspondents were busy today.*)

أَعْتَقِدُ إِنَّ مُدَرِّسي المَدْرَسة مُمْتازونَ.

(**'a3taqidu 'inna mudarrisii al-madrasa mumtaazuuna.** *I think that the school's teachers are excellent.*)

Including Adjectives in Your Complex 'iDaafas

Knowing how to put many words together in lengthy **'iDaafas** is a good starting point, but wouldn't it be nice to be able to describe the words in your **'iDaafa** with adjectives as well? If you answered with a resounding "yes!" you've come to the right place. In this section, I show you the rules for adding adjectives to your **'iDaafas.**

Looking at 'iDaafas with single adjectives

Adjectives in Arabic ordinarily follow the words they describe. (Chapter 6 covers adjectives in detail.) Here's an example showing how the two words usually appear together:

السَّيّارة السَّريعة (**as-sayyaara as-sarii3a;** *the fast car*)

However, an adjective isn't allowed to interrupt the flow of the **'iDaafa.** For this reason, if you want to describe a word in an **'iDaafa,** you must put the adjective after the **'iDaafa** itself. The adjective still needs to agree with its noun in gender, number, and definiteness. Here's a simple **'iDaafa** with a single adjective describing the first word in the **'iDaafa:**

نُصْح جَدَّتي الـمُفيد (**nuSH jaddatii al-mufiid;** *my grandmother's useful advice*)

In this example, الـمُفيد (**al-mufiid;** *useful*) is an adjective that's further describing the advice, not the grandmother. Notice that the word نُصْح (**nuSH;** *advice*) itself doesn't have the ال ('**alif laam**). It can't have the ال ('**alif laam**) because it's the head of an **'iDaafa.** The next word in the **'iDaafa,** however, جَدَّتي (**jaddatii;** *my grandmother*), is definite because it has the possessive pronoun suffix. If the final word in an **'iDaafa** is definite, the whole **'iDaafa** is definite. For that reason, the adjective describing the word نُصْح (**nuSH**) has to have the ال ('**alif laam**).

The only partial exception to the rule that nothing can interrupt the flow of the **'iDaafa** is when you use demonstrative adjectives, such as *this* or *that.* Because demonstrative adjectives usually come before the noun in Arabic, they can come between two words in an **'iDaafa.** Here's an example:

حَلّ هـذِهِ الـمُشْكِلة (**Hall haadhihi-l-mushkila;** *the solution of this problem*)

However, if the demonstrative adjective describes the head of the **'iDaafa,** it follows the **'iDaafa,** as you see here:

مِن وُجْهَة النَّظَر هـذِه (**min wujhati-n-naDHari haadhihi;** *from this point of view*)

Translate the following phrases from English into Arabic.

0. that street's dangerous intersection

A. مُفْتَرَق ذلِك الشّارِع الـخَطير (**muftaraq dhaalika-sh-shaari3 al-khaTiir**)

11. the book's final page _____

12. the car's big engine _____

13. this man's courage _____

14. the doctor's clean clinic _____

15. the color of the tall tree _____

16. my favorite class's teacher _____

17. the senator's final votes _____

18. the contract's lengthy negotiations _____

19. a plate of tasty food _____

Handling 'iDaafas with multiple adjectives

After reading the heading for this section, you're probably thinking: "How can I possibly use an adjective to describe both nouns in an **'iDaafa?**" I'm glad you asked! In this section, I demonstrate how you can add multiple adjectives to complex **'iDaafas** by expanding on a previous example about my grandmother. In this example, the adjective describing her advice comes after the **'iDaafa** itself:

نُصْح جَدَّتي المُفيد (**nuSH jaddatii al-mufiid;** *my grandmother's useful advice*)

However, I can use an adjective to describe my grandmother instead of an adjective describing her advice. In this case, the adjective still follows the whole **'iDaafa,** as in this example:

نُصْح جَدَّتي اللَّطيفة (**nuSH jaddatii al-laTiifa;** *my kindly grandmother's advice*)

If I want to add one adjective describing the advice and another adjective describing my grandmother, the rule is to add the adjectives — in reverse order — after the **'iDaafa.** In other words, the adjective describing my grandmother comes first, because *grandmother* is the final word in the **'iDaafa.** Then I add the adjective describing her advice. Look at how the adjective for the last word in the **'iDaafa** comes before the adjective for the first word:

نُصْح جَدَّتي اللَّطيفة المُفيد (**nuSH jaddatii al-laTiifa al-mufiid;** *my kindly grandmother's useful advice*)

If your **'iDaafa** has three or more words in it, you continue to add the adjectives — in reverse order — after the **'iDaafa,** as in this ridiculously complicated example:

مُدير مَكْتَبة الجامعة الأَمْريكيّة اللُّغَويّة الأَوَّل

(**mudiir maktabat al-jaami3a al-amriikiyya al-lughawiyya al-'awwal;** *the American university's linguistic library's first director* or *the first director of the American university's linguistic library*)

Constructing an **'iDaafa** as long and complicated as the preceding example isn't fun for anyone, even native writers. To avoid making an **'iDaafa** this long in the first place, you have the option of breaking up the **'iDaafa** with a preposition. Here's the same long example, but this time it's made a bit more manageable by splitting the subject off the **'iDaafa** with a preposition:

المُدير الأَوَّل لِمَكْتَبة الجامعة الأَمْريكيّة اللُّغَويّة

(**al-mudiir al-'awwal li-maktabat aljaami3a al-'amriikiyya al-lughawiyya;** *the first director of the American university's linguistic library* or *the first director to the American university's linguistic library*)

You're hosting a working luncheon with representatives from several companies and government entities. The place settings contain placards with the titles of several important guests. The placards were translated from English into Arabic by a co-worker who hasn't yet mastered the complex **'iDaafa** construction with adjectives. To save your company some embarrassment, indicate whether each of the following is correct or incorrect, and then make the corrections as needed. They range in difficulty from one adjective to three adjectives in an **'iDaafa:**

Q. الرَّئيس الولايات المُتَّحِدة (ar-ra'iis al-wilaayaat al-muttaHida; *the President of the United States*)

A. **Incorrect.** The placard should have been written like this: رَئيس الولايات المُتَّحِدة (ra'iis al-wilaayaat al-muttaHida)

20. السَّفير السَّابِق الأُرُدن (as-safiir as-saabiq al-'urdun; *the Former Ambassador of Jordan*)

_____

21. مُدير المَركَز التَّربية الإقْليمي الرَّئيسي الإبْتِدائِيّة (mudiir al-markaz at-tarbiya al-'iqliimii ar-ra'iisii al-'ibtidaa'iyya; *the Chief Director of the Regional Secondary Education Center*)

_____

22. نائِب الرَّئيس لإدارة التَّنْمية الإقْتِصادِيّة (naa'ib ar-ra'iis li-'idaarat at-tanmiya al-'iqtiSaadiyya; *the Vice President for the Economic Development Administration*)

_____

23. وَزيرة الدِّفاع الوَطَنِيّة (waziirat ad-difaaq al-waTaniyya; *the National Defense Minister*)

_____

Answer Key

1 وَظيفة زَوْجَتي (waDHiifat zawjatii)

2 كاتِب الكِتاب (kaatib al-kitaab)

3 بَيْت صَديقِهِ (bayt Sadiiqihi)

4 باب مَكْتَب الطّبيب (baab maktab aT-Tabiib)

5 هاتِف صَديقة أُمِّهِ (haatif Sadiifat 'ummihi)

6 مُدير مَكْتَبَة الجامعة (mudiir maktabat al-jaami3a)

7 نِظام نَقْل المَدينة (niDHaam naql al-madiina)

8 مُذيع بَرْنامَج الرّاديو (mudhii3 barnaamaj ar-raadiyu)

9 جَمال فَصْل الصَّيْف (jamaal faSl aS-Sayf)

10 أَهَمِّية رَأْي أَبي ('ahammiyat ra'y 'abii)

11 صَفْحة الكِتاب الأخيرة (SafHat al-kitaab al-'akhiira)

12 مُحَرِّك السَّيّارة الكَبير (muHarrik as-sayyaara al-kabiir)

13 شَجاعة هذا الرَّجُل (shajaa3at haadhaa-r-rajul)

14 عِيادة الطّبيب النَظيفة (3iyaadat aT-Tabiib an-naDHiifa)

15 لَوْن الشَّجَرة الطَّويلة (lawn ash-shajara aT-Tawiila)

16 مُدَرِّس صَفّي المُفَضَّل (mudarris Saffii al-mufaDDal)

17 أَصْوات الشَّيْخ الأخيرة ('aSwaat ash-shaykh al-'akhiira)

18 مُفاوَضات العَقْد الطَّويلة (mufaawaDaat al-3aqd aT-Tawiila)

19 صَحْن طَعام لَذيذ (SaHn Ta3aam ladhiidh)

20 **Incorrect.** The placard should have been written like this: سَفير الأُرْدُن السّابِق (**safiir al-'urdun as-saabiq**).

21 **Incorrect.** The placard should have been written like this: مُدير مَرْكَز التَّرْبية الإبْتِدائِيّة الإقْليمي الرَّئيسيّ (**mudiir markaz at-tarbiya al-'ibtidaa'iyya al-'iqliimii ar-ra'iisii**).

22 **Correct.**

23 **Incorrect.** The placard should have been written like this: وَزيرة الدِّفاع الوَطَنيّ (**waziirat ad-difaa3 al-waTanii**).

Chapter 8

Pronouns: Relatively Speaking

A good writer goes beyond just writing a subject, verb, and object. The world of subordinate clauses allows you to give important background on a topic, all within a single sentence. The relative clause lets you add levels of detail in your background explanation that go way beyond what adjectives alone can achieve.

Like other skills you acquire by working through this book, the use of the relative clause in Arabic distinguishes you as an accomplished writer. In this chapter, you discover the essential tricks for forming relative clauses correctly and precisely in Arabic.

Getting to Know the Singular Relative Pronoun

A *relative clause* is a secondary clause that tells you information about a word in the main sentence. Here's an example of a sentence with a relative clause in English: *The man, who just called me, is my brother.* The main sentence informs the reader that *The man is my brother.* The relative clause gives information about the man in the form of sub-clause.

Before you can compose a relative clause, you need to understand the components that make them up and the situations in which to include them. So in this section, I cover the elements of a relative clause and then discuss the masculine and feminine singular relative pronouns. At the end of the section, I discuss relative pronouns and the parts of speech. And, as usual, I include practice questions to help you sharpen your skills.

Dissecting relative clauses

The relative clause is always about someone or something in the sentence. The word being described further in this way is called the *antecedent.* As a rule, the antecedent comes before the relative clause and ordinarily is the word that immediately precedes the relative clause.

When you describe someone or something, you frequently use an adjective. You may, for instance, say that a man you met is "tall." Perhaps you want to describe the man even further and add that he's "tall and angry." Adjectives can take you a long way toward describing physical and other attributes.

Sometimes, however, what you want to describe to your reader isn't a visible attribute, but a fact concerning your topic. You may want to describe important background information to help your reader or listener understand the topic better. For instance, you may write that you met "the tall and angry man who came to the party with Fatima." This information may be significant if a second tall and angry man came to the party with Dalia!

The way you convey background information in this way is through a relative clause. If you remove the whole relative clause, what's left over is a separate and grammatical sentence. Here's an example in Arabic where the relative clause comes at the end of the sentence:

اللَّيْلَة الماضِية الْتَقَيْتُ بِالرَّجُلِ الطَّويل وَالغَضْبان اَلَّذي أتى إلى الحَفْلِة مَعَ. فاطِمة

(**al-layla al-maaDiya iltaqaytu bir-rajuli aT-Tawiili wa-l-ghaDbaan <u>alladhii</u> 'ataa 'ilaa-l-Haflati ma3a faaTima.** *Last night I met the tall and angry man <u>who</u> came to the party with Fatima.*)

Here's the same sentence without the relative clause. As you can see, it's still a complete thought:

اللَّيْلَة الماضِية الْتَقَيْتُ بِالرَّجُلِ الطَّويل وَالغَضْبان.

(**al-layla al-maaDiya iltaqaytu bir-rajuli aT-Tawiili wa-l-ghaDbaan.** *Last night I met the tall and angry man.*)

A relative clause can come in the middle of the sentence as well. Here's a sentence with the relative clause imbedded inside:

الرَّجُلُ الطَّويلُ وَالغَضْبان اَلَّذي أتى إلى الحَفْلِة مَعَ فاطِمة أَخْبَرَني نُكْتَةً.

(**a-rajul aT-Tawiil wa-l-ghaDbaan <u>alladhii</u> 'ata 'ila-l-Hafla ma3a faaTima 'akhbarani nuktatan.** *The tall and angry man <u>who</u> came to the party with Fatima told me a joke.*)

You can remove the relative clause from the middle and still have a full sentence:

الرَّجُلُ الطَّويلُ وَالغَضْبان أَخْبَرَني نُكْتَةً.

(**a-rajul aT-Tawiil wa-l-ghaDbaan 'akhbarani nuktatan.** *The tall and angry man told me a joke.*)

Use الَّذي (**alladhii**; *who/that*) or الَّتي (**allatii**; *who/that*) only when the antecedent is a definite noun — that is, it has the الـ (**'alif laam**; *the*), a possessive suffix, or it's the head of an **'iDaafa** that's definite. Arabic has a slightly different way of forming relative clauses for indefinite antecedents (see the later section "Looking at Other Relative Clauses" for details).

Masculine singular relative الَّذي (*alladhi*)

Arabic has separate relative pronouns for the different genders and numbers of potential antecedents. When the antecedent is a masculine singular noun in the definite state, whether it's a person or an object, use the pronoun الَّذي (**alladhii**; *who/that*). Check out the following examples:

الفِلْم الَّذي شاهَدْناهُ أَمْس كانَ رائِعاً.

(**al-film alladhii shaahadnaahu 'amsi kaana raa'i3an.** *The film that we saw yesterday was tremendous.*)

الرَّجُل الَّذي اِتَّصَلَ بي أَمْس قالَ لي نَفْس الشَّيْء.

(**ar-rajul alladhii ittaSala bii 'amsi qaala lii nafsa-sh-shay'.** *The man who called me yesterday told me the same thing.*)

Feminine singular relative الَّتي (*allatii*)

When the antecedent in a relative clause is a feminine singular definite noun, use the relative pronoun الَّتي (**allatii**; *who/that*). Here are three examples of sentences with feminine singular definite antecedents:

أُمّي الَّتي أَتّصِلُ بِها يَوْميّاً ما تَزالُ تَقْلَقُ عَلَيَّ.

(**'ummii allatii 'attaSilu bihaa yawmiyyan maa tazaalu taqlaqu 3alayya.** *My mother, whom I call daily, still worries about me.*)

اَللُّغَةُ الَّتي تَدْرُسُها هِيَ مُفيدةٌ جِدّاً في الشَّرْق الأَوْسَطِ.

(**al-lughatu allatii tadrusuhaa hiya mufiidatun jiddan fii-sh-sharqi -l'awsaTi.** *The language that you are studying is very useful in the Middle East.*)

Suppose you're writing an e-mail describing your vacation to a friend. Depending on the gender of the antecedent, write the correct form of the relative pronoun on the lines that are provided to you.

Q. الرِّسالة _____ أَكْتُبُها لَكَ فَهِيَ عَن عُطْلَتِنا. (**ar-risaalatu _____ 'aktubuhaa lakaa fa-hiya 3an 3uTlatinaa.** *The letter _____ I write to you is about our vacation.*)

A. الرِّسالة الَّتي أَكْتُبُها لَكَ فَهِيَ عَن عُطْلَتِنا. (**ar-risaalatu allatii 'aktubuhaa lakaa fa-hiya 3an 3uTlatinaa.** *The letter that I write to you is about our vacation.*)

New Message

Send | Cut | Copy | Paste | Undo | **abc✔** Check

أَحْمَد

(ʾaHmad; *Ahmad*)

1. العُطْلةُ ــــــــ إِنْتَظَرْناها وَصَلَتْ آخِيراً.

(al-3uTlatu _____ intaDHarnaahaa waSalat ʾakhiiran. *The vacation that we were waiting for finally arrived.*)

2. نُسافِرُ مَعَ ــــــــ كَتَبْتُ عَنْهُ في رِسالَتي السّابِقة.

(nusaafira ma3a jaarinaa _____ katabtu 3anhu fii risaalatii as-saabiqa. *We are traveling with our neighbor about whom I wrote in my previous letter.*)

3. السَّيّارةُ ــــــــ أجَّرْناها هِيَ كَبيرةٌ وَجَديدةٌ.

(as-sayyaaratu _____ ʾajjarnaahaa hiya kabiiratun wa-jadiidatun. *The car that we rented is big and new.*)

4. وَصَلْنا سَريعاً إلى الفُنْدُقِ ــــــــ إخْتارَهُ زَوْجي لَنا.

(waSalnaa sarii3an ʾilaa-l-funduqi _____ ikhtaarahu zawjii lanaa. *We arrived quickly at the hotel that my husband chose for us.*)

5. غُرْفَتُنا ــــــــ نَسْتَطيعُ أنْ نَرى مِنها الشّاطِئ هِيَ نَظيفة جِدّاً.

(ghurfatunaa _____ nastaTii3u ʾan naraa minhaa ash-shaaTiʾa hiya naDHiifa jiddan. *Our room, from which we can see the beach, is very clean.*)

6. سَأكْتُبُ مِن جَديد عَن المَكان ــــــــ قَرَّرْنا بِأنْ نَزورَهُ غَداً.

(sa-ʾaktubu min jadiid 3an al-makaani _____ qarrarnaa bi-ʾan nazuurahu ghadan. *I will write again about the place that we have decided to visit tomorrow.*)

المُخْلِصة

مَرْيم

(al-mukhliSa, maryam; *Sincerely, Maryam.*)

Singular relative pronouns and parts of speech

A relative pronoun in Arabic can appear anywhere a noun might. It could be the subject of its own verb. You could have a relative pronoun as the object of a verb within a relative clause. It also could be governed by a preposition.

The relative pronoun presents a situation in which the normally complicated Arabic language is considerably easier than English. Arabic has preserved case endings for almost all nouns, while English nouns are invariable. Arabic relative pronouns, however, are *nondeclinable* (meaning, they have a single form that can stand for the subject or object within a relative clause). You use the forms الَّذي (**alladhii**; *who/that*) or الَّتي (**allatii**; *who/that*) regardless of whether the relative pronoun is the subject or object in the relative clause. English, by contrast, has one form for the nominative, *who*, another for accusative or after prepositions, *whom*, and even a genitive relative pronoun, *whose*.

Relative pronoun as a subject

No matter what role the antecedent plays in the sentence, the relative pronoun describing it can be the subject of the relative clause. Here's a relative clause with the relative pronoun as a subject:

أُحِبُّ الكاتِبَ الَّذي كَتَبَ ذلِكَ الكِتابَ.

(**'uHibbu al-kaatiba alladhii kataba dhaalika-l-kitaaba.** *I love the author who wrote that book.*)

Relative pronoun as a direct object

An antecedent can be the object within a relative clause. Whenever a relative pronoun is the object, you then have to add an object pronoun either directly to the verb or to a preposition required by the verb. This produces the Arabic equivalent of saying "The man whom I met him" or "His book that he wrote it." This certainly does sound odd to an English-speaking person. But if you form a relative clause and forget to use these object pronouns, a more advanced reader of Arabic will certainly notice their absence.

The extra pronoun you add when the relative pronoun is an object or is governed by a preposition is an essential part of a fully grammatical relative clause in Arabic. Grammarians call the object pronoun used in this way a *resumptive pronoun*, meaning it resumes speaking about the antecedent.

The following are two examples of relative pronouns that are direct objects. I underline the resumptive pronoun in the Arabic so you can become accustomed to its use:

الرَّجُلُ الَّذي اِلتَقَيْتُ بِهِ في الحَفْلةِ كانَ طَويلاً وغَضْبانَ.

(**ar-rajulu alladhii iltaqaytu bihi fi-l-Haflati kaana Tawiilan wa-ghaDbaana.** *The man whom I met at the party was tall and angry.*)

قَرَأْتُ كِتابَهُ الَّذي كَتَبَهُ عَن هذا المَوْضوعِ.

(**qara'tu kitaabahu alladhii katabahu 3an haadhaa-l-mawDuu3i.** *I read his book that he had written on that subject.*)

Relative pronoun governed by a preposition

In English, relative pronouns can be governed by a preposition. Here are two examples in English:

> *The friend about whom I told you is getting married soon.*

> *She sent a letter to the uncle from whom she received the present.*

By contrast, Arabic doesn't put the preposition before the relative pronoun. Instead, you move the prepositional phrase into the relative clause and use the object suffix. Here are Arabic versions of the preceding English example sentences. I translate them into literal English here to show you where to put the prepositions. I've underlined the prepositions with their object suffixes so you can see how they compare to the English:

الصَّديقُ الَّذي أَخْبَرْتُكَ عَنْهُ سَوْفَ يَتَزَوَّجُ قَريباً.

(**aS-Sadiiqu alladhii 'akhbartuka <u>3anhu</u> sawfa yatazawwaju qariiban.** *The friend who I told you <u>about him</u> is getting married soon.*)

أَرْسَلَتْ رسالةً لِلْخال الَّذي حَصَلَتْ عَلى الهَديةِ مِنْهُ.

(**'arsalat risaalatan lil-khaali alladhii HaSalat 3ala-l-hadiyati <u>minhu</u>.** *She sent a letter to the uncle who she received the present <u>from him</u>.*)

Relative pronoun in the genitive

The relative pronoun in Arabic doesn't have a genitive case, but you can still use a relative clause to describe an antecedent that owns something. In English you use *whose* or *of whom* to form a relative clause describing ownership. Here's an example in English: *The colleague whose proposal we are considering wants to speak before the group.*

To express this sentence in Arabic, use the relative pronoun and put the possessive suffix on the object within the relative clause. Here's an Arabic version of the preceding example sentence. I've underlined the possessive suffix to show you how Arabic creates a relative pronoun in the genitive:

الزَّميلُ الَّذي نَهْتَمُّ بِاقْتِراحِهِ يُريدُ أَنْ يَتَكَلَّمَ أَمامَ اللَّجْنةِ.

(**az-zamiilu alladhii nahtammu bi-'iqtiraaHi<u>hi</u> yuriidu 'an yatakallama 'amaama al-lajnati.** *The colleague who we are considering <u>his</u> proposal wants to speak before the committee.*)

As you become more experienced with picking the correct relative pronoun for each gender, you can take it to the next level by adding the resumptive pronouns. Here's your chance to show off what you know by using these skills! Translate each of the following sentences into Arabic. Any words you don't know are in the dictionary at the back of the book.

0. The room I entered was very dark.

A. الغُرفةُ الَّتي دَخَلْتُها كانَتْ مُظْلِمةً جِدّاً. (**al-ghurfatu allatii dakhaltuhaa kaanat muDHlimatan jiddan.**)

7. The letter that I sent to my friend arrived after only two days.

_____

8. I wanted to study with the professor whose specialty is in Arabic.

_____

9. The pen with which he signed the contract was a gift from his grandfather.

_____

10. They submitted their proposal to the company that has a branch in Qatar.

_____

11. She looked for the solution that would lead to success.

_____

12. The sister with whom I visited Jordan wants to return there soon.

_____

13. He wore the shirt in which he got married.

_____

Examining Relative Clauses with Plural Antecedents

A relative clause can have a plural noun as its antecedent. Arabic has plural relative pronouns for such occasions. One peculiar grammatical trait of Arabic, however, is that the only time you actually use a plural relative pronoun is when the antecedent is both plural and animate. An _animate_ object is something alive, either a human or even an animal. An _inanimate_ object, by contrast, is something that isn't living, such as a book or a sofa. The dual relative pronouns are the only ones that have different forms depending on the case of the pronoun. For your reference, Table 8-1 shows the singular and plural forms of the relative pronoun.

Table 8-1	Singular and Plural Forms of the Relative Pronoun	
	Singular	*Plural*
Masculine	الّذي (**alladhii;** *who, whom, that*)	الّذينَ (**alladhiina;** *who, whom, that*)
Feminine	الّتي (**allatii;** *who, whom, that*)	اللَّواتي (**allawaati;** *who, whom, that*)

الَّذينَ *(alladhiina) with animate plurals*

Because you use the masculine plural relative pronouns for any group of humans that's either all male or (as is more common) of mixed gender, the masculine plural relative is overwhelmingly the most common plural form. All the rules you observe with the singular relative forms apply to its use. The antecedent has to be definite, plural, and animate. Consider the following examples:

المُراسِلونَ الَّذينَ كَتَبوا هذِهِ المَقالة سَيَفوزونَ بِجائِزَةٍ.

(al-muraasiluuna <u>alladhiina</u> katabuu hadhihi-l-maqaala sayafuuzuuna bi-jaa'izatin. *The correspondents <u>who</u> wrote that article will win an award.*)

سَلَّمْنا عَلى كُلّ الزُّوار الَّذينَ حَضَروا المُحاضَرة.

(sallamnaa 3ala kulli-z-zuwwaari <u>alladhiina</u> HaDaruu al-muHaaDarata. *We greeted all the visitors <u>who</u> attended the lecture.*)

You can additionally modify many plural nouns with the word كُلّ (kull; *all*). Here is an example:

رَأى الرَّئيسُ كُلَّ الزُّوّار.

(ra'aa ar-ra'iisu kulla-z-zuwwaari. *The president saw all the visitors.*)

Even though technically the plural noun is in 'iDaafa with كُلّ (kull) (a singular noun), you won't see grammatical agreement between كُلّ (kull) and relative pronouns. Instead, Arabic intuitively uses plural relative pronouns. Here's an example of a relative clause with كُلّ (kull). Note the use of the plural relative pronoun (underlined):

رَأى الرَّئيسُ كُلَّ الزُّوّار الَّذينَ حَضَروا إلى البَيْتِ الأَبْيَضِ.

(ra'aa ar-ra'iisu kulla-z-zuwwaari <u>alladhiina</u> HaDaruu 'ilaa-l-bayti- al-'abyaDi. *The president saw all the visitors <u>who</u> came to the White House.*)

الَّتي *(allatii) with inanimate plurals*

When you form a relative clause with inanimate plurals as the antecedent, use the feminine singular relative pronoun الَّتي (allatii; *who, whom, which, that*). If you need to use resumptive pronouns in these sentences, make sure they're feminine singular as well. Here are two examples:

باعَ الباعةُ كُلَّ المُنْتَجاتِ الَّتي أنْتَجَها المَصْنَعُ.

(baa3a al-baa3atu kulla-l-muntajaati <u>allatii</u> 'antajahaa al-maSna3u. *The salesmen sold all the products <u>that</u> the factory produced.*)

يُفَضِّلُ الأوْلاد الكُتُبَ الَّتي فيها الصُّوَرُ.

(yufaDDilu al-'awlaadu alkutuba <u>allatii</u> fiihaa aS-Suwaur. *The children prefer the books <u>that</u> have pictures.*)

In the following sentences, translate and write the sentences using the exact type of plural relative pronoun necessary.

Q. The writers who wrote the stories were my friends.

A. الكُتّاب اَلَّذينَ كَتَبوا القِصَص كانوا أَصْدِقائي. (al-kuttaabu alladhinna katabuu al-qiSas kaanuu 'aSdiqaa'ii.)

14. The students who heard the lecture learned much.

_____

15. He denied the rumors about which the reporter asked.

_____

16. The president praised the women who founded that college.

_____

17. The doctor examined all the patients who came to the hospital.

_____

18. Our company is improving the products that it sells.

_____

Looking at Other Relative Clauses

The beginning of this chapter shows you how Arabic handles relative clauses when the antecedent is a definite noun. But some relative clauses have indefinite antecedents or, for that matter, no stated antecedent at all. In the following sections, I show you how to write these kinds of relative clauses.

Indefinite antecedents in relative clauses

You form a relative clause with an indefinite antecedent exactly the same way you form a relative clause with a definite antecedent, except you don't use the relative pronoun. Because a relative pronoun can only have a definite antecedent, you leave the relative pronoun unstated in Arabic. (See the earlier section "Getting to Know the Singular Relative Pronoun" for details on how to form a relative clause with a definite antecedent.)

Here are examples of indefinite antecedents in relative clauses. The English translations have relative pronouns, but there's no stated word in the Arabic for the relative pronoun:

كَتَبْتُ رِسالةً لَم أُرْسِلُها.

(**katabtu risaalatan lam 'ursilhaa.** *I wrote a letter that I never sent.*)

بَقِيْتُ في فُنْدُق اقْتَرَحَهُ صَديقي عَلَيَّ.

(**baqaytu fii funduqin iqtaraHahu Sadiiqii 3alayya.** *I stayed in a hotel that my friend had suggested to me.*)

Topical antecedents in relative clauses

Sometimes the antecedent in a relative clause isn't a noun that's stated explicitly in the sentence. The very topic of a sentence can become the unstated antecedent. Luckily, each of these situations has a relative pronoun that tells you when to expect a relative clause without a stated antecedent. To help you spot the relative pronouns in this section, I underline them in the Arabic and the English.

Who

The particle مَنْ (**man**; *who*) can serve as a relative pronoun in cases where you want to form a relative clause referring to a previously unmentioned human or animate object. Here's an example of a sentence using this particle:

كانَ في الجُمْهور مَن بَحَثَ عَن إجابةٍ.

(**kaana fii-l-jumhuuri** <u>man</u> **baHatha 3an 'ijaabatin.** *There was in the crowd someone* <u>who</u> *sought an answer.*)

What

The word ما (**maa**; *what*) stands as a relative pronoun for indefinite objects that are unstated. Consider this example:

دَعَمْتُ ما كَتَبَ الصُّحُفيُّ.

(**da3amtu** <u>maa</u> **kataba aS-SuHufiyyu.** *I supported* <u>what</u> *the reporter wrote.*)

Which

The word مِمّا (**mimmaa**; *which*), which is the contraction of مِن (**min**; *from*) and ما (**maa**; *what*), can serve as a relative pronoun. It stands for concepts or ideas raised within the first part of the sentence. Check out the following example:

قَرَّرَ أَنْ يَدْرُسَ في باريس مِمّا أَحْزَنَ أُمَّهُ.

(**qarrara 'an yadrusa fii-baariis** <u>mimmaa</u> **'aHzana 'ummahu.** *He decided to study in Paris,* <u>which</u> *saddened his mother.*)

For each of the sentences in this exercise, look at the relative pronouns provided, select the one that grammatically fits, and write it in the blank.

اَلَّذِينَ ~~(alladhiina)~~   اَلَّذِي (alladhii)   اللَّواتي (allawaatii)   اَلَّتِي (allatii)

مَن (man)   ما (maa)   مِمّا (mimaa)

Q. اِسْتَمَعْنا لِلشُّيوخِ ـــــ تَكَلَّموا مَعَنا. (**istama3naa li-sh-shuyuukhi _____ takallamuu ma3anaa.** *We listened to the Senators _____ spoke with us.*)

A. اِسْتَمَعْنا لِلشُّيوخِ الَّذِينَ تَكَلَّموا مَعَنا. (**istama3naa li-sh-shuyuukhi <u>alladhiina</u> takallamuu ma3anaa.** *We listened to the Senators <u>who</u> spoke with us.*)

19. رَأَيْتُ هُناك ـــــ قالَ لي قِصَّةً. (**ra'aytu hunaaka _____ qaala lii qiSSatan.** *I saw there someone _____ told me a story.*)

20. لَمْ أَحْصُلْ عَلى رِسالةٍ مِن حَبيبَتي ـــــ أَقْلَقَني. (**lam 'aHSul 3alaa risaalatin min Habiibatii _____ 'aqlaqanii.** *I didn't get a letter from my girlfriend, _____ worried me.*)

21. لا أَسْتَطيعُ أَنْ أَفْهَمَ ـــــ حَدَثَ بَيْنَهُما. (**laa 'astaTii3u 'an 'afhama _____ Hadatha baynahumaa.** *I can't understand _____ happened between those two.*)

22. النِّساء ـــــ وَجَدْنَ الوَلَد أَنْقَذْنَهُ مِن المَوْتِ. (**an-nisaa' _____ wajadna al-walada 'anqadh-nahu mina-l-mawti.** *The women _____ found the boy saved him from death.*)

23. الأَماكِن ـــــ زُرتُها كانَتْ جَميلةٌ. (**al-'amaakin _____ zurtuhaa kaanat jamiilatun.** *The places _____ I visited were beautiful.*)

24. الشَّخْصُ ـــــ عَلَّمَني الكَثيرَ كانَ أَبي. (**ash-shakhSu _____ darrasani al-kathiira kaana 'abii.** *The person _____ taught me the most was my father.*)

Answer Key

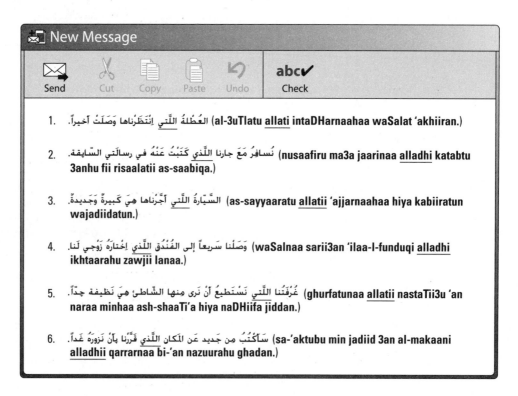

1. العُطْلَةُ اللّتِي اِنْتَظَرْناها وَصَلَتْ آخِيراً. (al-3uTlatu allati intaDHarnaahaa waSalat 'akhiiran.)

2. نُسافِرُ مَعَ جارِنا اللّذِي كَتَبْتُ عَنْهُ في رِسالَتي السّابِقة. (nusaafiru ma3a jaarinaa alladhi katabtu 3anhu fii risaalatii as-saabiqa.)

3. السّيّارةُ اللّتِي آجَّرْناها هِيَ كَبِيرةٌ وَجَدِيدةٌ. (as-sayyaaratu allatii 'ajjarnaahaa hiya kabiiratun wajadiidatun.)

4. وَصَلْنا سَرِيعاً إلى الفُنْدُق اللّذِي اِخْتارَهُ زَوْجي لَنا. (waSalnaa sarii3an 'ilaa-l-funduqi alladhi ikhtaarahu zawjii lanaa.)

5. غُرْفَتُنا اللّتِي نَسْتَطِيعُ أَنْ نَرى مِنها الشّاطِئ هِيَ نَظِيفة جِدّاً. (ghurfatunaa allatii nastaTii3u 'an naraa minhaa ash-shaaTi'a hiya naDHiifa jiddan.)

6. سَأَكْتُبُ مِن جَدِيد عَن المَكان اللّذِي قَرَّرْنا بِأَنْ نَزورَهُ غَداً. (sa-'aktubu min jadiid 3an al-makaani alladhii qarrarnaa bi-'an nazuurahu ghadan.)

7. الرّسالةُ الّتِي أَرْسَلْتُها لِصَديقي وَصَلَتْ بَعْدَ يَوْمَيْن فَقَط. (ar-risaalatu allatii 'arsaltuhaa li-Sadiiqii waSalat ba3da yawmayni faqaT.)

8. أَرَدْتُ أَنْ أَدْرُسَ مَعَ الأُسْتاذِ الّذِي تَخَصُّصُهُ اللُّغةَ العَرَبِيّةَ. ('aradtu 'an 'adrusa ma3a-l-'ustaadhi alladhii takhaSSuSuhu al-lughata al-3arabiyyata.)

9. القَلَم الّذِي وَقَّعَ العَقْد بِه كانَ هَدِية مِن جَدِّه. (al-qalam alladhii waqqa3a al-3aqda bihi kaana hadiyatun min jaddihi.)

10. سَلَّموا اِقْتِراحَهُم لِلشّركةِ الّتِي عِنْدَها فَرْعٌ في قَطَر. (sallamuu iqtiraaHahum li-sh-sharikati allatii 3indahaa far3un fii qaTar.)

11. بَحَثَتْ عَن الحَلّ الّذِي قَد يُؤَدّي إلى النّجاحِ. (baHathat 3an al-Halli alladhii qad yu'addii 'ilaa-n-najaaHi.)

12. الأُخْتُ الّتِي زُرْتُ الأُرْدُن مَعَها تُرِيدُ أَنْ تَرْجِعَ هُناكَ قَرِيباً. (al-'ukhtu allatii zurtu al-'urdun ma3ahaa turiidu 'an tarji3a hunaaka qariiban.)

13 لَبِسَ القَميصَ الَّذِي تَزَوَّجَ فيهِ. (labisa al-qamiiSa alladhii tazawwaja fiihi.)

14 الطُّلابُ الَّذِينَ سَمِعوا المُحاضَرةَ تَعَلَّموا الكَثيرَ مِنها. (aT-Tullaabu alladhiina sami3uu al-mu-Haadarata ta3allamuu al-kathiira minhaa.)

15 نَفى الإشاعاتِ الَّتي سَألَ الصُّحُفيَ عَنْها. (nafaa al-'ishaa3aati allatii sa'ala aS-SuHufii 3anhaa.)

16 مَدَحَ الرَّئيسُ النِّساءَ اللَّواتي أسَّسْنَ تِلْكَ الكُلِّيَةَ. (madaHa ar-ra'iisu an-nisaa'a allawaatii 'assasna tilka-l-kulliyata.)

17 تَفَحَّصَ الطَّبيبُ كُلَّ المَرْضى الَّذينَ حَضَروا إلى المُسْتَشْفى. (tafaHHaSa aT-Tabiibu kulla-l-marDaa alladhiina HaDaruu 'ilaa-l-mustashfaa.)

18 تُحَسِّنُ شَرِكَتُنا المُنْتَجاتِ الَّتي تَبيعُها. (tuHassinu sharikatunaa almuntajaati allatii tabii3uhaa.)

19 رَأيْتُ هُناك مَنْ قالَ لي قِصّةً. (ra'aytu hunaaka <u>man</u> qaala lii qiSSatan. *I saw there someone <u>who</u> told me a story.*)

20 لَمْ أَحْصُلْ عَلى رِسالةٍ مِن حَبيبَتي مِمّا أقْلَقَني. (lam 'aHSul 3alaa risaalatin min Habiibatii <u>mimmaa</u> 'aqlaqanii. *I didn't get a letter from my girlfriend, <u>which</u> worried me.*)

21 لا أسْتَطيعُ أنْ أفْهَم ما حَدَثَ بَيْنَهُما. (laa 'astaTii3u 'an 'afhama <u>maa</u> Hadatha baynahumaa. *I can't understand <u>what</u> happened between those two.*)

22 النِّساء اللَّواتي وَجَدْنَ الوَلَد أنْقَذْنَهُ مِن المَوْتِ. (an-nisaa' <u>allawaatii</u> wajadna al-walada 'anqadhnahu mina-l-mawti. *The women <u>who</u> found the boy saved him from death.*)

23 الأماكن الَّتي زُرْتُها كانَتْ جَميلةٌ. (al-'amaakin <u>allatii</u> zurtuhaa kaanat jamiilatun. *The places <u>that</u> I visited were beautiful.*)

24 الشَّخْصُ الَّذي عَلَّمَني الكَثيرَ كانَ أبي. (ash-shakhSu <u>alladhii</u> darrasani al-kathiira kaana 'abii. *The person <u>who</u> taught me the most was my father.*)

Part III
Staying Active: Forming Arabic Verbs

The 5th Wave   By Rich Tennant

"Mona's trying to form endings to Arabic
verbs. This from a woman who can't
form an ending to a conversation."

In this part . . .

*I*f you like to be part of the action, this is the part for
you. It's where you find everything you need to write
verbs of every size, shape, and especially, form in Arabic.
The ten forms of the Arabic verb will bow to your command after you master them here. I introduce those pesky
irregular verbs as well, but I show you that deep down
they're manageable, too. Discovering how to add an object
to your verb helps you polish your writing skills, so I
include a chapter on the object suffix. Finally, in this part,
you break out of the basic world of indicative verbs and
take on the task of using the subjunctive and the jussive
when Arabic calls for it.

Chapter 9

Forms and Functions: The Forms of the Arabic Verb

- -

In This Chapter

▶ Recognizing the structure of the Arabic verb forms

▶ Producing the past and present of the verb forms

- -

*E*very language has basic verbs to describe the actions of the world. But beyond simply using basic verbs, such as *eat, run,* and *sleep,* each language also has ways to nuance descriptions. In English, for example, you can refine verbs with prepositions, to produce statements such as *eat out, run on,* and *sleep in.* In some cases, just adding a preposition produces an idiomatic meaning quite separate from the basic verb by itself.

Similarly, Arabic has a way to change basic verbal roots to produce multiple meanings. Arabic, however, adds various prefixes, vowels, and doubled consonants to generate meanings such as *to cause to do something, to seek to do something,* or *to be done.* So in this chapter, you discover how to apply the changes that turn a verbal root into any of the different word patterns, creating various shades of meaning or even whole new verbs in the process.

Understanding the Forms of the Arabic Verb

The nine word patterns you read about in this chapter are called *forms* by English language linguists. These forms are usually distinguished by the use of Roman numerals, which is the convention that I use in this book. You likely became acquainted with the common Form I in your basic studies of Arabic. (If not, you can find a refresher on Form I in Chapter 2.)

An Arabic verb form is a word pattern created by the addition of extra consonants or long vowels. These extra elements, depending on the form, are added to the verbal root at the beginning of the word or in between the consonants of the verbal root.

Each of the forms has specific features that you'll come to recognize and associate with that form. I highlight the features for you in this chapter. This treatment of the features will allow you to remember the traits that can help you recognize a given form.

In order to understand how Arabic can create different meanings through elements such as prefixes, consider by analogy a similar development in English. The English language inherited numerous verbs from Latin, and these verbs come to the language already carrying various prepositional prefixes that radically change their meanings. Nowadays we don't even think about how some of these verbs are related to one another. Words have specific meanings for us in English today that aren't readily apparent from their etymologies alone.

For example, from Latin *capere,* meaning *to take,* we get these words: *receive, conceive,* and *perceive.* Similarly, from Latin *mittere,* meaning *to send,* we get *remit, commit,* and *permit.* And from Latin *formare,* meaning *to form,* we get *reform, conform,* and *perform.*

Form II

Form II is a common and easily recognizable verb form. As you're about to see, there's a visual flag on a Form II verb that helps you determine that you do, in fact, have a Form II verb on your hands. Here are the distinct traits of Form II:

- ✔ The second consonant of the root doubles, which is written by placing a ˝ (**shadda**) over the second consonant. Only two of the Arabic verb forms will have a ˝ (**shadda**) over the second consonant — Forms II and V. And Form V will have an additional prefix that Form II doesn't have.

- ✔ A ˌ (**kasra**) is added under the second consonant of the root in the present tense.

- ✔ A ´ (**Damma**) is added over the present tense prefixes.

Forget what the **kasra, Damma,** and **shadda** are? Check out Chapter 3.

The meaning of Form II

Form II can affect the root meaning of a verb in two ways. In some cases, it seems to imply an intensifying of the action. For example, consider the Form I verb, كَسَرَ (**kasara**), which means *to break.* The intensified Form II version of this verb is كَسَّرَ (**kassara**), which means *to shatter/smash.* Here's an example sentence using this verb:

كَسَّرَتِ الإِمْرَأَةُ الغَضْبانَةُ الزُّجاجَةَ عَلى الأَرْض.

(**kassarat al-'imra'atu al-ghaDbaanatu az-zujaajata 3alaa-l-'arDi.** *The angry woman smashed the bottle on the ground.*)

Other verbs in Form II are causative. For instance, the Form I verb, دَرَسَ (**darasa**; *to learn*), changes in Form II to دَرَّسَ (**darrasa**), which means *to teach* (or *to cause to learn*). Check out this example sentence:

أَشْكُرُ الرَّجُلَ الَّذي دَرَّسَني اللُّغةَ العَرَبِيَّة.

(**'ashkuru ar-rajula alladhii darrasanii al-lughata al-3arabiyyata.** *I thank the man who taught me the Arabic langauge.*)

You can observe the intensifying meaning of Form II when you compare Form I كَسَرَ (**kasara**; *to break*) to Form II كَسَّرَ (**kassara**; *to shatter*). But that doesn't mean you can take just any verbal root and put it into Form II with the intention of intensifying the meaning. In other words, a verbal root may occur in Form II or it may not. And if a verbal root doesn't occur in Form II, you can't create a new verb by putting it into Form II.

Producing Form II

Here are some other common and important verbs that occur in Form II. Unlike كَسَّرَ (**kassara**; *to shatter*), these verbs don't have any apparent meaning imparted to them by Form II:

سَلَّمَ (**sallama**; *to greet*)

غَيَّرَ (**ghayyara**; *to change*)

The following are some examples using these verbs:

سَلِّمْ لي عَلى زَوْجَتِكَ مِن فَضْلِكَ.

(**sallim lii 3alaa zawjatika min faDlika.** *Please convey my greetings to your wife.*)

غَيَّرتُ رَأيي سَريعاً.

(**ghayyartu ra'yii sarii3an.** *I changed my opinion quickly.*)

To produce Form II, you apply the steps I show you in the introduction to this section. All Arabic verb forms take the same suffixes and prefixes to form their past and present tenses. (If you're interested in reviewing past and present tense formation, you can visit Chapter 2.)

The following tables show the conjugation of دَرَّسَ (**darrasa**; *to teach*), which is a Form II verb. I show the conjugation in both past and present tense.

Past tense conjugation for دَرَّسَ (**darrasa**; *to teach*)	
دَرَّسْتُ (**'anaa darrastu**)	دَرَّسْنا (**naHnu darrasnaa**)
دَرَّسْتَ (**'anta darrasta**) دَرَّسْتِ (**'anti darrasti**)	دَرَّسْتُم (**'antum darrastum**) دَرَّسْتُنَّ (**'antunna darrastunna**)
دَرَّسَ (**huwa darrasa**) دَرَّسَتْ (**hiya darrasat**)	دَرَّسوا (**hum darrasuu**) دَرَّسْنَ (**hunna darrasna**)
هَلْ دَرَّسْتُم أَوْلادَكُم أَنْ يَتَكَلَّموا العَرَبِيّة؟ (**hal darrastum 'awlaadakum 'an yatakallamuu al-3arabiyya?** *Have you taught your children to speak Arabic?*)	

Present tense conjugation for دَرَّسَ (**darrasa**; *to teach*)	
أُدَرِّسُ (**'anaa 'udarrisu**)	نُدَرِّسُ (**naHnu nudarrisu**)
تُدَرِّسُ (**'anta tudarrisu**) تُدَرِّسينَ (**'anti tudarrisiina**)	تُدَرِّسونَ (**'antum tudarrisuuna**) تُدَرِّسنَ (**'antunna tudarrisna**)
يُدَرِّسُ (**huwa yudarrisu**) تُدَرِّسُ (**hiya tudarrisu**)	يُدَرِّسونَ (**hum yudarrisuuna**) يُدَرِّسنَ (**hunna yudarrisna**)
نُدَرِّسُ لِكَيْ نَتَعَلَّم. (**nudarrisu likay nata3allama.** *We teach that we might learn.*)	

The best way to internalize your production of each verb form in this chapter is to apply the steps you discover in each section immediately after you encounter them. For this exercise, I give you a pronoun and a verbal root. Write the past and present tenses of the Form II verb that correspond to the verbal root and the supplied pronoun in each item.

Q. هُوَ (**huwa**) / درس (**d-r-s**)

A. دَرَّسَ (**darrasa**; *he taught*) / يُدَرِّسُ (**yudarrisu**; *he teaches*)

1. أنا (**'anaa**) / سهل (**s-h-l**) _____

2. أَنْتَ (**'anta**) / غرب (**gh-r-b**) _____

3. أَنْتِ (**'anti**) / شجع (**sh-j-3**) _____

4. هُوَ (**huwa**) / خبر (**kh-b-r**) _____

5. هِيَ (hiya) / جدد (j-d-d) _____

6. نَحْنُ (naHnu) / مدن (m-d-n) _____

7. أَنْتُم ('antum) / نشف (n-sh-f) _____

8. هُم (hum) / طبق (T-b-q) _____

Form III

These are the distinct features of Form III:

- ✓ A long *a* vowel — written with an أَلِف ('alif) — comes after the first consonant of the root.
- ✓ A ِ (kasra) is added under the second consonant in the present tense.
- ✓ A ُ (Damma) is added over the prefixes in the present tense.

To read more about the أَلِف ('alif), flip to Chapter 3.

The meaning of Form III

Form III generally imparts a meaning of *trying to do something*. For example, consider the Form I verb, شَهِدَ (shahida; *to witness*). The Form III version, شاهَدَ (shaahada) means *to watch* or *to try to witness something*. Another example is the Form I verb صَدَقَ (Sadaqa; *to speak the truth*). The Form III version of this verb is صادَقَ (Saadaqa), meaning *to befriend, consent*.

Here are examples of sentences using these verbs:

شاهَدْنا فِلماً أَمْس.

(**shaahadnaa filman 'amsi.** *We watched a movie yesterday.*)

صادَقْتُ الجارَ الَّذي كانَ عَدُوّاً لي.

(**Saadaqtu al-jaara alladhii kaana 3aduwwan lii.** *I befriended the neighbor who used to be my enemy.*)

Here are three other useful verbs that occur in Form III:

رافَقَ (**raafaqa;** *to accompany*)

شارَكَ (**shaaraka;** *to share/take part in*)

The following are some examples using these verbs:

هَل تُرافِقُنـي إلى السّـوق؟

(**hal turaafiqunii 'ilaa-s-suuqi?** *Will you accompany me to the store?*)

يُشاركُ العُمّال في الضَّرب.

(**yushaariku al-3ummaal fi-D-Darb.** *The workers are taking part in the strike.*)

Producing Form III

The main distinguishing feature of Form III is the long **a** vowel, written with أَلِف (**'alif**), after the first consonant of your root. It's visible in both the present and past tenses.

The following tables show the conjugation of the Form III verb تابَعَ (**taaba3a;** *to continue*). I show the conjugation in both past and present tense.

Past tense conjugation for تابَعَ (**taaba3a;** *to continue*)	
تابَعْتُ ('**anaa taaba3tu**)	تابَعْنا (**naHnu taaba3naa**)
تابَعْتَ ('**anta taaba3ta**) تابَعْتِ ('**anti taaba3ti**)	تابَعْتُم ('**antum taaba3tum**) تابَعْتُنَّ ('**antunna taaba3tunna**)
تابَعَ (**huwa taaba3a**) تابَعَتْ (**hiya taaba3at**)	تابَعوا (**hum taaba3uu**) تابَعْنَ (**hunna taaba3na**)
تابَعَتْ جَدّتـي قِصَّتَها. (**taaba3at jaddatii qiSSatahaa.** *My grandmother continued her story.*)	

Present tense conjugation for تابَعَ (**taaba3a;** *to continue*)	
أُتابِعُ ('**anaa 'utaabi3u**)	نُتابِعُ (**naHnu nutaabi3u**)
تُتابِعُ ('**anta tutaabi3u**) تُتابِعينَ ('**anti tutaabi3iina**)	تُتابِعونَ ('**antum tutaabi3uuna**) تُتابِعْنَ ('**antunna tutaabi3na**)
يُتابِعُ (**huwa yutaabi3u**) تُتابِعُ (**hiya tutaabi3u**)	يُتابِعونَ (**hum yutaabi3uuna**) يُتابِعْنَ (**hunna yutaabi3na**)
لِماذا نُتابِعُ هذِه الحُجَّةَ؟ (**limaadhaa nutaabi3u haadhihi-l-Hujjata?** *Why do we continue this argument?*)	

For this exercise, I give you a pronoun and a verbal root. Write the past and present tenses of the Form III verb that correspond to the verbal root and the supplied pronoun in each item.

0. هُوَ (huwa) / بكر (b-k-r)

A. باكَرَ (baakara; *he anticipated*) / يُباكِرُ (yubaakiru; *he anticipates*)

9. أَنا ('anaa) / رفق (r-f-q) _____

10. أَنْتَ ('anta) / حسب (H-s-b) _____

11. أَنْتِ ('anti) / عقب (3-q-b) _____

12. هُوَ (huwa) / كتم (k-t-m) _____

13. هِيَ (hiya) / حكم (H-k-m) _____

14. نَحْنُ (naHnu) / بلغ (b-l-gh) _____

15. أَنْتُم ('antum) / درك (d-r-k) _____

16. هُم (hum) / فصل (f-S-l) _____

Form IV

Form IV is unusual because its past and present tenses each have different distinctive traits that you use to spot a verb in that category. The features of a Form IV verb are:

- A prefixed أ ('a) is added in the past tense only.
- A ◌ٌ (Damma) is added over the prefixes in the present tense.
- A ◌ِ (kasra) is added under the second consonant in the present tense.

The meaning of Form IV

Form IV reliably gives a causative meaning to a verbal root. In other words, if your verb root means *to cook,* the Form IV of that verb root would mean *to cause someone to cook (make someone cook).* For example, consider the Form I verb قَرَأ (qara'a), which means *to read.* The Form IV version of this word is أَقْرَأ ('aqra'a), meaning *to make someone read.* Another example is the Form I verb عَمِلَ (3amila; *to work*). The Form IV version of this verb is أَعْمَلَ ('a3mala), meaning *to put to work.*

The following are some example sentences that use these verbs:

هَل قَرَأْتِ قِصَّتَها الجَديدة؟

(**hal qara'ti qiSSatahaa al-jadiida?** *Have you read her new story?*)

لا. لِأَنَّ مُدَرِّسَتَنا ما أَقْرَأْتْنا هَذِهِ القِصّة.

(**laa. li'anna mudarrisatanaa maa 'aqra'atnaa haadhihi-l-qiSSa.** *No. Because our teacher didn't make us read this story.*)

These are some other useful verbs that occur in Form IV:

أَرْسَلَ ('**arsala;** *to send*)

أَعْلَنَ ('**a3lana;** *to announce/advertise*)

Here are some sentences using these Form IV verbs:

أَرْسِلْ لي رِسالةً حينَ تَحْصُل عَلى النَّتائِج.

('**arsil lii risaalatan Hiina taHsul 3alaa-n-nataa'ij.** *Send me a message when you get the results.*)

يُعلِنُ الطَّيَران عَن وُصول طائِرَتِهِ القادِمة مِن باريس.

(**yu3linu aT-Tayaraan 3an wuSuul Taa'iratihi al-qaadima min baariis.** *The airline is announcing the arrival of their plane coming from Paris.*)

Producing Form IV

Make sure to study the past and present tenses of the Form IV verb separately and internalize the different look and feel of them. In the past tense, note the use of the أَلِف ('**alif**) prefix. In the present tense, observe how the Form IV verb differs from Form I in the vowels alone.

The following tables show the conjugation of the Form IV verb أَكْمَلَ ('**akmala**), which means *to finish*. I show the conjugation in both past and present tenses.

Past tense conjugation for أَكْمَلَ ('akmala; to finish)	
أَكْمَلْتُ ('anaa 'akmaltu)	أَكْمَلْنا (naHnu 'akmalnaa)
أَكْمَلْتَ ('anta 'akmalta)	أَكْمَلْتُمْ ('antum 'akmaltum)
أَكْمَلْتِ ('anti 'akmalti)	أَكْمَلْتُنَّ ('antunna 'akmaltunna)
أَكْمَلَ (huwa 'akmala)	أَكْمَلوا (hum 'akmaluu)
أَكْمَلَتْ (hiya 'akmalat)	أَكْمَلْنَ (hunna 'akmalna)
ما أَكْمَلوا الواجِباتِ. (maa 'akmaluu al-waajibaati. They didn't finish the homework.)	

Present tense conjugation for أَكْمَلَ ('akmala; to finish)	
أُكْمِلُ ('anaa 'ukmilu)	نُكْمِلُ (naHnu nukmilu)
تُكْمِلُ ('anta tukmilu)	تُكْمِلُونَ ('antum tukmiluuna)
تُكْمِلِينَ ('anti tukmiliina)	تُكْمِلْنَ ('antunna tukmilna)
يُكْمِلُ (huwa yukmilu)	يُكْمِلُونَ (hum yukmiluuna)
تُكْمِلُ (hiya tukmilu)	يُكْمِلْنَ (hunna yukmilna)
مَتى تُكْمِلِينَ العَمَلَ اليَوْمَ؟	
(mataa tukmiliina al3amal al-yawma? *When do you finish work today?*)	

To help you improve your use of Forms IV, your teacher designed a matching exercise. You have a word bank with seven verbs in Form IV. Match each one with the sentence that fits the meaning best. ***Note:*** The exact form in the word bank isn't what you need to fill in the blank, because the context of the sentence will prompt you for a specific tense and person of the verb. Each verb will make the best sense in only one place.

أَصْبَحَ ('aSbaHa)   أَكْمَلَ ('akmala)   أَعْلَنَ ('a3lana)   أَزْعَجَ ('az3aja)

أَصْدَرَ ('aSdara)   أَدْخَلَ ('adkhala)   أَطْلَقَ ('aTlaqa)

0. بَعْدَ التَّخَرُّج أنا ـــــــــــ مُوَظَّفاً هُناك. (ba3da-t-takharruj 'anaa ـــــــــــ muwaDHDHafan hunaaka. *After graduation, I ـــــــــــ an employee there.*)

A. بَعْدَ التَّخَرُّج أنا أَصْبَحْتُ مُوَظَّفاً هُناك. (ba3da-t-takharruj 'anaa 'aSbaHtu muwaDHDHafan hunaaka. *After graduation, I <u>became</u> an employee there.*)

17. الصَّيّادُ ـــــــــــ النّارَ على الأَسَدِ أَمْس. (ـــــــــــ aS-Sayyaadu an-naara 3alaa-l-'asadi 'amsi. *The hunter ـــــــــــ at the lion yesterday.*)

18. ـــــــــــ كَلْبُ جاري دائماً. (ـــــــــــ kalbu jaarii daa'iman. *My neighbor's dog always ـــــــــــ me.*)

19. جُمْلَةً ـــــــــــ في رسالَةٍ. (ـــــــــــ jumlatan fii risaalatin. *I will ـــــــــــ a sentence into the message.*)

20. أنا ـــــــــــ الرّسالةَ وَأَرْسَلْتُها في نَفْس اليَوْم. ('anaa ـــــــــــ ar-risaalata wa-'arsaltuhaa fii nafsi-l-yawmi. *I ـــــــــــ the letter and sent it the same day.*)

21. ـــــــــــ الخَبَرُ عَن زيارَة السَّفير. (ـــــــــــ al-khabaru 3an ziyaarati as-safiiri. *The news will ـــــــــــ the visit of the ambassador.*)

22. المَطْبَعَة ـــــــــــ كِتابَها عَن عِلْم الأَحْياء حَديثاً. (ـــــــــــ al-maTba3a kitaabahaa 3an 3ilmi al-'aHyaa'i Hadiithan. *The printer recently ـــــــــــ her book about biology.*)

Form V

Form V is a very recognizable form. Form V presents the following distinct features:

- A ـَ (ta-) is prefixed onto the root.
- The second consonant of the root is doubled.
- A ـَ (fatHa) is added over the present tense prefixes.
- A ـَ (fatHa) is added over the second consonant of the root in both the present and past tenses.

The meaning of Form V

Form V serves as the reflexive or passive counterpart to Form II. What I mean is that when you have a verbal root in Form V, the same root will usually have a Form II with a similar meaning. Form V will be the *reflexive* (where the action is done by the subjects on themselves) or *passive* (where the action is done to the subject). For instance, consider the Form I verb عَلَّم (**3allama;** *to teach*). The Form V version of this verb is تَعَلَّم (**ta3allama**), which means *to learn* (or *to be taught*). The following is a sentence using this Form V verb:

أَتَعَلَّمْتَ سِرَّ النَّجاح؟

(**'ata3allamta sirra an-najaaHi?** *Have you learned the secret of success?*)

Here are some other useful verbs that occur in Form V:

تَعَرَّفَ (**ta3arrafa;** *to get to know/meet/become acquainted*)

تَضَمَّنَ (**taDammana;** *to include/contain*)

The following are some example sentences that show you how these Form V verbs are used:

تَعَرَّفْتُ عَلى جاري.

(**ta3arraftu 3alaa jaarii.** *I made the acquaintance of my neighbor.*)

يَتَضَمَّنُ الكِتاب مَعْلومات مُهِمّة.

(**yataDammanu al-kitaab ma3luumaat muhimma.** *The book contains important information.*)

Producing Form V

The Form V verb has the same distinctive doubling as the Form II verb, but it additionally has the distinctive تَ (**ta-**) prefix.

The following tables show the conjugation of the Form V verb تَكَلَّم (takallama; *to speak*). I show the conjugation in both past and present tenses.

Past tense conjugation for تَكَلَّم (takallama; *to speak*)	
تَكَلَّمْتُ ('anaa takallamtu)	تَكَلَّمْنا (naHnu takallamnaa)
تَكَلَّمْتَ ('anta takallamta)	تَكَلَّمْتُم ('antum takallamtum)
تَكَلَّمْتِ ('anti takallamti)	تَكَلَّمْتُنَّ ('antunna takallamtunna)
تَكَلَّمَ (huwa takallama)	تَكَلَّموا (hum takallamuu)
تَكَلَّمَتْ (hiya takallamat)	تَكَلَّمْنَ (hunna takallamna)
تَكَلَّمْتِ مَعَ أُمِّكِ أَمْسِ؟ (takallmti ma3a ummiki 'amsi? *Did you speak with your mother yesterday?*)	

Present tense conjugation for تَكَلَّم (takallama; *to speak*)	
أَتَكَلَّمُ ('anaa 'atakallamu)	نَتَكَلَّمُ (naHnu natakallamu)
تَتَكَلَّمُ ('anta tatakallamu)	تَتَكَلَّمونَ ('antum tatakallamuuna)
تَتَكَلَّمينَ ('anti tatakallamiina)	تَتَكَلَّمْنَ ('antunna tatakallamna)
يَتَكَلَّمُ (huwa yatakallamu)	يَتَكَلَّمونَ (hum yatakallamuuna)
تَتَكَلَّمُ (hiya tatakallamu)	يَتَكَلَّمْنَ (hunna yatakallamna)
سَيَتَكَلَّمونَ مَعاً بَعْدَ الإِجْتِماعِ. (sa-yatakallamuuna ma3an ba3da-l-'ijtimaa3i. *They will speak together after the meeting.*)	

For this exercise, I give you a pronoun and a verbal root. Write the past and present tenses of the Form V verb that correspond to the verbal root and the supplied pronoun in each item.

Q. هُوَ (huwa) / خرج (kh-r-j)

A. تَخَرَّجَ (takharraja; *he graduated*) / يَتَخَرَّجُ (yatakharraju; *he graduates*)

23. أنا ('anaa) / جند (j-n-d) _____

24. أَنْتَ ('anta) / ستر (s-t-r) _____

25. أَنْتِ ('anti) / قبل (q-b-l) _____

26. هُوَ (huwa) / لفت (l-f-t) _____

27. هِيَ (hiya) / مَلك (m-l-k) _____

28. نَحْنُ (naHnu) / نفض (n-f-D) _____

29. أَنْتُم ('antum) / كفل (k-f-l) _____

30. هُم (hum) / طبق (T-b-q) _____

Form VI

Form VI is produced by:

- Adding a prefixed تَ (ta-)
- Inserting a long **a** vowel after the first consonant of the root
- Using a ٰ (fatHa) over the second consonant in both the present and past tenses
- Using a ٰ (fatHa) over the prefixes in the present tense

The meaning of Form VI

Form VI is the reciprocal counterpart to Form III. Here's what I mean: If a verb is in Form VI, it describes people exchanging the action of a verb that exists in Form III. For example, consider the Form III verb حارَبَ (Haaraba), which means *to fight*. The Form VI version of this verb is تَحارَبَ (taHaaraba), which means *to fight one another*.

The following is an example sentence that uses this verb:

تَحارَبَ الجُنود كُلَّ اللَّيْلِة.

(**taHaaraba al-junuud kulla-l-laylati.** *The soldiers fought one another all night.*)

Here are some other useful verbs that occur in Form VI:

تَسالَمَ (**tasaalama;** *to make peace with one another*)

تَساءَلَ (**tasaa'ala;** *to ask oneself/inquire*)

Take a look at these example sentences:

تَسالَمَ الأَعْداء أخيراً.

(**tasaalama al-'a3daa' 'akhiiran.** *The enemies finally reconciled.*)

تَساءَلْتُ هَلْ سَأَذْهَبُ إلى الحَفْلَةِ أَمْ لا.

(**tasaa'altu hal sa-'adh-hab 'ilaa-l-Haflati 'am laa.** *I asked myself whether I would go to the party or not.*)

Producing Form VI

Watch for the long **a** vowel — written with أَلِف (**'alif**) — and the prefixed تَ (**ta-**) as the key points of Form VI.

The following tables show the conjugation of the Form VI verb تَبادَلَ (**tabaadala**), which means *to exchange*. I show the conjugation in both the past and present tenses.

Past tense conjugation for تَبادَلَ (tabaadala; *to exchange*)	
(’anaa tabaadaltu) تَبادَلْتُ	(naHnu tabaadalnaa) تَبادَلْنا
(’anta tabaadalta) تَبادَلْتَ	(’antum tabaadaltum) تَبادَلْتُمْ
(’anti tabaadalti) تَبادَلْتِ	(’antunna tabaadaltunna) تَبادَلْتُنَّ
(huwa tabaadala) تَبادَلَ	(hum tabaadaluu) تَبادَلوا
(hiya tabaadalat) تَبادَلَتْ	(hunna tabaadalna) تَبادَلْنَ
تَبادَلْنا نُسْخَتَيْ العَقْدِ. (tabaadalnaa nuskhatay al-3aqdi. *We exchanged the two copies of the contract.*)	

Present tense conjugation for تَبادَلَ (tabaadala; *to exchange*)	
(’anaa ’atabaadalu) أَتَبادَلُ	(naHnu natabaadalu) نَتَبادَلُ
(’anta tatabaadalu) تَتَبادَلُ	(’antum tatabaadaluuna) تَتَبادَلونَ
(’anti tatabaadaliina) تَتَبادَلينَ	(’antunna tatabaadalna) تَتَبادَلْنَ
(huwa yatabaadalu) يَتَبادَلُ	(hum yatabaadaluuna) يَتَبادَلونَ
(hiya tatabaadalu) تَتَبادَلُ	(hunna yatabaadalna) يَتَبادَلْنَ
مُمْكِن نَتَبادَلُ أَرْقامَ الهاتِف؟ (mumkin natabaadalu ’arqaama al-haatif? *Maybe we can exchange phone numbers?*)	

Form VI isn't terribly common, but you should try your hand at producing just a few of them so you're familiar with their patterns. Write the past and present tenses for the indicated pronouns and verbal roots.

Q. هُم (**hum**) / زحم (**z-H-m**)

A. تَزاحَموا (**tazaaHamuu**; *they crowded together*) / يَتَزاحَمونَ (**yatazaaHamuuna**; *they crowd together*)

31. أَنا (**'anaa**) / نول (**n-w-l**)

32. أَنْتَ ('anta) / شـرك (sh-r-k)

_____

33. هُم (hum) / لحـق (l-H-q)

_____

Form VII

To create Form VII, you have to:

- Prefix a ن (**nuun**) to the verb
- Prefix an أَلِف (**'alif**) + ِ (**kasra**) before the ن (**nuun**) in the past tense
- Add a َ (**fatHa**) over the prefixes in the present tense
- Add a ِ (**kasra**) under the second consonant of the root in the present tense

The meaning of Form VII

Form VII is relatively rare and can impart a passive meaning. In other words, when it exists, it means the action is done to the subject of the verb. For example, consider the Form I verb كَسَرَ (**kasara**), meaning _to break_ (_something_). The Form VII version of this verb is إنْكَسَرَ (**inkasara**), which means _to be broken_.

The following sentence shows how you can use this verb:

إنْكَسَرَ الباب عِنْدَما فَتَحْتُهُ.

(**inkasara al-baab 3indamaa fataHtuhu.** _The door became broken when I opened it._)

Here are some other common and important verbs that occur in Form VII:

إنْدَلَعَ (**indala3a**; _to break out_ [_war, fire_])

إنْبَغى (**inbaghaa**; _to be incumbent upon_)

Consider the following sentences, which show you how to use these common Form VII verbs:

كُنْتُ هُناك عِنْدَما إنْدَلَعَتْ الحَرْب.

(**kuntu hunaak 3indamaa indala3at al-Harb.** _I was there when the war broke out._)

يَنْبَغِي لِي أَنْ أَتَعَلَّمَ العَرَبِيّة.

(yanbaghii lii 'an 'ata3allama al-3arabiyya. *I must learn Arabic.*)

Producing Form VII

The feature of a Form VII verb is the prefixing of the ن (**nuun**). In the past, there's the additional أَلِف ('**alif**) before the ن (**nuun**). In the present, you find the ن (**nuun**) between the normal present tense prefix and the first consonant of your root.

The following tables show the conjugation of the Form VII verb اِنْكَسَر (**inkasara**), which means *to get broken*. I show the conjugation in both past and present tenses.

Past tense conjugation for اِنْكَسَر (inkasara; *to get broken*)	
اِنْكَسَرْتُ ('anaa inkasartu)	اِنْكَسَرْنا (naHnu inkasarnaa)
اِنْكَسَرْتَ ('anta inkasarta)	اِنْكَسَرْتُمْ ('antum inkasartum)
اِنْكَسَرْتِ ('anti inkasarti)	اِنْكَسَرْتُنَّ ('antunna inkasartunna)
اِنْكَسَرَ (huwa inkasara)	اِنْكَسَروا (hum inkasaruu)
اِنْكَسَرَتْ (hiya inkasarat)	اِنْكَسَرْنَ (hunna inkasarna)
وَقَعَتْ الصّورة وَانْكَسَرَتْ. (waqa3at aS-Suura wa-n-kasarat. *The picture fell and broke.*)	

Present tense conjugation for اِنْكَسَر (inkasara; *to get broken*)	
أَنْكَسِرُ ('anaa 'ankasiru)	نَنْكَسِرُ (naHnu nankasiru)
تَنْكَسِرُ ('anta tankasiru)	تَنْكَسِرونَ ('antum tankasiruuna)
تَنْكَسِرينَ ('anti tankasiriina)	تَنْكَسِرْنَ ('antunna tankasirna)
يَنْكَسِرُ (huwa yankasiru)	يَنْكَسِرونَ (hum yankasiruuna)
تَنْكَسِرُ (hiya tankasiru)	يَنْكَسِرْنَ (hunna yankasirna)
مُمْكِن تَنْكَسِرُ ذِراعُهُ. (mumkin tankasiru dhiraa3uhu. *His arm may be broken.*)	

Form VII verbs are rare, but knowing how to form them will be a boon when you really need one. For this exercise, I give you a pronoun and a verbal root. Write the past and present tenses of the Form VII verb that correspond to the verbal root and pronoun in each item.

Q. هُوَ (huwa) / دلع (d-l-3)

A. اِنْدَلَعَ (indala3a; *he was spoiled*) / يَنْدَلِعُ (yandali3u; *he is spoiled*)

34. هُوَ (huwa) / فجر (f-j-r) _____

35. هُوَ (huwa) / عطف (3-T-f) _____

36. هِيَ (hiya) / جبر (j-b-r) _____

Form VIII

Form VIII has the following distinct features:

- A ت (ta-) is inserted after the first consonant of the root.
- You have to prefix an أَلِف ('alif) + ِ (kasra) to the verb in the past tense.
- You use a َ (fatHa) over the prefixes in the present tense.
- You use a ِ (kasra) under the second consonant of the root in the present tense.

The meaning of Form VIII

Form VIII can be reflexive or passive. For example, consider the Form I verb رَفَعَ (rafa3a; *to lift*). The Form VIII version of this verb is اِرْتَفَعَ (irtafa3a), which means *to rise*.

The following is a sentence showing the use of this verb:

اِرْتَفَعَ البالونُ فَوْقَ البنايةِ الطَّويلةِ.

(irtafa3a al-baaluunu fawqa-l-binaayati aT-Tawiilati. *The balloon rose over the tall building.*)

Here are some other useful verbs that occur in Form VIII:

اِجْتَمَعَ (ijtama3a; *to meet [together]*)

اِنْتَقَلَ (intaqala; *to move*)

Check out these example sentences:

سَتَجْتَمِعُ اللَّجْنة مَرَّتَيْن في الشَّهُر القادِم.

(satajtami3u al-lajna marratayn fish-shahr alqaadim. *The committee will meet twice in the coming month.*)

اِنْتَقَلَتْ عائِلَتي إلى بَيْتٍ جَديدٍ.

(intaqalat 3aa'ilatii 'ilaa baytin jadiidin. *My family moved into a new house.*)

Producing Form VIII

Form VIII is the only Arabic verb form with what's called an *infix.* This means that the extra element, the consonant *t,* is inserted between the first and second consonants of the root. Be careful not to mistake a Form VIII verb for a verb with a ت (taa') as part of its root. Also be on the lookout for how similar a Form VIII verb with س (siin) as its first letter will look to a Form X verb. (You can read more about Form X later in this chapter.)

The following tables show the conjugation of perhaps the most common Form VIII verb, اِسْتَمَعَ (istama3a), which means *to listen.* I show the conjugation in both past and present tenses.

Past tense conjugation for اِسْتَمَعَ (istama3a; *to listen*)	
اِسْتَمَعْتُ ('anaa istama3tu)	اِسْتَمَعْنا (naHnu istama3naa)
اِسْتَمَعْتَ ('anta istama3ta)	اِسْتَمَعْتُمْ ('antum istama3tum)
اِسْتَمَعْتِ ('anti istama3ti)	اِسْتَمَعْتُنَّ ('antunna istama3tunna)
اِسْتَمَعَ (huwa istama3a)	اِسْتَمَعوا (hum istama3uu)
اِسْتَمَعَتْ (hiya istama3at)	اِسْتَمَعْنَ (hunna istama3na)
هَلْ اِسْتَمَعْتُمْ إلى الخَبَرِ عَنِ الزَّلْزَلِةِ؟ (hal istama3tum 'ilaa-l-khabar 3an al-zalzalati? *Did you listen to the news about the earthquake?*)	

Present tense conjugation for اِسْتَمَعَ (istama3a; *to listen*)	
أَسْتَمِعُ ('anaa 'astami3u)	نَسْتَمِعُ (naHnu nastami3u)
تَسْتَمِعُ ('anta tastami3u)	تَسْتَمِعونَ ('antum tastami3uuna)
تَسْتَمِعينَ ('anti tastami3iina)	تَسْتَمِعْنَ ('antunna tastami3na)
يَسْتَمِعُ (huwa yastami3u)	يَسْتَمِعونَ (hum yastami3uuna)
تَسْتَمِعُ (hiya tastami3u)	يَسْتَمِعْنَ (hunna yastami3na)
أَنا أَسْتَمِعُ إلى الصَّوْتِ خارِجاً مِنَ البَيْتِ. ('anaa 'astami3u 'ilaa-S-Sawti khaarijan min al-bayti. *I listen to the sound coming from the house.*)	

Now you have a chance to practice your formation of Form VIII verbs and your overall Arabic composition skills. Translate the following English sentences into Arabic. Each item requires you to generate a Form VIII verb.

_Q._ After the negotiations we finished the meeting.

_A._ بَعْدَ المُفاوَضاتِ تَخَتَّمْنا الإِجْتِماعَ. (**ba3da-l-mufaawaDaati takhattamnaa al-'ijtimaa3a.**)

37. I believe that the musical group is wonderful.

_____

38. My professor tested my knowledge.

_____

39. The United States elected a new president last year.

_____

40. Did you consider the problem before you responded?

_____

41. We celebrated her birthday at the restaurant.

_____

Form IX

Form IX exists in Arabic, but it occurs rarely. It's a way to describe the action of acquiring either a color or a bodily defect. Just so that you can recognize it if you ever come across it, the one distinct feature of a Form IX verb is a doubling of the third consonant in the verbal root, which is written by placing a ّ (**shadda**) over the third consonant. For example, consider the Form II verb حَمَّر (**Hammara;** _to redden_). The Form IX version of this verb is إِحْمَرَّ (**iHmarra**), which means _to turn red._

For your reference, here are sample forms of the past and present tenses of a Form IX verb:

Past Tense: إِحْمَرَّ (**huwa iHmarra;** _he turned red_)

Present Tense: تَحْمَرُّ (**hiya taHmarru;** _she turns red_)

Now check out this example of a Form IX verb in a sentence:

كانَ الجَوّ حارّاً جِدّاً فَهِيَ إِحْمَرَّتْ مِنَ الشَّمْسِ.

(**kaana-l-jawu Haarran jiddan fa-hiya iHmarrat mina-sh-shamsi.** _The weather was very hot, and so she turned red from the sun._)

Form X

Form X involves the following distinct features:

- Prefixing سْتَ (**sta-**) to the verb
- Prefixing an أَلِف ('**alif**) + ِ (**kasra**) before the سْتَ (**sta-**) prefix in the past tense
- Using َ (**fatHa**) over the present tense prefixes
- Using ِ (**kasra**) under the second consonant of the root in the present tense

The meaning of Form X

Form X implies the act of seeking for the action described by the verbal root. For example, consider the Form II verb فَسَّلَ (**fassala;** *to explain*). The Form X version of this verb is إِسْتَفْسَلَ (**istafsala**), which means *to seek an explanation.*

Here's an example sentence using this form of the verb:

لَمْ يَفْهَمْ كَيْفَ حَدَثَتْ الحادِثة فَهُوَ اِسْتَفْسَرَ عَنْ الأَسْباب.

(**lam yafham kayfa Hadathat al-Haaditha, fa-huwa istafsara 3an al-'asbaabi.** *He didn't understand how the accident occurred, so he sought an explanation as to the causes.*)

These are some other common and important verbs that occur in Form X:

إِسْتَشْهَد (**istash-hada;** *to be martyred/die in battle*)
إِسْتَغْرَق (**istaghraqa;** *to take/last*)

Check out the following sentences, which are examples of uses of these verbs:

اِسْتَشْهَدَ أَلْف جُنْدي في المَعْرَكة.

(**istash-hada alf jundi fii-l-ma3raka.** *A thousand soldiers died in the battle.*)

اِسْتَغْرَقَتْ الرِّحْلة يَوْمَيْن.

(**istaghraqat ar-riHla yawmayni.** *The trip took two days.*)

Producing Form X

Form X is one of the easiest forms to identify, because it includes a two-consonant prefix سْتَ (**sta-**) before the three consonants of the verbal root. In the past tense, you add the سْتَ (**sta-**) prefix, and then you add an additional short *i* vowel before that prefix, which is written with an أَلِف ('**alif**) and ِ (**kasra**). In the present tense, you add the سْتَ (**sta-**) prefix and then add the same present tense prefixes used for all the forms directly before the سْتَ (**sta-**) prefix.

The following tables show the conjugation of the Form X verb اِسْتَعْمَلَ (ista3mala; *to use*). The overall root meaning of عمل (**3-m-l**) is *to work*, so in Form X it means *to seek to work*, or *to use*. I show the conjugation in both the past and present tenses.

Past tense conjugation for اِسْتَعْمَلَ (ista3mala; *to use*)	
اِسْتَعْمَلْتُ ('anaa ista3maltu)	اِسْتَعْمَلْنا (naHnu ista3malnaa)
اِسْتَعْمَلْتَ ('anta ista3malta)	اِسْتَعْمَلْتُمْ ('antum ista3maltum)
اِسْتَعْمَلْتِ ('anti ista3malti)	اِسْتَعْمَلْتُنَّ ('antunna ista3maltunna)
اِسْتَعْمَلَ (huwa ista3mala)	اِسْتَعْمَلوا (hum ista3maluu)
اِسْتَعْمَلَتْ (hiya ista3malat)	اِسْتَعْمَلْنَ (hunna ista3malna)
هُوَ اِسْتَعْمَلَ هاتِفي ثُمّ تَرَكَ فَوْراً. (huwa ista3mala haatifii thumma taraka fawran. *He used my phone and then left immediately.*)	

Present tense conjugation for اِسْتَعْمَلَ (ista3mala; *to use*)	
أَسْتَعْمِلُ ('anaa 'asta3milu)	نَسْتَعْمِلُ (naHnu nasta3milu)
تَسْتَعْمِلُ ('anta tasta3milu)	تَسْتَعْمِلونَ ('antum tasta3miluuna)
تَسْتَعْمِلينَ ('anti tasta3miliina)	تَسْتَعْمِلْنَ ('antunna tasta3milna)
يَسْتَعْمِلُ (huwa yasta3milu)	يَسْتَعْمِلونَ (hum yasta3miluuna)
تَسْتَعْمِلُ (hiya tasta3milu)	يَسْتَعْمِلْنَ (hunna yasta3milna)
مُمْكِن أَسْتَعْمِلُ حاسِبَتَكِ حَتّى أَعُدَّ الحِسابَ؟ (mumkin 'asta3milu Haasibataki Hatta 'a3udda al-Hisaaba? *Could I use your calculator to add up the bill?*)	

For this exercise, I give you a pronoun and a verbal root. Write the past and present tenses of the Form X verb that correspond to the verbal root and pronoun in each item.

Q. هُوَ (huwa) / قبل (q-b-l)

A. اِسْتَقْبَلَ (istaqbala; *he greeted*) / يَسْتَقْبِلُ (yastaqbilu; *he greets*)

42. أَنا ('anaa) / فهم (f-h-m) _____

43. أَنْتَ ('anta) / خدم (kh-d-m) _____

44. أَنْتِ ('anti) / سلم (s-l-m) _____

45. هُوَ (huwa) / نبط (n-b-T) _____

46. هِيَ (hiya) / عجب (3-j-b) _____

47. نَحْنُ (naHnu) / درك (d-r-k) _____

Answer Key

1 سَهَّلْتُ (**sahhaltu;** *I facilitated*) / أُسَهِّلُ (**'usahhilu;** *I facilitate*)

2 غَرَّبْتَ (**gharrabta;** *you went away*) / تُغَرِّبُ (**tugharribu;** *you go away*)

3 شَجَّعْتِ (**shajja3ti;** *you encouraged*) / تُشَجِّعِينَ (**tushajji3iina;** *you encourage*)

4 خَبَّرَ (**khabbara;** *he notified*) / يُخَبِّرُ (**yukhabbiru;** *he notifies*)

5 جَدَّدَت (**jaddadat;** *she renewed*) / تُجَدِّدُ (**tujaddidu;** *she renews*)

6 مَدَّنّا (**madannaa;** *we civilized*) / نُمَدِّنُ (**numaddinu;** *we civilize*)

7 نَشَّفْتُمْ (**nashshaftum;** *you dried*) / تُنَشِّفُونَ (**tunashshifuuna;** *you dry*)

8 طَبَّقوا (**Tabbaquu;** *they covered*) / يُطَبِّقونَ (**yuTabbiquuna;** *they cover*)

9 رافَقْتُ (**raafaqtu;** *I accompanied*) / أُرافِقُ (**'uraafiqu;** *I accompany*)

10 حاسَبْتَ (**Haasabta;** *you settled an account*) / تُحاسِبُ (**tuHaasibu;** *you settle an account*)

11 عاقَبْتِ (**3aaqabti;** *you punished*) / تُعاقِبِينَ (**tu3aaqibiina;** *you punish*)

12 كاتَمَ (**kaatama;** *he hid*) / يُكاتِمُ (**yukaatimu;** *he hides*)

13 حاكَمَتْ (**Haakamat;** *she prosecuted*) / تُحاكِمُ (**tuHaakimu;** *she prosecutes*)

14 بالَغْنا (**baalaghnaa;** *we exaggerated*) / نُبالِغُ (**nubaalighu;** *we exaggerate*)

15 دارَكْتُمْ (**daaraktum;** *you outran*) / تُداركونَ (**tudaarikuuna;** *you outrun*)

16 فاصَلوا (**faaSaluu;** *they bargained*) / يُفاصِلونَ (**yufaaSiluuna;** *they bargain*)

17 أَطْلَقَ الصَّيّادُ النّارَ على الأسَدِ أمْس. (**'aTlaqa aS-Sayyaadu an-naara 3alaa-l-'asadi 'amsi.** *The hunter <u>shot</u> at the lion yesterday.*)

18 يُزْعِجُني كَلْبُ جاري دائماً. (**yuz3ijunii** kalbu jaarii daa'iman. *My neighbor's dog always <u>bothers</u> me.*)

19 سَأُدْخِلُ جُمْلَةً فِي رِسَالَةٍ. (**sa-'udkhilu** jumlatan fii risaalatin. *I will <u>insert</u> a sentence into the message.*)

20 أَنا أَكْمَلْتُ الرِّسَالَةَ وَأَرْسَلْتُها فِي نَفْس اليَوْم. ('anaa **'akmaltu** ar-risaalata wa-'arsaltuhaa fii nafsi-l-yawmi. *I <u>finished</u> the letter and sent it the same day.*)

21 سَيُعْلِنُ الخَبَرُ عَنْ زِيَارَةِ السَّفِير. (**sa-yu3linu** al-khabaru 3an ziyaarati as-safiiri. *The news will <u>announce</u> the visit of the ambassador.*)

22 أَصْدَرَتْ المَطْبَعَة كِتابَها فِي عِلْم الأَحْياء حَدِيثاً. ('**aSdarat** al-maTba3a kitaabahaa fii 3ilmi al-'aHyaa'i Hadiithan. *The printer recently <u>published</u> her book about biology.*)

23 تَجَنَّدْتُ (**tajannadtu**; *I was drafted*) / أَتَجَنَّدُ ('**atajannadu**; *I am drafted*)

24 تَسَتَّرْتَ (**tasattarta**; *you were concealed*) / تَتَسَتَّرُ (**tatasattaru**; *you are concealed*)

25 تَقَبَّلْتِ (**taqabbalti**; *you received*) / تَتَقَبَّلِينَ (**tataqabbaliina**; *you receive*)

26 تَلَفَّتَ (**talaffata**; *he turned around*) / يَتَلَفَّتُ (**yatalaffatu**; *he turns around*)

27 تَمَلَّكَتْ (**tamallakat**; *she owned*) / تَتَمَلَّكُ (**tatamallaku**; *she owns*)

28 تَنَفَّضْنا (**tanaffaDnaa**; *we trembled*) / نَتَنَفَّضُ (**natanaffaDu**; *we tremble*)

29 تَكَفَّلْتُمْ (**takaffaltum**; *you vouched for*) / تَتَكَفَّلونَ (**tatakaffaluuna**; *you vouch for*)

30 تَطَبَّقوا (**taTabbaquu**; *they were closed*) / يَتَطَبَّقونَ (**yataTabbaquuna**; *they are closed*)

31 تَناوَلْتُ (**tanaawaltu**; *I obtained*) / أَتَناوَلُ ('**atanaawalu**; *I obtain*)

32 تَشارَكْتَ (**tashaarakta**; *you participated together*) / تَتَشارَكُ (**tatashaaraku**; *you participate together*)

33 تَلاحَقوا (**talaaHaquu**; *they pursued each other*) / يَتَلاحَقونَ (**yatalaaHaquuna**; *they pursue each other*)

34 اِنْفَجَرَ (**infajara**; *it exploded*) / يَنْفَجِرُ (**yanfajiru**; *it explodes*)

35 اِنْعَطَفَ (**in3aTafa**; *it was bent*) / يَنْعَطِفُ (**yan3aTifu**; *it is bent*)

36 اِنْجَبَرَتْ (injabarat; *she was mended*) / تَنْجَبِرُ (tanjabiru; *she is mended*)

37 أَعْتَقِدُ إِنَّ الفِرْقَةَ الموسيقيّة مُمْتازَةٌ. ('a3taqidu 'inna-l-firqata al-musiqiyyata mumtaazatun.)

38 اِمْتَحَنَ أُسْتاذي مَعْلوماتي. (imtaHana 'ustaadhii ma3luumatii.)

39 اِنْتَخَبَتْ الولايات المُتَّحِدة رَئيساً جَديداً في السَّنةِ الماضيةِ. (intakhabat al-wilaayaat al-muttaHida ra'iisan jadiidan fii-s-sanati al-maaDiyati.)

40 هَلْ اِعْتَبَرْتَ المُشْكِلة قَبْل أَنْ أَجَبْتَ؟ (hal i3tabarta al-mushkila qabla 'an 'ajabta?)

41 اِحْتَفَلْنا بعيد ميلادِها في المَطْعَم. (iHtafalnaa bi-3iid miilaadihaa fii-l-maT3ami.)

42 أَسْتَفْهِمُ (astafhimu; *I seek understanding*) / اِسْتَفْهَمْتُ (istafhamtu; *I sought understanding*)

43 اِسْتَخْدَمْتَ (istakhdamta; *you utilized*) / تَسْتَخْدِمُ (tastakhdimu; *you utilize*)

44 اِسْتَسْلَمْتِ (istaslamti; *you surrendered*) / تَسْتَسْلِمينَ (tastaslimiina; *you surrender*)

45 اِسْتَنْبَطَ (istanbaTa; *he discovered*) / يَسْتَنْبِطُ (yastanbiTu; *he discovers*)

46 اِسْتَعْجَبَتْ (ista3jabat; *she was amazed*) / تَسْتَعْجِبُ (tasta3jibu; *she is amazed*)

47 اِسْتَدْرَكْنا (istadraknaa; *we rectified*) / نَسْتَدْرِكُ (nastadriku; *we rectify*)

Chapter 10

Exploring Irregularity in Arabic Verbs

· ·

· ·

*I*f you grew up speaking English, you never had to think about how maddeningly irregular the language can be. People who learn English as a second language don't have it so easy. They learn that if you want to put a verb in the past tense, you can just add *-ed,* such as in *walked.* But if the verb already ends in *e,* you just add a *d,* as in *baked.* If only that were the end of it! Instead you come across words like *see,* which in the past tense is *saw.* The last straw comes when you realize that with *go,* the past tense (*went*) is from a completely different verb. Every language has its irregularities, but English is among the worst offenders.

So you won't be surprised to find out that Arabic also has irregular forms. Unlike English, however, the so-called irregularity in Arabic just amounts to a different set of rules when a few of the consonants appear in a verb. This chapter shows you how to confidently form any Arabic verb, regardless of these pesky irregularities.

Grasping Verb Weakness in Arabic

The verbs you encounter in this chapter are irregular in the sense that they don't play by the same rules as the so-called "regular" verbs (see Chapters 2 and 9 for more on these run-of-the-mill verbs). Many Arabic grammar books prefer to call these irregular verbs *weak.* There's a good reason for using that adjective to refer to these verbs. You probably recall from your basic Arabic studies that Arabic verbs have three consonants onto which you add the various suffixes and prefixes to indicate who's performing the action of the verb.

Just a few consonants, however, are soft enough in their pronunciation that they can't quite carry the vowels the same way as the others. For example, a *w* is a whole lot weaker in pronunciation than, say, a *d.* With a *w,* you're bending air in your mouth, but you aren't touching your tongue against something as you do with letters such as *d*. The three Arabic consonants that yield irregularities from the expected forms are the أَلِف ('alif), the واو (waaw), and the ياء (yaa').

In this chapter, I show you the forms of weak verbs in their past and present tenses. Other chapters in this book cover forms of the verb, such as imperative forms (Chapter 11), verbal nouns (Chapter 15), and participles (Chapter 18). The weak verb forms of each of those are discussed in their respective chapters.

Discovering Initial Weak Verbs

Weak consonants can affect a verb no matter where they appear in a sentence. So in this section, I show you the various problems that weak consonants cause when they come in the first, or *initial,* position.

Verbs with initial ء (hamza)

Verbs with an initial glottal stop, which is written with a ء (**hamza**), have the least amount of change overall from the regular pattern. A *glottal stop* is that little catch you have in the back of your throat before you start a word with a vowel. Even though we don't think of the *glottal stop* as a consonant in English, in Arabic it's treated as such. It may seem surprising to you that something we don't even see as a consonant is still able to carry almost all the normal vowels of the Arabic verb.

The irregularity of the initial **hamza** verb stems from the inability of Arabic to have two أَلِف ('alifs) in a row. Forms such as the first person singular present in Form I and all the past tense of Form IV replace the two **'alifs** with a آ (**madda**). (For more information on the **madda**, see Chapter 3.) The only other thing to be on the look out for with initial **hamza** verbs is the change in spelling when the **hamza** appears over the واو (**waw**) seat in the present tense of Forms II, III, and IV.

The hamza with Form 1 verbs

The following tables showing the past and present conjugations of the common Form I verb أَكَلَ (**akala**; *to eat*) demonstrate how an initial **hamza** verb behaves.

Past conjugation for أَكَلَ (akala; *to eat*)	
أَكَلْتُ ('anaa 'akaltu)	أَكَلْنا (naHnu 'akalnaa)
أَكَلْتَ ('anta 'akalta)	أَكَلْتُمْ ('antum 'akaltum)
أَكَلْتِ ('anti 'akalti)	أَكَلْتُنَّ ('antunna 'akaltunna)
أَكَلَ (huwa 'akala)	أَكَلوا (hum 'akaluu)
أَكَلَتْ (hiya 'akalat)	أَكَلْنَ (hunna 'akalna)
أَكَلَ الوَلَد الطَّعام سَريعاً جِدّاً. (akala al-walad aT-Ta3aam sarii3an jiddan. *The boy ate the food very fast.*)	

Present conjugation for أَكَلَ (akala; *to eat*)	
آكُلُ ('anaa 'aakulu)	نَأْكُلُ (naHnu na'kulu)
تَأْكُلُ ('anta ta'kulu)	تَأْكُلُونَ ('antum ta'kuluuna)
تَأْكُلِينَ ('anti ta'kuliina)	تَأْكُلْنَ ('antunna ta'kulna)
يَأْكُلُ (huwa ya'kulu)	يَأْكُلُونَ (hum ya'kuluuna)
تَأْكُلُ (hiya ta'kulu)	يَأْكُلْنَ (hunna ta'kulna)
آكُلُ الخُبْزَ كُلّ يَوْم. ('aakulu al-khubz kull yawm. *I eat bread every day.*)	

As you can see from the previous tables, there's only one form in the present tense where a verb with an initial **hamza** isn't what you would have expected. That form is the first person singular. Here's why: Arabic doesn't permit two **'alifs** to stand next to one another. Because of that fact, the first person singular form replaces the double **'alif** with a **madda**.

The hamza with Form II verbs

Form II is a case where the initial **hamza** will only cause spelling irregularity. An initial **hamza** in a Form II verb is normal in the past tense, but it uses the **waaw** seat in the present. The following tables show the past and present conjugations of the Form II verb أَخَّرَ (**'akhkhara;** *to delay*).

Past conjugation for أَخَّرَ ('akhkhara; *to delay*)	
أَخَّرْتُ ('anaa 'akhkhartu)	أَخَّرْنا (naHnu 'akhkharnaa)
أَخَّرْتَ ('anta 'akhkharta)	أَخَّرْتُم ('antum 'akhkhartum)
أَخَّرْتِ ('anti 'akhkharti)	أَخَّرْتُنَّ ('antunna 'akhkhartunna)
أَخَّرَ (huwa 'akhkhara)	أَخَّروا (hum 'akhkharuu)
أَخَّرَتْ (hiya 'akhkharat)	أَخَّرْنَ (hunna 'akhkharna)
أَخَّرَتْ زِيارَتَهَ عِنْدَما سَمِعَتْ الخَبَر. ('akhkharat ziyaaratahaa 3indamaa sami3at al-khabar. *She delayed her visit when she heard the news.*)	

Present conjugation for أَخَّرَ ('akhkhara; *to delay*)	
أُؤَخِّرُ ('anaa 'u'akhkhiru)	نُؤَخِّرُ (naHnu nu'akhkhiru)
تُؤَخِّرُ ('anta tu'akhkhiru)	تُؤَخِّرونَ ('antum tu'akhkhiruuna)
تُؤَخِّرينَ ('anti tu'akhkhiriina)	تُؤَخِّرْنَ ('antunna tu'akhkhirna)
يُؤَخِّرُ (huwa yu'akhkhiru)	يُؤَخِّرونَ (hum yu'akhkhiruuna)
تُؤَخِّرُ (hiya tu'akhkhiru)	يُؤَخِّرْنَ (hunna yu'akhkhirna)
تُؤَخِّرُ المَشاكِلُ وُصولَنا لِلْأَسَف. (tu'akhkhiru al-mashaakil wuSuulanaa lil'asaf. *Unfortunately the problems are delaying our arrival.*)	

Take note of the present tense in the previous table, and get used to seeing the **hamza** over a **waaw** seat outside of Form I. Anytime there's a ´ (**Damma**), the **hamza** will be written over a **waaw** as you see in the table.

The hamza with Form III and IV verbs

In Forms III and IV, the spelling irregularities of the **hamza** will be shown in two ways. First, the inability to have two consecutive 'alifs forces the use of a **madda** in the past tense of a Form III or IV verb. Secondly, the **hamza** is written over a **waaw** seat in the present of a Form III or Form IV verb. The following tables show the past and present conjugations for the Form IV verb آكَلَ ('aakala; *to feed*).

Past conjugation for آكَلَ ('aakala; *to feed*)	
آكَلْتُ ('anaa 'aakaltu)	آكَلْنا (naHnu 'aakalnaa)
آكَلْتَ ('anta 'aakalta)	آكَلْتُمْ ('antum 'aakaltum)
آكَلْتِ ('anti 'aakalti)	آكَلْتُنَّ ('antunna 'aakaltunna)
آكَلَ (huwa 'aakala)	آكَلوا (hum 'aakaluu)
آكَلَتْ (hiya 'aakalat)	آكَلْنَ (hunna 'aakalna)
آكَلَتْني أُمّي جَيِّداً جِدّاً. ('aakalatnii 'ummii jayyidan jiddan. *My mother fed me very well.*)	

Present conjugation for آكَلَ ('aakala; *to feed*)	
أُوْكِلُ ('anaa 'u'kilu)	نُوْكِلُ (naHnu nu'kilu)
تُوْكِلُ ('anta tu'kilu)	تُوْكِلونَ ('antum tu'kiluuna)
تُوْكِلينَ ('anti tu'kiliina)	تُوْكِلْنَ ('antunna tu'kilna)
يُوْكِلُ (huwa yu'kilu)	يُوْكِلونَ (hum yu'kiluuna)
تُوْكِلُ (hiya tu'kilu)	يُوْكِلْنَ (hunna yu'kilna)
تُوْكِلُنا فَلافِل عادَةً عِنْدَما نَزورُها. (tu'kilunaa falaafil 3aadatan 3indamaa nazuuruhaa. *She usually feeds us falafel when we visit her.*)	

Looking at the table showing the past tense, just remember that whenever you have a **madda**, it's because Arabic doesn't like two 'alifs in a row. So an initial **madda** is an excellent hint that the first consonant of the verb is an **'alif.**

The simple act of writing out the irregular verbs immediately after you study each type helps lock them in your memory. So in this exercise, write the past and present tenses for each root, pronoun, and form of the verb as indicated.

Q. أمر ('-m-r) / هُوَ (**huwa**) / Form III

A. يُوَامِرُ (yu'aamiru; *he consults*); آمَرَ ('aamara; *he consulted*)

1. أَمِل ('-m-l) / أَنا ('anaa) / Form I

2. أَلِم ('-l-m) / نَحْنُ (naHnu) / Form IV

3. أَخَذ ('-kh-dh) / أَنا ('anaa) / Form I

4. أَجِر ('-j-r) / هُم (hum) / Form IV

5. أَزِر ('-z-r) / أَنْتَ ('anta) / Form III

Verbs with initial واو *(waaw)*

The واو (**waaw**) is a *weak wittle wetter.* You're going to see it behave in three ways. It will disappear entirely in some cases, assimilate into a doubled *t* in others, and just turn into a long *u* vowel elsewhere. An initial **waaw** causes significantly more changes to a verb than the initial **hamza,** which is described earlier in the chapter.

Some grammarians call initial **waaw** verbs *assimilating verbs,* because, as I said, assimilation is one of the things that an initial **waaw** verb will do. Other linguists, myself included, prefer to label all the irregular verbs with their most accurate description. If the issue is an initial **waaw,** that's what I call the verb.

The waaw with Form 1 verbs

In Form I, the **waaw** disappears in the present tense, but is stable in the past tense. In the following tables, I show you an example of how the **waaw** behaves with the Form I verb وَصَل (**waSala;** *to arrive*). The conjugations are shown in the following tables.

Past conjugation for وَصَل (waSala; *to arrive*)	
وَصَلْتُ ('anaa waSalatu)	وَصَلْنا (naHnu waSalnaa)
وَصَلْتَ ('anta waSalta)	وَصَلْتُم ('antum waSaltum)
وَصَلْتِ ('anti waSalti)	وَصَلْتُنَّ ('antunna waSaltunna)
وَصَل (huwa waSala)	وَصَلوا (hum waSaluu)
وَصَلَت (hiya waSalat)	وَصَلْنَ (hunna waSalna)
وَصَلَ الطَّرْد بَعْدَ يَوْمَيْن فَقَطْ.	
(waSala aT-Tard ba3da yawmayni faqaT. *The package arrived after only two days.*)	

Present conjugation for وَصَلَ (waSala; to arrive)	
أَصِلُ ('anaa 'aSilu)	نَصِلُ (naHnu naSilu)
تَصِلُ ('anta taSilu)	تَصِلونَ ('antum taSiluuna)
تَصِلينَ ('anti taSiliina)	تَصِلنَ ('antunna taSilna)
يَصِلُ (huwa yaSilu)	يَصِلونَ (hum yaSiluuna)
تَصِلُ (hiya taSilu)	يَصِلنَ (hunna yaSilna)
مَتى تَصِلُ الطّائِرة؟ (mattaa taSilu aT-Taa'ira? When does the plane arrive?)	

Note the present tense in the previous table. Whenever you have a verb that seems to be missing a consonant to make up a nice triliteral root, consider the possibility that it's an initial **waaw** like you see here.

The waaw with Form IV verbs

Verbs with initial **waaw** are completely regular in Forms II and III, so we can skip over those. الحَمْدُ لله. (al-Hamdu lillah. *Praise God.*) But in Form IV, an initial **waaw** causes some problems in the present tense. What you'll see is that the **waaw** becomes a long *u* vowel following the prefix. Take a look at the following conjugation tables for the Form IV verb أوْضَحَ ('awDaHa; *to make clear/explain*).

Past conjugation for أوْضَحَ ('awDaHa; to make clear/explain)	
أوْضَحْتُ ('anaa 'awDaHtu)	أوْضَحْنا (naHnu 'awDaHnaa)
أوْضَحْتَ ('anta 'awDaHta)	أوْضَحْتُمْ ('antum 'awDaHtum)
أوْضَحْتِ ('anti 'awDaHti)	أوْضَحْتُنَّ ('antunna 'awDaHtunna)
أوْضَحَ (huwa 'awDaHa)	أوْضَحوا (hum 'awDaHuu)
أوْضَحَتْ (hiya 'awDaHat)	أوْضَحْنَ (hunna 'awDaHna)
أوْضَحَ نائِب الرَّئيس غِياب السَّفيرِ عَنِ الإجْتِماعِ. ('awDaHa naa'ib ar-ra'iis ghiyaaba as-safiiri 3ani-l-'ijtimaa3i. *The vice president explained the ambassador's absense from the meeting.*)	

Present conjugation for أوْضَحَ ('awDaHa; to make clear/explain)	
أوْضِحُ ('anaa 'uuDiHu)	نُوضِحُ (naHnu nuuDiHu)
تُوضِحُ ('anta tuuDiHu)	تُوضِحونَ ('antum tuuDiHuuna)
تُوضِحينَ ('anti tuuDiHiina)	تُوضِحْنَ ('antunna tuuDiHna)
يُوضِحُ (huwa yuuDiHu)	يُوضِحونَ (hum yuuDiHuuna)
تُوضِحُ (hiya tuuDiHu)	يُوضِحْنَ (hunna yuuDiHna)
سَتَفْهَمُ عِنْدَما أوْضِحُ رَأيي. (sa-tafhamu 3indamaa 'uuDiHu ra'yii. *You will understand when I explain my opinion.*)	

Notice that in the past tense, the initial **waaw** verb is regular in Form IV. But it turns into a long *u* vowel (written with **waaw**) in the present tense.

The waaw with Form VIII verbs

The initial **waaw** is regular in Forms V, VI, and VII. But if you thought regularity would run the table, think again! In Form VIII, an initial **waaw** assimilates into the تاء (**taa'**) you put after the first consonant in Form VIII, producing a doubled **taa'** in both the past and present tenses. The doubled **taa'** is written with a ّ (**shadda**). (For more on doubled letters, consult the information on the **shadda** in Chapter 3.) An example in which this happens is the verb إتَّصَلَ (**'ittaSala**; *to call*), which is shown in the following conjugation tables.

Past conjugation for إتَّصَلَ (**'ittaSala**; *to call*)	
إتَّصَلْتُ ('anaa 'ittaSaltu)	إتَّصَلْنا (naHnu 'ittaSalnaa)
إتَّصَلْتَ ('anta 'ittaSalta)	إتَّصَلْتُمْ ('antum 'ittaSaltum)
إتَّصَلْتِ ('anti 'ittaSalti)	إتَّصَلْتُنَّ ('antunna 'ittaSaltunna)
إتَّصَلَ (huwa 'ittaSala)	إتَّصَلوا (hum 'ittaSaluu)
إتَّصَلَتْ (hiya 'ittaSalat)	إتَّصَلْنَ (hunna 'ittaSalna)
إتَّصَلْتُ بِأَبِي بَعْدَ أَنْ وَصَلْتُ إلى الأُرْدُن. (ittaSaltu bi-'abii ba3da 'an waSaltu 'ilaa-l-'urdun. *I called my father after I got to Jordan.*)	

Present conjugation for إتَّصَلَ (**'ittaSala**; *to call*)	
أتَّصِلُ ('anaa 'attaSilu)	نتَّصِلُ (naHnu nattaSilu)
تتَّصِلُ ('anta tattaSilu)	تتَّصِلونَ ('antum tattaSiluuna)
تتَّصِلينَ ('anti tattaSiliina)	تتَّصِلْنَ ('antunna tattaSilna)
يتَّصِلُ (huwa yattaSilu)	يتَّصِلونَ (hum yattaSiluuna)
تتَّصِلُ (hiya tattaSilu)	يتَّصِلْنَ (hunna yattaSilna)
أتَّصِلُ بِأخي في عيد ميلادِهِ. ('attaSilu bi-'akhii fii 3iid milaadihi. *I call my brother on his birthday.*)	

Make sure to remember that an initial **waaw** verb in Form VIII is one of the few that has its particular irregularity in both past and present tenses. That doubled **taa'** turns into your friend when you realize it's a huge red flag for an initial **waaw** verb in Form VIII.

Here's your chance to produce the most irregular of the initial **waaw** forms. In this exercise, write the past and present tenses of the verb indicated by the root, pro-noun, and verb form that I give you.

Q. وضع (**w-D-3**) / أنْتِ ('**anti**) / Form I

A. تَضَعينَ (**taDa3iina**; *you put*); وَضَعْتِ (**waDa3ti**; *you put*)

6. ورق (**w-r-q**) / أنا (**'anaa**) / Form I

_____

7. وزن (**w-z-n**) / نَحْنُ (**naHnu**) / Form IV

_____

8. وحد (**w-H-d**) / أنا (**'anaa**) / Form VIII

_____

9. وجد (**w-j-d**) / هُم (**hum**) / Form I

_____

10. وثق (**w-th-q**) / هِيَ (**hiya**) / Form IV

_____

11. وجه (**w-j-h**) / أنْتُم (**'antum**) / Form VIII

_____

Getting to Know Medial Weak Verbs

In this section, you meet the most challenging type of irregular verbs in Arabic: the _medial weak verbs_. _Medial_ simply means _in the middle_. Why is this name significant? Well, as you know, most Arabic verbs (and nouns) are made up of three consonants. When the middle consonant is a واو (**waaw**) or a ياء (**yaa'**), more often than not something besides a **waaw** or a **yaa'** is used in that place. However, the original **waaw** or **yaa'** may reappear in some of the forms. You'll see some books call these _hollow verbs,_ because the medial **waaw** or **yaa'** will sometimes give the appearance that the verb is hollowed out.

Verbs with medial waaw

Verbs that have medial **waaw** are more common than verbs with medial **yaa'**, so I start with them. For some reason, the statistics overall in the Arabic language are that the **yaa'** as an actual consonant in the triliteral root is fairly rare. In the following section, I explain how the medial **waaw** behaves in each of the forms affected by it.

The medial waaw in Form 1

In Form I, the medial **waaw** can take two different shapes. In one shape, the medial **waaw** will tend to stay as either a long or short _u_ vowel. The important and useful verb قالَ (**qaala**; _to say_) — which comes from the root قول (**q-w-l**) — behaves this way.

Here are the features of a medial **waaw** verb that prefers the long or short _u_ vowel in place of the **waaw**:

✔ The **waaw** only appears in the present tense and even then only as a long *u* vowel.

✔ The long *u* vowel in the present tense is reduced to a ´ (**Damma**) in the two feminine plural forms.

✔ In the past tense, you see a long *a* whenever the final consonant *l* has a vowel and a short *u* whenever the final consonant has a ˚ (**sukuun**).

The following tables show the past and present conjugations of قالَ (**qaala**; *to say*).

Past conjugation for قالَ (qaala; to say)	
قُلْتُ ('anaa qultu)	قُلْنا (naHnu qulnaa)
قُلْتَ ('anta qulta)	قُلْتُمْ ('antum qultum)
قُلْتِ ('anti qulti)	قُلْتُنَّ ('antunna qultunna)
قالَ (huwa qaala)	قالوا (hum qaaluu)
قالَتْ (hiya qaalat)	قُلْنَ (hunna qulna)
قُلْتُ لَكَ الحَقَّ. (qultu laka al-Haqq. *I told you the truth.*)	

Present conjugation for قالَ (qaala; to say)	
أَقولُ ('anaa 'aquulu)	نَقولُ (naHnu naquulu)
تَقولُ ('anta taquulu)	تَقولونَ ('antum taquuluuna)
تَقولينَ ('anti taquuliina)	تَقُلْنَ ('antunna taqulna)
يَقولُ (huwa yaquulu)	يَقولونَ (hum yaquuluuna)
تَقولُ (hiya taquulu)	يَقُلْنَ (hunna yaqulna)
تَقولُ النِّساءُ إنَّهُنَّ مُوافِقاتٌ مَعكِ. (taquulu an-nisaa' 'innahunna muwaafiqaat ma3aki. *The women say that they agree with you.*)	

Make sure to notice that in the present tense, you can see all three consonants of the root in all but the feminine plural forms.

The verb نامَ (**naama**; *to sleep*) shows you the second style a verb with medial **waaw** can display in Form I. Here, the medial **waaw** will become an *a* or *i* vowel. The features of verbs like نامَ (**naama**) are:

✔ Instead of a **Damma** in the past tense, you use a ِ (**kasra**).

✔ In the present tense, you have a long *a* vowel (written with an ألِف [**'alif**]) in place of the long *u* (written with **waaw**).

✔ The feminine plural forms reduce the long *a* to a ´ (**fatHa**).

To read more about the **Damma, kasra,** and **fatHa,** check out Chapter 3.

The following tables show the conjugations of نامَ (**naama**; *to sleep*).

Past conjugation for نامَ (**naama**; *to sleep*)	
نِمْتُ ('**anaa nimtu**)	نِمْنا (**naHnu nimnaa**)
نِمْتَ ('**anta nimta**)	نِمْتُمْ ('**antum nimtum**)
نِمْتِ ('**anti nimti**)	نِمْتُنَّ ('**antunna nimtunna**)
نامَ (**huwa naama**)	ناموا (**hum naamuu**)
نامَتْ (**hiya naamat**)	نِمْنَ (**hunna nimna**)
ما نِمْتُ جَيِّداً جِدّاً اللّيْلة الماضِية.	
(**maa nimtu jayyidan jiddan al-layla al-maaDiya.** *I didn't sleep very well last night.*)	

Present conjugation for نامَ (**naama**; *to sleep*)	
أَنامُ ('**anaa 'anaamu**)	نَنامُ (**naHnu nanaamu**)
تَنامُ ('**anta tanaamu**)	تَنامونَ ('**antum tanaamuuna**)
تَنامينَ ('**anti tanaamiina**)	تَنَمْنَ ('**antunna tanamna**)
يَنامُ (**huwa yanaamu**)	يَنامونَ (**hum yanaamuuna**)
تَنامُ (**hiya tanaamu**)	يَنَمْنَ (**hunna yanamna**)
لا نَنامُ في الصَّفّ أَبَداً.	
(**laa nanaamu fii-S-Saff 'abadan.** *We never sleep in class.*)	

Even though you don't see the **waaw** at all with this verb, the only verb that can have a long *a* (written with '**alif**) in the present tense of Form I is a medial **waaw**. So, look at that long *a* and always remember it's secretly a **waaw**.

The particular style a medial **waaw** verb uses is predetermined. You can't just select one or the other. A verb either follows the pattern of قالَ (**qaala**) or نامَ (**naama**). A dictionary can tell you the style a verb follows.

The medial waaw in Form IV

A medial **waaw** causes no irregularity in Forms II and III. But Form IV is a different matter. In Form IV, the medial **waaw** vanishes altogether. Here are the guidelines to remember in this case:

- ✔ In the past tense, the **waaw** is replaced with a long *a* whenever the third consonant has a vowel.

- ✔ Forms with a **sukuun** over the third consonant reduce the vowel to a **fatHa**.

- ✔ In the present tense, you encounter a long *i* vowel (written with **yaa'**), except for the feminine plural forms, which reduce it to a **kasra**.

The verb أَجَابَ ('ajaaba; *to answer*) is a good example of how a Form IV medial **waaw** verb is formed. The following tables show the conjugations.

Past conjugation for أَجَابَ ('ajaaba; *to answer*)	
أَجَبْتُ ('anaa 'ajabtu)	أَجَبْنا (naHnu 'ajabnaa)
أَجَبْتَ ('anta 'ajabta)	أَجَبْتُمْ ('antum 'ajabtum)
أَجَبْتِ ('anti 'ajabti)	أَجَبْتُنَّ ('antunna 'ajabtunna)
أَجَابَ (huwa 'ajaaba)	أَجَابوا (hum 'ajaabuu)
أَجَابَتْ (hiya 'ajaabat)	أَجَبْنَ (hunna 'ajabna)
أَجَابَتْ السُّؤَال سَريعاً. ('ajaabat as-su'aal sarii3an. *She answered the question quickly.*)	

Present conjugation for أَجَابَ ('ajaaba; *to answer*)	
أُجيبُ ('anaa 'ujiibu)	نُجيبُ (naHnu nujiibu)
تُجيبُ ('anta tujiibu)	تُجيبونَ ('antum tujiibuuna)
تُجيبينَ ('anti tujiibiina)	تُجِبْنَ ('antunna tujibna)
يُجيبُ (huwa yujiibu)	يُجيبونَ (hum yujiibuuna)
تُجيبُ (hiya tujiibu)	يُجِبْنَ (hunna yujibna)
لِماذا لا تُجيبُني؟ (limaadhaa laa tujiibunii? *Why don't you answer me?*)	

Take a mental note of the past and present tenses of أَجَابَ ('ajaaba) because they show you at a glance how medial **waaw** appears in the forms after Form I. Whenever you see long *a* and long *i* between two consonants, you have a medial **waaw** or medial **yaa'** verb. But because medial **yaa'** is relatively rare, it's probably a medial **waaw**.

The medial waaw in Forms VII and VIII

Like Form IV, Forms VII and VIII are other cases of the completely vanished medial **waaw**. Like the second style for Form I, the **waaw** is replaced with a long *a* everywhere except:

- ✔ Past tense forms with **sukuun** over the third consonant
- ✔ The feminine plural forms in the present tense

The verb إنْقادَ (**inqaada**; *to obey*) demonstrates how to make the Form VII of a medial **waaw** verb. The following tables show you the conjugations.

Past conjugation for اِنْقَادَ (inqaada; to obey)	
اِنْقَدْتُ ('anaa inqadtu)	اِنْقَدْنا (naHnu inqadnaa)
اِنْقَدْتَ ('anta inqadta)	اِنْقَدْتُم ('antum inqadtum)
اِنْقَدْتِ ('anti inqadti)	اِنْقَدْتُنَّ ('antunna inqadtunna)
اِنْقَادَ (huwa inqaada)	اِنْقَادوا (hum inqaaduu)
اِنْقَادَتْ (hiya inqaadat)	اِنْقَدْنَ (hunna inqadna)
اِنْقَدْنا لِمُدَرِّسِنا. (inqadnaa li-mudarrisinaa. *We obeyed our teacher.*)	

Present conjugation for اِنْقَادَ (inqaada; to obey)	
آنْقَادُ ('anaa 'anqaadu)	نَنْقَادُ (naHnu nanqaadu)
تَنْقَادُ ('anta tanqaadu)	تَنْقَادونَ ('antum tanqaaduuna)
تَنْقَادينَ ('anti tanqaadiina)	تَنْقَدْنَ ('antunna tanqadna)
يَنْقَادُ (huwa yanqaadu)	يَنْقَادونَ (hum yanqaaduuna)
تَنْقَادُ (hiya tanqaadu)	يَنْقَدْنَ (hunna yanqadna)
هَلْ تَنْقَادُ لِجَدِّكَ؟ (hal tanqaadu li-jaddika? *Do you obey your grandfather?*)	

Here you see how the long *a* continues to be a reliable marker for a lost **waaw**.

The verb اِعْتَادَ (i3taada; *to be accustomed to*) is a good example of the Form VIII of a medial **waaw** verb. See the tables for the conjugations.

Past conjugation for اِعْتَادَ (i3taada; to be accustomed to)	
اِعْتَدْتُ ('anaa i3tadtu)	اِعْتَدْنا (naHnu i3tadna)
اِعْتَدْتَ ('anta i3tadta)	اِعْتَدْتُم ('antum i3tadtum)
اِعْتَدْتِ ('anti i3tadti)	اِعْتَدْتُنَّ ('antunna i3tadtunna)
اِعْتَادَ (huwa i3taada)	اِعْتَادوا (hum i3taaduu)
اِعْتَادَتْ (hiya i3taadat)	اِعْتَدْنَ (hunna i3tadna)
ما اِعْتَدْتُ عَلَى الطَّقْس في مِصْر. (maa i3tadtu 3alaa-T-Taqs fii miSr. *I didn't become accustomed to the weather in Egypt.*)	

Present conjugation for أَعْتَاد (i3taada; *to be accustomed to*)	
أَعْتَادُ ('anaa 'a3taadu)	نَعْتَادُ (naHnu na3taadu)
تَعْتَادُ ('anta ta3taadu)	تَعْتَادونَ ('antum ta3taaduuna)
تَعْتَادينَ ('anti ta3taadiina)	تَعْتَدْنَ ('antunna ta3tadna)
يَعْتَادُ (huwa ya3taadu)	يَعْتادونَ (hum ya3taaduuna)
تَعْتَادُ (hiya ta3taadu)	يَعْتَدْنَ (hunna ya3tadna)
يَعْتادونَ أَنْ يَأْكُلوا كَثيراً. (ya3taaduuna 'an ya'kuluu kathiiran. *They are accustomed to eating a lot.*)	

When you see a verb in Form VIII, resist the urge to assume that the **taa'** appearing after the first consonant is part of the root. Keep in mind that any long *a* vowel in the past or present tense is likely hiding a **waaw** instead.

The medial waaw in Form X

Medial **waaw** verbs in Form X follow the same rules as Form IV. Here are the rules:

- In the past tense, the **waaw** is replaced with a long *a* whenever the third consonant has a vowel.

- Forms with a **sukuun** over the third consonant reduce the vowel to a **fatHa**.

- In the present tense, you encounter a long *i* vowel (written with **yaa'**), except for the feminine plural forms, which reduce it to a **kasra**.

The verb اسْتَقام (istaqaama; *to stand up*) is an example of a Form X verb. The following are the conjugation tables for the verb.

Past conjugation for اسْتَقَام (istaqaama; *to stand up*)	
اسْتَقَمْتُ ('anaa istaqamtu)	اسْتَقَمْنا (naHnu istaqamnaa)
اسْتَقَمْتَ ('anta istaqamta)	اسْتَقَمْتُمْ ('antum istaqamtum)
اسْتَقَمْتِ ('anti istaqamti)	اسْتَقَمْتُنَّ ('antunna istaqamtunna)
اسْتَقامَ (huwa istaqaama)	اسْتَقاموا (hum istaqaamuu)
اسْتَقامَتْ (hiya istaqaamat)	اسْتَقَمْنَ (hunna istaqamna)
اسْتَقَمْتُ في الإجْتِماع وَقَدَّمْتُ اقْتِراحي. (istaqamtu fii-l-ijtimaa3 wa-qaddamtu iqtiraaHii. *I stood up in the meeting and offered my proposal.*)	

Present conjugation for اِسْتَقامَ (istaqaama; to stand up)	
أَسْتَقيمُ ('anaa 'astaqiimu)	نَسْتَقيمُ (naHnu nastaqiimu)
تَسْتَقيمُ ('anta tastaqiimu)	تَسْتَقيمونَ ('antum tastaqiimuuna)
تَسْتَقيمينَ ('anti tastaqiimiina)	تَسْتَقِمْنَ ('antunna tastaqimna)
يَسْتَقيمُ (huwa yastaqiimu)	يَسْتَقيمونَ (hum yastaqiimuuna)
تَسْتَقيمُ (hiya tastaqiimu)	يَسْتَقِمْنَ (hunna yastaqimna)
عِنْدَما نَسْتَقيمُ مَعاً سَنَكونُ أَقْوِياء. (3indamaa nastaqiimu ma3an sanakuunu 'aqwiyaa'. *When we stand up together we will be strong.*)	

Form X is another example of the need to never disregard the clue of having a long *a* or long *i* in the verb. I've seen many students try to make the سين (**siin**) or تاء (**taa'**) of Form X part of the root.

Verbs with medial yaa'

Verbs with a medial **yaa'** are somewhat rare in the language. But there are a few of them that are common and important verbs. A medial **yaa'** presents its own peculiar irregularities to your verb formation. A verb with medial **yaa'** in Form I follows these guidelines:

- A long *a* vowel takes the place of the **yaa'** in the past tense when the third consonant has a vowel.
- The long *a* vowel in the past tense reduces to a **kasra** when the third consonant has a **kasra**.
- A long *i* vowel takes the place of the **yaa'** in the present tense.
- The long *i* vowel in the present reduces to a **kasra** with the feminine plural forms.

The following conjugation table shows an example using the verb باعَ (**baa3a**; *to sell*).

Past conjugation for باعَ (baa3a; to sell)	
بِعْتُ ('anaa bi3tu)	بِعْنا (naHnu bi3naa)
بِعْتَ ('anta bi3ta)	بِعْتُمْ ('antum bi3tum)
بِعْتِ ('anti bi3ti)	بِعْتُنَّ ('antunna bi3tunna)
باعَ (huwa baa3a)	باعوا (hum baa3uu)
باعَتْ (hiya baa3at)	بِعْنَ (hunna bi3na)
باعَ زَوْجي سَيّارَتَهُ لِأَخيهِ. (baa3a zawjii sayyaaratahu li-'akhiihi. *My husband sold his car to his brother.*)	

Present conjugation for باعَ (**baa3a**; *to sell*)	
أَبيعُ (**'anaa 'abii3u**)	نَبيعُ (**naHnu nabii3u**)
تَبيعُ (**'anta tabii3u**) تَبيعينَ (**'anti tabii3iina**)	تَبيعونَ (**'antum tabii3uuna**) تَبِعْنَ (**'antunna tabi3na**)
يَبيعُ (**huwa yabii3u**) تَبيعُ (**hiya tabii3u**)	يَبيعونَ (**hum yabii3uuna**) يَبِعْنَ (**hunna yabi3na**)
هَلْ يَبيعونَ القَهْوة هُناكَ أَمْ لا؟ (**hal yabii3uuna al-qahwa hunaaka 'am laa?** *Do they sell coffee there or not?*)	

The main thing to concentrate on in the previous charts is the vowel over the prefixes in the present tense. If you see a **fatHa** over the prefix, and then a long *i* where you may have expected a medial consonant, it means that you have a Form I medial **yaa'** verb on your hands. If you see a **Damma,** you have a Form IV irregular verb.

In Forms IV, VII, VIII, and X, verbs with medial **yaa'** behave exactly the same as Form IV, VII, VIII, and X medial **waaw** verbs.

For each of the following items, create the past and present tenses of the verbs indicated by the root, pronoun, and verb form that I give you.

0. فوت (**f-w-t**) / هُم (**hum**) / Form I

A. يَفوتونَ (**yafuutuuna**; *they go by*); فاتوا (**faatuu**; *they went by*)

12. سير (**s-y-r**) / هِيَ (**hiya**) / Form I

_____

13. ثور (**th-w-r**) / نَحْنُ (**naHnu**) / Form IV

_____

14. طوع (**T-w-3**) / أَنْتَ (**'anta**) / Form X

_____

15. عوذ (**3-w-dh**) / هُم (**hum**) / Form I

_____

16. رود (**r-w-d**) / أنَا (**'anaa**) / Form IV

_____

17. روح (**r-w-H**) / هُوَ (**huwa**) / Form VIII

_____

Working with Final Weak Verbs

When the weak consonants واو (**waaw**) or يَاء (**yaa'**) appear as the final consonant in an Arabic verb root, they create a series of irregularities in your verb production. I explain verbs with both consonants in the following sections. You may see verbs with a final **waaw** or **yaa'** called _defective verbs_ in other books. This really isn't a good way to reference them, because they aren't defective at all. Rather, the final weak consonant just presents its own distinct patterns.

Verbs with final waaw

In Form I, verbs with a **waaw** as their third (and final) consonant follow these rules:

- ✔ Forms with ° (**sukuun**) over the third consonant are normal, and the **waaw** appears as a full consonant.

- ✔ The **waaw** disappears in the past tense third person feminine singular.

- ✔ The **waaw** turns into a long _a_ (written as an أَلِف [**'alif**]) in the past tense third person masculine singular.

- ✔ The past tense third person masculine plural is a consonantal **waaw**.

- ✔ All present tense forms without a suffix replace the **waaw** with a long _u_ vowel.

- ✔ The **waaw** disappears in the present tense second person feminine singular.

As an example, the following tables show the conjugations of the Form I verb دَعا (**da3aa;** _to call, invite_).

Past conjugation for دَعا (da3aa; _to call, invite_)	
دَعَوْتُ (**'anaa da3awtu**)	دَعَوْنا (**naHnu da3awnaa**)
دَعَوْتَ (**'anta da3awta**)	دَعَوْتُم (**'antum da3awtum**)
دَعَوْتِ (**'anti da3awti**)	دَعَوْتُنَّ (**'antunna da3awtunna**)
دَعا (**huwa da3aa**)	دَعَوْا (**hum da3aw**)
دَعَت (**hiya da3at**)	دَعَوْنَ (**hunna da3awna**)
دَعَوْتُ صَديقي إلى أنْ يُساعِدَني. (**da3awtu Sadiiqii 'ilaa 'an yusaa3idanii.** _I called on my friend to help me._)	

Present conjugation for دَعا (da3aa; *to call, invite*)	
أَدْعو ('anaa 'ad3uu)	نَدْعو (naHnu nad3uu)
تَدْعو ('anta tad3uu)	تَدْعونَ ('antum tad3uuna)
تَدْعينَ ('anti tad3iina)	تَدْعونَ ('antunna tad3uuna)
يَدْعو (huwa yad3uu)	يَدْعونَ (hum yad3uuna)
تَدْعو (hiya tad3uu)	يَدْعونَ (hunna yad3uuna)
نَدْعو كُلّ أَصْدِقاءَنا إلى الحَفْلة. (nad3uu kull 'aSdiqaa'anaa 'ilaa-l-Hafla. *We invite all our friends to the party.*)	

Note that a final **waaw** verb is the only case in the whole Arabic language where the masculine and feminine plural forms are identical. Verbs with final **waaw** behave as if they have a final **yaa'** in all the other Forms. To see what changes that means for you, consult the next section on final **yaa'** verbs.

Verbs with final yaa'

Much more irregular than final **waaw** verbs (see the previous section) are those with a **yaa'** as the third and final consonant. They're more irregular than final **waaw** verbs in that there are three different styles that a final **yaa'** verb can follow. And you don't have your choice as to which of the three styles you prefer. Instead, if a verb has a final **yaa'**, you need to determine which of the three it is in order to correctly state it in the past and present in Form I.

The final yaa' in Form 1

I show you the verb بَكى (**bakaa**; *to cry*) as an example of the first style of a final **yaa'** verb. The traits of this style of final **yaa'** verb are a tendency for the **yaa'** to be a consonant in a closed syllable when suffixes are added to the past tense and for the **yaa'** to appear as a long *i* vowel in the present tense. The following tables show the conjugations of بَكى (**bakaa**; *to cry*).

Past conjugation for بَكى (bakaa; *to cry*)	
بَكَيْتُ ('anaa bakaytu)	بَكَيْنا (naHnu bakaynaa)
بَكَيْتَ ('anta bakayta)	بَكَيْتُم ('antum bakaytum)
بَكَيْتِ ('anti bakayti)	بَكَيْتُنَّ ('antunna bakaytunna)
بَكى (huwa bakaa)	بَكَوْا (hum bakaw)
بَكَتْ (hiya bakat)	بَكَيْنَ (hunna bakayna)
بَكَيْتُ أَثْناءَ الفيلم. (bakaytu 'athnaa' al-fiilm. *I cried during the movie.*)	

Present conjugation for بَكى (bakaa; to cry)	
أَبْكي ('anaa 'abkii)	نَبْكي (naHnu nabkii)
تَبْكي ('anta tabkii)	تَبْكونَ ('antum tabkuuna)
تَبْكينَ ('anti tabkiina)	تَبْكينَ ('antunna tabkiina)
يَبْكي (huwa yabkii)	يَبْكونَ (hum yabkuuna)
تَبْكي (hiya tabkii)	يَبْكينَ (hunna yabkiina)
هَلْ تَبْكينَ أَمْ تَضْحَكينَ؟ (hal tabkiina 'am taDHakiina? Are you crying or laughing?)	

In the next style of final **yaa'** verb, the **yaa'** appears usually as a long *i* vowel in the past tense and as an أَلِف مَكْسورة ('**alif maksura**) in many present tense forms. For this style of verb, I use the verb نَسِيَ (**nasiya**; *to forget*), whose conjugations you can see in the following tables.

Past conjugation for نَسِيَ (nasiya; to forget)	
نَسيتُ ('anaa nasiitu)	نَسينا (naHnu nasiinaa)
نَسيتَ ('anta nasiita)	نَسيتُمْ ('antum nasiitum)
نَسيتِ ('anti nasiiti)	نَسيتُنَّ ('antunna nasiitunna)
نَسِيَ (huwa nasiya)	نَسوا (hum nasuu)
نَسِيَتْ (hiya nasiyat)	نَسينَ (hunna nasiina)
هَلْ نَسيتُمْ عُنْواني؟ (hal nasiitum 3unwaanii? Have you forgotten my address?)	

Present conjugation for نَسِيَ (nasiya; to forget)	
أَنْسى ('anaa 'ansaa)	نَنْسى (naHnu nansaa)
تَنْسى ('anta tansaa)	تَنْسَوْنَ ('antum tansawna)
تَنْسَيْنَ ('anti tansayna)	تَنْسَيْنَ ('antunna tansayna)
يَنْسى (huwa yansaa)	يَنْسَوْنَ (hum yansawna)
تَنْسى (hiya tansaa)	يَنْسَيْنَ (hunna yansayna)
أَنْسى الأَرْقام دائِماً. ('ansaa al-'arqaam daa'iman. I always forget numbers.)	

The third style of final **yaa'** verb is essentially a hybrid of the previous two. It forms its past tense like بَكى (**bakaa**; *to cry*) and its present tense like نَسِيَ (**nasiya**; *to forget*). The following conjugation tables for سَعى (**sa3aa**; *to make an effort*) show you what I mean.

Past conjugation for سَعى (sa3aa; *to make an effort*)	
سَعَيْتُ ('anaa sa3aytu)	سَعَيْنا (naHnu sa3aynaa)
سَعَيْتَ ('anta sa3ayta)	سَعَيْتُمْ ('antum sa3aytum)
سَعَيْتِ ('anti sa3ayti)	سَعَيْتُنَّ ('antunna sa3aytunna)
سَعى (huwa sa3aa)	سَعَوْا (hum sa3aw)
سَعَتْ (hiya sa3at)	سَعَيْنَ (hunna sa3ayna)
هَلْ سَعَيْتِ وَراءَ الدِّراسة؟ (hal sa3ayti waraa' ad-diraasa? *Did you make an effort to study?*)	

Present conjugation for سَعى (sa3aa; *to make an effort*)	
أَسْعى ('anaa 'as3aa)	نَسْعى (naHnu nas3aa)
تَسْعى ('anta tas3aa)	تَسْعَوْنَ ('antum tas3awna)
تَسْعَيْنَ ('anti tas3ayna)	تَسْعَيْنَ ('antunna tas3ayna)
يَسْعى (huwa yas3aa)	يَسْعَوْنَ (hum yas3awna)
تَسْعى (hiya tas3aa)	يَسْعَيْنَ (hunna yas3ayna)
هُوَ يَسْعى لأَنْ يَتَكَلَّمَ بِبُطْء. (huwa yas3aa li-'an yatakallama bi-buT'. *He is making an effort to speak slowly.*)	

The final yaa' in Forms II–X

Verbs with either final **waaw** or final **yaa'** each have the same endings in Forms II–X. Essentially, the final **waaw** verbs act as if they were final **yaa'**. Forms II, III, IV, VIII, and X use the same endings as the Form I verb بَكى (**bakaa;** *to cry*). In the following conjugation tables, I show you the Form IV verb أَخْفى ('**akhfaa;** *to hide*) as an example.

Past conjugation for أَخْفى ('akhfaa; *to hide*)	
أَخْفَيْتُ ('anaa 'akhfaytu)	أَخْفَيْنا (naHnu 'akhfaynaa)
أَخْفَيْتَ ('anta 'akhfayta)	أَخْفَيْتُمْ ('antum 'akhfaytum)
أَخْفَيْتِ ('anti 'akhfayti)	أَخْفَيْتُنَّ ('antunna 'akhfaytunna)
أَخْفى (huwa 'akhfaa)	أَخْفَوْا (hum 'akhfaw)
أَخْفَتْ (hiya 'akhfat)	أَخْفَيْنَ (hunna 'akhfayna)
أَخْفَتِ المَوْضوع مِن أُمِّها. ('akhfat al-mawDuu3 min 'ummihaa. *She hid the situation from her mother.*)	

Present conjugation for أَخْفَى ('akhfaa; *to hide*)	
أُخْفِي ('anaa 'ukhfii)	نُخْفِي (naHnu nukhfii)
تُخْفِي ('anta tukhfii)	تُخْفُونَ ('antum tukhfuuna)
تُخْفِينَ ('anti tukhfiina)	تُخْفِينَ ('antunna tukhfiina)
يُخْفِي (huwa yukhfii)	يُخْفُونَ (hum yukhfuuna)
تُخْفِي (hiya tukhfii)	يُخْفِينَ (hunna yukhfiina)
نُخْفِي مالَنا عِنْدَما نَرى صَديقَنا. (nukhfii maalanaa 3indamaa Sadiiqanaa. *We hide our money when we see our friend.*)	

Final weak verbs in Forms V, VI, and VII use the same endings with the exception of having an **'alif maksura** in place of the final *i* in the present tense. For example, look at the conjugation tables for تَسَمَّى (**tasammaa**; *to be named*).

Past conjugation for تَسَمَّى (tasammaa; *to be named*)	
تَسَمَّيْتُ ('anaa tasammaytu)	تَسَمَّيْنا (naHnu tasammaynaa)
تَسَمَّيْتَ ('anta tasammayta)	تَسَمَّيْتُم ('antum tasammaytum)
تَسَمَّيْتِ ('anti tasammayti)	تَسَمَّيْتُنَّ ('antunna tasammaytunna)
تَسَمَّى (huwa tasammaa)	تَسَمَّوْا (hum tasammaw)
تَسَمَّتْ (hiya tasammat)	تَسَمَّيْنَ (hunna tasammayna)
تَسَمَّى أَحْمَد مِثلَ جَدِّهِ. (tasammaa 'aHmad mithla jaddihi. *He was named Ahmad like his grandfather.*)	

Present conjugation for تَسَمَّى (tasammaa; *to be named*)	
أَتَسَمَّى ('anaa 'atasammaa)	نَتَسَمَّى (naHnu natasammaa)
تَتَسَمَّى ('anta tatasammaa)	تَتَسَمَّوْنَ ('antum tatasammawna)
تَتَسَمَّيْنَ ('anti tatasammayna)	تَتَسَمَّيْنَ ('antunna tatasammayna)
يَتَسَمَّى (huwa yatasammaa)	يَتَسَمَّوْنَ (hum yatasammawna)
تَتَسَمَّى (hiya tatasammaa)	يَتَسَمَّيْنَ (hunna yatasammayna)
هَلْ تَتَسَمَّيْنَ فاطِمة أَمْ هُدى؟ (hal tatasammayna faaTima 'am hudaa? *Are you named Fatima or Huda?*)	

Notice that the only difference between the masculine and feminine plural forms in the previous tables is the consonant before the final **-na** prefix — **waaw** for masculine and **yaa'** for feminine.

Now it's time to reinforce what you've discovered about final weak verbs with a bit of practice forming them. For each of the following items, create the past and present tenses of the verbs indicated by the root, pronoun, and verb form that I give you.

Q. خفى (**k-f-y**) / هُوَ (**huwa**) / Form VII

A. يَخْتَفِي (**yakhtafii**; *he disappears*); اِخْتَفَى (**ikhtafaa**; *he disappeared*)

18. كفى (**k-f-y**) / هُوَ (**huwa**) / Form I

_____

19. رجو (**r-j-w**) / نَحْنُ (**naHnu**) / Form I

_____

20. شري (**sh-r-y**) / أَنْتَ (**'anta**) / Form VIII

_____

21. بَقي (**b-q-y**) / أَنْتُم (**'antum**) / Form I

_____

22. مضى (**m-D-y**) / أَنا (**'anaa**) / Form IV

_____

23. فضو (**f-D-w**) / هُوَ (**huwa**) / Form V

_____

Touching on Geminate Verbs

Sometimes a verb has the same consonant in the second and final position. Because you essentially have twin consonants in one verb, these are called *geminate* verbs (like my zodiac sign, Gemini). Some linguists call these *doubled verbs,* but this name isn't helpful because there's plenty of doubling that goes on in Arabic apart from the nature of the root (such as the doubling of the middle consonant in Form II).

With geminate verbs in Forms II, III, V, and VI, there's no irregularity at all. In those forms, you can just use all three consonants normally, even though the second and third consonants are identical. In those forms, you have both consonants living side by side. But in Form I, a geminate verb will sometimes assimilate the two identical twins into one doubled consonant.

In Form I, there's no irregularity when you put a suffix that begins in a consonant on the verb. But with other suffixes and in all present tense forms except the feminine plural, the second and third consonants contract into one doubled consonant. To show you how this appears, I include a conjugation table of the Form I verb عَدَّ (**3adda;** *to count*).

Past conjugation for عَدَّ (3adda; *to count*)	
عَدَدْتُ (’anaa 3adadtu)	عَدَدْنا (naHnu 3adadnaa)
عَدَدْتَ (’anta 3adadta)	عَدَدْتُم (’antum 3adadtum)
عَدَدْتِ (’anti 3adadti)	عَدَدْتُنَّ (’antunna 3adadtunna)
عَدَّ (huwa 3adda)	عَدُّوا (hum 3adduu)
عَدَّت (hiya 3addat)	عَدَدْنَ (hunna 3adadna)
عَدَدْتُ الزُّوَّارَ هُناكَ. (3adadtu az-zuwwaara hunaaka. *I counted the visitors there.*)	

Present conjugation for عَدَّ (3adda; *to count*)	
أَعُدُّ (’anaa ’a3uddu)	نَعُدُّ (naHnu na3uddu)
تَعُدُّ (’anta ta3uddu)	تَعُدُّونَ (’antum ta3udduuna)
تَعُدِّينَ (’anti ta3uddiina)	تَعُدُدْنَ (’antunna ta3dudna)
يَعُدُّ (huwa ya3uddu)	يَعُدُّونَ (hum ya3udduuna)
تَعُدُّ (hiya ta3uddu)	يَعُدُدْنَ (hunna ya3dudna)
هِيَ تَعُدُّ المال مِنْ بَيْع السَّيّارة. (hiya ta3uddu al-maal min bay3 as-sayyaara. *She counts the money from the sale of the car.*)	

In Forms IV, VII, VIII, and X, the second and third consonants also contract in the past tense whenever the suffix begins with a vowel. In the present tense, it contracts except in the feminine plural forms. I use the verb اِسْتَمَرَّ (**istamarra**; *to continue*) to show you what I mean.

Past conjugation for اِسْتَمَرَّ (istamarra; *to continue*)	
اِسْتَمْرَرْتُ (’anaa istamrartu)	اِسْتَمْرَرْنا (naHnu istamrarnaa)
اِسْتَمْرَرْتَ (’anta istamrarta)	اِسْتَمْرَرْتُم (’antum istamrartum)
اِسْتَمْرَرْتِ (’anti istamrarti)	اِسْتَمْرَرْتُنَ (’antunna istamrartunna)
اِسْتَمَرَّ (huwa istamarra)	اِسْتَمَرُّوا (hum istamarruu)
اِسْتَمَرَّت (hiya istamarrat)	اِسْتَمْرَرْنَ (hunna istamrarna)
اِسْتَمَرَّت الحَفْلة لِمُدَّة ثَلاث ساعات. (istamarrat al-Hafla limuddat thalaath saa3aat. *The party continued for three hours.*)	

Present conjugation for اِسْتَمَرَّ (istamarra; *to continue*)	
أَسْتَمِرُّ (’anaa ’astamirru)	نَسْتَمِرُّ (naHnu nastamirru)
تَسْتَمِرُّ (’anta tastamirru)	تَسْتَمِرُّونَ (’antum tastamirruuna)
تَسْتَمِرِّينَ (’anti tastamirriina)	تَسْتَمْرِرْنَ (’antunna tastamrirna)
يَسْتَمِرُّ (huwa yastamirru)	يَسْتَمِرُّونَ (hum yastamirruuna)
تَسْتَمِرُّ (hiya tastamirru)	يَسْتَمْرِرْنَ (hunna yastamrirna)
هَلْ تَسْتَمِرُّ فِي دِراسَتِكَ؟	
(hal tastamirru fii diraasatika? *Do you continue in your studies?*)	

The way to master the geminate verbs is to notice that the twin consonants double up whenever there's a vowel after them. When there's no vowel (such as when you have a consonant suffix), the twins insist on their individuality and both get pronounced.

You're writing an e-mail describing your vacation to a friend. Fill in the blanks in the e-mail with the irregular verbs I provide. You'll use each of the items once. Each one will best fit the context somewhere in the e-mail.

أَضاعـوا-	يَجِبُ	نَزورَ	كُنْتُ	مَشَيْنا
(’aDaa3uu)	(yajibu)	(nazuura)	(kuntu)	(mashayna)

أَشْتَرِيَ	أَصِفَ	نُريدُ	أَسْتَطيعُ	
(’ashtariya)	(’aSifa)	(nuriidu)	(’astaTii3u)	

Q. عِنْدي مُشْكِلة لأنَّ الْمُوَظَّفينَ _____ حَقائِبي في الْمَطار. (3indii mushkila li’anna-l-muwaDHDHafiina _____ Haqaa’ibii fii-l-maTaar.)

A. عِنْدي مُشْكِلة لأنَّ الْمُوَظَّفينَ أَضاعـوا حَقائِبي في الْمَطار. (3indii mushkila li’anna-l-muwaDHDHafiina ’aDaa3uu Haqaa’ibii fii-l-maTaar. *I have a problem because the employees* <u>lost</u> *my luggage at the airport.*)

New Message

| Send | Cut | Copy | Paste | Undo | abc✔ Check |

أَحْمَد

لا _____ أَنْ _____ 24. جَمالَ البَحْر هُنا

_____

لكنْ أَوَّلاً _____ أَنْ _____ مَلابِسَ جَديدةً .25

_____

غَداً نَحْنُ _____ أَنْ _____ صَديقاً كانَ زَوْجي في الجَيْش مَعَهُ .26

_____

أَمْس _____ قَليلاً في القَرْية القَريبة مِن الشّاطيء .27

_____

لَوْ _____ غَنيةً لأَرَدْتُ أَنْ أَسْكُنَ هَنا كُلّ السَنة .28

_____

الخُلِصة

مَرْيم

Answer Key

1 أَمَلُ ('aamulu; *I hope*); أَمَلْتُ ('amaltu; *I hoped*)

2 نُؤْلِمُ (nu'limu; *we cause pain*); آلَمْنا ('aalamna; *we caused pain*)

3 آخُذُ ('aakhudhu; *I take*); أَخَذْتُ ('akhadhtu; *I took*)

4 يُؤْجِرونَ (yu'jiruuna; *they rent out*); آجَروا ('aajaruu; *they rented out*)

5 تُؤازِرُ (tu'aaziru; *you help*); آزَرْتَ ('aazarta; *you helped*)

6 أُورِقُ ('uuriqu; *I sprout*); أَوْرَقْتُ ('awraqtu; *I sprouted*)

7 نَزِنُ (nazinu; *we weigh*); وَزَنّا (wazanna; *we weighed*)

8 أَتَّحِدُ ('attaHidu; *I join in*); اِتَّحَدْتُ (ittaHadtu; *I joined in*)

9 يَجِدونَ (yajiduuna; *they find*); وَجَدوا (wajaduu; *they found*)

10 تُوثِقُ (tuuthiqu; *she ties*); أَوْثَقَتْ ('awthaqat; *she tied*)

11 تَتَّجِهونَ (tattajihuuna; *you head for*); اِتَّجَهْتُمْ (ittajahtum; *you headed for*)

12 تَسيرُ (tasiiru; *she runs*); سارَتْ (saarat; *she ran*)

13 نُثيرُ (nuthiiru; *we agitate*); أَثَرْنا ('atharna; *we agitated*)

14 تَسْتَطيعُ (tastaTii3u; *you are able*); اِسْتَطَعْتَ (istaTa3ta; *you were able*)

15 يَعوذونَ (ya3uudhuuna; *they seek protection*); عاذوا (3aadhuu; *they sought protection*)

16 أُريدُ ('uriidu; *I want*); أَرَدْتُ ('aradtu; *I wanted*)

17 يَرْتاحُ (yartaaHu; *he rests*); اِرْتاحَ (irtaaHa; *he rested*)

18 يَكْفي (yakfii; *it's enough*); كَفى (kafaa; *it was enough*)

19 نَرْجو (narjuu; *we hope*); رَجَوْنا (rajawna; *we hoped*)

20 تَشْتَري (**tashtarii**; *you buy*); اِشْتَرَيْتَ (**ishtarayta**; *you bought*)

21 تَبْقُونَ (**tabquuna**; *you remain*); بَقَيْتُم (**baqaytum**; *you remained*)

22 أُمْضي ('**umDii**; *I sign*); أَمْضَيْتُ ('**amDaytu**; *I signed*)

23 يَتَفَضّى (**yatafaDDaa**; *he has leisure*); تَفَضّى (**tafaDDaa**; *he had leisure*)

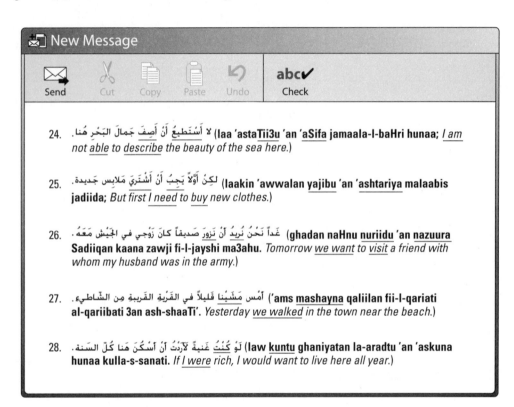

✉ New Message

| Send | Cut | Copy | Paste | Undo | abc✔ Check |

24. لا أَسْتَطِيعُ أَنْ أَصِفَ جَمالَ البَحْرِ هُنا. (**laa 'astaTii3u 'an 'aSifa jamaala-l-baHri hunaa;** *I am not able to describe the beauty of the sea here.*)

25. لكِنْ أَوَّلاً يَجِبُ أَنْ أَشْتَرِيَ مَلابِس جَديدة. (**laakin 'awwalan yajibu 'an 'ashtariya malaabis jadiida;** *But first I need to buy new clothes.*)

26. غَداً نَحْنُ نُريدُ أَنْ نَزورَ صَديقاً كانَ زَوْجي في الجَيْش مَعَهُ. (**ghadan naHnu nuriidu 'an nazuura Sadiiqan kaana zawji fi-l-jayshi ma3ahu.** *Tomorrow we want to visit a friend with whom my husband was in the army.*)

27. أَمْس مَشَيْنا قَليلاً في القَرْيَة القَريبة مِن الشّاطِيء. ('**ams mashayna qaliilan fii-l-qariati al-qariibati 3an ash-shaaTi'.** *Yesterday we walked in the town near the beach.*)

28. لَوْ كُنْتُ غَنِيَّةً لأَرَدْتُ أَنْ أَسْكُنَ هَنا كُلَّ السَنة. (**law kuntu ghaniyatan la-aradtu 'an 'askuna hunaa kulla-s-sanati.** *If I were rich, I would want to live here all year.*)

Chapter 11

Using the Imperative in Commands

In This Chapter
▶ Using formal and informal commands in Arabic
▶ Producing imperative forms for regular verbs
▶ Understanding the forms of irregular Arabic imperatives

1 bet in your average day you tell other people what to do hundreds of times. For example, if you're a parent, you tell your kids to behave or to do their homework. Or, if you're a student, you tell your roommates to pick up their clothes or to turn down their music. Now, I'm sure you're appropriately polite about it. I mean, even if you're a boss with lots of employees who answer to you, you've noticed that just barking orders doesn't always get the desired result (unless, of course, you're in the military!). You do better to at least add "please" to your request. And, chances are, when you tell someone what to do, you aren't really so much telling them directly what to do as asking them in a roundabout way. You may say something like, "Would you please have this project done by close of business?" You may even ask that dreaded question, "Would you like to take out the trash?"

This chapter discusses the verb forms known as *commands* or *imperatives.* You first see how to work with verbs that have three strong consonants. Then later in the chapter, you uncover the changes to make when one of the three consonants is weak. Arabic also uses forms of the jussive mood to produce *prohibitions* (negative commands, such as "Don't stay out too late") as well as hortatory commands (suggestions like "Let's go out sometime"). You can explore the jussive forms and the ways you can use the jussive in Chapter 13.

As in English, Arabic has ways to form commands along the entire spectrum of directness and courtesy. In this chapter, you discover how to use and form a command for any verb and every occasion, whether you need to direct it to a close friend or a dignitary you just met. So, please get ready. Would you like to begin?

Addressing People Properly with Commands

When you give any type of command, you're addressing another person (unless you're talking to a pet). You may be talking to one person, two friends, or 20 strangers, but a command is something you direct to other people. So many other things in Arabic can be about inanimate objects or people who aren't even in the room. But, generally speaking, a command is, by definition, an utterance directed at another human. (You can, of course, direct a command to your dogs. And they can even understand simple commands. But I'll leave that for another book: *Training Your Pets with Arabic Commands For Dummies!* Or, maybe not.)

A command by definition is a request for action on the part of someone else. But you can't really *make* anyone else do something. Just like in English, asking someone to do something in Arabic can run the spectrum of barking an order to asking for things as nicely as possible. Think of the difference, for instance, between these two sentences:

Finish your homework!

Would you be so good as to finish your homework, please?

The writer of both sentences has the same intention and hoped for outcome, but the tone of each is very different.

When to use the command form

As a general rule of thumb, Arabic courtesies for commands are the same as in English. In other words, don't give a straight-out command to someone in Arabic if you wouldn't command that person in English. At the very least, don't forget to add a word for "please" if you direct a command at someone. If you're in a setting like a taxi cab, restaurant, or hotel lobby, you can use command forms with employees, but omitting "please" is needlessly rude. Here are some examples of commands you might use in such settings:

اِحْمِلْ حَقيبَتي إلى غُرْفَتي مِن فَضْلِكَ.

(**iHmil Haqiibatii 'ilaa ghurfatii, min faDlika.** *Carry my bag to my room, please.*)

مِن فَضْلِكِ أَخْبِري الطَّبّاخَ بِأَنَّ الطَّعامَ كانَ مُمتازاً.

(**min faDliki 'akhbirii aT-Tabbaakha bi'anna aT-Ta3aama kaana mumtaazan.** *Please tell the cook that the food was wonderful.*)

The preceding examples involve singular imperatives. You can generally use singular forms with a close friend or family member as well as with employees commonly understood to be in a servile position. ***Remember:*** You never have any reason to omit the courtesy of the word "please."

When to use the polite alternatives to the command form

Just as in English, formal communication requires you to ask for things in a more round about way. When you write a business letter, you ordinarily stick to a level of courtesy beyond singular commands. The way Arabic kicks formality up a notch is to use the plural command. Just as the Queen of England can say of herself, "We are not amused," using plural forms directed at a single person is seen as a polite way to ask for things. Here is an example of a plural command used for politeness:

مِن فَضْلِكُم السَّيِّد مُبارَك أَعْذِروني لِغِيابي عَن الإجْتِماعِ أَمْسِ.

(**min faDlikum, as-sayyid mubaarak, 'a3dhiruuni 3an ghiyaabi 3an al-'ijtimaa3i 'amsi.** *Please, Mr. Mubarak, forgive me for my absence from the meeting yesterday.*)

Creating Commands of Regular Verbs

You write or speak commands with the intention of getting someone to do something. It makes sense that a language would use the simplest and most concise form of a verb to do that. Think about English for a moment. You change vowels and add suffixes to the verb *to tell* depending on the tense. Someone *tells* a story. Yesterday he *told* a story. Right now she's *telling* a story. But if you need to use the verb as a command, you use the most basic form available, and say "*Tell* me something." Arabic is much the same. In this section, I show you how to strip the present tense of the verb down to its most basic form, the command.

Producing Form 1 regular verb commands

Form I verbs are the most common type in the Arabic language. (I cover the ten forms of the Arabic verb in Chapter 9.) I start with Form I verbs because they're the most likely form you'll face when writing and reading in Arabic. (You use a different final step to produce the commands for Forms II through X.) If you know how to form the present tense, forming the command won't be difficult for you. If you're rusty on the present tense, review it in Chapter 2.

A command is something you say to another person. And when you talk to another person, you use the second person present tense forms. Depending on whether you're talking to one male, one female, or a mixed group of people, you use one of the four second person present tense forms of the verb. So there are four command forms, corresponding to the four second person present tense verbs. You shorten the second person present tense form of the verb to arrive at the command forms by following these steps:

1. **Remove any suffix that follows a long vowel.**

2. **Shorten one more form, the second person masculine singular, by removing the final vowel, the ´ (Damma), and replacing it with the ˚ (sukuun), which indicates that it has no vowel at all.**

3. **Add an أَلِف ('alif) after the واو (waaw) of the masculine plural form.**

   Arabic always adds an **'alif** after the long *u* sound of a plural verb; it has no pronunciation value.

4. **Remove the present-tense prefix from all four second person present tense verb forms.**

5. **Identify the vowel after the second consonant of your verb and follow these instructions:**

- If the vowel is an *a* (written with ´ [**fatHa**]), add a short *i* vowel (written with an **'alif** and a ˛ [**kasra**]) at the beginning of the word.

- If the vowel is an *i* (written with **kasra**), add a short *i* vowel (written with an **'alif** and a **kasra**) at the beginning of the word.

- If the vowel is a *u* (written with a **Damma**), add a short *u* vowel at the beginning of the word (written with an **'alif** and a **Damma**).

When you follow these five steps for the Form I verb ذَهَبَ (**dhahaba**; *to go*), you produce the commands in Table 11-1.

Table 11-1	Imperative of ذَهَبَ (dhahaba; *to go*), a Form I Verb
Present Tense	**Imperative**
تَذْهَبُ ('anta tadh-habu; *You go*)	اِذْهَبْ (idh-hab; *Go!*)
تَذْهَبِينَ ('anti tadh-habiina; *You go*)	اِذْهَبِي (idh-habii; *Go!*)
تَذْهَبُونَ ('antum tadh-habuuna; *You go*)	اِذْهَبوا (idh-habuu; *Go!*)
تَذْهَبْنَ ('antunna tadh-habna; *You go*)	اِذْهَبْنَ (idh-habna; *Go!*)

The verb دَخَلَ (**dakhala**; *to enter*) has a ´ (**Damma**) after the second consonant in the present tense. Follow the five steps from earlier in the chapter to produce the command forms, which you can see in Table 11-2.

Table 11-2	Imperative of دَخَلَ (dakhala; *to enter*), a Form I Verb
Present Tense	**Imperative**
تَدْخُلُ ('anta tadkhulu; *You enter*)	اُدْخُلْ (udkhul; *Enter!*)
تَدْخُلِينَ ('anti tadkhuliina; *You enter*)	اُدْخُلِي (udkhulii; *Enter!*)
تَدْخُلُونَ ('antum tadkhuluuna; *You enter*)	اُدْخُلوا (udkhuluu; *Enter!*)
تَدْخُلْنَ ('antunna tadkhulna; *You enter*)	اُدْخُلْنَ (udkhulna; *Enter!*)

Here are examples of a few sentences showing the command forms in action:

اِقْرَأْ الكِتابَ.

(**iqra' al-kitaaba.** *Read the book.*)

اُكْتُبْنَ أَسْماءَكُنَّ.

(**uktubna asmaa'akunna.** *Write your names.*)

This exercise lets you apply the five steps of command production that I explain earlier. For each item, I give you a second person present tense verb for Form I. Your job is to turn each one into the command form that matches the gender and number of the present tense verb you start with.

Q. تَعْمَلُ (**ta3malu;** *You work*)

A. اِعْمَلْ (**i3mal!** *Work!*)

1. تَجْلِسونَ (**tajlisuuna;** *You sit*) _____

2. تَفْعَلينَ (**taf3aliina;** *You do*) _____

3. تَدْرُسُ (**tadrusu;** *You study*) _____

4. تَشْكُرُ (**tashkuru;** *You thank*) _____

5. تَلْعَبْنَ (**tal3abna;** *You play*) _____

6. تَسْكُتُ (**taskutu;** *You're silent*) _____

7. تَكْتُبونَ (**taktubuuna;** *You write*) _____

8. تَضْرِبينَ (**taDribiina;** *You type*) _____

9. تَسْمَحُ (**tasmaHu;** *You permit*) _____

10. تَسْمَعونَ (**tasma3uuna;** *You hear*) _____

Producing regular verb commands for Forms II, III, V, and VI

To produce the commands of Forms II, III, V, and VI, you use some of the same steps you use to produce commands of Form I verbs (see the previous section). The difference is that you can stop after Step 4 with these verbs because the first consonant has a vowel. The fifth step is necessary only when Steps 2 through 4 leave an initial consonant without a vowel.

Here are the steps you take to produce commands for Forms II, III, V, and VI:

1. **Starting from the end of the verb, remove any suffix that follows a long vowel.**

2. **Shorten up one more form, the second person masculine singular, by removing the final vowel, the ُ (Damma), and replacing it with the ْ (sukuun), which indicates that it now has no vowel at all.**

3. **Add an** أَلِف **('alif) after the** واو **(waaw) of the masculine plural form.**

   Arabic always adds an **'alif** after the long *u* sound of a plural verb; it has no pronunciation value.

4. **Remove the present-tense prefix from all four second person present tense verb forms.**

Table 11-3 shows the commands for the Form II verb دَرَّسَ (**darrasa;** *to teach*).

Table 11-3 Imperative of دَرَّسَ (darrasa; *to teach*), a Form II Verb

Present Tense	Imperative
تُدَرِّسُ ('anta tudarrisu; *You teach*)	دَرِّس (darris; *Teach!*)
تُدَرِّسِينَ ('anti tudarrisiina; *You teach*)	دَرِّسِي (darrisii; *Teach!*)
تُدَرِّسُونَ ('antum tudarrisuuna; *You teach*)	دَرِّسُوا (darrisuu; *Teach!*)
تُدَرِّسْنَ ('antunna tudarrisna; *You teach*)	دَرِّسْنَ (darrisna; *Teach!*)

Table 11-4 shows the commands for the Form III verb سَاعَدَ (saa3ada; *to help*).

Table 11-4 Imperative of سَاعَدَ (saa3ada; *to help*), a Form III Verb

Present Tense	Imperative
تُسَاعَدُ ('anta tusaa3idu; *You help*)	سَاعِد (saa3id; *Help!*)
تُسَاعَدِينَ ('anti tusaa3idiina; *You help*)	سَاعِدي (saa3idii; *Help!*)
تُسَاعَدونَ ('antum tusaa3iduuna; *You help*)	سَاعِدوا (saa3iduu; *Help!*)
تُسَاعَدْنَ ('antunna tusaa3adna; *You help*)	سَاعِدْنَ (saa3idna; *Help!*)

Table 11-5 shows the commands for the Form V verb تَكَلَّمَ (takallama; *to speak*).

Table 11-5 Imperative of تَكَلَّمَ (takallama; *to speak*), a Form V Verb

Present Tense	Imperative
تَتَكَلَّمُ ('anta tatakallamu; *You speak*)	تَكَلَّم (takallam; *Speak!*)
تَتَكَلَّمِينَ ('anti tatakallamiina; *You speak*)	تَكَلَّمي (takallamii; *Speak!*)
تَتَكَلَّمونَ ('antum tatakallamuuna; *You speak*)	تَكَلَّموا (takallamuu; *Speak!*)
تَتَكَلَّمْنَ ('antunna tatakallamna; *You speak*)	تَكَلَّمْنَ (takallamna; *Speak!*)

Table 11-6 shows the commands of the Form VI verb تَبَادَلَ (tabaadala; *to exchange*).

Table 11-6 Imperative of تَبَادَلَ (tabaadala; *to exchange*), a Form VI Verb

Present Tense	Imperative
تَتَبَادَلُ ('anta tatabaadalu; *You exchange*)	تَبَادَلْ (tabaadal; *Exchange!*)
تَتَبَادَلِينَ ('anti tatabaadaliina; *You exchange*)	تَبَادَلي (tabaadalii; *Exchange!*)
تَتَبَادَلونَ ('antum tatabaadaluuna; *You exchange*)	تَبَادَلوا (tabaadaluu; *Exchange!*)
تَتَبَادَلْنَ ('antunna tatabaadalna; *You exchange*)	تَبَادَلْنَ (tabaadalna; *Exchange!*)

Now I give you a chance to practice producing the commands of verbs in Forms II, III, V, and VI. Produce the command that corresponds to the second person present tense form I give you.

0. تُكَلِّفُ (**tukallifu**; *You entrust*)

A. كَلِّفْ (**kallif!** *Entrust!*)

11. تَتَحَسَّنونَ (**tataHassanuuna**; *You improve*) _____

12. تُقَرِّرُ (**tuqarriru**; *You decide*) _____

13. تَتَراسَلُ (**tataraasalu**; *You correspond*) _____

14. تُلاحِظونَ (**tulaaHiDHuuna**; *You notice*) _____

15. تُمَرِّنُ (**tumarrinu**; *You practice*) _____

Producing regular verb commands for Forms IV, VII, VIII, IX, and X

Removing the present tense prefixes from Forms IV, VII, VIII, IX, and X leaves behind a consonant without a vowel. But Arabic doesn't accept consonants without vowels at the beginnings of words. To solve the problem, you need another step to complete your command production. So to create the commands for these verbs, you have to follow the first four steps from the earlier section, "Producing Form I regular verb commands," and then add the new Step 5. Here are the steps to follow:

1. **Starting from the end of the verb, remove any suffix that follows a long vowel.**

2. **Shorten up one more form, the second person masculine singular, by removing the final vowel, the ´ (Damma), and replacing it with the ° (sukuun), which indicates that it now has no vowel at all.**

3. **Add an أَلِف ('alif) after the واو (waaw) of the masculine plural form.**

   Arabic always adds an **'alif** after the long u sound of a plural verb; it has no pronunciation value.

4. **Remove the present-tense prefix from all four second person present tense verb forms.**

5. **Add the past-tense prefix specific to each form.**

I give you an example for four of the forms in this section; see Tables 11-7, 11-8, 11-9, and 11-10.

Table 11-7 Imperative of أَكْمَلَ (akmala; *to complete*), a Form IV Verb

Present Tense	Imperative
تُكْمِلُ ('anta tukmilu; *You complete*)	أَكْمِلْ ('akmil; *Complete!*)
تُكْمِلِينَ ('anti tukmiliina; *You complete*)	أَكْمِلِينَ ('akmilii; *Complete!*)
تُكْمِلُونَ ('antum tukmiluuna; *You complete*)	أَكْمِلُوا ('akmiluu; *Complete!*)
تُكْمِلْنَ ('antunna tukmilna; *You complete*)	أَكْمِلْنَ ('akmilna; *Complete!*)

Table 11-8 Imperative of اِنْكَسَرَ (inkasara; *to break*), a Form VII Verb

Present Tense	Imperative
تَنْكَسِرُ ('anta tankasiru; *You break*)	اِنْكَسِرْ (inkasir; *Break!*)
تَنْكَسِرِينَ ('anti tankasiriina; *You break*)	اِنْكَسِرِي (inkasirii; *Break!*)
تَنْكَسِرُونَ ('antum tankasiruuna; *You break*)	اِنْكَسِرُوا (inkasiruu; *Break!*)
تَنْكَسِرْنَ ('antunna tankasirna; *You break*)	اِنْكَسِرْنَ (inkasirna; *Break!*)

Table 11-9 Imperative of اِسْتَمَعَ (istama3a; *to listen*), a Form VIII Verb

Present Tense	Imperative
تَسْتَمِعُ ('anta tastami3u; *You listen*)	اِسْتَمِعْ (istami3; *Listen!*)
تَسْتَمِعِينَ ('anti tastami3iina; *You listen*)	اِسْتَمِعِي (istami3ii; *Listen!*)
تَسْتَمِعُونَ ('antum tastami3uuna; *You listen*)	اِسْتَمِعُوا (istami3uu; *Listen!*)
تَسْتَمِعْنَ ('antunna tastami3na; *You listen*)	اِسْتَمِعْنَ (istami3na; *Listen!*)

Table 11-10 Imperative of اِسْتَعْمَلَ (ista3mala; *to use*), a Form X Verb

Present Tense	Imperative
تَسْتَعْمِلُ ('anta tasta3milu; *You use*)	اِسْتَعْمِلْ (ista3mil; *Use!*)
تَسْتَعْمِلِينَ ('anti tasta3miliina; *You use*)	اِسْتَعْمِلِي (ista3milii; *Use!*)
تَسْتَعْمِلُونَ ('antum tasta3miluuna; *You use*)	اِسْتَعْمِلُوا (ista3miluu; *Use!*)
تَسْتَعْمِلْنَ ('antunna tasta3milna; *You use*)	اِسْتَعْمِلْنَ (ista3milna; *Use!*)

Now I give you a chance to practice producing the commands of verbs in Forms IV, VII, VIII, IX, and X. Produce the command that corresponds to the second person present tense form I give you.

Q. تَسْتَعْمِلينَ (**tasta3miliina;** *You use*)

A. إِسْتَعْمِلي (**ista3milii!** *Use!*)

16. تَنْتَقِلينَ (**tantaqiliina;** *You move*) _____

17. تُعْلِنينَ (**tu3liniina;** *You announce*) _____

18. تَسْتَقْبِلونَ (**tastaqbiluuna;** *You greet*) _____

19. تُشْرِفُ (**tushrifu;** *You supervise*) _____

20. تَنْتَخِبونَ (**tantakhibuuna;** *You elect*) _____

Making Commands with Weak Verbs

Verb forms in Arabic are quite regular whenever you have three strong consonants in the root. However, whenever one of the so-called "weak" letters appears, the verb can become irregular. Commands are no different. If you aren't familiar with the ways weak letters change the verb, you can review the topic in Chapter 10.

Commanding with the initial أَلِف ('alif) and initial واو (waaw)

When you have an أَلِف ('**alif**) or a واو (**waaw**) as the first consonant, it simply drops off when you create a command for Form I verbs. Tables 11-11 and 11-12 show some examples.

Table 11-11	Imperative of أَكَلَ ('akala; *to eat*), a Form I Verb
Present Tense	***Imperative***
تَأْكُلُ ('**anta ta'kulu;** *You eat*)	كُلْ (**kul;** *Eat!*)
تَأْكُلينَ ('**anti ta'kuliina;** *You eat*)	كُلي (**kulii;** *Eat!*)
تَأْكُلونَ ('**antum ta'kuluuna;** *You eat*)	كُلوا (**kuluu;** *Eat!*)
تَأْكُلْنَ ('**antunna ta'kulna;** *You eat*)	كُلْنَ (**kulna;** *Eat!*)

Table 11-12	Imperative for وَضَعَ (waDa3a; *to put*), a Form I Verb
Present Tense	**Imperative**
تَضَعُ ('anta taDa3u; *You put*)	ضَعْ (Da3; *Put!*)
تَضَعِينَ ('anti taDa3iina; *You put*)	ضَعِي (Da3ii; *Put!*)
تَضَعُونَ ('antum taDa3uuna; *You put*)	ضَعُوا (Da3uu; *Put!*)
تَضَعْنَ ('antunna taDa3na; *You put*)	ضَعْنَ (Da3na; *Put!*)

In other verb forms, commands from initial أَلِف ('alif) and initial واو (waaw) verbs are no more irregular than the present tense from which you form them. Here are a few examples of commands from initial أَلِف ('alif) and initial واو (waaw) verbs. The third example shows you how an initial واو (waaw) Form VIII verb is regular in its production:

ضَعْ حَقيبَتي في الزاوِيةِ مِن فَضْلِكَ.

(**Da3 Haqiibatii fi-l-zaawiyati, min faDlika.** *Put my bag in the corner, please.*)

كُلوا يا أَوْلاد.

(**kuluu yaa 'awlaad.** *Eat up, children.*)

اِتَّجِهْ إِلَى الْيَسار عِنْدَ الْمُفْتَرِق.

(**ittajih 'ilaa-l-yasaari 3inda-l-muftaraqi.** *Head to the left at the corner.*)

Commanding with medial weak verbs

A *medial weak verb* is a verb with a واو (**waaw**) or a ياء (**yaa'**) as its second consonant. To produce the command of a medial weak verb, you follow the same first four steps as demonstrated in other sections of this chapter. But then you have a unique fifth step in which you reduce the long middle vowel for the masculine singular and feminine plural forms. The feminine singular and masculine plural commands are finished with just the first four steps.

If the medial vowel is written with واو (**waaw**), replace it with ُ (**Damma**). Table 11-13 shows the commands of a common verb of this type.

Table 11-13	Imperative of قالَ (qaala; *to say*), a Form I Medial Weak Verb
Present Tense	**Imperative**
تَقولُ ('anta taquulu; *You say*)	قُلْ (qul; *Say!*)
تَقولِينَ ('anti taquuliina; *You say*)	قولي (quulii; *Say!*)
تَقولونَ ('antum taquuluuna; *You say*)	قولوا (quuluu; *Say!*)
تَقُلْنَ ('antunna taqulna; *You say*)	قُلْنَ (qulna; *Say!*)

If the medial vowel is written with يَاء (**yaa'**), replace it with ِ (**kasra**). Table 11-14 shows examples of commands for a verb with a medial يَاء (**yaa'**).

Table 11-14   Imperative of بَاعَ (baa3a; *to sell*), a Form I Medial Weak Verb

Present Tense	Imperative
تَبِيعُ (’anta tabii3u; *You sell*)	بِعْ (bi3; *Sell!*)
تَبِيعِينَ (’anti tabii3iina; *You sell*)	بِيعِي (bii3ii; *Sell!*)
تَبِيعُونَ (’antum tabii3uuna; *You sell*)	بِيعُوا (bii3uu; *Sell!*)
تَبِعْنَ (’antunna tabi3na; *You sell*)	بِعْنَ (bi3na; *Sell!*)

If the medial vowel is written with أَلِف ('alif), put ◌َ (fatHa) in its place for the masculine singular and feminine plural command forms. Table 11-15 shows commands for this type of verb.

**Table 11-15   Imperative of خَافَ (khaafa; *to be afraid*),
a Form I Medial Weak Verb**

Present Tense	Imperative
تَخَافُ (’anta takhaafu; *You are afraid*)	خَفْ (khaf; *Be afraid!*)
تَخَافِينَ (’anti takhaafiina; *You are afraid*)	خَافِي (khaafii; *Be afraid!*)
تَخَافُونَ (’antum takhaafuuna; *You are afraid*)	خَافُوا (khaafuu; *Be afraid!*)
تَخَفْنَ (’antunna takhafna; *You are afraid*)	خَفْنَ (khafna; *Be afraid!*)

The same reductions in vowel length that take place in Form I also occur in Forms II–X. Table 11-16 shows an example of a Form IV verb command from a medial weak verb.

**Table 11-16   Imperative of أَجَابَ ('ajaaba; *to reply*),
a Form IV Medial Weak Verb**

Present Tense	Imperative
تُجِيبُ (’anta tujiibu; *You reply*)	أَجِبْ (’ajib; *Reply!*)
تُجِيبِينَ (’anti tujiibiina; *You reply*)	أَجِيبِي (’ajiibii; *Reply!*)
تُجِيبُونَ (’antum tujiibuuna; *You reply*)	أَجِيبُوا (’ajiibuu; *Reply!*)
تُجِبْنَ (’antunna tujibna; *You reply*)	أَجِبْنَ (’ajibna; *Reply!*)

Commanding with the final واو (waaw) and ياء (yaa')

Verbs with a final واو (**waaw**) or final ياء (**yaa'**) form their command forms with the same first four steps as every other verb with only one exception: The final long vowel of the masculine singular reduces to a short vowel.

If the final vowel is written with ياء (**yaa'**), it reduces to ِ (**kasra**). Table 11-17 shows commands for this type of verb.

Table 11-17	**Imperative of بَكَى (bakaa; *to cry*), a Form I Final Weak Verb**
Present Tense	**Imperative**
تَبْكي ('anta tabkii; *You cry*)	اِبْكِ (ibki; *Cry!*)
تَبْكينَ ('anti tabkiina; *You cry*)	اِبْكي (ibkii; *Cry!*)
تَبْكونَ ('antum tabkuuna; *You cry*)	اِبْكوا (ibkuu; *Cry!*)
تَبْكينَ ('antunna tabkiina; *You cry*)	اِبْكينَ (ibkiina; *Cry!*)

If the final vowel is written with واو (**waaw**), it reduces to ُ (**Damma**). Table 11-18 gives you the commands for this type of verb.

Table 11-18	**Imperative of دَعا (da3aa; *to call*), a Form I Final Weak Verb**
Present Tense	**Imperative**
تَدْعو ('anta tad3uu; *You call*)	اُدْعُ (ud3u; *Call!*)
تَدْعينَ ('anti tad3iina; *You call*)	اُدْعي (ud3ii; *Call!*)
تَدْعونَ ('antum tad3uuna; *You call*)	اُدْعوا (ud3uu; *Call!*)
تَدْعونَ ('antunna tad3uuna; *You call*)	اُدْعونَ (ud3uuna; *Call!*)

If the final vowel is written with أَلِف مَكْسورة ('**alif maksuura**), it reduces to َ (**fatHa**). In Table 11-19, I show you the commands of a verb of this type.

Table 11-19	Imperative of تَحَدّى (taHadda; *to provoke*), a Form V Final Weak Verb	
Present Tense		**Imperative**
تَتَحَدّى (’anta tataHaddaa; *You provoke*)		تَحَدَّ (taHadda; *Provoke!*)
تَتَحَدّيْنَ (’anti taHaddayna; *You provoke*)		تَحَدّي (taHaddii; *Provoke!*)
تَتَحَدّوْنَ (’antum tahaddawna; *You provoke*)		تَحَدّوا (tahaddaw; *Provoke!*)
تَتَحَدّيْنَ (’antunna tatahaddayna; *You provoke*)		تَحَدّيْنَ (taHaddayna; *Provoke!*)

Your doctor is giving you a prescription to help you get over a cold, and she also wants you to be in better shape. Use everything I cover in this chapter to fill in the blanks with the proper command prompted by the present tense verb on the first line. The answer key shows you both the masculine and feminine singular answers for these prescription points.

John Doe, M.D.
Physician • St. Mary's Clinic

Rx

21. تَشْرَبُ (tasrabu; *You drink.*)
   (_____ كَثيراً مِنَ الماء kathiiran mina-l-maa’)

22. تَأْخُذُ (ta’khudhu; *You take.*)
   حَبَّتَيْن مِنَ الأَسْبِرِين _____) Habbatayni mina-l-’asbiriina)

23. تَتَجَنّبُ (tatajannabu; *You avoid.*)
   (_____ الحَلَوَيات al-Halawayaati)

24. تَنامُ (tanaamu; *You sleep.*)
   ٨ ساعاتٍ كُلَّ لَيْلةٍ _____) 8 saa3aatin kulla laylatin)

25. تُمَرّنُ (tumarrinu; *You exercise.*)
   ٣ مَرّات كُلَّ أُسْبوع _____) 3 marraat kulla ’usbuu3in)

_____
Signature

Answer Key

1 اِجْلِسـوا (**ijlisuu!** *Sit!*)

2 اِفْعَـلي (**if3alii!** *Do!*)

3 أُدْرُسْ (**udrus!** *Study!*)

4 أُشْكُرْ (**ushkur!** *Thank!*)

5 اِلْعَبْنَ (**il3abna!** *Play!*)

6 أُسْكُتْ (**uskut!** *Be quiet!*)

7 اُكْتُبُوا (**uktubuu!** *Write!*)

8 اِضْرِبي (**iDribii!** *Type!*)

9 اِسْمَحْ (**ismaH!** *Permit!*)

10 اِسْمَعوا (**isma3uu!** *Hear!*)

11 تَحَسَّنـوا (**taHassanuu!** *Improve!*)

12 قَرِّرْ (**qarrir!** *Decide!*)

13 تَراسَـلْ (**taraasal!** *Correspond!*)

14 لاحِظـوا (**laaHiDHuu!** *Notice!*)

15 مَرِّنْ (**marrin!** *Practice!*)

16 اِنْتَقِـلي (**intaqilii!** *Move!*)

17 أَعْلِـني (**'a3linii!** *Announce!*)

18 اِسْتَقْبِـلوا (**istaqbiluu!** *Greet!*)

19 أَشْرِفْ (**'ashrif!** *Supervise!*)

20 اِنْتَخِبوا (**intakhibuu!** *Elect!*)

John Doe, M.D.
Physician • St. Mary's Clinic

R𝑥

21. إِشْرَبْ (**ishrab.** *Drink lots of water.*) / إِشْرَبي (**ishrabii.** *Drink lots of water.*)

22. خُذْ (**khudh.** *Take two aspirin.*) / خُذي (**khudhii.** *Take two aspirin.*)

23. تَجَنَّبْ (**tajannab.** *Avoid sweets.*) / تَجَنَّبي (**tajannabii.** *Avoid sweets.*)

24. نَمْ (**nam.** *Sleep 8 hours every night.*) / نَامي (**naamii.** *Sleep 8 hours every night.*)

25. مَرِّنْ (**marrin.** *Exercise 3 times every week.*) / مَرِّني (**marrinii.** *Exercise 3 times every week.*)

_____
Signature

Chapter 12

Writing to the Point with Object Suffixes and Pronouns

. . . .

In This Chapter

▶ Changing nouns with possessive suffixes

▶ Forming object suffixes on verbs

▶ Adding suffixes to prepositions

. . . .

"**H**ow can you correct this sentence to make this sentence more concise?" That's easy! Just don't repeat the words "this sentence!" After you've referred to something once, you can usually replace it with a pronoun in the second reference. For example, you may write something like this: "How can you correct this sentence to make *it* more concise?"

You use pronouns so often in your speaking and writing that you probably don't even think about them. Like so many things in a language, the most common things can frequently be the most irregular. For instance, consider the fact that English preserves different forms of pronouns depending on whether the pronoun is a subject or an object. And so, you write "*He* celebrates *his* birthday with *me*," but then "*I* saw *him* at the party."

 Like English, Arabic also has different forms of pronouns depending on whether the pronoun is the subject or the object of the verb. In Arabic, however, only the subject pronouns will be separate words. Every other type of pronoun will be a suffix on a verb or preposition. In this chapter, you discover everything you need to tighten your writing by effortlessly adding object pronouns to verbs and prepositions.

Forms of the Object Suffix

Object suffixes that are added to a verb are almost identical to the possessive pronoun suffixes. If you're rusty on the possessive pronoun suffixes, you may want to study them before working through this chapter. I discuss them in Chapter 2.

I show you the minor difference between object suffixes and possessive pronoun suffixes before letting you see all the forms together. Then I show you just a few minor tweaks to the system that you'll encounter before you can declare yourself an expert on the object suffixes.

Note: Because the focus of this chapter is the object suffixes, I will not use all of the formal final endings on the nouns and verbs.

Using nii instead of ii

The object suffixes themselves depart from the possessive pronoun suffixes in only one place: the first person singular. When you put the possessive pronoun for *my* on a noun in Arabic, the ending is ي (**ii**). But when you want to describe in Arabic how someone saw *me*, the ending you put on the verb is نـي (**nii**). Here's an example of this suffix in use. I underline the ending so you can locate it easily:

أَخْبَرَنِي عَن البِنَاية الَّتِي يَعْمَلُ فيهَا.

(**'akhbaranii 3an al-binaaya allatii ya3amlu fiihaa.** *He told me about the building in which he works.*)

Table 12-1 shows a run-through of the object suffixes using the third person past tense verb, زَارَ (**zaara**; *he visited*), as an example.

Table 12-1	Object Suffixes	
English Object Pronoun	*Object Suffix*	*Example*
me	نِي (-nii)	زَارَنِي (zaaranii; *he visited me*)
you (MS)	كَ (-ka)	زَارَكَ (zaaraka; *he visited you*)
you (FS)	كِ (-ki)	زَارَكِ (zaaraki; *he visited you*)
him	ـهُ (-hu)	زَارَهُ (zaarahu; *he visited him*)
her	ها (-haa)	زَارَها (zaarahaa; *he visited her*)
us	نا (-naa)	زَارَنا (zaaranaa; *he visited us*)
you (MP)	كُم (-kum)	زَارَكُم (zaarakum; *he visited you*)
you (FP)	كُنَّ (-kunna)	زَارَكُنَّ (zaarakunna; *he visited you*)
them (MP)	هُم (-hum)	زَارَهُم (zaarahum; *he visited them*)
them (FP)	هُنَّ (-hunna)	زَارَهُنَّ (zaarahunna; *he visited them*)

Replacing the ´ (Damma) with a ِ (kasra)

You need to make one minor adjustment in the vowel of a few of the object suffixes. Arabic doesn't like having a *u* vowel (written with the ´ [**Damma**]) after the *i* vowel, or ِ (**kasra**). So it changes the *u* to another *i*. (Linguists call this *euphony*, meaning, it sounds nicer.) So where you might have expected رَأَيْتِهُ (**ra'aytihu**; *you saw him*), you instead get رَأَيْتِهِ (**ra'aytihi**). Three conditions cause this euphonic change to happen. You will see it after:

✔ a short *i* (written with ِ [**kasra**])

✔ a long *i* (written with ياء [**yaa'**])

✔ a closed syllable ending in *y* (written with a ياء [**yaa'**] and a ْ [**sukuun**])

Here are two examples:

هَل تَرَكْتِهِم في السَّيّارة؟

(**hal tarakt*ihim* fii-s-sayyara?** *Did you leave them in the car?*)

رَأَيْتِهِ هُناكَ ٱلَيْسَ كَذلِكَ؟

(**ra'ayt*ihi* hunaka, 'alaysa kadhaalika?** *You saw him there, isn't that so?*)

Looking at the disappearing ألِف ('alif)

The change I explain in this section is only a matter of spelling. You ordinarily write an extra ألِف ('**alif**) after the third person masculine plural in the past tense:

أَكَلوا الطَّعامَ. ('**akal*uu* aT-Ta3aama.** *They ate the food.*)

When you add an object suffix, however, you just remove that extra ألِف ('**alif**) and add your object suffix:

أَكَلوهُ. ('**akal*uuhu*.** *They ate it.*)

Here are a few more examples:

كَتَبوا رَسائِلَهُم ثُمَّ أَرْسَلوها لأَصْدِقائِهِم.

(**katabuu rasaa'ilahum thumma 'arsal*uuhaa* li-'aSdiqaaiihim.** *They wrote their letters and then sent them to their friends.*)

البَيْت جَديد لِكِن باعوهُ عَلى كُلِّ حال.

(**al-bayt jadiid, laakin baa3*uuhu* 3alaa kulli Haal.** *The house is new, but they sold it anyway.*)

Changing tum to tumuu

The change I explain in this section is a little more involved than the magical disappearing ألِف ('**alif**) trick. When you write the second person masculine plural ending, you use the ending **tum**. Here's an example:

أَكَلْتُم الطَّعامَ. ('**akal*tum* aT-Ta3aama.** *You ate the food.*)

When you add an object suffix to a verb with the second person masculine plural ending, however, you change the verb ending to **tumuu**, as in this example:

أَكَلْتُموهُ. ('**akal*tumuuhu*.** *You ate it.*)

Here are two more examples to demonstrate the different ending:

أَرْسَلْتُ الطَّرْد مُنْذُ أُسْبوع. آرَأَيْتُموهُ بَعْد؟

(**'arsaltu aT-Tard mundhu usbuu3. 'ara'aytumuuhu ba3d?** *I sent the package a week ago. Have you seen <u>it</u> yet?*)

أَعْجَبَتْني تِلْكَ المَقالة. هَل قَرَأْتُموها أَيْضاً؟

(**'a3jabatni tilka-l-maqaala. hal qara'tumuuhaa 'ayDaN?** *I loved that article. Have you also read <u>it</u>?*)

Now it's your turn to have fun with object suffixes. In the following exercise, I give you a verb and a pronoun. Take the verb and add to it the object suffix that corresponds to the pronoun next to it.

Q. أَشْرَبُ (**'ashrabu**; *I drink*) / هُوَ (**huwa**; *it*)

A. أَشْرَبُهُ (**'ashrabuhu**; *I drink it*)

1. رَأَتْ (**ra'at**; *she saw*) / نَحْنُ (**naHnu**; *we*)

_____

2. أَخْبَروا (**'akhbaruu**; *they told*) / أَنا (**'anaa**; *I*)

_____

3. أَرْسَلْتِ (**'arsalti**; *you sent*) / هُم (**hum**; *they*)

_____

4. رافَقْتُ (**raafaqtu**; *I accompanied*) / هِيَ (**hiya**; *she*)

_____

5. تَرَكْنا (**taraknaa**; *we left*) / أَنْتُم (**'antum**; *you*)

_____

6. سَمِعْتُم (**sami3tum**; *you heard*) / هُوَ (**huwa**; *he*)

_____

7. كَلَّم (**kallama**; *he spoke with*) / أَنا (**'anaa**; *I*)

_____

8. تُحِبُّ (**tuHibbu**; *she loves*) / أَنْتَ (**'anta**; *you*)

_____

9. نُكَلِّفُ (**nukallifu**; *we entrust*) / أَنْتِ (**'anti**; *you*)

_____

10. تُؤْمِنُ (**tu'minu**; *you believe*) / هُم (**hum**; *they*)

_____

Important verbs using object suffixes

After you're comfortable with putting the object suffixes on verbs, you're ready to use some important Arabic idiomatic verbs that require object suffixes. I show you two of the most common and useful verbs in this category. The proper use of these verbs will distinguish your Arabic use.

The Arabic verb أَعْجَبَ (**'a3jaba**; *to please*) functions exactly the same as Spanish **gustar.** The thing liked will actually be the subject of the verb and the thing that likes it will be the direct object, expressed as an object suffix. In your basic Arabic studies, you may have learned to say you like something using أُحِبُّ (**'uHibbu**; *I like/love*). This usage isn't wrong, but it isn't as formal and proper as أَعْجَبَ (**'a3jaba**). (This verb is a Form IV verb, which you can review in Chapter 9.) Here are two examples that use this verb:

يُعْجِبُني المَطْعَم.

(**yu3jibunii al-maT3am.** *I like the restaurant.* [literally, *The restaurant pleases me.*])

أَعْجَبَتْنا السَّيّارة.

(**'a3jabatnaa as-sayyaara.** *We liked the car.* [literally, *The car pleased us.*])

Another important idiomatic verb to include in your Arabic vocabulary is وَصَلَ (**waSala**; *to arrive*). This verb is a Form I verb but it's irregular because it has a واو (**waaw**) as the first consonant of its root (you can refresh your memory on irregular verbs in Chapter 10). An idiomatic usage of وَصَلَ (**waSala**) requires you to use object suffixes. When you get something in the mail, the preferable idiom in Arabic is to say, *The letter arrived [to] me.* Here's the Arabic equivalent:

وَصَلَتْني الرِّسالة.

(**waSalatnii ar-risaala.** *I received the letter.*)

 Whenever a language behaves differently than our native language, it's difficult to break out of our normal mode of thinking. Resist the natural temptation to make yourself the grammatical subject when you remark that you like something or got something in the mail. Instead, think backwards from how English works. For example, avoid thinking *I like* or *I receive.* Instead, write *pleases me* and *arrived me.* If you use the verbs in this section correctly, these idioms will distinguish you as having a good command of Modern Standard Arabic.

Your Arabic teacher knows how important it is for you to master the idioms covered in this section. So, she's giving you a pop quiz in which you have to form several sentences with each verb. For each question, you get a noun, a verb, and a pronoun. The noun is the grammatical subject and the pronoun is the object. Create the indicated Arabic sentence for both the past and present tenses.

0. الفول (al-fuul) / أَعْجَبَ ('a3jaba) / هُم (hum)

A. أَعْجَبَهُم الفول. ('a3jabahum al-fuul. *They liked beans.*) / يُعْجِبُهُم الفول. (yu3jibuhum al-fuul. *They like beans.*)

11. صَديقَتي (Sadiiqii) / أَعْجَبَ ('a3jaba) / أنا ('anaa)

_____

12. الكِتاب (al-kitaab) / أَعْجَبَ ('a3jaba) / هُوَ (huwa)

_____

13. الدَّرّاجة (ad-darraaja) / أَعْجَبَ ('a3jaba) / هِيَ (hiya)

_____

14. البِناية (al-binaaya) / أَعْجَبَ ('a3jaba) / أَنْتُم ('antum)

_____

15. القَلَم (al-qalam) / أَعْجَبَ ('a3jaba) / أنْتِ ('anti)

_____

16. الطَّعام (aT-Ta3aam) / أَعْجَبَ ('a3jaba) / هُم (hum)

_____

17. رسالَتي (risaalatii) / وَصَلَ (waSala) / أَنْتُم ('antum)

_____

18. طَرْدُنا (Tardunaa) / وَصَلَ (waSala) / هِيَ (hiya)

_____

19. المَجَلّة (al-majalla) / وَصَلَ (waSala) / هُوَ (huwa)

_____

20. الرَّسائل (ar-rasaa'il) / وَصَلَ (waSala) / أنا ('anaa)

_____

21. البَرْقِيّة (al-barqiyya) / وَصَلَ (waSala) / أَنْتَ (’anta)

_____

22. البِطاقة (al-baTaaqa) / وَصَلَ (waSala) / نَحْنُ (naHnu)

_____

Connecting Prepositions with Object Pronouns

You use pronouns with prepositions because you can write more concisely with them. The rule we follow in English is to use the same form of the pronoun after prepositions as we would use for direct objects. For example, you may say, _I met my friend in the park and went <u>with him</u> to dinner._

While English uses object pronouns after prepositions, Arabic puts the possessive pronouns on prepositions as a suffix.

In this section, you explore the two types of prepositions in Arabic and see how the possessive pronoun suffixes team up with them.

Indeclinable prepositions

The type of preposition that's most common and easiest to learn in Arabic is called the _indeclinable preposition._ Characteristics of indeclinable prepositions include at least one of the following:

- They're spelled with only one or two letters.
- They end in a long vowel.

Besides taking possessive pronoun suffixes, indeclinable prepositions can be used with nouns. I introduce you to a couple of indeclinable prepositions, underlining them for you to help you spot them:

خَرَجْتُ مِنَ البَيْت وَمَشَيْتُ إلى الحَديقة.

(**kharajtu <u>mina</u>-l-bayt wa-mashaytu <u>’ilaa</u> al-Hadiiqa.** _I went out <u>from</u> the house and walked <u>to</u> the park._)

رَأَتْ صَديقَتَها في السَّيّارة.

(**ra’at Sadiiqatahaa <u>fii</u>-s-sayyaara.** _She saw her friend <u>in</u> the car._)

The possessive suffixes are added to the prepositions with just a few irregularities. Here are some guidelines to keep in mind:

- Before the suffix ي (**ii;** *me, my*), indeclinable prepositions ending in ن (**nuun**) double that **nun.** For example, مِن (**min;** *from*) becomes مِنّي (**minni;** *from me*).

- Instead of ي (**ii;** *me, my*), you add يَ (**-ya;** *me, my*) to prepositions ending in a long vowel. You write the يَ (**-ya**) with a ّ (**shadda**) whenever the final vowel is a long *i* (written with ياء [**yaa'**]). Here are two examples: فيَّ (**fiiyya;** *in me*) and إلَيَّ ('**ilayya;** *to me*).

Table 12-2 shows the suffixes of the indeclinable preposition بِ (**bi-;** *with*). Note that the vowel of the forms هُ (**hu**) and هُم (**hum**) changes to *i* to match the vowel of the preposition.

Table 12-2	Indeclinable Prepositions
Suffix	**Preposition + Suffix**
ي (-ii)	بي (**bii;** *with me*)
كَ (-ka)	بِكَ (**bika;** *with you*)
كِ (-ki)	بِكِ (**biki;** *with you*)
هُ (-hu) / ه (-hi)	بِه (**bihi;** *with him*)
ها (-haa)	بِها (**bihaa;** *with her*)
نا (-naa)	بِنا (**binaa;** *with us*)
كُم (-kum)	بِكُم (**bikum;** *with you*)
هُم (-hum) / هِم (-him)	بِهِم (**bihim;** *with them*)

Here are some other indeclinable prepositions:

- سِوى (**siwaa;** *other than*)
- كَ (**ka-;** *like*)
- عَن (**3an;** *about*)
- حَتّى (**Hatta;** *until*)
- مَعَ (**ma3a;** *with*)
- إلى ('**ilaa;** *to*)

A final ألِف مَكسورة ('**alif maksuura**) is hiding a final ياء (**yaa'**) that existed in the distant past. When you put any type of suffix on a word with final ألِف مَكسورة ('**alif maksuura**), the ياء (**yaa'**) reappears. (This is similar to how you pronounce the usually silent final *s* in French words when a vowel immediately follows.)

Understanding suffixes on prepositions with a final ('alif maksuura) أَلِف مَكْسُورَة

REMEMBER

When a preposition ends in أَلِف مَكْسُورَة ('**alif maksuura**), the يَاء (**yaa'**) becomes a final consonant, onto which you then put your possessive pronoun suffixes. Table 12-3 shows an example of when this happens with the preposition عَلى (**3alaa**; *on/onto*). Note the use of the suffix يَ (**ya**) in place of ي (**ii**), as well as و (**hi**) for ه (**hu**) and هِم (**him**) for هُم (**hum**) in response to the final يَاء (**yaa'**).

Table 12-3	Adding Suffixes on a Preposition with a Final أَلِف مَكْسُورَة ('alif maksuura)
Suffix	**Preposition + Suffix**
ي (-ii) / يَ (-ya)	عَلَيَّ (3alayya; *on me*)
كَ (-ka)	عَلَيْكَ (3alayka; *on you*)
كِ (-ki)	عَلَيْكِ (3alayki; *on you*)
ه (-hu) / و (-hi)	عَلَيْهِ (3alayhi; *on him*)
ها (-haa)	عَلَيْها (3alayhaa; *on her*)
نا (-naa)	عَلَيْنا (3alaynaa; *on us*)
كُم (-kum)	عَلَيْكُم (3alaykum; *on you*)
هِم (-him) / هُم (-hum)	عَلَيْهِم (3alayhim; *on them*)

Dealing with the preposition لِ (li-; to)

The preposition لِ (**li-**; *to*) picks up the vowel ﹷ (**fatHa**) when you add suffixes that begin in consonants. Table 12-4 shows what the preposition looks like after you add the ﹷ (**fatHa**).

Table 12-4	Adding Suffixes to the Preposition لِ (li-; to)
Suffix	**Preposition + the fatHa**
ي (-ii)	لِي (lii; *to me*)
كَ (-ka)	لَكَ (laka; *to you, MS*)
كِ (-ki)	لَكِ (laki; *to you, FS*)
ه (-hu)	لَهُ (lahu; *to him*)
ها (-haa)	لَها (lahaa; *to her*)
نا (-naa)	لَنا (lanaa; *to us*)
كُم (-kum)	لَكُم (lakum; *to you, MP*)
هُم (-hum)	لَهُم (lahum; *to them, MP*)

Declinable prepositions

Think for a moment about the English preposition *beside*. You may have noticed that this preposition is related to the noun *side*. The English language also has *inside* and *outside*. These prepositions began their careers as nouns. Similarly, Arabic has several nouns that function as quasi-prepositions. They're called *declinable prepositions*. They're called this because they "decline," that is to say they take the genitive case just like nouns if you put another preposition in front of them. (You can encounter the genitive case in more detail in Chapter 4.)

Here are two examples of the declinable preposition قُرْبَ (**qurba**; *near*) used by itself:

وَجَدوهُ قُرْبَ البَيْت.

(**wajaduuhu qurba-l-bayti.** *They found him near the house.*)

لاحَظَتْهُ قُرْبَه.

(**laaHaDHathu qurbahu.** *She noticed him near it.*)

The thing that makes the declinable prepositions different from the indeclinable types is that they can take prepositions themselves. Like all words following prepositions, the declinable prepositions take on the final *i* vowel of the genitive case.

In the following two examples, I put the preposition **bi-** on the declinable preposition قُرْب (**qurba**). Notice that the meaning doesn't change at all. The only thing that changes about the declinable preposition itself is that the final vowel changes from *a* to *i* because it takes on the genitive case after the prepositional prefix.

وَجَدوهُ يقُرْب البَيْت.

(**wajaduuhu bi-qurbi-l-bayt.** *They found him near the house.*)

لاحَظَتْهُ يقُرْبِه.

(**laaHaDHathu bi-qurbihi.** *She noticed him near it.*)

Here are some other declinable prepositions. Notice that one feature of the declinable prepositions is that all of them end in *a* when they stand by themselves:

- ✔ مِثْلَ (**mithla**; *like*)
- ✔ بَيْنَ (**bayna**; *between*)
- ✔ قُرْبَ (**qurba**; *near*)
- ✔ أَمامَ (**'amaama**; *in front of*)
- ✔ بَعْدَ (**ba3da**; *after*)

- ✔ قَبْلَ (**qabla**; *before*)
- ✔ وَراءَ (**waraa'a**; *behind*)
- ✔ خِلالَ (**khilaala**; *during*)
- ✔ عِنْدَ (**3inda**; *at*)
- ✔ دون (**duuna**; *without*)

In this exercise, you're writing an e-mail to your friend Ahmad that requires you to use several prepositions with object pronouns. The context of each sentence tells you which preposition in your word bank is the best choice as well as what object pronoun to add. To determine what the best preposition is, you may have to consult your dictionary to see what prepositions are used with the verbs in this e-mail. You have a variety of declinable and indeclinable prepositions to choose from, but each one makes the best sense in only one spot.

لَكَ ~~(laka)~~   مِن (min)   أمامَ ('amaam)   إلى ('ilaa)   ب (bi-)

على (3alaa)   بِدون (bi-duuni)   مَعَ (ma3a)   في (fii)

0. يا صَديقي! أَنا قُلْتُ ـــــ الحَقّ.

(yaa Sadiiqii! 'anaa qultu _____ al-Haqq)

A. يا صَديقي! أَنا قُلْتُ لَكَ الحَقّ.

(yaa Sadiiqii! 'anaa qultu <u>laka</u> al-Haqq. *My friend! I told <u>you</u> the truth.*)

New Message

Send | Cut | Copy | Paste | Undo | abc✔ Check

أَهْلاً يا صَديقي أَحْمَد

('ahlan yaa Sadiiqii 'aHmad)

23. _____ يَجِبُ أَنْ أَشْتَرِيَ دَفْتَراً جَديداً. رُبَّما تُريد الذَّهاب

(yajibu 'an 'ashtarii daftaran jadiidan. rubbamaa turiid adh-dhahaab _____)

24. _____ أَمّا أَنا فَلا أُريد الذَّهاب

('amma 'anaa fa-laa 'uriid adh-dhahaab _____)

25. لكن لا تَعْرِف عُنْوانِي الجَديد. وَأَنْتَ بِحاجة _____ إذا أَرَدْتَ أَنْ تَجِد بَيْتي.

(laakin laa ta3rif 3unwaanii al-jadiid. wa-'anta bi-Haaja _____

'idha 'aradta 'an tajid baytii.)

26. _____ أَرْسِلُ لي رَقَم الهاتِف وَسَأَتَّصِل

('arsil lii raqam al-haatif wa-sa'attaSil_____)

27. _____ سَمِعْتُ عَن مُشْكِلَتِكَ وَكُنْتُ أُفَكِّر

(sami3tu 3an muskilatika wa-kuntu 'ufakkir _____)

28. _____ كُلّ التَفاصيل . أُريدُ أَنْ أَتَعَلَّمَ

('uriid 'an 'ata3allam _____ kull at-tafaaSiil.)

29. _____ وَنَسْتَطيعُ أَنْ نَجِد حَلّاً عَن المَوْضوع

(wa-nastaTii3u 'an najid Hallan 3an al-mawDuu3 _____)

30. _____ أَمّا زَوْجَتَكَ فَسَلِّمُ لي

('ammaa zawjatuka fa-sallim lii _____)

إلى اللِّقاء

ilaa-l-liqaa'
[Sign your own name in Arabic]

_____

Answer Key

1 رَأَتْنا (ra'atnaa; *She saw us*)

2 أَخْبَروني ('akhbaruunii; *They told me*)

3 أَرْسَلْتِهِم ('arsaltihim; *You sent them*)

4 رافَقْتُها (raafaqtuhaa; *I accompanied her*)

5 تَرَكْناكُم (taraknaakum; *We left you*)

6 سَمِعْتُموهُ (sami3tumuuhu; *You heard him*)

7 كَلَّمَني (kallamanii; *He spoke with me*)

8 تُحِبُّكَ (tuHibbuka; *She loves you*)

9 نُكَلِّفُكِ (nukallifuki; *We entrust you*)

10 تُؤْمِنُهُم (tu'minuhum; *You believe them*)

11 تُعْجِبُني صَديقَتي. / أَعْجَبَتْني صَديقَتي. ('a3jabatnii Sadiiqatii. *I liked my friend.*) / (tu3jibunii Sadiiqatii. *I like my friend.*)

12 أَعْجَبَهُ الكِتاب. / يُعْجِبُهُ الكِتاب. ('a3jabahu al-kitaab. *He liked the book.*) / (yu3jibuhu al-kitaab. *He likes the book.*)

13 أَعْجَبَتْها الدَّرّاجة. / تُعْجِبُها الدَّرّاجة. ('a3jabathaa ad-darraaja. *She liked the bicycle.*) / (tu3jibu-haa ad-darraaja. *She likes the bicycle.*)

14 أَعْجَبَتْكُم البِناية. / تُعْجِبُكُم البِناية. ('a3jabatkum al-binaaya. *You liked the building.*) / (tu3jibu-kum al-binaaya. *You like the building.*)

15 أَعْجَبَكِ القَلَم. / يُعْجِبُكِ القَلَم. ('a3jabaki al-qalam. *You liked the pen.*) / (yu3jibuki al-qalam. *You like the pen.*)

16 أَعْجَبَهُم الطَّعام. / يُعْجِبُهُم الطَّعام. ('a3jabahum aT-Ta3aam. *They liked the food.*) / (yu3jibuhum aT-Ta3aam. *They like the food.*)

17 وَصَلَتْكُم رِسالَتي. / تَصِلُكُم رِسالَتي. (waSalatkum risaalatii. *You received my letter.*) / (taSilu-kum risaalatii. *You receive my letter.*)

18 وَصَلَها طَرْدُنا. / يَصِلُها طَرْدُنا. (waSalahaa Tardunaa. *She received our package.*) / (yaSiluhaa Tardunaa. *She receives our package.*)

19 وَصَلَتْهُ المَجَلّة. / تَصِلُهُ المَجَلّة. (waSalathu al-majalla. *He received the magazine.*) / (taSiluhaa al-majalla. *He receives the magazine.*)

20 وَصَلَتْني الرَّسائِل. / تَصِلُني الرَّسائِل. (waSalatnii ar-rasaa'il. *I received the letters.*) / (taSilunii ar-rasaa'il. *I receive the letters.*)

21 وَصَلُكَ البَرْقِيّة. (**waSalatka al-barqiyya.** *You received the telegram.*) / . تَصِلُكَ (**taSiluka al-barqiyya.** *You receive the telegram.*)

22 وَصَلَتْنا البَطاقة. (**waSalatnaa al-baTaaqa.** *We received the card.*) / . تَصِلُنا البَطاقة (**taSilunaa al-baTaaqa.** *We receive the card.*)

Translation of letter:

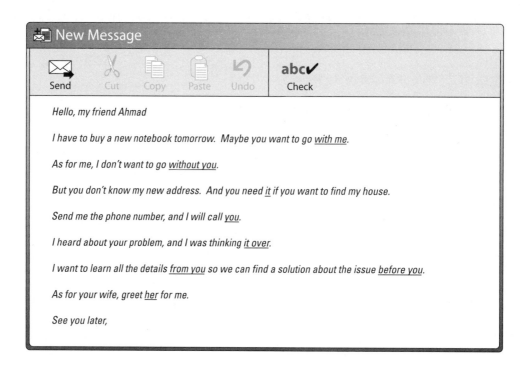

Hello, my friend Ahmad

I have to buy a new notebook tomorrow. Maybe you want to go <u>with me</u>.

As for me, I don't want to go <u>without you</u>.

But you don't know my new address. And you need <u>it</u> if you want to find my house.

Send me the phone number, and I will call <u>you</u>.

I heard about your problem, and I was thinking <u>it over</u>.

I want to learn all the details <u>from you</u> so we can find a solution about the issue <u>before you</u>.

As for your wife, greet <u>her</u> for me.

See you later,

23 مَعِي (**ma3ii;** *with me*)

24 بِدُونِكَ (**bi-duunika;** *without you*)

25 إِلَيْهِ (**'ilayhi;** *[to] it*)

26 بِكَ (**bika;** *[with] you*)

27 فِيها (**fiihaa;** *about [in] it*)

28 مِنْكَ (**minka;** *from you*)

29 أَمامَكَ (**'amaamaka;** *before you*)

30 عَلَيْها (**3alayhaa;** *unto her*)

Chapter 13

The Indicative, Jussive, and Subjunctive Moods of the Arabic Verb

....

In This Chapter

▶ Recognizing the indicative mood

▶ Producing the subjunctive mood

▶ Forming the jussive mood

....

Have you ever heard someone say something like, "I wish I was in Cairo right now!" Or maybe, "If only I can see the pyramids!" You understand what they mean, but you also sense that something's a bit off in their sentences. Better word choices would have been, "I wish I *were* . . ." and "If only I *could* . . ." Words like *should, would, could,* and *were* in English are the last vestiges we have left of something called *mood* in language. That's right; your professor isn't the only one who can be moody.

Modern Standard Arabic has three moods: indicative, subjunctive, and jussive. In Arabic, mood refers to whether the action of the verb has happened or is just something you want to happen. There's only one mood for the past tense verb: the indicative. The logic behind this is that anything reported as having happened must, by definition, be indicative, because indicative is the mood for reporting realities.

A verb, as you see in this chapter, doesn't really change its meaning when used in these moods. Instead, the various moods simply give you the correct expression of the verb for the different situations you face. In this chapter, you discover how to create the three moods easily, and you figure out when and how to use them.

Setting the Record Straight with the Indicative Mood

In your everyday use of any language, you tend to talk about realities. You tell your friends what you did over the weekend. You tell your significant other that you love him or her. When you use language this way, you're using the *indicative mood,* which means that the action of the verb

✔ Has actually taken place

✔ Is currently taking place

✔ Will indeed take place

The past tense you encountered in your basic studies is indicative because the action is over. The action definitely happened, and you're using the past tense to describe it.

Take special note that a ´ (**Damma**) appears over four of the present indicative forms: the first person singular and plural, the second person singular masculine, and the third person singular masculine. The verbs ending in ´ (**Damma**) can be converted into the other two moods by changing only the ´ (**Damma**). (You can read more about the ´ [**Damma**] in Chapter 3.)

The following table shows you the present indicative of the Form I verb شَكَرَ (**shakara**; *to thank*).

شَكَرَ (**shakara**; *to thank*)	
أَشْكُرُ ('anaa 'ashkuru)	نَشْكُرُ (naHnu nashkuru)
تَشْكُرُ ('anta tashkuru) تَشْكُرِينَ ('anti tashkuriina)	تَشْكُرُونَ ('antum tashkuruuna) تَشْكُرْنَ ('antunna tashkurna)
يَشْكُرُ (huwa yashkuru) تَشْكُرُ (hiya tashkuru)	يَشْكُرُونَ (hum yashkuruuna) يَشْكُرْنَ (hunna yashkurna)
أَشْكُرُ مُدَرِّسِي لِمُساعَدَتِهِ. ('ashkuru mudarrisii limusaa3adatihi. *I thank my teacher for his help.*)	

Hypothesizing with the Subjunctive Mood

The *subjunctive mood* is used to convey the idea of being subjective or hypothetical. You need the subjunctive, for instance, when you wish something would happen. Here are a few examples in English of the subjunctive in action:

I wish he would tell me what happened.

If only I could go along with them.

It's important that he travel tomorrow.

Notice that in the third example, the subjunctive in English is different from the indicative *he travels.* The subjunctive doesn't impart a new meaning to the verb. Rather, it's just the correct version of the verb for certain situations. If you make a mistake and use the indicative instead of the subjunctive in English, people will understand you. In fact, many folks may not even notice the error. The same thing is true of

Arabic. But because I know that you want to stand out from the crowd, I show you how to create the subjunctive in Arabic and when to use it.

Forming the subjunctive of regular verbs

The subjunctive involves changing the suffixes of a verb. No matter which one of the ten verb forms you have, the suffixes are all the same. For that reason, forming the subjunctive is the same for all ten verb forms. To produce the subjunctive of regular verbs, you have to do the following:

- ✔ Change any final ´ (**Damma**) to ˊ (**fatHa**).
- ✔ Remove the suffix نَ (**na**) or نِ (**ni**) after any long vowel, and add a superfluous أَلِف (**'alif**) after any resulting final واو (**waaw**).
- ✔ Leave the final نَ (**na**) of the feminine plural verbs alone. These verbs are the same in all three moods.

The following table shows you what you get after applying the previous guidelines to the verb شَكَرَ (**shakara**; *to thank*).

شَكَرَ (shakara; *to thank*)	
أَشْكُرَ ('anaa 'ashkura)	نَشْكُرَ (naHnu nashkura)
تَشْكُرَ ('anta tashkura) تَشْكُرِي ('anti tashkurii)	تَشْكُرُوا ('antum tashkuruu) تَشْكُرْنَ ('antunna tashkurna)
يَشْكُرَ (huwa yashkura) تَشْكُرَ (hiya tashkura)	يَشْكُرُوا (hum yashkuruu) يَشْكُرْنَ (hunna yashkurna)
يَجِبُ أَنْ أَشْكُرَ مُدَرِّسِي لِمُساعَدَتِهِ. (yajibu 'an 'ashkura mudarrisii limusaa3adatihi. *It is necessary that I thank my teacher for his help.*)	

Forming the subjunctive of irregular verbs

The subjunctive mood is only irregular with verbs that have a weak final letter (for more on irregular verbs see Chapter 10). Even then, only a few verbs require an adjustment to the normal rules that you use to produce the subjunctive.

It's easier to show you the indicative and subjunctive of final weak verbs side by side and point out how the final weak letter altered the verb. Table 13-1 shows the present indicative and subjunctive versions of the Form I final واو (**waaw**) verb دَعَا (**da3aa**; *to call*).

Table 13-1	Comparing the Subjunctive and Present Indicative of دَعا (da3aa; *to call*), a Final واو (waaw) Verb	
Subjunctive	*Present Indicative*	
تَدْعي ('anti tad3ii; [*that*] you call)	تَدْعينَ ('anti tad3iina; *you call*)	
يَدْعُوَ (huwa yad3uwa; [*that*] he call)	يَدْعو (huwa yad3uu; *he calls*)	
تَدْعُوَ (hiya tad3uwa; [*that*] she call)	تَدْعو (hiya tad3uu; *she calls*)	
نَدْعُوَ (naHnu nad3uwa; [*that*] we call)	نَدْعو (naHnu nad3uu; *we call*)	
يَدْعوا (hum yad3uu; [*that*] they call)	يَدْعونَ (hum yad3uuna; *they call*)	

When you remove the endings after long vowels, the subjunctive verbs with final واو (**waaw**) are completely regular. The only tricky verbs are those that have a final long *u* vowel — written with a واو (**waaw**). To produce these subjunctive verbs you:

✔ Turn the واو (**waaw**) into a consonant and add the ´ (**fatHa**) of the subjunctive.

✔ Put a ´ (**Damma**) over the middle consonant of the root.

Verbs with a final ياء (**yaa'**) are irregular in one of two ways. First off, if the verb has an أَلِف مَكْسورَة ('**alif maksuura**) as the final vowel in the present indicative, the subjunctive won't change at all. Table 13-2 shows the subjunctive and present indicative of the Form I final ياء (**yaa'**) verb نَسِيَ (**nasiya**; *to forget*).

Table 13-2	Comparing the Subjunctive and Present Indicative of نَسِيَ (nasiya; *to forget*), a Final ياء (yaa') Verb	
Subjunctive	*Present Indicative*	
تَنْسَي ('anti tansay; [*that*] you forget)	تَنْسَيْنَ ('anti tansayna; *you forget*)	
يَنْسى (huwa yansaa; [*that*] he forget)	يَنْسى (huwa yansaa; *he forgets*)	
تَنْسى (hiya tansaa; [*that*] she forget)	تَنْسى (hiya tansaa; *she forgets*)	
يَنْسَوْا (hum yansaw; [*that*] they forget)	يَنْسَوْنَ (hum yansawna; *they forget*)	

However, when a final ياء (**yaa'**) verb has a final long *i* vowel — written with ياء (**yaa'**) — in the present, the final ياء (**yaa'**) becomes a consonant in the subjunctive version. For example, Table 13-3 shows the subjunctive and present indicative of the Form I verb, بَكى (**bakaa**; *to cry*), with a final long *i* vowel.

Table 13-3	Comparing the Subjunctive and Present Indicative of بَكَى (bakaa; *to cry*), a Final يَاء (yaa') Verb	
Subjunctive	*Present Indicative*	
تَبْكِي ('anti tabkii; [*that*] *you cry*)	تَبْكِينَ ('anti tabkiina; *you cry*)	
يَبْكِيَ (huwa yabkiya; [*that*] *he cry*)	يَبْكِي (huwa yabkii; *he cries*)	
تَبْكِيَ (hiya tabkiya; [*that*] *she cry*)	تَبْكِي (hiya tabkii; *she cries*)	
يَبْكُوا (hum yabkuu; [*that*] *they cry*)	يَبْكُونَ (hum yabkuuna; *they cry*)	

Using the subjunctive

You use the subjunctive whenever you want to express a situation that may or may not have happened. The subjunctive in Arabic is always introduced by certain conjunctions, just as it is always preceded in Spanish by the conjunction **que.** Most of the time, you use subjunctive after the conjunction أَنْ ('an; *that*) in constructions expressing wishes. Other conjunctions that precede the subjunctive express purpose clauses. In this section, I show you how to form these important and common constructions in Arabic.

As a rule of thumb, you don't need to worry about whether the subjunctive is warranted or not. Instead, whenever you naturally find yourself in need of one of the conjunctions that I demonstrate in this section, you put the verb that follows it in the subjunctive.

Working with the conjunction أَنْ ('an; that)

The conjunction أَنْ ('an; *that*) follows a verb expressing wish, necessity, or command. In the following example, note that the verb following أَنْ ('an) is in the subjunctive:

يَجِبُ أَنْ نُسَافِرَ قَرِيباً.

(**yajibu 'an nusaafira qariiban.** *It is necessary that we travel soon.*)

I translated the preceding example into English very literally to demonstrate how the Arabic expresses *that* in a sentence. A better English translation of any sentence with the subjunctive is frequently to not express the word *that* at all and render the subjunctive as an infinitive. For example, the translation for the previous example may sound like this: *We have to travel soon.*

Arabic uses subjunctive in the preceding sentence construction because the example sentence (*It is necessary that we travel soon*) isn't really talking about the fact of the action; there may be no traveling that actually occurs. The sentence instead is talking about the potential need for travel. As such, this is what is called an *irreal situation.* The action may or may not happen at all, and we may not even want the action to happen.

Here are several examples of sentences using the conjunction أَنْ ('an) followed by a subjunctive verb describing irreal situations:

هَل سَأَلْتِهِ أَنْ يُرْسِلَ الرّسالةَ؟

(**hal sa'altihi 'an yursila ar-risaalata?** *Did you ask him to send the letter?*)

يُريدُ أَنْ يَدْرُسَ فـي اليابان.

(**yuriidu 'an yadrusa fii-l-yaabaani.** *He wants to study in Japan.*)

Sometimes a verb requires a preposition for its object. When such a verb precedes a subjunctive, you can just put the preposition directly in front of the conjunction أَنْ ('an; *that*). Here are some examples with أَنْ ('an; *that*) plus a preposition:

لا يَسْمَحُ لـي أَبـي بِأَنْ أَتْرُكَ المَدْرَسةَ.

(**laa yasmaHu lii 'abii bi-'an 'atruka al-madrasata.** *My father won't permit me to leave school.*)

تَتَمَكَّنُ مِن أَنْ تَتَكَلَّمَ الإِنْكـليزيّةَ.

(**tatamakkanu min 'an tatakallama al-inkliiziyyata.** *She is able to speak English.*)

Expressing purpose in the subjunctive with a few more conjunctions

The subjunctive is the appropriate mood to describe any situation that isn't yet a concrete fact. That holds true for sentences in which you want to express purpose as well. If I say, for instance, "They stayed at the library in order to complete the task," you don't actually know from the sentence whether they completed the task. All you really know is that they completed an action for the purpose of completing another. For all we know, they got to chatting and still have lots of work to do! For that reason, you use the subjunctive in Arabic, along with conjunctions that essentially mean *in order to,* to express purpose in Arabic.

Here are examples of the conjunctions you can use with subjunctive verbs following:

✔ حَتّى (**Hattaa;** *until/in order to*)
✔ كَيْ / لِكَيْ (**kay/likay;** *in order to*)
✔ لِ (**li-;** *to*)

And now here are examples using those conjunctions:

بَقَوا فـي المَكْتَبِة حَتّى يُكْمِلوا المُهمّةَ.

(**baqaw fii-l-maktabati <u>Hatta yukmiluu</u> almuhimmata.** *They stayed at the library <u>in order to complete</u> the task.*)

يُريدُ أَنْ يُغَيِّر مَوْعِد طائِرَتِه لِكَـيْ يَرْجِعَ فـي يَوْم السَبْتِ.

(**yuriidu 'an yughayyira maw3ida Taa'iratihi <u>likay yarji3a</u> fii yawmi as-sabti.** *He wants to change his plane <u>in order to return</u> on Saturday.*)

تَعْمَلُ في وَظيفَتَيْن لِتَكْسِبَ مالاً كَثيراً.

(ta3malu fii waDHiifatayni li-taksiba maalan kathiiran. *She works two jobs in order to earn a lot of money.*)

A friend has just sent you an e-mail. Find and underline cases where he should have used subjunctive. You'll find 11 different mistakes. Then in the blanks provided, write the proper verb he should have used. As you'll soon see, your friend's problems run deeper than ignorance of the subjunctive!

Q. The first mistake, أشْرَحُ, is underlined for you.

A. أشْرَحَ (**'ashraHa**; *[that] I explain*)

صَديقي.

أُريدُ أنْ أشْرَحُ لَكَ ما حَدَثَ أمْس.

لكِنْ أوَّلاً يَجِبُ أنْ تَفْهَمُ المَوْضوعَ.

كُنْتُ أعْمَلُ في المَكْتَب ضارباً عَلى الحاسوب.

أرَدْتُ أنْ أطْبَعُ مَقالاً لكِنْ ما كانَ عِنْدي وَرَق.

ذَهَبْتُ إلى المَخْزَن لِكَيْ أجِدُ عُلبةَ وَرَق.

وَصَلَتْ هُناكَ في نَفْس الوَقْت مُساعِدةُ المُدير حَتّى تَبْحَثُ عَن قَلَم.

أمّا أنا فَأُحِبُّها فِعْلاً لكِنْ لَمْ أُخْبِرْها أبَداً.

أرَدْتُ أنْ تُلاحِظَني فَحاوَلْتُ أنْ أقولُ لَها "هَل يُمْكِنُ أنْ أساعدكَ؟"

لكِنْ قَلْبي قالَ شَيْئاً آخَر وَسَمِعْتُ هذِه الكَلِمات خارِجةً مِنّي: "هَل يُمْكِنُ أنْ أقَبِّلُكِ؟"

هِيَ احْمَرَّتْ وَتَرَكَتْني هُناكَ. فَوْراً طَرَدَني المُدير مِن الشَّرِكة.

والآن يَجِبُ أنْ أجِدُ وَظيفةً جَديدةً.

تَكَلَّمْتُ مَعَ رَجُل في المَكْتَب القَريب مِن مَكْتَبي السّابِق.

يُمْكِنُ أنْ يُعطونَني وَظيفةً هُناكَ.

أُريدُ أنْ أحْصُلُ عَلى وَظيفةٍ هُناكَ لِكَيْ أرى الفَتاةَ مِن حين إلى حين.

أحْمَد

1. _____

2. _____

3. _____

4. _____

5. _____

6. _____

7. _____

8. _____

9. _____

10. _____

11. _____

Taking Charge with the Jussive Mood

The *jussive mood* is named as such because one of its uses is to create polite commands. Unlike the subjunctive, we don't have even a trace of a jussive in English.

Like the subjunctive, the jussive in Arabic doesn't so much have a meaning but a proper context. Instead, there are a number of constructions in which jussive is the correct version of the verb to use. In this section, I show you how to create the jussive version of the verb and when you should use it.

Forming the jussive of regular verbs

You produce the jussive by making changes to the suffixes of the verb. Because all ten forms of the Arabic verb use the same suffixes, the process of creating the jussive is the same for all ten forms. To generate the jussive of a Form I regular verb, you do the following:

- ✔ Change any final ´ (**Damma**) to ˚ (**sukuun**).

- ✔ Remove the suffix نَ (**na**) or نِ (**ni**) after any long vowel. Add a superfluous أَلِف ('**alif**) after any resulting final وَاو (**waaw**).

- ✔ Leave the final نَ (**na**) of the feminine plural verbs alone. These verbs are the same in all three moods.

With the exception of the verbs that you change to ´ (**sukuun**), the jussive and subjunctive forms are identical when you have three strong consonants in the root.

When you apply the previous three rules to the verb شَكَرَ (**shakara**; *to thank*), the conjugations look like those in the following table.

شَكَرَ (shakara; to thank)	
أَشْكُر ('anaa 'ashkur)	نَشْكُر (naHnu nashkur)
تَشْكُر ('anta tashkur)	تَشْكُروا ('antum tashkuruu)
تَشْكُري ('anti tashkurii)	تَشْكُرْنَ ('antunna tashkurna)
يَشْكُر (huwa yashkur)	يَشْكُروا (hum yashkuruu)
تَشْكُر (hiya tashkur)	يَشْكُرْنَ (hunna yashkurna)
لَأَشْكُرْ مُدَرِّسي لِمُساعَدَتِه.	
(li'ashkur mudarrisii limusaa3adatihi. *I should thank my teacher for his help.*)	

Forming the jussive mood of irregular verbs

The real hallmark of the jussive versions of the verb is that they're attempting to shorten the verb wherever possible. When you have three strong consonants, the only way to shorten the verb is to remove all final vowels and the prefixes before long vowels. Some of the irregular verbs, however, give the jussive the opportunity to reduce the verbs even further.

Final weak verb reductions

Like the subjunctive, final weak verbs are fair game for this reduction. The basic rules you use to reduce final weak verbs in the jussive are as follows:

✔ When there's a final long *u* — written with a واو (**waaw**) — it reduces to a ´ (**Damma**).

✔ When there's a final long *a* — written with an أَلِف مَكْسورة ('**alif maksuura**) — it reduces to a ´ (**fatHa**).

✔ When there's a final long *i* — written with a ياء (**yaa'**) — it reduces to a , (**kasra**).

Table 13-4 shows you what you get after you apply the rules to the final weak verb دَعا (**da3aa**; *to call*). Because the jussive is used for many different constructions and expressions, I won't translate the jussive verbs differently than the indicative.

Table 13-4	Comparing the Jussive and Present Indicative of دَعا (da3aa; *to call*), a Final Weak Verb
Jussive	*Present Indicative*
تَدْعِي ('anti tad3ii; *you call*)	تَدْعِينَ ('anti tad3iina; *you call*)
يَدْعُ (huwa yad3u; *he calls*)	يَدْعُو (huwa yad3uu; *he calls*)
تَدْعُ (hiya tad3u; *she calls*)	تَدْعُو (hiya tad3uu; *she calls*)
يَدْعوا (hum yad3uu; *they call*)	يَدْعونَ (hum yad3uuna; *they call*)

Table 13-5 compares the jussive and present indicative of the final weak verb نَسِيَ (**nasiya**; *to forget*).

Table 13-5	Comparing the Jussive and Present Indicative of نَسِيَ (nasiya; *to forget*), a Final Weak Verb
Jussive	*Present Indicative*
تَنْسَيْ ('anti tansay; *you forget*)	تَنْسَيْنَ ('anti tansayna; *you forget*)
يَنْسَ (huwa yansa; *he forgets*)	يَنْسى (huwa yansaa; *he forgets*)
تَنْسَ (hiya tansa; *she forgets*)	تَنْسى (hiya tansaa; *she forgets*)
يَنْسَوْا (hum yansaw; *they forget*)	يَنْسَوْنَ (hum yansawna; *they forget*)

Table 13-6 shows the jussive and present indicative forms of the final weak verb بَكى (**bakaa**; *to cry*) side by side.

Table 13-6	Comparing the Jussive and Present Indicative of بَكى (bakaa; *to cry*), a Final Weak Verb
Jussive	*Present Indicative*
تَبْكِي ('anti tabkii; *you cry*)	تَبْكِينَ ('anti tabkiina; *you cry*)
يَبْكِ (huwa yabki; *he cries*)	يَبْكي (huwa yabkii; *he cries*)
تَبْكِ (hiya tabki; *she cries*)	تَبْكي (hiya tabkii; *she cries*)
يَبْكوا (hum yabkuu; *they cry*)	يَبْكونَ (hum yabkuuna; *they cry*)

Medial weak verb reductions

In addition to dropping off the suffixes, verbs with a medial weak letter also reduce their medial vowels in the jussive. (Check out Chapter 10 for more on medial weak verbs.) You produce the jussive of a medial weak verb with the following rules:

✔ Any verb with a ´ (**sukuun**) on the third consonant in the jussive reduces its medial long vowel.

✔ A medial long *u* — written with واو (**waaw**) — reduces to a ´ (**Damma**).

✔ A medial long *a* — written with أَلِف (**'alif**) — reduces to a ´ (**fatHa**).

✔ A medial long *i* — written with يَاء (**yaa'**) — reduces to a ˌ (**kasra**).

✔ The medial long vowel in all other jussive verbs remains.

Table 13-7 shows what you get after you apply these rules to the medial weak verb قَالَ (**qaala**; *to say*).

Table 13-7	Comparing the Jussive and Present Indicative of قَالَ (qaala; *to say*), a Medial Weak Verb
Jussive	**Present Indicative**
تَقُولِي ('**anti taquulii**; *you say*)	تَقُولِينَ ('**anti taquuliina**; *you say*)
يَقُلْ (**huwa yaqul**; *he says*)	يَقُولُ (**huwa yaquulu**; *he says*)
تَقُلْ (**hiya taqul**; *she says*)	تَقُولُ (**hiya taquulu**; *she says*)
يَقُولُوا (**hum yaquuluu**; *they say*)	يَقُولُونَ (**hum yaquuluuna**; *they say*)

Table 13-8 shows side by side the jussive and present indicative forms of the medial weak verb نَامَ (**naama**; *to sleep*).

Table 13-8	Comparing the Jussive and Present Indicative of نَامَ (naama; *to sleep*), a Medial Weak Verb
Jussive	**Present Indicative**
تَنَامِي ('**anti tanaamii**; *you sleep*)	تَنَامِينَ ('**anti tanaamiina**; *you sleep*)
يَنَمْ (**huwa yanam**; *he sleeps*)	يَنَامُ (**huwa yanaamu**; *he sleeps*)
تَنَمْ (**hiya tanam**; *she sleeps*)	تَنَامُ (**hiya tanaamu**; *she sleeps*)
يَنَامُوا (**hum yanaamuu**; *they sleep*)	يَنَامُونَ (**hum yanaamuuna**; *they sleep*)

Table 13-9 shows the jussive and present indicative forms of the final weak verb أَجَابَ ('**ajaaba**; *to answer*).

Table 13-9	Comparing the Jussive and Present Indicative of أَجَابَ ('ajaaba; *to answer*), a Medial Weak Verb	
Jussive	*Present Indicative*	
تُجِيبِي ('anti tujiibii; *you answer*)	تُجِيبِينَ ('anti tujiibiina; *you answer*)	
يُجِبْ (huwa yujib; *he answers*)	يُجِيبُ (huwa yujiibu; *he answers*)	
تُجِبْ (hiya tujib; *she answers*)	تُجِيبُ (hiya tujiibu; *she answers*)	
يُجِيبُوا (hum yujiibuu; *they answer*)	يُجِيبُونَ (hum yujiibuuna; *they answer*)	

Geminate irregularity

One curious irregularity in the jussive comes when you have the same second and third consonant in the root. These verbs, which are called *geminate* verbs (see Chapter 10), would have had a ˘ (**sukkun**) over a doubled letter. However, this really isn't possible to pronounce. As a result, you actually have to add a ´ (**fatHa**) as the final vowel. The result is that the jussive and subjunctive of a geminate verb are identical.

Table 13-10 shows side by side the present indicative and jussive/subjunctive versions for the geminate verb عَدَّ (**3adda;** *to count*).

Table 13-10	Comparing the Jussive/Subjunctive and Present Indicative of عَدَّ (3adda; *to count*), a Geminate Verb	
Jussive/Subjunctive	*Present Indicative*	
تَعُدِّي ('anti ta3uddii; *you count*)	تَعُدِّينَ ('anti ta3uddiina; *you count*)	
يَعُدَّ (huwa ya3udda; *he counts*)	يَعُدُّ (huwa ya3uddu; *he counts*)	
تَعُدَّ (hiya ta3udda; *she counts*)	تَعُدُّ (hiya ta3uddu; *she counts*)	
يَعُدُّوا (hum ya3udduu; *they count*)	يَعُدُّونَ (hum ya3udduuna; *they count*)	

Using the jussive mood

A handy use of the jussive is to create indirect commands. To produce an indirect command, you add the particle لِ (**li-;** *to*) to the jussive. Often, you can translate the resulting verb with the sense of *let's do something*. Here's a demonstration of this use of the jussive:

لِنَتَكَلَّمْ مَعاً.

(**linatakallam ma3an.** *Let's speak together.*)

Often, you see the particle فَ (**fa-**) attached before the لِ (**li-**), which then takes a ْ (**sukuun**). Here is an example:

فَلْنَذْهَبْ.

(**falnadh-hab.** *Let's go.*)

Several of the more important uses of the jussive are covered in other chapters of this book. For example, to see the use of jussive to create a negative command and produce a negated past tense, refer to Chapter 17. To see the jussive used in a conditional sentence, consult Chapter 14.

For each of the following items, I give you a pronoun and verb in the present indicative. Produce the correct jussive verb for each.

Q. يُشاهِدونَ (**yushaahiduuna**)

A. يُشـاهِدوا (**yushaahiduu;** *they watch*)

12. يَقـولُ (**yaquulu**) _____

13. نَبْنـي (**nabnii**) _____

14. تَخـافُ (**takhaafu**) _____

15. تُجيـبُ (**tujiibu**) _____

16. أَتَكَلَّمُ (**'atakallamu**) _____

17. يَسْتَطيعُ (**yastaTii3u**) _____

18. يَنْسـى (**yansaa**) _____

19. تَلْتَقـي (**taltaqii**) _____

20. تَكْتُبونَ (**taktabuuna**) _____

21. يَذْهَبْنَ (**yadh-habna**) _____

22. يَدُلُّ (**yadullu**) _____

23. نَكـونُ (**nakuunu**) _____

24. يَشْـكُرونَ (**yashkuruuna**) _____

25. أَجِـدُ (**'ajidu**) _____

Answer Key

صَديقي،

أُريدُ أَنْ أَشْرَحَ لَكَ ما حَدَثَ أَمْس.

لكِنْ أَوَّلاً يَجِبُ أَنْ تَفْهَمَ المَوْضوعَ.

كُنْتُ أَعْمَلُ في المَكْتَب ضارِباً عَلى الحاسوب.

أَرَدْتُ أَنْ أَطْبَعَ مَقالاً لكِنْ ما كانَ عِنْدي وَرَق.

ذَهَبْتُ إلى المَخْزَن لِكَيْ أَجِدَ عُلْبةَ وَرَق.

وَصَلَتْ هُناكَ في نَفْس الوَقْتِ مُساعِدةُ المُدير حَتّى تَبْحَثَ عَن قَلَم.

أمّا أنا فَأُحِبُّها فِعْلاً لكِنْ لَمْ أُخْبِرْها أَبَداً.

أَرَدْتُ أَنْ تُلاحِظَني فَحاوَلْتُ أَنْ أَقولَ لَها "هَل يُمْكِنُ أَنْ أُساعِدَكِ؟"

لكِنْ قَلْبي قالَ شَيْئاً آخَر وَسَمِعْتُ هذِهِ الكَلِماتِ خارِجةً مِنّي: "هَل يُمْكِنُ أَنْ أُقَبِّلَكِ؟"

هِيَ احْمَرَّتْ وَتَرَكَتْني هُناك. فَوْراً طَرَدَني المُديرُ مِن الشَّرِكة.

وَالآنَ يَجِبُ أَنْ أَجِدَ وَظيفةً جَديدةً.

تَكَلَّمْتُ مَعَ رَجُل في المَكْتَب القَريب مِن مَكْتَبي السّابِق.

يُمْكِنُ أَنْ يُعطونَني وَظيفةً هُناك.

أُريدُ أَنْ أَحْصُلَ عَلى وَظيفةٍ هُناكَ لِكَيْ أَرى الفَتاةَ مِن حين إلى حين.

أَحْمَد

(My friend,
I want to explain to you what happened yesterday. But first you need to understand the situation. I was working at the office typing on the computer. I wanted to print an article, but I didn't have paper. I went to the storeroom to find a box of paper. At the same time the director's assistant arrived there to look for a pen. As for me, I am really in love with her, but I have never told her. I wanted her to notice me, so I tried to say to her: "May I help you?" But my heart said something else, and I heard these words coming from me: "May I kiss you?" She turned red and left me there. The director immediately fired me from the company. So now I need to find a new job. I spoke with a man in the office near my former office. And they may give me a job there. I want to get a job there so that I see the young lady from time to time.)

1 تَفْهَمَ (**tafhama**; *you understand*)

2 أَطْبَعَ ('**aTba3a**; *I print*)

3 أَجِدَ ('**ajida**; *I find*)

4 تَبْحَثَ (**tabHatha**; *she looks for*)

5 تُلاحِظَني (**tulaaHiDHanii**; *she notices me*)

6 أَقولَ ('**aquula**; *I say*)

7 أُساعِدَكِ ('**usaa3idaki**; *I help you*)

8 أُقَبِّلَكِ ('**uqabbilaki**; *I kiss you*)

9 أَجِدَ ('**ajida**; *I find*)

10 يُعطوني (**yu3Tuunii**; *they give me*)

11 أَحْصُلَ ('**aHSula**; *I get*)

12 يَقُلْ (**yaqul**; *he says*)

13 نَبْنِ (**nabni**; *we build*)

14 تَخَفْ (**takhaf**; *you are afraid*)

15 تُجِبْ (**tujib**; *she answers*)

16 أَتَكَلَّمْ ('**atakallam**; *I speak*)

17 يَسْتَطِعْ (**yastaTi3**; *he is able*)

18 يَنْسَ (**yansa**; *he forgets*)

19 تَلْتَقِ (**taltaqi**; *she meets*)

20 تَكْتُبوا (**taktubuu**; *you write*)

21 يَذْهَبْنَ (**yadh-habna**; *they go*)

22 يَدُلَّ (**yadulla;** *he points*)

23 نَكُنْ (**nakun;** *we are*)

24 يَشْكُروا (**yashkuruu;** *they thank*)

25 أجِدْ ('**ajid;** *I find*)

Part IV

Enlivening Your Writing with Particles

The 5th Wave   By Rich Tennant

In this part . . .

Big things sometimes come in small packages. In this part, you find the same to be quite true of the Arabic particles. In this part's chapters, you discover how to use small but mighty words to form sentences such as conditionals. You also add valuable words, including conjunctions, to your inventory. I provide a chapter on the verbal noun, which is the smallest form of the verb but important for many parts of speech. Negation is also important in communication, so I show you how to add *not* to any type of sentence. Finally, you discover the forms of the participle in Arabic.

Chapter 14

Forming Conditional Sentences

. . . .

In This Chapter

▶ Discovering the parts of a conditional sentence

▶ Examining simple conditional sentences

▶ Dealing with contrary to fact conditionals

▶ Applying the jussive to conditional sentences

▶ Recognizing the conditional particle إِنْ ('in) in Classical Arabic

. . . .

If you've worked through the preceding chapters, you've practiced quite a bit of Arabic! Just think: If you hadn't picked up a copy of *Intermediate Arabic For Dummies,* you would have missed all the fun!

The preceding two sentences are conditional sentences. What's that, you ask? A *conditional sentence* is one that discusses hypothetical situations and their consequences.

Whenever you describe a situation in English that may or may not happen, you usually form a sentence that starts with the word *if.* However, forming conditional sentences in Arabic requires you to choose the correct word for *if.* You also have to determine which tense and mood is the best choice for the conditional sentence you want to express.

This chapter gives you the information you need to confidently enter the Arabic world of "what if?" You'll encounter the parts of the conditional sentence, a list of Arabic words for *if,* and some handy tips for selecting the correct type of verb to go in your sentence.

Seeing the Condition and Result in Sentences

Anytime you use the word *if,* you're talking about a hypothetical situation (something that may or may not happen). These conditional sentences each have two parts. Grammarians call the part of the sentence introduced by the word *if* the *protasis.* This is the part of the sentence that affects the outcome of the second part, which is called the *apodosis.* In this book, I call them the *condition clause* and the *result clause* as shown in Table 14-1.

Table 14-1	The Main Parts of Conditional Sentences
Protasis (Condition Clause)	**Apodosis (Result Clause)**
If I had lived in Roman times,	I would have liked to have been a gladiator.
If I have the time,	I will surely come to your party.

In English, the condition clause and the result clause can actually come in reverse order and still produce a conditional sentence. For example, consider this sentence: *You won't learn as quickly if you don't complete the practice exercises.*

The first part of the sentence (*You won't learn as quickly . . .*) is the result clause of the second part of the sentence (*. . . if you don't complete the practice exercises*), which is the condition clause. In this sentence, you can also replace the word *if* with *unless* without changing the meaning. So, one half of the sentence tells you what may or may not happen, and the other half tells you the result.

In Arabic, the result clause comes before the condition clause much more rarely than in English. That's not to say it's never done, but that construction is definitely not as common as in English.

Forming Simple Conditional Sentences in Arabic

In Arabic, conditional sentences can take on two basic forms:

- ✔ Simple
- ✔ Contrary to fact

In this section, I discuss simple conditional sentences. You can read about contrary to fact conditional sentences in the later section, "Getting to Know Contrary to Fact Conditional Sentences."

A *simple conditional* sentence describes a situation that could have happened or still could happen. For example, "If I have the time, I will surely come to your party." In the condition clause of this example, it isn't yet clear whether the person will have the time (and thus whether he or she will come to the party). A simple conditional sentence includes two primary variations: past tense indicative and jussive. And, of course, there are some exceptions and twists!

English has one workhorse word to introduce conditional sentences: *if*. English distinguishes between different types of conditional situations through the use of grammatical moods. By contrast, Arabic uses different words to introduce conditional sentences, depending on whether they're simple or contrary to fact. Because most conditional sentences are of the simple type, you will most often use the Arabic word for *if* reserved for this style of conditional sentence: إذا (**'idha**).

Be careful not to form an Arabic simple conditional sentence with a word for word substitution of English words and tenses. Someone reading what you write in this case will probably still understand what you mean, but he or she will also be aware that your Arabic needs help.

In this section, I show you the Arabic word that's used for *if* in simple conditional sentences. I also walk you through the past indicative and show you how to add a negative to a simple conditional sentence.

Using إذا ('idha) for if

If learning the word for *if* was all you needed to know in order to write simple conditional sentences in Arabic, you would be set up for success. But I have good news and bad news. The bad news is that writing simple conditional sentences is just a little more complicated than simply knowing the Arabic word for *if*. But the good news is that you form conditional sentences in Arabic without needing to understand any new forms of the verb. In fact, you just have to get used to using the past tense for everything, even when you're referring to the present or future. See what I mean about past tense in the later section "Applying past tense indicative."

Modern Standard Arabic has a special word for *if* that's used when you want to form a simple conditional sentence. That word is إذا (**'idha**). And in Arabic, the condition clause usually comes first. To finish the job of creating your simple conditional sentence, all you have to do next is state the verbs of both the conditional clause and the result clause in the past tense.

Applying past tense indicative

To get a feel for how conditional sentences would sound in English with only past tense verbs, take a look at the following examples:

> *If you studied this book, you learned many things.*
>
> *If I saw my friend, I was happy.*
>
> *If he wanted, he was able to come too.*

These sentences (translated literally) may seem strange to English speakers. On the face of it, you may wonder how the speaker has forgotten whether he saw his friend. But this is just how Arabic forms simple conditional sentences. What the Arabic means here is this: *If I see my friend, I will be happy.* The Arabic, however, puts both verbs in the past tense.

In the following Arabic versions of the same sentences, the verbs are really past tense, but a good English translation of past tense verbs in a conditional sentence is to express them as present tense:

إذا دَرَسْتَ هذا الْكِتاب تَعَلَّمْتَ أَشْياء كَثيرَة.

(**'idhaa darasta hadha-l-kitaab, ta3alamta'ashyaa' kathiira.** *If you study this book, you'll learn many things.*)

إذا رَأَيْتُ صَدِيقِي كُنْتُ مَسْرُوراً.

(**'idhaa ra'aytu Sadiiqii, kuntu masruuran.** *If I see my friend, I'll be happy.*)

إذا اِرادَ اِسْتَطاعَ أَنْ يَحْضُرَ أَيْضاً.

(**'idhaa araada, istaTaa3a 'an yaHDura 'ayDan.** *If he wants, he can come too.*)

Using past tense this way may seem a bit confusing at first, but once you get used to it, you'll be grateful that simple conditional sentences in Arabic are so easy. After all, in many languages, an entirely new form of the verb is required for this situation. In Arabic, on the other hand, you just need to use the most basic form of the verb.

Using the past tense in both the condition and result clauses is the most common method of forming conditional sentences in Arabic. A simple conditional sentence, however, can involve other tenses in the result clause. You may, for instance, use imperative or future tense. Just remember that when you do use something besides the past tense in a simple conditional sentence, you must add the prefix فَ (**fa-**) to the result clause.

Here are a few examples of other tenses in the result clauses of simple conditional sentences:

إذا اِسْتَطَعْتُ فَقُلْ لِي سَرَّكَ مِن فَضْلِكَ.

(**'idhaa istaTa3ta, <u>fa-qul</u> lii sirraka min faDlika.** *If you can, please <u>tell</u> me your secret.*)

إذا أَرْدْتَ فَسَأَقولُهُ لَكَ.

(**'idhaa 'aradta, <u>fa-sa'aquuluhu</u> laka.** *If you want, I will tell it to you.*)

So you can identify them easily, I underline the verbs that are in some other tense besides past. In the first example, you have an imperative. In the second case, you can see a future tense verb. Each one, as per the requirement, has the prefix فَ (**fa-**) on it first.

Adding a negative to a simple conditional sentence

When you need to add a negative to your simple conditional sentence, you can't use the normal negative particle ما (**maa;** *not*) with the past tense verb. Instead, you use لَمْ (**lam;** *not*) plus the jussive forms of the verb in the condition clause. (For more on using لَمْ [**lam**] to negate sentences, check out Chapter 17.) You also have to add the prefix فَ (**fa-**) to the result clause (as I discuss in the previous section).

Here are a few examples:

إذا لَمْ يَزُرْ جَدَّتَهُ فَلَنْ تَكونَ مَسْرورَةً مَعَهُ.

(**'idhaa lam yazur jaddatahu, fa-lan takuna masruuratan ma3ahu.** *If he doesn't visit his grandmother, she won't be happy with him.*)

إذا لَمْ تَكُنْ مُتَأَكِّداً مِنْ إجابَتِكَ فَلا تُخَمِّنْ.

(**'idhaa lam takun muta'akkidan min 'ijaabatika, fa-laa tukhammin.** *If you aren't sure about your answer, don't guess.*)

For each of the English sentences I give you in the following practice set, translate them into Arabic using the word إذا (**'idha**). For items 1–5, use the past tense of the verb in both the condition clause and the result clause. In item 6 you need to use a negative verb (covered in Chapter 17). For item 7, use a command (go to Chapter 11 if you're uncertain about these). Item 8 requires a future tense (which you can discover in Chapter 2).

Q. If you agree, we would do that.

A. إذا كُنْتَ مُوافِقاً فَعَلنا ذلكَ. (**'idhaa kunta muwaafiqan fa3alnaa dhaalika.**)

1. If we go to the restaurant, I'd eat the falafel.

_____

2. If I have time, I'd do that for you.

_____

3. If she can come, we'd speak together.

_____

4. If you want to know the answer, you should ask the question.

_____

5. If he is here tomorrow, we would complete the work.

_____

6. If he doesn't arrive soon, we will start without him.

_____

7. If she says something, don't doubt it.

_____

8. If the weather is nice tomorrow, we will go to the park.

_____

Getting to Know Contrary to Fact Conditional Sentences

In most simple conditional sentences, there's at least the potential for the condition to come true. The *contrary to fact conditional,* on the other hand, involves things that can never be true at all. An English example would be something like this: *If I had lived in Roman times, I would have liked to have been a gladiator.* Until time travel exists outside of science fiction, neither you nor I will be able to actually go back to the days of yore.

Here are some additional English examples about circumstances that didn't happen or could never happen (okay, maybe you *could* become a king, but it isn't likely):

If I were king, things would be different.

If I had gone to the party (but I didn't), I would have seen my friend there.

 The good news for you is that contrary to fact conditional sentences are even easier to form in Arabic than they are in English. After all, sometimes in English you hear someone say, "If I was in charge, things would be different." But if you're in tune to your grammar, you know that this is wrong! The correct statement is, "If I *were* in charge, things would be different." English has a special form of certain verbs that's used when you form contrary to fact conditionals. In this particular case, "were" is the subjunctive form, used in English to properly form conditions contrary to fact. Creating contrary to fact sentences in Arabic is much easier than all that. In Arabic, all you need to do is use a different word for *if* and use the past tense in both parts of the sentence.

In this section, I show you the Arabic word used for *if* in contrary to fact conditional sentences. I also explain how to be negative and contrary at the same time.

Expressing contrary to fact conditionals with لَوْ (law)

Arabic has a word for *if* that's reserved only for use in contrary to fact conditional sentences. That word is لَوْ (**law**), and it's translated as *if,* just like the word إذا (**'idhaa**) within simple conditional sentences.

 When creating contrary to fact sentences in Arabic, you have to use the prefix لَ (**la-**). You put the لَ (**la-**) at the beginning of the result clause, but you don't translate it. It's just a stylistic conjunction required by Arabic at this particular spot.

To express a contrary to fact conditional sentence in Arabic, follow these steps:

1. Introduce the condition clause with the particle لَوْ (**law**).

2. Add the prefix لَ (**la-**) to the result clause.

3. Use the past tense in both the condition and result clauses.

Here are a few examples of contrary to fact conditional sentences:

لَوْ ذَهَبْتُ إلى مِصْر لَرَأَيْتُ الأَهْرام.

(**law** <u>**dhahabtu**</u> **'ilaa miSr,** <u>**lara'aytu**</u> **al-ahraam.** *If I had gone to Egypt, I would have seen the Pyramids.*)

لَوْ رَأى ذلكَ الفيلم لَكانَ مُوافِقاً مَعـي.

(**law** <u>**ra'a**</u> **hadha-l-film,** <u>**lakaana**</u> **muwaafiqan ma3ii.** *If he had seen that movie, he would have agreed with me.*)

لو كانَ عِنْدَهُمْ مِلْيون دولار لَشْتَروا البَيْت.

(**law** <u>**kaana**</u> **3indahum milyuun dolaar, la-**<u>**shtaruu**</u> **al-bayt.** *If they had a million dollars, they would buy the house.*)

In the previous examples, I underline the two past tense verbs of the conditional and result clauses. You can see that in each case, there's the addition of the prefix لَ (**la-**) before the second past tense verb. Also note, however, that the English translation reflects the unreal situation posed by a contrary to fact sentence.

Adding the negative to contrary to fact conditional sentences

When you need to add a negative to your contrary to fact conditional sentence, you use لَمْ (**lam**; *not*) plus the jussive forms of the verb in the condition clause, and ما (**maa**; *not*) plus the past tense in the result clause. To read more about the use of ما (**maa**) and لَمْ (**lam**; *not*), flip to Chapter 17.

In the following examples, I underline the verbs, preceded by their words for *not* so that you can easily spot them:

لو لَمْ أُرسِلْ الطَّرْد يَوْم الخَميس لَما وَصَلَ لِحَبيبَتي أمْس.

(**law** <u>**lam 'ursil**</u> **aT-Tard yawm al-khamiis** <u>**lamaa waSala**</u> **liHabiibatii 'amsi.** *If I hadn't sent the package on Thursday, my girlfriend would not have received it yesterday.*)

لو فازَتْ فِرْقَتي لَما كُنْتُ حَزيناً الآنَ.

(**law faaza firqatii** <u>**lamaa kuntu**</u> **Haziinan al'aana.** *If my team had won, I wouldn't be sad right now.*)

In this practice set, I give you several simple conditional sentences. Convert them into contrary to fact conditional sentences by replacing إذا ('**idha**) with لَوُ (**law**) and adding the particle لَ (**la-**) to the result clause. Then translate your newly created contrary to fact conditional sentence into English.

Q. إِذَا ذَهَبْنَا إِلَى الْمَطْعَم أَكَلْتُ الفَلَافِل. ('**idhaa dhahabnaa 'ilaa-l-maT3am 'akaltu al-falaafil.** *If we go to the restaurant, I would eat the falafel.*)

A. لَوْ ذَهَبْنَا إِلَى الْمَطْعَم لَأَكَلْتُ الفَلَافِل. (**law dhahabnaa 'ilaa-l-maT3am la'akaltu al-falaafil.** *If we had gone to the restaurant, I would have eaten the falafel.*)

9. إِذَا كَانَ عِنْدي الوَقْت فَعَلْتُ ذلِكَ لَكَ. ('**idhaa kaana 3indii al-waqt fa3altu dhaalika laka.** *If I have time, I'd do that for you.*)

_____

10. إِذَا حَضَرَتْ تَكَلَّمْنَا مَعاً. ('**idhaa HaDarat takallamnaa ma3an.** *If she comes, we'd speak together.*)

_____

11. إِذَا كَانَ الجَوّ لَطِيفاً غَداً فَسَنَذْهَبُ إِلَى الحَدِيقة. ('**idhaa kaana al-jaww laTiifan ghadan fa-sanadh-habu ilaa-l-Hadiiqa.** *If the weather is nice tomorrow* [change to *yesterday*], *we will go to the park.*)

_____

Tackling the Jussive in Simple Conditional Sentences

Jussive comes from a Latin word meaning *to order*. You can use the jussive mood in what are very polite orders, such as فَلْنَذْهَب (**falnadh-hab;** *Let's go*). Because the jussive is a mood that you can use in unreal situations, the jussive can be used in simple conditional sentences. A simple conditional sentence using jussive won't impart a meaning different from one using just past tense (to see the use of past tense verbs refer to the earlier section "Applying past tense indicative"). But you want to know how to form a conditional sentence with jussive so you can vary your own writing style and also make sense of conditional sentences formed with jussive that you come across in your reading.

To use the jussive in a conditional sentence, you can start with a past tense verb in the condition clause, just like you would for a simple conditional sentence (see the earlier section "Forming Simple Conditional Sentences in Arabic" for more information). In the result clause, you use a jussive form of the verb, following the addition of the particle فَ (**fa-**).

The particle فَ (**fa-**) is left untranslated, because it's a stylistic necessity of Arabic in a simple conditional sentence with the jussive, not a meaning-bearing word as such. However, فَ (**fa-**) does have the translatable meaning of *and so/and then* in other contexts. (To discover further details about the use of فَ (**fa-**), see Chapter 15.)

Here are a few examples of simple conditional sentences using the jussive in the result clause:

إِذَا دَرَسْتَ هَذَا الْكِتَابَ فَتَتَعَلَّمْ أَشْيَاءَ كَثِيرَةً.

(**'idhaa <u>darasta</u> hadha-l-kitaab, <u>fatata3allam</u>** 'ashyaa' kathiira. *If you study this book, you'd learn many things.*)

إِذَا رَأَيْتُ صَدِيقِي فَأَكُنْ مَسْرُوراً.

(**'idhaa <u>ra'aytu</u> Sadiiqii, <u>fa'akun</u>** masruuran. *If I see my friend, I'd be happy.*)

إِذَا ارَادَ فَيَسْتَطِعْ أَنْ يَحْضُرَ اَيْضاً.

(**'idhaa <u>araada</u>, <u>fayastaTi3</u>** 'an yaHDura 'ayDan. *If he wants, he can come too.*)

In the previous examples, I underline the verbs to help you quickly locate them. Notice that all the verbs in the condition clause are past tense. The result clauses, however, have verbs in the jussive, each one preceded by the particle فَ (**fa-**).

Until you have fully mastered the jussive, get in the habit of just using past tense for all your conditional sentences. It's grammatically correct, and it's easier to work with than the jussive.

The following sentences are conditionals that currently use past tense in both parts. Rewrite each sentence, adding the prefix فَ (**fa-**) to the result clause and changing the verb in that clause to the jussive.

0. إِذَا كُنْتُ مُوَافِقاً فَعَلْنَا ذَلِكَ. (**'idhaa kunta muwaafiqan fa3alnaa dhalika.**)

A. إِذَا كُنْتُ مُوَافِقاً فَنَفْعَلْ ذَلِكَ. (**'idhaa kunta muwaafiqan fanaf3al dhalika.** *If you agree, we would do that.*)

12. إِذَا قَرَأُوا رِسَالَتِي عَرَفُوا الْجَوَابَ. (**'idhaa qara'uu risaalatii, 3arafuu al-jawaab.**)

_____

13. إِذَا زُرْنَا الْمَتْحَف تَعَلَّمْنَا كَثِيراً. (**'idhaa zurnaa al-matHaf, ta3allamnaa kathiiran.**)

_____

14. إِذَا دَرَسْتَ أَكْثَر نَجَحْتَ فِي الْإِمْتِحَان. (**'idhaa darasta akthar, najaHta fi-l-imtHaan.**)

_____

15. إِذَا أَكَلْتَ كَثِيراً صِرْتَ مَرِيضاً. (**'idhaa 'akalta kathiran Sirta mariiDan.**)

_____

16. إِذَا اِشْتَرَيْتُ حَاسُوب جَدِيد كُنْتُ فَقِيراً. (**'idhaa ishtaraytu Haasuub jadiid kuntu faqiiran.**)

_____

Finding إِنْ ('in) in Classical Conditional Sentences

At one time, إِذَا ('**idha**) was used to imply more potential for the conditional sentence coming true. By contrast, إِنْ ('**in**) implied a more hypothetical situation. In Modern Standard Arabic today, however, إِذَا ('**idha**) has become the standard word for all conditional sentences. You may see إِنْ ('**in**) used in classical texts, but it's no longer a commonly used word. It survives today within the phrase you should use whenever referring to the future: إِنْ شَاء اللّٰه ('**in shaa' 'allah;** *if God wills it*). (To see more about the use and formation of the future tense, visit Chapter 2.) But don't get in the habit of using إِنْ ('**in**) regularly in your own writing. It would make it sound overly formal and maybe even stuffy. I'm only showing you this particle so you recognize it when you see it in classical texts and quotes.

Answer Key

1 إذا ذَهَبْنا إلى المُطْعَم أكَلْتُ الفَلافِل. ('idhaa dhahabnaa 'ilaa-l-maT3am 'akaltu al-falaafil.)

2 إذا كانَ عِنْدي الوَقْت فَعَلْتُ ذلِكَ لَكَ. ('idhaa kaana 3indii al-waqt fa3altu dhaalika laka.)

3 إذا حَضَرَتْ تَكَلَّمْنا مَعاً. ('idhaa HaDarat takallamnaa ma3an.)

4 إذا أرَدْتَ أنْ تَعْرِفَ الجَواب سَأَلْتَ السُّؤال. ('idhaa 'aradta 'an ta3rifa al-jawaab sa'alta as-su'aal.)

5 إذا كانَ هُنا غَداً أكْمَلْنا الشُّغْل. ('idhaa kaana hunaa ghadan 'akmalnaa al-3amal.)

6 إذا لَمْ يَصِل قَريباً فَسَنَبْدَأُ بِدونِه. ('idhaa lam yaSil qariiban fa-sanabda'u biduunihi.)

7 إذا قالَتْ شَيْئاً فَلا تَتَشَكَّكْ بِه. ('idhaa qaalat shay'an fa-laa tatashakkak bihi.)

8 إذا كانَ الجَوّ لَطيفاً غَداً فَسَنَذْهَبُ إلى الحَديقة. ('idhaa kaana al-jaww laTiifan ghadan fa-sanadh-habu ilaa-l-Hadiiqa.)

9 لَوْ كانَ عِنْدي الوَقْت لَفَعَلْتُ ذلِكَ لَكَ. (law kaana 3indii al-waqt lafa3altu dhaalika laka. *If I had had time, I would have done that for you.*)

10 لَوْ حَضَرَتْ لَتَكَلَّمْنا مَعاً. (law HaDarat latakallamnaa ma3an. *If she had come, we would have spoken together.*)

11 لَوْ كانَ الجَوّ لَطيفاً أمْس لَذَهَبْنا إلى الحَديقة. (law kaana al-jaww laTiifan 'ams ladhahabnaa ilaa-l-Hadiiqa. *If the weather had been nice yesterday, we would have gone to the park.*)

12 إذا قَرَأوا رِسالَتي فَيَعْرِفوا الجَواب. ('idhaa qara'uu risaalatii fa-ya3rifuu aljawaab. *If they read my letter, they'll know the answer.*)

13 إذا زُرْنا المَتْحَف فَنَتَعَلَّم كَثيراً. ('idhaa zurnaa al-matHaf fa-nata3allam kathiiran. *If we visit the museum, we'll learn a lot.*)

14 إذا دَرَسْتَ أكْثَر فَتَنْجَحْ في الإمْتِحان. (idha darasta 'akthar fa-tanjaH fii-l-imtiHaan. *If you study more, you'll pass the test.*)

15 إذا أكَلْتَ كَثيراً فَتَصِرْ مَريضاً. ('idhaa 'akalta kathiran fa-taSir mariiDan. *If you eat a lot, you'd get sick.*)

16 إذا اشْتَرَيْتُ حاسوباً جَديداً فَأَكُنْ فَقيراً. ('idhaa ishtaraytu Haasuuban jadiidan fa'akun faqiiran. *If I buy a new computer I'd be poor.*)

Chapter 15

Picking Up the Pieces Using Particles and Partitives

In This Chapter

▶ Discovering simple and temporal conjunctions

▶ Looking into Arabic partitive nouns

Two particular pieces of Arabic grammar come together in this chapter: particles and partitives. Arab grammarians traditionally divided their language into just three categories: nouns, verbs, and, well, everything else. The name they gave to this "everything else" category is حُروف (**Huruuf**), meaning *particles*. If you've read through other chapters of this book, you've probably already seen many things that qualify as particles. Just like particles of dust in the air, Arabic particles are everywhere!

In the first part of this chapter, I give you an overview of Arabic particles. Then I focus on two important types of particles: simple and temporal conjunctions. *Conjunctions* are those words you use to bind or divide parts of your sentence. The most basic and important of the conjunctions is و (**wa-;** *and*). But I explain several others that you can use to polish your Arabic writing.

In the second part of the chapter, I present the Arabic partitive nouns. *Partitives* are the words you use to talk about "parts" of a noun. In other words, they indicate whether you're discussing *all, some,* or *most* of something.

Examining Arabic Particles

There's a reason that the Arabic word for particle, حُروف (**Huruuf**), is the same word used for *letters* (of the alphabet). It's because they're both tiny little things. Languages tend to use small words for important and common tasks and reserve multiple syllable words for rarer things. Imagine how tired your tongue would be at the end of the day if the word for *and* were as long as *antidisestablishmentarianism*! Many different types of words qualify as particles. Included are prepositions, conjunctions, and even words such as لا (**laa;** *no/not*), which makes a verb negative. I show you the particles for making sentences negative in Chapter 17. And you can explore prepositions in detail in Chapter 12.

Pulling Sentences Together Using Arabic Conjunctions

Arabic offers you a variety of ways to join words. Sometimes you just need to bind two words with و (wa-; *and*). Other times you need something more sophisticated than that. So, in this section, I delve into the most common conjunctions that you may encounter and use to combine words and longer phrases. I break them down into two categories: simple and temporal.

Simple conjunctions

What grammarians call *simple conjunctions* are those words that either join or separate words and phrases in a sentence. Now, just because they're called *simple* doesn't mean they aren't important. You're about to see that these words can give you some powerful ways to express yourself in Arabic. The most common simple conjunctions, which I show you in the following sections, include the following: *and, when, and/and so/and then, but, or,* and *because.* I also toss in a few other essential conjunctions that fall into the miscellaneous category.

و (wa-; and)

The conjunction و (wa-; *and*) is probably the most important conjunction of all. You add و (wa-) as a prefix to words when you want to say *and.* Here's an example of this powerful conjunction in action:

ذَهَبَ أَحْمَدُ وَمَرْوان إلى المَلْعَب وَبَعْدَ ذلِكَ رَجَعا إلى البَيْت.

(dhahaba 'aHmadu <u>wa</u>-marwaan 'ilaa-l-mal3ab <u>wa</u>-ba3da dhaalika raja3aa 'ilaa-l-bayt. *Ahmad <u>and</u> Marwan went to the stadium, <u>and</u> after that they returned to the house.*)

Notice that the conjunction in the previous example joins two people, Ahmad and Marwan, but also joins two clauses together the second time it occurs.

Here's a useful trick you can perform with the conjunction و (wa-). You can create a circumstantial clause just by joining a few words or a separate sentence to your main sentence with **wa-.**

A *circumstantial clause* is a phrase or sentence that tells your reader some important background information (the circumstances) about your main topic. For instance, I could tell you that I went to France. But if I tell you that I went to France *when I was in college,* I would be adding information that's circumstantial to my main topic (going to France). You can create a circumstantial clause in Arabic by putting و (wa-) in place of *when* in the example I just used. Here's the Arabic equivalent:

ذَهَبْتُ إلى فَرَنْسا وَأَنا في الكُلِّية.

(dhahabtu 'ilaa faransaa <u>wa</u>-'anaa fii-l-kulliya. *I went to France <u>when</u> I was in college.*)

Keep in mind that it isn't the case that وَ (**wa-**; *and*) means *when* just because we translate it that way in English. Rather, Arabic uses the conjunction to create a circumstantial clause. Here are more examples of the conjunction **wa-** creating circumstantial clauses:

تَعَلَّمَتْ تِلْكَ اللُّغة وَهِيَ طالِبةٌ في الجامِعة.

(**ta3allamat tilka-l-lugha wa-hiya Taalibatun fi-l-jaami3a.** *She learned that language when she was a student at the university.*)

نَزَلَ مِن الطّائِرة وَهُوَ يَتَكَلَّمُ مَعَ صَديقِهِ.

(**nazala min aT-Taa'ira wa-huwa yatakallamu ma3a Sadiiqihi.** *He got off the plane while talking with his friend.*)

فَ (fa-; and/and so/and then)

In addition to وَ (**wa-**), Arabic has the conjunction فَ (**fa-**), which also translates as *and* in many contexts. The main difference between the two is that فَ (**fa-**) ordinarily implies that the two things you're binding together are happening in a certain order. Most of the time, you use فَ (**fa-**) to put together two phrases that happen one after another. In this case, you can translate فَ (**fa-**) as simply *and,* or you could translate it as *and so* or *and then* (depending on what sounds best in that context). Like **wa-**, you attach **fa-** as a prefix to the first word in your new clause.

Here are a few examples of فَ (**fa-**) in action:

ذَهَبَ أَحْمَدُ وَمَرْوان إلى المَلْعَب فَرَجَعا إلى البَيْت.

(**dhahaba 'aHmadu wa-marwaan 'ilaa-l-mal3ab fa-raja3a 'ilaa-l-bayt.** *Ahmad and Marwan went to the stadium, and then they returned to the house.*)

لَيْسَ عِنْدي خُبْزٌ فَيَجِبُ أَنْ آذْهَبَ إلى السّوق.

(**laysa 3indii khubzun fa-yajib 'an 'adh-haba 'ilaa-s-suuq.** *I don't have bread, and so I need to go to the market.*)

Notice that the conjunctions here are identical. It's the English context that requires slightly different translations. In the first example, the conjunction focuses on the temporal relationship between the clauses. In the second example, the main point is the logical connection between the clauses. But the Arabic conjunction is the same for both.

لٰكِنْ / لٰكِنَّ (laakin/laakinna; but)

Arabic has two forms of the word for *but.* Those two forms are لٰكِنْ (**laakin**) and لٰكِنَّ (**laakinna**).

The word لٰكِنْ (**laakin**) is the simple version of *but* in Arabic. You can simply insert it as a separate word between two clauses when you want to express exclusion. It can occur before a verb or a noun in the nominative case (unlike لٰكِنَّ [**laakinna**], which requires accusative).

Here are a few examples of لـكِنْ (laakin):

يُريدونَ اَنْ يَأْكُلوا هُناكَ لِكِنْ لَيْسَ عِنْدَهُم مالٌ كَثيرٌ.

(yuriiduuna 'an ya'kuluu hunaaka, <u>laakin</u> laysa 3indahum maalun kathiirun. *They want to eat there, <u>but</u> they don't have much money.*)

تَدْرُسُ فاطِمة الرِّياضِيّات لِكِنْ يَدْرُسُ أخوها الهَنْدَسة.

(tadrusu faaTima aririyaaDiyaat, <u>lakin</u> yadrusu 'akhuhaa al-handasa. *Fatima studies mathematics, <u>but</u> her brother studies engineering.*)

لـكِنّ (laakinna) also means *but;* however, it behaves differently than لـكِنْ (laakin). لـكِنّ (laakinna) can't be followed immediately by a verb. Instead, you have to follow it with the subject of the verb, either a noun (in the accusative case) or an object pronoun attached to لـكِنّ (laakinna).

Here are some examples of لـكِنّ (laakinna):

يُعجِبُني الفيلم لِكِنّ المُمَثّلينَ يُزعِجونَني كَثيراً.

(yu3jibuni al-fiilm, <u>laakinna</u>-l-mumaththiliina yuz3ijuunani kathirran. *I like the film, <u>but</u> the actors really bother me.*)

تَشْرُبُ زَوْجَتي كَثيراً مِن الشّاي لِكِنّني أَفَضّلُ القَهْوة.

(tashrubu zawjatii kathiiran min ash-shaay, <u>laakinnanii</u> 'ufaDDilu al-qahwa. *My wife drinks a lot of tea, <u>but</u> I prefer coffee.*)

There are two equally valid ways of adding the object pronoun for أنا ('anaa; *I*) and نَحْنُ (naHnu; *we*). One way is to assimilate the initial *n* sound into the doubled *n* of lakinna. The other way is to keep them as separate sounds. There's no difference in meaning and no time when either option is more correct than the other. This example illustrates your options:

لِكِنّي (laakinni; *but I . . .*)

لِكِنّني (laakinnanii; *but I . . .*)

أَوْ/أَمْ ('aw/'am; or)

The words أَوْ ('aw) and أَمْ ('am) both mean *or*. The only difference between them is that you use أَمْ ('am) when you need to express *or* within a question. By contrast, you use أَوْ ('aw) in any sentence that isn't a question.

Here's an example using أَوْ ('aw):

سَأَكْتُبُ رسالةً اليَوْم أَوْ سَأَتّصِلُ بِحَبيبتي.

(sa'aktubu risaalatan al-yawm, '<u>aw</u> sa'attaSilu biHabiibatii. *I will write a letter today, <u>or</u> I will call my girlfriend.*)

And to better understand the distinction between the two, check out this example that uses أَمْ ('am):

هَلْ تَذْهَبينَ مَعَنا إلى السّينَما أَمْ لا؟

(hal tadh-habiina ma3anaa 'ila-s-siinama '<u>am</u> laa? *Will you go to the cinema with us <u>or</u> not?*)

لِأَنَّ (li'anna; because)

The word for *because* in Arabic is لِأَنَّ (li'anna). Like لكِنَّ (laakinna; *but*), which is discussed earlier in the chapter, you use an accusative noun immediately after لِأَنَّ (li'anna). Or you can also add an object pronoun to it (see Chapters 4 and 12 for more on object pronouns). If you have a verb after the conjunction, you put the object pronoun on first. If you have a noun as a subject, it goes immediately after the conjunction and is expressed in the accusative case.

Here are two examples:

الـمَصـرِفُ مَقـفـولٌ لِأَنَّ الـيَوْمَ هُـوَ عـيد الـعُمّـال.

(**al-maSrifu maqfuulun li'anna al-yawma huwa 3iid al'3ummaal.** *The bank is closed today because it's Labor Day.*)

الأَوْلاد جـائِـعـونَ جِدّاً لِأَنَّـهُم لَمْ يَأْكُـلـوا بَعْـد.

(**al-'awlaad jaa'i3uuna jiddan li'annahum lam ya'kuluu ba3d.** *The children are very hungry because they haven't eaten yet.*)

Temporal conjunctions

Temporal conjunctions bind clauses together with the information of *when* they happened or in what order. In Modern Standard Arabic, the most common temporal conjunction to express the concept of *when* something happened is عِنْدَما (3indamaa). Here are a couple examples to illustrate its use:

كُنْتُ صَغيراً عِنْدَما اِشْتَرَيْنا ذلِكَ الـبَيْت.

(**kuntu Saghiiran 3indamaa ishtaraynaa dhalika-l-bayt.** *I was young when we bought that house.*)

سَنَسْتَقْبِلُ أخانا عِنْدَما يَصِلُ إلى الـمَطار.

(**sa-nastaqbilu akhaana 3indamaa yaSilu 'ilaa-l-maTaar.** *We'll greet our brother when he arrives at the airport.*)

You can create conjunctions in Arabic to say that something happened before or after something else by adding temporal prepositions to the conjunction أَنْ ('an).

Here's an example using قَبْلَ أَنْ (qabla 'an; *before*):

عَـمِلَ أبي لِـمُدّة خَمْـسـينَ سَـنة قَبْلَ أَنْ تَقـاعَـدَ.

(**3amila 'abii li-muddat khamsiina sana qabla 'an taqaa3ada.** *My father worked fifty years before he retired.*)

Here's an example using بَعْدَ أَنْ (ba3da 'an; *after*):

سـافَـرَتْ إلى قَطَر بَعْدَ أَنْ غادَرَتِ الـكُـوَيْت.

(**saafarat 'ila qaTar ba3da 'an ghaadarat al-kuwayt.** *She traveled to Qatar after she left Kuwait.*)

مُنْذُ (**mundhu**) is another temporal conjunction. You may recall seeing this particle as a preposition that means *ago,* as in this example:

اِلْتَقَيْتُ بِهِ مُنْذُ ثَلاث سَنَوات.

(**iltaqaytu bihi mundhu thalaath sanawaat.** *I met him three years ago.*)

As a temporal conjunction, however, مُنْذُ (**mundhu**) means *since:*

قَدْ أَحْبَبْتُهُ مُنْذُ اِلْتَقَيْتُ بِهِ.

(**qad 'aHbabtuhu mundhu iltaqaytu bihi.** *I've liked him since I met him.*)

In the following practice set, I give you a number of sentences with missing conjunctions. Each sentence is best completed by inserting one of the conjunctions supplied in the word bank. You may need to add object suffixes from clues elsewhere in the sentence. Each word is used once. لِأَنَّ (**li'anna**), however, is used once in the example and once in the actual practice set. Write the sentence with the conjunction on the line provided.

قَبْلَ أَنْ (**qabla 'an**)	أَوْ (**'aw**)	لكِنَّ (**laakinna**)	لِأَنَّ (**li'anna**)
فَـ (**fa-**)	وَ (**wa-**)	عِنْدَما (**3indamaa**)	أَمْ (**'am**)

Q. هُوَ تَعْبان جِدّاً ـــــــ لَمْ يَنَمْ جَيِّداً. (**huwa ta3baan jiddan _____ lam yanam jayyidan.**)

A. هُوَ تَعْبان جِدّاً لِأَنَّهُ لَمْ يَنَمْ جَيِّداً. (**huwa ta3baan jiddan li'annahu lam yanam jayyidan.** *He's very tired because he didn't sleep well.*)

1. لَيْسَ عِنْدي مالٌ كَثيرٌ ـــــــ لَيْسَ عِنْدي وَظيفَةٌ. (**laysa 3indii maalun kathiirun _____ laysa 3indii waDHiifatun.**)

   _____

2. تُريدينَ أَنْ تَأْكُلي وَرَق عِنَب ـــــــ سَمَك مَشْوي؟ (**turiidina 'an ta'kulii waraq 3inab _____ samak mashwii?**)

   _____

3. أَنا مَشْغول جِدّاً الْيَوْم ـــــــ لا أَسْتَطيعُ أَنْ أَذْهَبَ مَعَكَ. ('**ana mashghul jiddan al-yawm _____ laa 'astaTi3u 'an 'adh-haba ma3aka.**)

   _____

4. نَحْنُ بِحاجة إلى أَقْلام ـــــــ نَكْتُبَ الرَّسائِل. (**naHnu bi-Haaja 'ilaa 'aqlaam _____ naktuba ar-rasaa'il.**)

   _____

5. اِتَّصِلْ بِي _____ تَصِلُ إلى المَحَطّة. ('ittaSil bii _____ taSilu 'ilaa-l-maHaTTa.)

_____

6. سَأَشْـرَبُ الماء _____ القَهْوة. (sa'ashrabu al-maa' _____ al-qahwa.)

_____

7. اِكْتَسَبَتْ خِبْرة كَثيرة _____ هِيَ مُوَظّفة فـي هذِهِ الشَّركة. (iktasabat khibra kathirra _____ hiya muwaDHDHafa fii haadhihi-sh-sharika.)

_____

8. سَيّارَتُها جَديدة _____ سَيّارَتَهُ قَديمة. (sayyaaratuhaa jadiida, _____ sayyaaratahu qadiima.)

_____

Parceling Noun Quantity with the Arabic Partitives

You've probably heard the old adage, "You can fool some of the people all of the time, and all of the people some of the time, but you can not fool all of the people all of the time." Whoever first said these words (they've been attributed to Abraham Lincoln and P.T. Barnum), made extensive use of a class of nouns known as *partitives*. Partitives in English frequently are used with the preposition *of* to express how much of something you have.

In some languages, such as Spanish, partitives are adjectives. Arabic partitives, however, behave in much the same way as English partitives. For example, you may say *all of, some of,* or *most of* something. In the same way, Arabic partitives come directly in front of the noun that they're modifying. There are Arabic partitives to express all the potential quantities of a noun that English expresses. Really, all you need to do is learn them as vocabulary items, and you're more than halfway to mastering them.

The Arabic partitives are a strange class of nouns. They function grammatically as nouns, having case, but they're somewhat defective in that they don't themselves have a plural. Instead, they convey the various shades of partitive meaning to whatever nouns you place immediately after them.

To use an Arabic partitive, you put the partitive in an **'iDaafa** construction with the noun you want to modify. The meaning of the partitive can change depending on whether its noun is singular or plural and whether it has the ال ('alif laam). I explain exactly how you change the translation as I show you each individual partitive. (If you want to review the formation of the **'iDaafa,** check out Chapter 7. For more on the ال ['alif laam], refer to Chapter 2.)

In this section, I show you how to use the Arabic partitives meaning *all, some/part,* and *most.*

Forming sentences with كُلّ (kull; all)

To express the phrase *all of the food* in Arabic, you take the partitive noun كُلّ (**kull;** *all*) and put the word الطَّعام (**aT-Ta3aam;** *the food*) directly after it. So the phrase looks like this: كُلّ الطَّعام (**kull aT-Ta3aam;** *all [of] the food*).

كُلّ (**kull**) can take the object suffixes (see Chapters 2 and 12) like any noun. You put object pronoun suffixes on this partitive when you want to express, for instance, *all of it* (as opposed to *all of the pie*) or *all of them*. Look at a few examples:

أمّا أصْدِقائي فَكُلُّهُم هُنا.

(**'amma 'aSdiqaa'ii fa-kulluhum hunaa.** *As for my friends, they're all here.*)

أكَلَ الوَلَد الكاتو كُلَّهُ.

(**'akala al-walad al-kaatuu kullahu.** *The boy ate the cake — all of it.*)

To show you how كُلّ (**kull;** *all*) works, I present the slightly different meanings it takes when it's followed by a definite or indefinite noun.

Using كُلّ (kull) with a definite noun

When you combine كُلّ (**kull**) with a definite singular noun, the partitive can be translated as *the whole*. With a definite plural noun, you would translate it as *all [of] the*. Here are some phrases using the partitive كُلّ (**kull**):

كُلّ النّاس (**kull an-naas;** *all [of] the people*)

كُلّ العالَم (**kull al-3aalam;** *the whole world*)

كُلّ الأيّام (**kull al-'ayyaam;** *all [of] the days*)

كُلّ اليَوْم (**kull al-yawm;** *the whole day*)

كُلّ اللَّيْل (**kull al-layl;** *the whole night*)

كُلّ السَّنة (**kull as-sana;** *the whole year*)

كُلّ الصَّفّ (**kull aS-Saff;** *the whole class*)

Using كُلّ (kull) with an indefinite noun

When an indefinite noun follows كُلّ (**kull**), it means *each* or *every*. Here are several example phrases for you:

كُلّ يَوْم (**kull yawm;** *every day*)

كُلّ شَخْص (**kull shakhS;** *each person*)

كُلّ سَنة (**kull sana;** *every year*)

كُلّ أحَدٍ (**kull aHadin;** *every one/each one*)

Creating reciprocal phrases with بَعْض (ba3D; some/part)

Like other partitives, بَعْض (**ba3D**) — which means *some* or *part of* something — precedes the noun it describes in an **'iDaafa** construction. Here are several examples to show you how to use بَعْض (**ba3D**):

بَعْض الوَقْت (**ba3D al-waqt;** *some of the time*)

بَعْض النّاس (**ba3D an-naas;** *some of the people*)

بَعْض الأيّام (**ba3D al-'ayyaam;** *some of the days*)

بَعْض (**ba3D**) with a possessive suffix gives you this useful reciprocal phrase:

بَعْضُهُم بَعْضاً (**ba3Duhum ba3Dan;** *one another/each other*)

What's a *reciprocal phrase,* you ask? It's a phrase in which you express action that's done between two subjects. You usually translate it with *each other* or *one another.*

With the exception of the way you translate بَعْض (**ba3D**) in a reciprocal phrase, this partitive can always be translated as *some.*

Writing with مُعْظَم (mu3DHam) and أَغْلَب ('aghlab)

The Arabic words مُعْظَم (**mu3DHam**) and أَغْلَب (**'aghlab**) both mean *most.* There isn't difference in meaning between them, and neither is more correct in any given context. The meaning stays the same regardless of the noun that follows it. Just as with كُلّ (**kull;** *all*) and بَعْض (**ba3D;** *some*) in the preceding sections, you use مُعْظَم (**mu3DHam**) and أَغْلَب (**'aghlab**) in an **'iDaafa** with the noun you want to modify. Here are a few examples:

مُعْظَم الطَّعام (**mu3DHam aT-Ta3aam;** *most [of] the food*)

أَغْلَب الطُّلاب (**'aghlab aT-Tullaab;** *most [of] the students*)

أَغْلَب المَشاكِل (**'aghlab al-mashaakil;** *most [of] the problems*)

To help you practice your use of the partitive nouns visually, in this exercise I show you a number of objects circled in different ways. For each picture, I give you a number of phrases — only one of which expresses the reality in the picture with the appropriate Arabic partitive. Select the item that best matches how the objects are circled, and then translate the Arabic phrase into English.

Q.

(A) كُلّ الأَقْلام (kull al-'aqlaam)

(B) كُلّ قَلَم (kull qalam)

(C) مُعْظَم الأَقْلام (mu3DHam al-'aqlaam)

A. **(C)** مُعْظَم الأَقْلام (mu3DHam al-'aqlaam; *most of the pencils*)

9.

(A) كُلّ صورة (kull Suura)

(B) كُلّ الصُّوَر (kull aS-Suwar)

(C) بَعْض الصُّوَر (ba3D aS-Suwar)

_____

10.

(A) كُلّ النِّساء (kull an-nissa')

(B) بَعْض النِّساء (ba3D an-nisaa')

(C) مُعْظَم النِّساء (mu3DHam an-nisaa')

_____

11.

(A) كُلّ الرِّجال (kull ar-rijaal)

(B) بَعْض الرَّجُل (ba3D ar-rajul)

(C) مُعْظَم الرِّجال (mu3DHam ar-rijaal)

_____

12.

(A) كُلّ الصُّحون (kull al-aS-SuHuun)

(B) بَعْض الصُّحون (ba3D aS-SuHuun)

(C) كُلّ صَحْن (kull SaHn)

_____

13.

(A) كُلّ السّاعات (kull as-saa3aat)

(B) أَغْلَب السّاعات ('aghlab as-saa3aat)

(C) كُلّ ساعة (kull saa3a)

_____

14.

(A) مُعْظَم بَيْت (mu3DHam bayt)

(B) كُلّ البَيْت (kull al-bayt)

(C) كُلّ البُيوت (kull al-buyuut)

_____

15.

(A) كُلّ سَيّارة (kull sayyaara)

(B) كُلّ السَّيّارات (kull as-sayyaaraat)

(C) أَغْلَب السَّيّارات ('aghlab as-sayyaaraat)

_____

16.

(A) كُلّ كِتاب (kull kitaab)

(B) بَعْض الكُتُب (ba3D al-kutub)

(C) كُلّ الكُتُب (kull al-kutub)

_____

Answer Key

1 لَيْسَ عِنْدي مالٌ كَثيرٌ لِأَنَّني لَيْسَ عِنْدي وَظيفَةٌ. (laysa 3indii maalun kathiirun <u>li'annanii</u> laysa 3indii waDHiifatun. *I don't have much money <u>because</u> I don't have a job.*)

2 تُريدينَ أَنْ تَأْكُلي وَرَق عِنَب أَمْ سَمَك مَشْوي؟ (turiidina 'an ta'kulii waraq 3inab <u>'am</u> samak mashwii? *Do you want to eat stuffed grape leaves <u>or</u> grilled fish?*)

3 أَنا مَشْغول جِدّاً اليَوْم فَلا أَسْتَطيعُ أَنْ أَذْهَبَ مَعَكَ. ('ana mashghul jiddan al-yawm <u>fa-laa</u> 'astaTi3u 'an 'adh-haba ma3aka. *I am very busy today, <u>and so</u> I can't go with you.*)

4 نَحْنُ بِحاجة إلى أَقْلام قَبْلَ أَنْ نَكْتُبَ الرَّسائِل. (naHnu bi-Haaja 'ilaa 'aqlaam <u>qabla 'an</u> naktuba ar-rasaa'il. *We need pens <u>before</u> we write the letters.*)

5 اتّصِلْ بي عِنْدَما تَصِلُ إلى المَحَطّة. (ittaSil bii <u>3indamaa</u> taSilu 'ilaa-l-maHaTTa. *Call me <u>when</u> you get to the station.*)

6 سَأَشْرَبُ الماء أَوْ القَهْوة. (sa'ashrabu al-maa' <u>'aw</u> al-qahwa. *I will drink water <u>or</u> coffee.*)

7 اِكْتَسَبَتْ خِبْرة كَثيرة وَهِيَ مُوَظَّفة في هذِه الشَّرِكة. (iktasabat khibra kathirra <u>wa</u>-hiya muwaDHDHafa fii haadhihi-sh-sharika. *She gained a lot of experience <u>while</u> she was an employee at this company.*)

8 سَيّارَتُها جَديدة لكِنَّ سَيّارَتَهُ قَديمة. (sayyaaratuhaa jadiida, <u>laakinna</u> sayyaaratahu qadiima. *Her car is new, <u>but</u> his car is old.*)

9 (A) كُلّ صورة (**kull Suura**; *each picture*)

10 (C) مُعْظَم النِّساء (**mu3DHam an-nisaa'**; *most of the women*)

11 (A) كُلّ الرِّجال (**kull ar-rijaal**; *all of the men*)

12 (B) بَعْض الصُّحون (**ba3D aS-SuHuun**; *some of the plates*)

13 (B) أَغْلَب السّاعات ('**aghlab as-saa3aat**; *most of the clocks*)

14 (C) كُلّ البُيوت (**kull al-buyuut**; *all of the houses*)

15 (A) كُلّ سَيّارة (**kull sayyaara**; *each car*)

16 (B) بَعْض الكُتُب (**ba3D al-kutub**; *some of the books*)

Chapter 16

Uncovering the Source of the Verbal Noun

In This Chapter

▶ Getting to know verbal nouns

▶ Creating verbal nouns for all the forms of the Arabic verb

▶ Using verbal nouns in your writing

*I*n English, when you write about actions as abstract or complex concepts, you're using verbal nouns. For example, in the maxim, "To err is human, to forgive divine," the words *err* and *forgive* are verbal nouns. They represent both abstract and complex actions. This is different from using a verb such as "Run!" which indicates a pretty simple and clear action.

Arabic has a system of verbal nouns that allows you to express abstract or complex concepts concisely. The Arabic word for the verbal noun is مَصْدَر (**maSdar**), which literally means *source*. You can think of the verbal noun as the source or most basic form of any verb. In this chapter, you discover how to produce the **maSdar** for any verb that you need to use. You also encounter how to use the **maSdar** in several important sentence structures.

Understanding the Basics of Verbal Nouns

Before you can begin using the Arabic **maSdar** in your writing, you first need to wrap your brain around it. A veteran linguist at the National Security Agency once told me that the key to understanding the Arabic verbal noun is to view it as more verb than noun. The **maSdar** is indeed a noun in form, though; it can take all the cases of the noun. (For more on the cases, flip to Chapter 4.) But a verbal noun in Arabic doesn't just describe an action. Instead, it's a way of expressing action. In Arabic, for instance, you frequently use a verbal noun where English would use a form of the verb called an *infinitive*. Like all verbs in Arabic, the verbal noun is quite varied in its shape in Form I, and remarkably regular in Forms II through X.

To help you understand verbal nouns from a grammatical standpoint, I start by describing their formations and uses in English. Verbal nouns are derived from verbs, and they describe the act of performing whatever their verbs mean. Grammarians use the term *gerund* in English to describe verbal nouns that end *-ing*. Think of the advice

"Seeing is believing." In this example, *seeing* and *believing* are gerunds being used as verbal nouns.

You can also use infinitives as verbal nouns. In English, you form the infinitive by putting the preposition *to* in front of the most basic form of the verb. You use the infinitive when you want to complete the action of certain auxiliary verbs. For example, when you say "I want . . ." you finish your thought with an infinitive (such as "to eat a nice juicy steak"). Consider the infinitive's use in the following maxim: "To err is human." In this example, *to err* is an infinitive, but it's representing the concept of erring.

While English uses more than one type of word as a verbal noun (such as the gerunds and infinitives in the previous examples), an Arabic verb has one verbal noun but can use that one verbal noun as both a gerund and even as an infinitive. Each of the ten Arabic verb forms has its own verbal noun, but you can think of them as verbal nouns of different verbs, even though they're derived from the same verbal root.

Grammatically, a verbal noun is a noun. You use it in both English and Arabic the same way you use other more concrete nouns. Here's an example of the same verb expressed once with a tangible object and then with a verbal noun as its object:

> *I like <u>stuffed grape leaves</u>.*
>
> *I like <u>eating</u> in Arab restaurants.*

I underline the direct objects of the verb in the previous examples. In the first example, the verb, *like,* has as its direct object a tangible (and delicious) concrete thing — stuffed grape leaves. In the second example, however, the object of the verb is an action that I like doing. The two sentences are identical in their deep grammatical structures (each one having a verb and a direct object). But they're quite different in that the second example shows the versatility of using a verbal noun to express succinctly what could have been a much more complex sentence if done verbally (for example, *I like it when I eat in Arab restaurants*).

Producing the maSdar in the Forms

Producing a **maSdar** is easy. All you need to know is the word pattern used by the particular verbal root in Form I or the regular word pattern used by each of the other verb forms. You can then simply substitute the consonants of your verbal root for the consonants in the dummy root فعل (**f-3-l**). (To discover more about this root to produce word patterns, visit Chapter 2.) Here are several examples of this substitution:

Pattern	Verbal Root	maSdar	English
تَفْعيل (**taf3iil**)	وقع (**w-q-3**)	تَوْقيع (**tawqii'**)	to sign
إفْعال (**'if3aal**)	كمل (**k-m-l**)	إكْمال (**'ikmaal**)	to complete
مُفاعَلة (**mufaa3ala**)	سعد (**s-3-d**)	مُساعَدة (**musaa3ada**)	to help

After you see how to align the consonants one by one with the location within the word pattern of the dummy root فعل (**f-3-l**), you can take any supplied pattern and produce the **maSdar.** Notice how the consonants in each verbal root replace the consonants of the dummy root فعل (**f-3-l**) to produce a word that essentially rhymes with the pattern.

The Arabic verb comes in ten forms. Each one of them has its own **maSdar** to master. The Arabic verb is also subject to various irregularities depending on the relative strength or weakness of the consonants in each verbal root. In this section, you encounter everything you need to know to produce the **maSdar,** not only of the regular verb in all ten forms, but also of the irregular verb.

Creating the maSdar of regular verbs

To succeed with the **maSdar** of the regular verb, all you need to know is the principle of substituting consonants within the word patterns with the dummy root. The **maSdar** almost always preserves the distinct elements you use to recognize the form of the verb. (For more on the ten forms of the Arabic verb, go to Chapter 9.)

Form 1

The **maSdar** of Form I verbs is unpredictable. I know it's frustrating to have to memorize random patterns for these verbs. But do know that the rest of the forms are completely regular and predictable.

No single word pattern is reserved for the Form I **maSdar.** Arabic uses an enormous variety of word patterns to produce it. And unfortunately, from a verbal root alone, you can't infallibly predict what shape that root's Form I **maSdar** will take. As a result, you ultimately have to memorize the **maSdar** of the basic and important verbs in Form I. To show you the possibilities, here are several Form I verbal nouns of some basic and important verbs:

ذَهاب (**dhahaab;** *to go*)

دُخول (**dukhuul;** *to enter*)

عَمَل (**3amal;** *to work*)

دِراسة (**diraasa;** *to study*)

Forms II–X

The **maSdar** in Forms II–X are regular and a little easier to master than Form I. In Table 16-1, I present the **maSdar** for some verbs in Forms II–X. In the "Pattern" column, I provide the word pattern that you use to produce each form's **maSdar.** The present tense is provided as a reference to remind you about the distinct features you find in each of the ten verb forms. Now, you can't exactly extrapolate the **maSdar** from any particular part of the verb. Instead, you need to memorize the word patterns for each of the ten forms.

Table 16-1		The maSdar in Forms II–X		
Form	**Present**	**maSdar**	**Pattern**	**English**
II	يُدَرِّسُ (yudarrisu)	تَدْرِيس (tadriis)	تَفْعِيل (taf3iil)	to teach
III	يُشَاهِدُ (yushaahidu)	مُشَاهَدة (mushaahada)	مُفَاعَلة (mufaa3ala)	to watch
IV	يُعْلِنُ (yu3linu)	إِعْلان ('i3laan)	إِفْعال ('if3aal)	to announce
V	يَتَكَلَّمُ (yatakallamu)	تَكَلُّم (takallum)	تَفَعُّل (tafa33ul)	to speak
VI	يَتَبَادَلُ (yatabaadalu)	تَبَادُل (tabaadul)	تَفَاعُل (tafaa3ul)	to exchange
VII	يَنْكَسِرُ (yankasiru)	إِنْكِسار (inkisaar)	إِنْفِعال (infi3aal)	to break
VIII	يَسْتَمِعُ (yastami3u)	إِسْتِماع (istimaa3)	إِفْتِعال (ifti3aal)	to listen
IX	يَحْمَرُّ (yaHmarru)	إِحْمِرار (iHmiraar)	إِفْعِلال (if3ilaal)	to turn red
X	يَسْتَعْمِلُ (yasta3milu)	إِسْتِعْمال (isti3maal)	إِسْتِفْعال (istif3aal)	to use

In this exercise, I give you the three consonants of a regular verb root and the word pattern of a **maSdar** (using the consonants فعل [**f-3-l**]). Substitute the consonants and write the resulting **maSdar** form as I did for you in Table 16-1.

0. Verbal root: علق (**3-l-q**); **maSdar** pattern: تَفْعِيل (**taf3iil**); verb form: II; English: *to hang*

A. تَعْلِيق (**ta3liiq**)

1. Verbal root: دخل (**d-kh-l**); **maSdar** pattern: إِفْعال (**'if3aal**); verb form: IV; English: *to insert*

2. Verbal root: خدم (**kh-d-m**); **maSdar** pattern: إِسْتِفْعال (**istif3aal**); verb form: X; English: *to utilize*

3. Verbal root: خرج (**kh-r-j**); **maSdar** pattern: تَفَعُّل (**tafa33ul**); verb form: V; English: *to graduate*

4. Verbal root: سـفر (**s-f-r**); maSdar pattern: مُفـاعَـلة (**mufaa3ala**); verb form: III; English: *to travel*

_____

5. Verbal root: كـلـف (**k-l-f**); maSdar pattern: تَفـْعـيل (**taf3iil**); verb form: II; English: *to entrust*

_____

6. Verbal root: حـفـل (**H-f-l**); maSdar pattern: اِفـْتـِعـال (**ifti3aal**); verb form: VIII; English: *to celebrate*

_____

7. Verbal root: خبـر (**kh-b-r**); maSdar pattern: إِفـْعـال (**'if3aal**); verb form: IV; English: *to tell*

_____

8. Verbal root: مرن (**m-r-n**); maSdar pattern: تَفـْعـيل (**taf3iil**); verb form: II; English: *to train*

_____

9. Verbal root: بصر (**b-S-r**); maSdar pattern: تَفَعـُّل (**tafa33ul**); verb form: V; English: *to ponder*

_____

10. Verbal root: نقل (**n-q-l**); maSdar pattern: اِفـْتـِعـال (**ifti3aal**); verb form: VIII; English: *to move*

_____

Creating the maSdar of irregular verbs

Arabic verbs are considered irregular if one or more of the three consonants of the verbal root are weak enough in pronunciation that they affect the form of the verb. When you produce the **maSdar** with a root containing a weak letter, you still use the same word patterns as the regular verb. You just have to make a few adjustments because of the weak letters.

Form 1

Just as with regular verbs, the irregular Form I **maSdar** is unpredictable and has to be memorized separately. A dictionary can give you this information.

Here are the **maSdar** forms of several important irregular verbs in Form I:

كَـوْن (**kawn**; *to be*)

وُصـول (**wuSuul**; *to arrive*)

بَـيْـع (**bay3**; *to sell*)

شِـراء (**shiraa'**; *to buy*)

In many cases, verbs that are irregular in their present or past tenses are completely regular in their **maSdar** forms. Geminate verbs, for instance, split up the doubled letter to produce a regular **maSdar**. Here are examples of geminate verbs with the letters doubled in the past tense and split up in the **maSdar**:

اِسْتَمَرَّ (**istamarra**; *he continued*)

اِسْتِمْرار (**istimraar**; *to continue*)

You can read more about geminate verbs in Chapter 10.

Initial واو (waaw) or ياء (yaa') verbs (Forms VIII, IV and X)

The **maSdar** of a verb with an initial واو (**waaw**) or ياء (**yaa'**) isn't terribly difficult to spot. Initial **waaw** or **yaa'** verbs keep the assimilation that they ordinarily have in Form VIII. However, in Forms IV and X, they turn their initial consonant into a long *i* vowel, which is written with ياء (**yaa'**). Here are some examples:

Form	Verbal Root	Present	maSdar	English
VIII	وصل (w-S-l)	يَتَّصِلُ (yattaSilu)	اِتّصال (ittiSaal)	to call
IV	وجب (w-j-b)	يوجِبُ (yuujibu)	إيجاب ('iijaab)	to obligate
X	ورد (w-r-d)	يَسْتَوْرِدُ (yastawridu)	اِسْتيراد (istiiraad)	to import

Note the doubled تاء (**taa'**), which is the distinctive feature of an initial واو (**waaw**) verb in Form VIII. The long *i* vowel — written with ياء (**yaa'**) — in the Form IV and X **maSdar** of an initial واو (**waaw**) verb can take some getting used to. Remember that the ياء (**yaa'**) and the واو (**waaw**) behave similarly in the irregular verbs, so it's no surprise that a واو (**waaw**) turns into a ياء (**yaa'**).

Medial واو (waaw) or ياء (yaa') verbs (Forms IV and X)

Medial واو (**waaw**) or ياء (**yaa'**) verbs in Forms IV and X turn the medial letter into a long *a* vowel (written with an أَلِف ['**alif**]) and add a تاء مَرْبوطَة (**taa' marbuuTa**). Check out a few examples:

Form	Verbal Root	Present	maSdar	English
IV	قوم (q-w-m)	يُقيمُ (yuqiimu)	إقامة ('iqaama)	to elevate
X	قوم (q-w-m)	يَسْتَقيمُ (yastaqiimu)	اِسْتِقامة (istiqaama)	to stand upright

Arabic likes its roots to have three consonants. When the weakness of a consonant makes it disappear, as you see it do by turning into a long *a* vowel in the previous table, the language compensates by adding something. The تاءمَرْبوطَة (**taa' marbuuTa**) gives the **maSdar** here an extra syllable to make up for the lost letter.

Final واو (waaw) or ياء (yaa') verbs (Forms II and III)

Final واو (**waaw**) or ياء (**yaa'**) verbs add a تاء مَرْبوطَة (**taa' marbuuTa**) in Forms II and III as shown in these examples:

Form	Verbal Root	Present	maSdar	English
II	ربو (r-b-w)	يُرَبّي (yurabbii)	تَرْبِية (tarbiya)	to educate
III	ندو (n-d-w)	يُنادي (yunaadii)	مُناداة (munaadaa)	to call out

The key to recognizing the **maSdar** of a final واو (**waaw**) or ياء (**yaa'**) verb in Forms II and III is to note that most of the normal shape of the **maSdar** is still present with them. Just be careful not to mistake the form تَرْبِية (**tarbiya**) for a feminine adjective (for more information on adjectives, check out Chapter 6).

Final واو (waaw) or ياء (yaa') verbs (Forms IV, VII, VIII and X)

In Forms IV, VII, VIII, and X, final واو (**waaw**) or ياء (**yaa'**) verbs turn the final letter into a long *a* — written with أَلِف (**'alif**) — followed by ء (**hamza**). Check out these examples:

Form	Verbal Root	Present	maSdar	English
IV	جري (j-r-y)	يُجْري (yujrii)	إجْراء ('ijraa')	to implement
VII	عزو (3-z-w)	يَنْعَزى (yan3azaa)	إنْعِزاء ('in3izaa')	to console oneself
VIII	عني (3-n-y)	يَعْتَني (ya3tanii)	إعْتِناء ('i3tinaa')	to feel concern for
X	قصو (q-S-w)	يَسْتَقْصي (yastaqSii)	إسْتِقْصاء (istiqSaa')	to examine

As you can see in the previous examples, the final واو (**waaw**) or ياء (**yaa'**) is replaced by the distinctly recognizable long *a* and ء (**hamza**). The key to finding a word in a dictionary is knowing what root it comes from. If you ever run across such a form in your reading, it's a good bet that a final long *a* and ء (**hamza**) are hiding a final واو (**waaw**) or ياء (**yaa'**).

Final واو (waaw) or ياء (yaa') verbs (Forms V and VI)

In Forms V and VI, final واو (**waaw**) or ياء (**yaa'**) verbs remove the final letter altogether and replace it with كَسْرَتَيْن (**kasratayn**). The **kasratayn** turns into a full long *i* vowel — written with ياء (**yaa'**) — when the **maSdar** is the head of an 'iDaafa or has the ال ('**alif laam**). Here are two examples:

Form	Verbal Root	Present	maSdar	English
V	قصو (q-S-w)	يَتَقَصّى (yataqaSSaa)	تَقَصٍّ (taqaSSin)	to inquire
			تَقَصّي (taqaSSii)	to inquire
VI	قضي (q-D-y)	يَتَقاضى (yataqaaDaa)	تَقاضٍ (taqaaDin)	to claim
			تَقاضي (taqaaDii)	to claim

To help you note the alternate forms, I've placed the Form V and VI final واو (**waaw**) or ياء (**yaa'**) **maSdar** directly below the form with **kasratayn**. The version with the final long vowel is the one you will actually see more commonly, because the **maSdar** will tend to take on the ال ('**alif laam**) in actual use. (To see more about adding the ال ['**alif laam**] to the **maSdar**, continue to the next section, "Incorporating the **maSdar** in Your Writing.")

Incorporating the maSdar in Your Writing

The Arabic **maSdar** is a powerful tool for expressing yourself succinctly. In this section, I show you ways to use a **maSdar** as a noun, describing actions vividly in the three cases. I also show you ways to replace longer verbal clauses with a **maSdar**. Finally, you discover how to coordinate the use of your **maSdar** with important auxiliary verbs, which shows you can express a polished literary style.

Using the maSdar as a noun

Like in English, every verbal noun in Arabic can be used as a noun that describes an action rather than a physical object. In fact, as a noun, a **maSdar** can appear in any place you might use another noun. In other words, it can be used in all three cases: nominative, accusative, and genitive. The verbal noun sometimes denotes a concept only translatable as a noun. Other times, the verbal noun could be replaced with a form of a verb to create a sentence of the same meaning. I explain how to use a **maSdar** with all three cases in the following sections.

The maSdar as a nominative noun

A **maSdar** in the nominative case can be the subject of a nominal sentence or the subject of a verb. A **maSdar** with a تاء مَرْبوطة (**taa' marbuuTa**) is treated as a feminine noun. A verbal noun in Arabic is usually in the *definite state,* meaning it has the ال ('**alif laam**) prefix (the equivalent of the English word *the*). (To see how to add the ال ['**alif laam**] to nouns, flip to Chapter 2.) In other words, unless the verbal noun is the first member of an '**iDaafa,** it either has the ال ('**alif laam**) or a possessive suffix.

Here's an example of the **maSdar** being used in the nominative case (the **maSdar** is underlined):

الدِّراسةُ كُلَّ يَوْمٍ مُهِمّةٌ.

(**<u>ad-diraasatu</u> kulla yawmin muhimmatun.** <u>Studying</u> *every day is important.*)

The maSdar as an accusative object noun

Just as a verbal noun can be the subject of a verb, it can also be the object, which means it's in the accusative case. Here are two examples of verbal nouns in the accusative case and serving as objects to verbs (the **maSdar** is underlined):

أُحِبُّ الأَكْلَ في مَطاعِم عَرَبيّة.

(**'uHibbu <u>al-'akl</u> fii maTaa3im 3arabiyya.** *I love <u>eating</u> in Arab restaurants.*)

بَدَأَتْ زِيارَتَها في المَتْحَف.

(**bada'at <u>ziyaaratahaa</u> fii-l-matHafi.** *She began <u>her visit</u> at the museum.*)

Notice that in the first example, the English gerund would be interchangeable with the infinitive *to eat.* In that example, the verbal noun is functioning as a verbal complement within the sentence. In the other example, the verbal noun is rendered much more as a noun. This displays the versatility of verbal nouns in Arabic.

The maSdar as a genitive noun

A verbal noun can appear in the genitive case after prepositions or as the second member of an 'iDaafa. Here are two examples of verbal nouns in the genitive case (the **maSdar** is underlined):

كانَتْ نَتيجَة عَمَلِها مُؤَثِّرة.

(**kaanat natiijat-3amaliha mu'aththiratan.** *The result of <u>her work</u> was impressive.*)

نامَ جَيِّداً بَعْدَ عَوْدَتِه من الرَّحْلة.

(**naama jayyidan ba3da 3awdatihi min ar-riHlati.** *He slept well after <u>his return</u> from the trip.*)

Notice that in the second example, another perfectly good translation would be to render the verbal noun as a verbal phrase: *He slept well after he returned from the trip.*

As long as you understand what the Arabic is actually doing on a grammatical level, you should feel free to translate more freely than a literal word for word rendering.

Creating purpose clauses with the maSdar

The **maSdar** gives you a convenient way to express a *purpose clause* (a clause that describes the reason or intention for doing something) that would otherwise require a longer sentence. You can add the preposition ل (**li-**; *to*) to a **maSdar** and use it as an infinitive. This **maSdar** can stand in the place of a longer clause formed using the subjunctive. Here are a few examples:

ذَهَبْتُ إلى مِصْر لِكَيْ أَدْرُسَ هُناكَ.

(**dhahabtu 'ila miSr likay 'adrusa hunaaka.** *I went to Egypt in order that I might study there.*)

ذَهَبْتُ إلى مِصْر لِلدِّراسة هُناكَ.

(**dhahabtu 'ila miSr <u>lid-diraasati</u> hunaaka.** *I went to Egypt to <u>study</u> there.*)

In the previous examples, it only takes one less syllable to use the **maSdar** in the purpose clause. Even so, learning to use the **maSdar** instead of the subjunctive is an efficient way to write. After all, there may be times when you won't know the subjunctive form of an irregular verb. The **maSdar** will likely be easier to remember.

Sometimes, you may want to form a purpose clause with an object. In this case, you can add an object to your purpose clause by putting your **maSdar** in an 'iDaafa with the intended object. (See Chapter 7 for more on the 'iDaafa.) Consider this literal translation of an 'iDaafa added to the earlier example:

ذَهَبْتُ إلى مِصْر لِدراسة العَرَبِيّة هُناكَ.

(**dhahabtu 'ila miSr li-<u>diraasat-al-3arabiyya</u> hunaaka.** *I went to Egypt for <u>the study of Arabic</u> there.*)

The "study of Arabic" is essentially the same thing as "studying Arabic." Here are some other examples of purpose clauses with **'iDaafas** as objects:

دَخَلَتْ الغُرْفة لِتَبْليغِ الرَّئيس عَن المُكالَمة.

(**dakhalat al-ghurfata litabliighi-r-ra'iisi 3an al-mukaalama.** *She entered the room to* <u>inform the president</u> *about the call.*)

يَجِبُ أَنْ تَكْتُبَ رسالةً لِوالِدَيْكَ لِتَهْدِئة أَعْصابِهِما.

(**yajibu 'an taktuba risaalatan li-waalidayka** <u>li-tahdi'ati a3Saabihimaa</u>. *You should write a letter to your parents* <u>in order to calm their nerves</u>.)

Making use of the maSdar with an auxiliary verb

A feature especially common in Arabic media is the use of the **maSdar** with certain auxiliary verbs. They're common in newspapers because they provide a way to concisely express certain constructions. In this section, I show you one auxiliary verb that is so pervasively used in literary Arabic that knowing it is essential as you begin to read and write at the intermediate level. The auxiliary verb you want to know is قامَ بِ (**qaama bi;** *to rise*).

The verb قامَ (**qaama**) means *to rise*. This verb can have numerous idiomatic uses, especially when you add a prepositional phrase to it. When you follow the verb قامَ (**qaama**) with the preposition بِ (**bi-;** *with, by*) plus **maSdar**, it denotes the concept of performing or undertaking an action. In many cases, it isn't even necessary to add the sense of performing or undertaking to your translation. You can just translate the **maSdar** as if it were the main verb of the sentence.

Here are a few examples of قامَ بِ (**qaama bi-**) with a **maSdar**:

قامَ الرَّئيس بِتَوْقيع المُعاهدة.

(**qaama ar-ra'iis** <u>bi-tawqii3i-l-mu3aahada</u>. *The president* <u>signed</u> *the treaty.*)

قاموا بِالبَحْث عَن الذَّهَب.

(**qaamuu** <u>bi-l-baHthi</u> 3an adh-dhahabi. *They undertook* <u>to search</u> *for the gold.*)

Remember that the **maSdar** is the real verb of the sentence when it's used with the auxiliary verbs. In the first example, I don't translate the auxiliary at all, because it isn't necessary. In the second example, I render it with the verb *to undertake;* though *They searched for the gold* would be a valid translation.

Almost all of the following sentences use one or more examples of the **maSdar.** See if you can arrange the sentences into the order that best makes a coherent story. To do so, first write the English translation below each sentence, and then write the letters of each sentence in the correct order to make a story in the space provided.

A. لٰكِنْ قَبْلَ شُرْب عَصير التُّفّاح سَمِعْتُ ضَرْباً عَلَى الباب. (laakin qabla shurb 3aSiir at-tuffaaH, sami3tu Darban 3alaa-l-baab.)

_____

B. فَقُمْتُ بِتَحْضير الفَطور. (fa-qumtu bi-taHDiir alfaTuur.)

_____

C. فَتَحْتُهُ وَرَأَيْتُ صَديقي مُصْطَفى. (fataHtuhu wa-ra'aytu Sadiiqii muSTafaa.)

_____

D. "لا تَعْرِفُ أَنَّ هُدى سَتَكونُ هُناكَ أَيْضاً؟" قالَ لي. ("laa ta3rifu 'anna hudaa sa-takuunu hunaaka 'ayDan?" qaala lii.)

_____

E. بَعْدَ أَكْل بَيْضَتَيْن لاحَظْتُ أَنَّني كُنْتُ عَطْشان أَيْضا. (ba3da-'akl-bayDatayn, laa HaDHtu 'annani kuntu 3aTshaan 'ayDan.)

_____

F. اِعْتَبَرْتُ السُّؤال. (i3tabartu as-su'aal.)

_____

G. ذَكَرْتُ الإمْرَأَة الجَميلة الذَّكِيّة الَّتي اِلْتَقَيْتُ بِها الأُسْبوع الماضي. (dhakartu al-imra'a al-jamiila adh-dhakiyya allatii iltaqaytu bihaa al-'usbuu3 al-maaDii.)

_____

H. "لِماذا لَمْ تَقُلْ ذلِكَ أَوَّلاً؟" أَجَبْتُهُ. "فَلْنَذْهَبْ!" ("limaadhaa lam taqul dhaalika 'awwalan?" 'ajabtuhu. "falnadh-hab!")

_____

I. اِسْتَيْقَظْتُ مِن النَّوْم وَكُنْتُ جائِعاً جِدًا. (istayqaDHtu min an-nawm wa-kuntu jaa'i3an jiddan.)

_____

J. هُوَ قالَ "أَذْهَبُ اليَوْم لِلدِّراسة في المَكْتَبة. هَل تُريدُ الذَّهاب مَعي؟" (huwa qaala, "'adh-habu alyawm lid-diraasa fii-l-maktaba. hal turiidu adh-dhaaba ma3ii?")

_____

K. فَبَدَأْتُ البَحْثَ عَن شَرابٍ في الثَّلاجة. (fa-bada'tu albaHth 3an sharaabin fii-th-thallaaja.)

_____

L. "لا، شُكْراً" قُلْتُ لَهُ. ("laa, shukran," qultu lahu.)

_____

11. Write the letters in the correct order here: _____

Answer Key

1 إدْخال ('**idkhaal**)

2 اِسْتِخْدام (**istikhdaam**)

3 تَخَرُّج (**takharruj**)

4 مُسافَرة (**musaafara**)

5 تَكْليف (**takliif**)

6 اِحْتِفال (**iHtifaal**)

7 إخْبار ('**ikhbaar**)

8 تَمْرين (**tamriin**)

9 تَبَصُّر (**tabaSSur**)

10 اِنْتِقال (**intiqaal**)

11 The correct order of story is: I, B, E, K, A, C, J, F, L, D, G, H. The following are the literal translations of each line.

I اِسْتَيْقَظْتُ مِن النَّوْم وَكُنْتُ جائِعاً جِدّاً. (**istayqaDHtu min an-nawm wa-kuntu jaa'i3an jiddan.** *I awoke from sleep, and I was very hungry.*)

B فَقُمْتُ بِتَحْضير الفَطور. (**fa-qumtu bi-taHDiir alfaTuur.** *So I prepared the breakfast.*)

E بَعْدَ أكْل بَيْضَتَيْن لاحَظْتُ أنَّني كُنْتُ عَطْشان أيْضاً. (**ba3da-'akl-bayDatayn, laaHaDHtu 'annani kuntu 3aTshaan 'ayDan.** *After eating two eggs, I noticed that I was thirsty also.*)

K فَبَدَأْتُ البَحْث عَن شَراب في الثَّلاجة. (**fa-bada'tu albaHth 3an sharaabin fii-l-thallaaja.** *So I began the search for a drink in the refrigerator.*)

A لكِنْ قَبْلَ شُرْب عَصير التُّفّاح سَمِعْتُ ضَرْباً عَلى الباب. (**laakin qabla shurb 3aSiir at-tuffaaH, sami3tu Darban 3alaa-l-baab.** *But before drinking the apple juice, I heard a knock on the door.*)

C فَتَحْتُهُ وَرَأيْتُ صَديقي مُصْطَفى. (**fataHtu wa-ra'aytu Sadiiqii muSTafaa.** *I opened it and saw my friend Mustafa.*)

J هُوَ قالَ "أذْهَبُ اليَوْم لِلدِّراسة في المَكْتَبة. هَلْ تُريدُ الذَّهاب مَعي؟" (**huwa qaaala, "'adh-habu alyawm lid-diraasa fii-l-maktaba. hal turiidu adh-dhaaba ma3ii?"** *He said, "I'm going today to study at the library. Do you want to go with me?"*)

F. اِعْتَبَرْتُ السُّؤال. (**i3tabartu as-su'aal.** *I considered the question.*)

L. "لا، شُكْراً" قُلْتُ لَهُ. (**"laa, shukran," qultu lahu.** *"No, thanks," I said to him.*)

D. "لا تَعْرِفُ أَنَّ هُدى سَتَكونُ هُناكَ أَيْضاً؟" قالَ لي. (**"laa ta3rifu 'anna hudaa sa-takuunu hunaaka 'ayDan?" qaala lii.** *"Don't you know that Huda will be there too?" he said to me.*)

G. ذَكَرْتُ الاِمْرَأَة الجَميلة الذَّكِيّة الَّتي اِلْتَقَيْتُ بِها الأُسْبوع الماضي. (**dhakartu al-imra'a al-jamiila adh-dhakiyya allatii iltaqaytu bihaa al'usbuu3 al-maaDii.** *I thought about the beautiful and intelligent woman whom I had met last week.*)

H. "لِماذا لَمْ تَقُلْ ذلِكَ أَوَّلاً؟" أَجَبْتُهُ. "فَلْنَذْهَبْ!" (**"limaadhaa lam taqul dhaalika 'awwalan?" 'ajabtuhu. "falnadh-hab!"** *"Why didn't you say that first?" I answered him. "Let's go!"*)

Chapter 17

Being Positive About Adding the Negative to Arabic Sentences

If you ask your boss for a raise, you're hoping, of course, to hear the word *yes.* And if you call that special someone for a date, you'd like to hear an enthusiastic *sure!* What you don't want to hear is that one dreaded word: *no.* Negative sentences have received a bad rap because they so often stand in the way of what you want in life. But negative sentences can be positive. Perhaps your boss says, "I've been thinking you *don't* make enough money here." Or, maybe your sweetheart says to you, "There's *no one* else in the world I'd rather go out with."

However you look at it, adding *no* or *not* to a sentence is important. In this chapter, you discover that Arabic adds *no* or *not* in a number of ways. In the first part of the chapter, you see that you need to use different words for *no* and *not* and different moods of the verb, depending on whether you want to negate past, present, or future tenses. In the second half of the chapter, you experience the different ways nouns and adjectives are negated. I can't guarantee you'll always hear the answer you hope for in life, but I'll at least try to make your experience of the negative in Arabic a positive one.

Putting a Negative Spin on Verbs

Telling your readers that something didn't happen is at least as valuable as being able to report what did. In English, you add the word *not,* usually directly in front of your verb, and you've done the job. Arabic, however, offers you a few more techniques. In this section, I show you how to negate in the past, present, and future tenses as well as how to negate commands.

Before you begin encountering the ways you add *not* to verbs, make sure you're comfortable with the jussive and subjunctive forms of the verb. (I explain them in considerable detail in Chapter 13.)

Don't do it! Writing the negative command

Unlike in English, in Arabic you can't tell someone not to do something just by putting the word *not* with the command. Instead, you have to put the word لا (**laa**) in front of the second person jussive forms.

Here are some examples of negative commands:

لا تَقولي ذلكَ!

(**laa** taquulii dhaalika! <u>*Don't*</u> *say that!*)

لا تَمْش إلى المَدْرَسة إذا كُنْتَ مَريضاً.

(**laa** tamshi 'ilaa-l-madrasa 'idha kunta mariiDan. <u>*Don't*</u> *go to school if you're sick.*)

لا تَنْسَ عيد ميلادي!

(**laa** tansa 3iid milaadii! <u>*Don't*</u> *forget my birthday!*)

لا تَتَأخَّروا!

(**laa** tata'akhkharuu! <u>*Don't*</u> *be late!*)

The way it wasn't: Negating the past tense

The past tense is the only timeframe in which Arabic gives you two options for adding *not* to your sentence. In each case, you put the word that means *not* directly in front of the verb form required by the negative.

Putting ما *(maa) before a past tense verb*

The first and easiest way to negate a past tense verb is to put the word ما (**maa;** *not*) before your verb. Here are several examples of ما (**maa**) plus a past tense verb:

ما كانَ جائعاً عِنْدَما وَصَلَ إلى المَطْعَم.

(**maa** kaana jaa'i3an 3indamaa waSala 'ilaa-l-mat3am. *He was <u>not</u> hungry when he arrived at the restaurant.*)

ما شَرِبْتُ القَهْوة لأنّي أُفَضِّلُ الشَّاي.

(**maa** sharibtu al-qahwa li'anni 'ufaDDilu al-shaay. *I did <u>not</u> drink the coffee because I prefer tea.*)

ما سافَروا إلى الأُرْدُن مَعَ جَدَّتِهِمْ.

(**maa** saafaruu 'ilaa-l-'urdun ma3a jaddatihim. *They did <u>not</u> travel to Jordan with their grandmother.*)

The handy thing about using ما (**maa**) plus the past tense verb is that this option allows you to just add one word to a fairly basic form of the verb. Because you probably picked up the past tense early in your Arabic studies, negating it with this method is easy enough.

Negating with لَمْ (lam) plus the jussive mood

The other way to negate the past tense involves using a form of the verb you probably didn't encounter until later in your Arabic studies: the jussive (see Chapter 13 if you need a refresher). If you put the word لَمْ (**lam;** *not*) directly in front of a jussive verb, you can translate the sentence just as if it were a past tense verb with ما (**maa**), which I discuss in the previous section.

The jussive on its own isn't a past tense verb. Only when you put لَمْ (**lam**) in front of the jussive does it take on a past tense meaning.

Here are some examples that use لَمْ (**lam**) plus the jussive. (***Note:*** I use the same examples in the preceding section to show you the past tense with ما [**maa**]. Notice that the translation is identical).

لَمْ يَكُنْ جائِعاً عِنْدَما وَصَلَ إلى المَطْعَم.

(**lam yakun jaa'i3an 3indamaa waSalam 'ilaa-l-mat3am.** *He was* <u>not</u> *hungry when he arrived at the restaurant.*)

لَمْ يُسافِروا إلى الأُرْدُن مَعَ جَدَّتِهمْ.

(**lam yusaafiruu 'ilaa-l-'urdun ma3a jaddatihim.** *They did* <u>not</u> *travel to Jordan with their grandmother.*)

Adding ما (**maa**) to negate a past tense verb is a bit less formal than using لَمْ (**lam**) plus the jussive mood. However, ما (**maa**) isn't colloquial Arabic. You're likely to encounter both these methods, and you should know how to produce both equally well.

Putting the word ما (**maa**) in front of a past tense verb doesn't involve much of a challenge. The more valuable skill is turning a past tense verb into a negative with the jussive option. For each of the past tense verbs I give you here, add لَمْ (**lam**) and replace the past tense verb with the corresponding jussive form. You'll find one practice problem that's already negative with ما (**maa**). In that case, replace the ما (**maa**) accordingly.

Q. شَرِبْتَ (**sharibta;** *you drank*)

A. لَمْ تَشْرَبْ (**lam tashrab;** *you didn't drink*)

1. قالَ (**qaala;** *he said*) _____

2. إسْتَطاعوا (**istaTaa3uu;** *they could*) _____

3. كُنّا (**kunnaa;** *we were*) _____

4. تَكَلَّمْتُمْ (**takallamtum;** *you [P] spoke*) _____

5. أرادوا (**'araaduu;** *they wanted*) _____

6. ما سافَرْتُ (**maa saafartu;** *I didn't travel*) _____

7. سَمِعْتِ (**sami3ti;** *you [FS] heard*) _____

8. وَجَدَتْ (**wajadat;** *she found*) _____

Not happening: Negating the present tense

Negating the present tense isn't difficult. I just did it in English! Luckily, it's just as easy in Arabic. All you have to do is add the word for *not* and you're in business. And because Arabic doesn't even have a present tense of the most basic verb of all, *to be*, you get a special verb just for when you need to say, *to not be.*

Using لا (laa) with most verbs

When you're dealing with the present timeframe and need to add the word *not,* you need only place the word لا (**laa**) in front of your verb. Here are two examples of negated present tense verbs:

لا يُريدُ أَنْ يَذْهَبَ مَعَنا لِأَنَّهُ مَريض.

(**laa yuriidu 'an yadh-haba ma3ana li'annahu mariiD.** *He does <u>not</u> want to go with us because he's sick.*)

لا أَسْكُنُ في بَيْتٍ بَلْ في شَقَّةٍ.

(**laa 'askunu fii baytin bal fii shaqqatin.** *I do <u>not</u> live in a house, but rather an apartment.*)

Not having or being: Applying لَيْسَ (laysa)

Because Arabic has no present tense form of the verb *to be,* you use a special negative particle لَيْسَ (**laysa**) to express concepts such as *he is not . . . .* (See Chapter 15 for more on particles.) The curious thing about لَيْسَ (**laysa**) is that although you use it as a negative form of the present tense, it has past tense endings on it. Like the verb كانَ (**kaana;** *to be*), لَيْسَ (**laysa**) uses the accusative case in the predicate. Check out the verb table for the conjugation of this word.

لَيْسَ (laysa; not to be)	
لَسْتُ ('anaa lastu)	لَسْنا (naHnu lasna)
لَسْتَ ('anta lasta)	لَسْتُمْ ('antum lastum)
لَسْتِ ('anti lasti)	لَسْتُنَّ ('antunna lastunna)
لَيْسَ (huwa laysa)	لَيْسوا (hum laysuu)
لَيْسَتْ (hiya laysat)	لَسْنَ (hunna lasna)
لَسْتُ عَطْشان الآن. (lastu 3aTshaan al'aan. I'm <u>not</u> thirsty right now.)	

Here are a couple of examples of using لَيْسَ (**laysa**) to negate *to be:*

لَيْسَ الفيلم جَيِّداً جِدّاً.

(**laysa**-l-film jayyidan jiddan. *The movie is not very good.*)

لَمْ يَدْرُسْ الطُّلاب فَلَيْسوا مُسْتَعِدّينَ لِلامْتِحان.

(**lam yadrusu aT-Tullaab, fa-laysuu musta3iddiin li-limtiHaan.** *The students didn't study, so they're not prepared for the test.*)

You can also use لَيْسَ (**laysa**) in the sense of *there isn't* [*something*]:

لَيْسَ هُناكَ شَيْءٌ عَلى الطّاولة.

(**laysa** hunaaka 'shay'un 3alaa-Taawila. *There is not anything on the table.*)

The word لَيْسَ (**laysa**) is also useful for negating عِنْدَ (**3inda;** *to have*). Consider these examples:

لَيْسَ عِنْدي مُشْكِلة.

(**laysa** 3indii muskila. *I have no problem.*)

لَيْسَ عِنْدَنا الوَقْت الآن.

(**laysa** 3indana al-waqt al'aan. *We do not have the time right now.*)

Not meant to be: Negating the future tense

To add the word *not* in the future tense, you need to use a special word for *not:* لَنْ (**lan**). You put it directly in front of the subjunctive form of the verb. (Refer to Chapter 13 for more on the subjunctive.) Here are some examples of sentences with future tense followed by a sentence with negated verbs in the subjunctive mood:

سَأُرْسِلُ لَكَ الرِّسالة. (**sa'ursilu laka ar-risaala.** *I will send you the letter.*)
لَنْ أُرْسِلَ لَكَ الرِّسالة. (**lan** 'ursila lahu ar-risaala. *I will not send you the letter.*)

سَيَصِلونَ إلى المَطار فِي السّاعة التّاسِعة. (**sa-yaSiluuna 'ilaa-l-maTaar fii-s-saa3a at-taasi3a.** *They will arrive at the airport at nine o'clock.*)

لَنْ يَصِلوا إلى المَطار فِي السّاعة التّاسِعة. (**lan** yaSiluu 'ilaa-l-maTaar fii-s-saa3a at-taasi3a. *They will not arrive at the airport at nine o'clock.*)

The following sentences contain no negatives. Change each one into its negative equivalent. If you have a present tense verb, all you need to do is put ﻻ (**laa**) before the verb. If it's a present tense nominal sentence, you need to add a form of لَيْسَ (**laysa**). (For more on nominal sentences, see Chapter 2.) If the verb has a future tense, you need to add لَنْ (**lan**) and change the verb into the subjunctive. Good luck!

0. أنا حَزين. ('**anaa Haziin.** *I'm sad.*)

A. لَسْتُ حَزيناً. (**lastu Haziinan.** *I'm not sad.*)

9. هُوَ مُهِمّ. (**huwa muhimm.** *He's interesting.*)

_____

10. يَقْرَأُ الكِتاب. (**yaqra'u al-kitaab.** *He reads the book.*)

_____

11. سَنَزورُها غَداً. (**sanazuuruhaa ghadan.** *We'll visit her tomorrow.*)

_____

12. عِنْدي هاتِف. (**3indii haatif.** *I have a phone.*)

_____

13. نَحْنُ مُوافِقونَ. (**naHnu muwaafiquuna.** *We agree.*)

_____

14. تَدْرُسُ كَثيراً. (**tadrusu kathiiran.** *She studies a lot.*)

_____

15. سَتَرْجِعُ سَريعاً. (**satarji3u sarii3an.** *You'll return quickly.*)

_____

16. سَيَكونُ هُناكَ. (**sayakuunu hunaaka.** *He'll be there.*)

_____

Turning Nouns and Adjectives Negative

It isn't only verbs that get negated in a language. In English, for instance, we have the sayings "No man is an island," "Hell hath no fury," and "there's no crying in baseball" (unless you're like me, a Cubs fan), which negate nouns and gerunds. In Arabic, you also can add a negative thought to things besides verbs. With an assortment of negative particles, you'll be able to make nouns and adjectives negative.

Making simple nouns negative with ﻻ (laa)

Put the ordinary negative particle ﻻ (**laa**) in front of nouns when you're forming a sentence that speaks of an exception. Here's an example to illustrate this somewhat formal construction:

لا صَديقَ لي إلّا مُصْطَفى.
(**laa Sadiiqa lii 'illaa muSTafaa.** *I have no friend except Mustafa.*)

The use of لا (**laa**) before a noun produces a few other useful words and phrases, such as the following:

لا شَكَّ (**laa shakka;** *no doubt*)

لا بُدَّ (**laa budda;** *it's inevitable* [*that*])

Understanding how to negate verbal nouns

Verbal nouns are nouns that describe an action in abstract terms. They're frequently in the form of a gerund, such as *seeing is believing*. They can also be nouns, such as *agreement* and *composition* (see Chapter 16).

When you need to add a negative to the phrase you're expressing with the verbal noun, you use the special word عَدَم (**3adam**). All on its own, this word would be translated as *nothingness* or *nonexistence*. When you put a verbal noun in an **'iDaafa** with عَدَم (**3adam**), you essentially express the nonexistence of that verbal noun's action. (Flip to Chapter 7 for more on the **'iDaafa** construction.)

Take a look at a couple examples of verbal nouns negated with عَدَم (**3adam**):

يَعْتَذِرُ أَحْمَد عَنْ عَدَم دِراسَتِهِ في مِصْر.

(**ya3tadhiru 'aHmad 3an 3adam diraasatihi fii miSr.** *Ahmad apologizes for <u>not</u> studying in Egypt.*)

شَرَحْتُ لِأُمّي سَبَبَ عَدَم زِيارَتي الأُسْبوع الماضي.

(**sharaHtu li-ummii sababa 3adam ziyaaratii al'usbuu3 al-maaDii.** *I explained to my mother the reason I did <u>not</u> visit last week.*)

Generating negative adjectives

In English, you can turn an adjective into a negative by adding a prefix such as *un-*, as in changing *acceptable* to *unacceptable*. You can also use *non-* in certain cases, as in *binding* and *nonbinding*. In Arabic, however, you negate an adjective by putting it in an **'iDaafa** with the word غَيْر (**ghayr**).

Here are some examples of adjectives negated with غَيْر (**ghayr**):

هذا غَيْر صَحيح.
(**haadha ghayr SaHiiH.** *That's <u>un</u>true.*)

أَنا غَيْر مُسْتَعِدّ.
(**'anaa ghayr musta3idd.** *I'm <u>un</u>prepared.*)

فَرَحُها غَيْر مَحْدود.
(**faraHuhaa ghayr maHduud.** *Her joy is <u>un</u>bounded.*)

Your friend is readying a newspaper ad for the grand opening of his restaurant. He has asked you to proofread it. Keep an eye out for any errors he made in the use of the negative. Circle them and write in the blanks which word he should have written. Then rewrite the sentence with correct word filled in.

Q. لا سَتَتَكَلَّمُ هذِهِ اللُّغة. **(laa satatakallamu haadhihi-l-lugha.)**

A. Error: لا سَتَتَكَلَّمُ **(laa satatakallamu)** / لَنْ تَتَكَلَّمَ هذِهِ اللُّغة. **(lan tatakallama haadhihi-l-lugha.** *You will not speak this language.)*

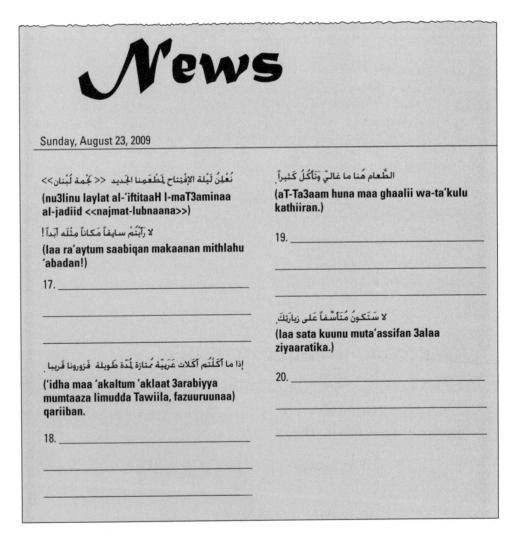

News

Sunday, August 23, 2009

نُعْلِنُ لَيْلة الإفْتِتاح لِمَطْعَمِنا الجَديد ﴿﴿نَجْمة لُبْنان﴾﴾
(nu3linu laylat al-'iftitaaH l-maT3aminaa al-jadiid <<najmat-lubnaana>>)

لا رَأَيْتُم سابِقاً مَكاناً مِثْلَه أَبَداً!
(laa ra'aytum saabiqan makaanan mithlahu 'abadan!)

17. _____

_____

إذا ما أَكَلْتُم أَكَلات عَرَبِيّة مُتازة لِمُدّة طَويلة فَزورونا قَريبا .
('idha maa 'akaltum 'aklaat 3arabiyya mumtaaza limudda Tawiila, fazuuruunaa) qariiban.

18. _____

_____

_____

الطّعام هُنا ما غالي وَتَأكُلَ كَثيراً .
(aT-Ta3aam huna maa ghaalii wa-ta'kulu kathiiran.)

19. _____

_____

لا سَتَكونُ مُتَأَسِّفاً عَلى زِيارَتِكَ.
(laa sata kuunu muta'assifan 3alaa ziyaaratika.)

20. _____

_____

Answer Key

1 لَمْ يَقُلْ (**lam yaqul**; *he didn't say*)

2 لَمْ يَسْتَطِعـوا (**lam yastaTi3uu**; *they couldn't*)

3 لَمْ نَكُنْ (**lam nakun**; *we weren't*)

4 لَمْ تَتَكَلَّموا (**lam tatakallamuu**; *you [P] didn't speak*)

5 لَمْ يُريدوا (**lam yuriiduu**; *they didn't want*)

6 لَمْ أُسافِرْ (**lam 'usaafir**; *I didn't travel*)

7 لَمْ تَسْمَعي (**lam tasma3ii**; *you [FS] didn't hear*

8 لَمْ تَجِدْ (**lam tajid**; *she didn't find*)

9 لَيْسَ مُهِمّاً. (**laysa muhimman.** *He's not interesting.*)

10 لا يَقْرَأُ الكِتاب. (**laa yaqra'u al-kitaab.** *He doesn't read the book.*)

11 لَنْ نَزورَها غَداً. (**lan nazuurahaa ghadan.** *We won't visit her tomorrow.*)

12 لَيْسَ عِنْدي هاتِف. (**laysa 3indii haatif.** *I don't have a phone.*)

13 لَسْنا مُوافِقينَ. (**lasnaa muwaafiqiina.** *We don't agree.*)

14 لا تَدْرُسُ كَثيراً. (**laa tadrusu kathiiran.** *She doesn't study a lot.*)

15 لَنْ تَرْجِعَ سَريعاً. (**lan tarji3a sarii3an.** *You won't return quickly.*)

16 لَنْ يَكونَ هُناكَ. (**lan yakuna hunaaka.** *He won't be there.*)

Sunday, August 23, 2009

17. الإفْتِتاح لِمَطْعَمِنا الجَديد << نَجْمة لُبْنان >>
نُعْلِنُ لَيْلة

(nu3linu laylat al-'iftitaaH l-maT3aminaa al-jadiid <<najmat-lubnaana>>)

[or] لَمْ تَرَوْا سابقاً مَكاناً مِثْلَه آبداً !
ما رَأَيْتُمْ

(maa ra'aytum [or] lam taraw saabiqan makaanan mithlahu 'abadan!)

We announce the opening night of our new restaurant <<The Star of Lebanon>> You've never before seen a place like it!

18. لِمُدّة طَويلة فَزورونا قَريباً إذا لَمْ تَأكُلوا.
أكَلات عَرَبِيّة مُمتازة

('idha lam ta'kuluu 'aklaat 3arabiyya mumtaaza limudda Tawiila, fa-zuuruunaa qariiban.)

If you haven't eaten excellent Arab dishes for a long time, visit us soon.

19. [or] غَيْر غال وَتَأكُلُ كَثيراً الطَّعام
هُنا ما لَيْسَ غالِياً

(aT-Ta3aam huna laysa ghaaliyan [or] ghayr ghaalin wa-ta'kulu kathiiran.)

The food here isn't expensive, and you'll eat a lot.

20. لَنْ تَكونَ مُتَأسّفاً عَلى زيارَتِكَ.

(lan takuna muta'assifan 3alaa ziyaaratika.)

You will not be sorry for your visit.

Chapter 18

Active and Passive Participles

Have you ever been the recipient of that old prank where someone calls you, pretending to be from the electrical company, and asks if your refrigerator is running? You answer, "Why, yes it is!" The caller then responds, "Well, you better go catch it!" The joke hinges on ambiguity in English over the use of participles.

In this chapter, you discover everything you need to know about using participles in Arabic. One thing you see is that Arabic participles don't have any of the ambiguity that the electrical joke depends on.

You may already know the endings you put on the Arabic participles. Participles take that series of endings called the *sound plurals*. They're called *sound* plurals because they're regular and predictable (as in the phrase *safe and sound*). After you master a few simple steps, you'll be producing Arabic active and passive participles for every one of the ten verb forms.

In this chapter, you also encounter the ways you use participles in your Arabic writing. Forming active and passive participles accurately and using them correctly is a valuable skill because it allows you to dramatically expand your ability to describe the world around you.

Acting or Acted Upon: Comparing Active and Passive Participles

A convenient definition of a *participle* is that it's a version of a verb that functions as an adjective. You can use *to eat* as a verb in the present tense to say *John eats too fast.* You can use it in the past tense to say *Yesterday I ate too much.* And you can use it in the future tense to say *We'll eat at a great restaurant tonight.* But a participle lets you take that same verb and make it describe not the action itself but someone or something doing that action. An *active* participle describes someone currently doing that action. A *passive* participle describes something an action has been done upon.

In English, you form all active participles with the suffix *-ing.* With a participle you can write, "*Eating* his meal, John noticed a fly in his soup." Or, "In the corner of the restaurant, he saw two people kissing." In both of these cases, the participle is really an adjective. Passive participles take the same action and describe someone as having experienced that action. With passive participles you can talk about taking home the rest of your *half-eaten* meal. You can also ask the waiter whether the tip is *included*.

English and Arabic share the fact that their participles are used as adjectives. Arabic, however, has separate versions of the participle depending on whether the participle is describing a male versus a female or one person versus a crowd. This fact isn't surprising, because Arabic distinguishes for gender and number in the rest of its adjectives as well. Another key difference is that Arabic doesn't form the participle with a simple ending as English does. Instead, Arabic uses the endings to mark gender and number. In Arabic you put the participle together by adding prefixes or changing the vowels, depending on the type of verb you're using to create your participle.

Creating Forms of the Participle

Within each form, you have two kinds of participles:

- ✔ **Active:** An *active participle* (also called the *present participle* in English) describes an action that's currently happening. In English, these end with *-ing*. The proverb "A *rolling* stone gathers no moss" shows you how the active participle is really used as an adjective.

- ✔ **Passive:** A *passive participle* (also called the *past participle* in English) describes an action as already completed. Consider the two passive participles in the proverb "A penny *saved* is a penny *earned*." A passive participle is a short way to say that an action has been accomplished on something. "A penny having been saved is a penny having been earned" is just unnecessarily long.

In this section, I show you how to form active and passive participles for the basic Form I verb, both regular and irregular. Because Forms II–X are more similar to each other than any of them are to Form I, I also show you the relatively easy task of forming participles for regular and irregular verbs in those forms.

Producing Form 1 active participles of regular verbs

To make the active participle of a Form I regular verb, take the three consonants that make up your verb (the verbal root) and add the following:

- ✔ A long *a* — written with an ألِف ('**alif**) — after the first consonant of the root
- ✔ A ِ (**kasra**) under the second consonant

Following these two rules produces the word pattern فاعِل (**faa3il;** *one doing*).

You use different versions of the participle when you need to use participles for the different genders and numbers of nouns. Here are examples of all the versions of a sample Form I active participle showing all the endings of the participle, including the final vowels. Only the masculine plural has a special and different form for its accusative/genitive plural. Here's the active participle of داخِل (**daakhil;** *entering*), a regular Form I verb:

	Masculine (Nom.)	*Masculine (Acc./Gen.)*	*Feminine*
Singular	داخِلٌ (**daakhilun**)		داخِلَةٌ (**daakhilatun**)
Plural	داخِلونَ (**daakhiluuna**)	داخِلينَ (**daakhiliina**)	داخِلاتُ (**daakhilaatu**)

Producing Form I active participles of irregular verbs

Some weak consonants produce Form I active participles that are different from those of the regular verb. In the following sections, I show you a few representative forms of irregular participles and let you in on a few tricks to produce them.

Handling irregularities with verbs rooted in واو (waaw) or ياء (yaa')

Even in English, when you make the sounds *w* and *y,* your lips and tongue don't completely touch anything. They're pretty weak sounds in comparison to, say, something meaty like a *d* or a *g.* In Arabic, these weak consonants, the واو (**waaw**) and the ياء (**yaa'**), tend to turn into other consonants or disappear altogether when the verb takes on different shapes. The Arabic verb has three consonants, and a واو (**waaw**) or ياء (**yaa'**) can appear in any of the three positions: first, second, or final.

If the واو (**waaw**) or ياء (**yaa'**) is the first consonant of the root, there's no irregularity in Form I. Here's an example:

واقِف (**waaqif;** *stopping*)

If the واو (**waaw**) or ياء (**yaa'**) is the second consonant of the root, you can produce your Form I active participle by just turning the واو (**waaw**) or ياء (**yaa'**) into a ء (**hamza**).

Here are a few examples using masculine singular active participles. I transliterate the three consonants of the root with lowercase letters for you and separate them with hyphens so you can see the position of the weak letters clearly:

Participle (MS)	*Verbal Root*	*English Participle*
بائِع (**baa'i3**)	بيع (**b-y-3**)	[*one*] *selling; (a salesperson)*
قائِل (**qaa'il**)	قول (**q-w-l**)	[*one*] *saying*

If the واو (**waaw**) or ياء (**yaa'**) is the final consonant of the root, you can produce the Form I active participles by turning the واو (**waaw**) or ياء (**yaa'**) into a final long *i* vowel. The masculine singular indefinite form is written with تَنْوِين (**tanwiin**), but it becomes a long *i* when you add an ال (**'alif laam**). Here are a few examples:

Masculine	*Feminine*	*Verbal Root*	*English Participle*
راجٍ (**raajin**)	راجِية (**raajiiya**)	رجو (**r-j-w**)	[*one*] *hoping*
باكٍ (**baakin**)	باكِية (**baakiiya**)	بكي (**b-k-y**)	[*one*] *weeping*

Producing participles from geminate verbs

Sometimes a verb has the very same consonant in the second and final position. Because you essentially have twin consonants in one verb, these are called *geminate verbs* (like my zodiac sign, Gemini). You can discover more about the irregular shapes a geminate verb can have in Chapter 10.

To produce the active participle of a Form I geminate verb, you do the following:

✔ Insert a long *a* — written with أَلِف (**'alif**) — after the first consonant of the verbal root.

✔ Write the identical second and third consonants as a single doubled letter — written with ّ (**shadda**).

Here's an example:

Masculine	*Feminine*	*Verbal Root*	*English Participle*
عادّ (**3aadd**)	عادّة (**3aadda**)	عدد (**3-d-d**)	*counting*
مادّ (**maadd**)	مادّة (**maadda**)	مدد (**m-d-d**)	*stretching*

Producing Form 1 passive participles of regular verbs

You form the passive participle of a Form I verb with the following steps:

✔ Attach the prefix مَ (**ma-**) to the first consonant of the root.

✔ Add a ْ (**sukuun**) to the first consonant.

✔ Insert a long *u* vowel — written with واو (**waaw**) — after the second consonant of the root.

Following these rules produces the word pattern مَفْعول (**maf3uul**). Here are the forms of a sample Form I passive participle, مَدْخول (**madkhuul;** *entered*):

مَدْخول (**madkhuul,** MS)
مَدْخولة (**madkhuula,** FS)
مَدْخولونَ (**madkhuuluna,** MP)
مَدْخولات (**madkhuulaat,** FP)

In this practice, take the supplied verbal root and write the four versions of the active participle and the four versions of the passive participle (the masculine singular, the feminine singular, the masculine plural, and the feminine plural).

0. فقـد (**f-q-d;** *to lose*)

A. Active (*losing*): فاقـد (**faaqid**); فاقِـدة (**faaqida**); فاقـدونَ (**faaqiduuna**); فاقِـدات (**faaqidaat**)

Passive (*lost*): مَفْـقـود (**mafquud**); مَفْـقـودة (**mafquuda**); مَفْـقـودونَ (**mafquuduuna**); مَفـقـودات (**mafquudaat**)

1. شـرب (**sh-r-b;** *to drink*)

Active (*drinking*): _____

Passive (*drunk*): _____

2. علـم (**3-l-m;** *to know*)

Active (*knowing*): _____

Passive (*known*): _____

3. خرج (**kh-r-j;** *to exit*)

Active (*exiting*): _____

Passive (*exited*): _____

4. ترك (**t-r-k;** *to leave*)

Active (*leaving*): _____

Passive (*left*): _____

5. بحث (**b-H-th;** *to search*)

Active (*searching*): _____

Passive (*searched*): _____

6. وصل (**w-S-l;** *to arrive*)

Active (*arriving*): _____

Passive (*arrived*): _____

7. كتب (**k-t-b;** *to write*)

Active (*writing*): _____

Passive (*written*): _____

8. ربط (**r-b-T**; *to connect*)

Active (*connecting*): _____

Passive (*connected*): _____

Producing Form 1 passive participles of irregular verbs

When a weak consonant is in the initial position, there are no irregularities with the passive participles in Form I. Here's an example: مَوْقوف (**mawquuf**; *stopped*).

However, the irregular verbs do cause a few difficulties when you need to create Form I passive participles. Like the active participles, these problems occur only when the second or final letter is weak.

Working with the second consonant

For the passive participle of a verb that has a weak consonant in the second syllable, you just turn the medial consonant into a long vowel. Here are some roots and their masculine singular passive participles:

Passive Participle (MS)	Verbal Root	English
مَبيع (**mabii3**)	بيع (**b-y-3**)	*selling*
مَقول (**maquul**)	قول (**q-w-l**)	*said*

Working with the final consonant

The passive participle of a final ياء (**yaa'**) verb turns the final consonant into a long *i* vowel. The passive participle of a final واو (**waaw**) verb preserves the واو (**waaw**). Here are a couple of examples:

Masculine	Feminine	Verbal Root	English
مَبْنيّ (**mabniyyun**)	مَبْنيّة (**mabniyya**)	بني (**b-n-y**)	*built*
مَدْعوّ (**mad3uwwun**)	مَدْعوّة (**mad3uwwa**)	دعو (**d-3-w**)	*called*

Working with geminate verbs

The passive participles of geminate verbs have no irregularity, because the twin letters are kept separate by the shape of the passive participle. Here's an example:

مَعْدود (**ma3duud**; *counted,* MS)

مَعْدودة (**ma3duuda**; *counted,* FS)

Producing active participles for regular verbs in Forms II–X

After mastering the steps to create the active and passive participle for Form I verbs, you can produce all the rest of the Forms with just a few common rules. (If you aren't familiar with the rules for producing the ten forms, see Chapter 9 before tackling the participles.)

To produce an active participle of verbs in Forms II–X, follow these steps:

1. Start with the third person singular present verb.

   For instance, start with the Form V verb يَتَكَلَّمُ (**yatakallamu**; *he speaks*).

2. Remove the verbal prefix (the ياء [**yaa'**] and its vowel) and add the prefix مُ (**mu-**).

   For example, يَتَكَلَّمُ (**yatakallamu**) becomes مُتَكَلَّمُ (**mutakallamu**).

3. In Forms V and VI, change the ◌َ (**fatHa**) of the second consonant to a ◌ِ (**kasra**).

   For example, مُتَكَلَّمُ (**mutakallamu**) becomes مُتَكَلِّمُ (**mutakallimu**).

4. Remove the ◌ُ (**Damma**) from the third consonant and add the sound endings.

   For instance, مُتَكَلِّمُ (**mutakallimu**) becomes مُتَكَلِّم (**mutakallim**), مُتَكَلِّمة (**mutakallima**), مُتَكَلِّمونَ (**mutakallimuuna**), and مُتَكَلِّمات (**mutakallimaat**), all of which mean *speaking*.

With just these four rules, you can produce all the active participles of Forms II–X. Table 18-1 shows you sample participles in Forms II–X. Because the sound endings are so regular, I just show you the masculine and feminine singular versions.

Table 18-1	Active Participles of Forms II–X		
Form	**Masculine Singular**	**Feminine Singular**	**English**
II	مُدَرِّس (mudarris)	مُدَرِّسة (mudarrisa)	[one] teaching
III	مُشاهِد (mushaahid)	مُشاهِدة (mushaahida)	[one] viewing
IV	مُشرِف (mushrif)	مُشرِفة (mushrifa)	[one] supervising
V	مُتَخَرِّج (mutakharrij)	مُتَخَرِّجة (mutakharrija)	[one] graduating
VI	مُتَزايِد (mutazaayid)	مُتَزايِدة (mutazaayida)	[one] increasing
VII	مُنكَسِر (munkasir)	مُنكَسِرة (munkasira)	[one] breaking
VIII	مُستَمِع (mustami3)	مُستَمِعة (mustami3a)	[one] listening
IX	مُحمَرّ (muHmarr)	مُحمَرّة (muHmarra)	[one] turning red
X	مُستَعمِل (musta3mil)	مُستَعمِلة (musta3mila)	[one] using

Producing passive participles for regular verbs in Forms II–X

The passive participles of Forms II–X are produced the same way as the active with one exception. Rule #3 from the previous list of steps will be the following for passive participles: Change the **kasra** of the second consonant of the root to a **fatHa.** (In Forms V and VI, you just leave it as it is.)

In other words, the only difference between an active and a passive participle in Forms II–X is the vowel of the second consonant of the root. Forms VII and IX have no passive at all. Table 18-2 shows sample passive participles for the forms that have a passive.

Table 18-2	Passive Participles of Forms II–X		
Form	**Masculine Singular**	**Feminine Singular**	**English**
II	مُدَرَّس (mudarras)	مُدَرَّسة (mudarrasa)	[one] taught
III	مُشاهَد (mushaahad)	مُشاهَدة (mushaahada)	[one] viewed
IV	مُشرَف (mushraf)	مُشرَفة (mushrafa)	[one] supervised
V	مُتَخَرَّج (mutakharraj)	مُتَخَرَّجة (mutakharraja)	[one] graduated
VI	مُتَزايَد (mutazaayad)	مُتَزايَدة (mutazaayada)	[one] increased
VII	rare	rare	
VIII	مُستَمَع (mustama3)	مُستَمَعة (mustama3a)	[one] listened to
IX	rare	rare	
X	مُستَعمَل (musta3mal)	مُستَعمَلة (musta3mala)	[one] used

Producing active participles for irregular verbs in Forms II–X

Irregular verbs pose even less difficulty in Forms II–X than they do in Form I. Internalize just a few tricks, and you'll be recognizing and producing them easily.

Working with weak first and second consonants

There are no special rules for creating active participles for verbs with weak first or second consonants in Forms II–X. Following the same four rules you use for regular verbs (see the preceding section) produces the correct forms because any irregularity is already present in the third person singular present tense form you start with.

Working with a weak final consonant

As with Form I participles, when the واو (**waaw**) or ياء (**yaa'**) is the final consonant of the root, you can produce the active participles by simply turning the واو (**waaw**) or ياء (**yaa'**) into a final long *i* vowel. Here's an example:

Masculine	Feminine	Verbal Root	English
مُلْتَق (**multaqin**)	مُلْتَقِية (**multaqiiya**)	لقي (**l-q-y**)	[one] meeting
مُبْكٍ (**mubkin**)	مُبْكِية (**mubkiya**)	بكي (**b-k-y**)	[one] causing tears

Producing passive participles for irregular verbs in Forms II–X

As with the active participle, there are no special rules for generating the passive participle of a verb with an irregularity in the first consonant. But like active participles, passive participles of irregular verbs present a few curious issues. In the following sections, I show you the peculiar cases to be on the lookout for.

Working with the second consonant

To produce the passive participles of medial واو (**waaw**) or ياء (**yaa'**) verbs in the other forms, just put a long *a* vowel — written with an أَلِف (**'alif**) — in the place of the medial letter. The following are a few examples using masculine singular passive participles. (*Note:* The passive participles of abstract concepts will sometimes look more like adjectives than participles.)

Passive Participle (MS)	Verbal Root	English
مُسْتَطاع (**mustaTaa3**)	طوع (**T-w-3**)	possible
مُقام (**muqaam**)	قوم (**q-w-m**)	set up

Working with the final consonant

In Forms II–X, the passive participles of a final واو (**waaw**) or ياء (**yaa'**) verb have a final أَلِف مَكْسورة (**'alif maksuura**) in the masculine and a long *a* (written with an أَلِف [**'alif**]) in the feminine. Here's an example:

Masculine	Feminine	Verbal Root	English
مُنْتَدَّى (**muntadan**)	مُنْتَداة (**muntadaa**)	ندو (**n-d-w**)	meeting point
مُخْتَفَّى (**mukhafan**)	مُخْتَفاة (**mukhtafaa**)	خفي (**kh-f-y**)	hiding place

Writing with Particles

To get a good grasp of how to use participles, you need to keep in mind exactly what they are. A *participle* is a verb that's given the endings of an adjective. As such, participles don't describe the action itself. Instead, a participle is primarily describing a noun in terms of an action that the noun is either doing or has had done to it.

The following can help you keep track of the main ways you use participles in your writing:

✔ As adjectives (their primary function)

✔ As nouns (as a logical extension from the adjective)

✔ As verbs

Using participles as adjectives

Participles function as adjectives in all ten of the Arabic verb forms. Some words you may have already encountered as adjectives are actually participles.

English and Arabic both can use participles as adjectives. The adjective *exciting* has the same *-ing* ending as the participle *drinking*. One difference, however, is that Arabic uses participles in place of adjectives for meanings that English speakers wouldn't expect a participle to convey.

In the following examples, I underline in the English the adjective that uses a participle in the Arabic

كانَ الطَّقْسُ حاراً جِداً أَمْس.

(**kaana-T-Taqsu** <u>haaran</u> **jiddan 'amsi.** *The weather was very <u>hot</u> yesterday.*)

صَديقُكَ الجَديدُ مُؤَدَّب أَلَيْسَ كَذلِكَ؟

(**Sadiiquka al-jadiidu** <u>mu'addab</u>, **'alaysa kadhaalika?** *Your new friend is <u>polite</u>, isn't he?*)

Using participles as nouns

Many adjectives in Arabic have come over time to be used as nouns in their own right. A classic example in Arabic is the participle مُدَرِّس (**mudarris**; *teaching*). Over time, the meaning of this participle changed to denote *one who teaches,* that is, *a teacher.* If you ask Arabic speakers or writers to tell you what مُدَرِّس (**mudarris**) means, their first and immediate answer will be *teacher.* Even so, if those same speakers or writers need to form the participle of the verb يُدَرِّس (**yudarris**; *to teach*), they'll form the word مُدَرِّس (**mudarris**) for that as well because it still remains a participle.

Unlike Arabic, English doesn't like to use participles as nouns. Instead, English speakers tend to use a class of nouns called the *nomen agentis,* the "noun of doing." To form these, you add *-er* to the end of the word. Words such as *teacher, singer,* and *baker* are examples.

Here are several example sentences that use participles as full nouns in Arabic:

لَمْ يَرْجِعْ العامِلُ بَعْدَ الإِجْتِماعِ.

(**lam yarji3 al-3aamilu ba3da al-'ijtimaa3i.** *The worker* [one working] *didn't return after the meeting.*)

أَعْلَنَ المُذيعُ أَنَّ الطّائِرةَ قَدْ هَبَطَتْ.

('**a3lana al-mudhii3u 'anna-T-Taa'irata qad habaTat.** *The announcer* [one announcing] *reported that the plane had landed.*)

Using participles as verbs

In many cases, a present participle can stand in the place of a verb. This usage antici-pates the evolution of the participle into the present tense of the verb in most spoken Arabic dialects. Here's an example in which the word translated as *sitting* is the parti-ciple being used as a verb:

الإِمْرَأَةُ جالِسةٌ تَحْت الشَّجَرةِ.

(**al-'imra'atu jaalisatun taHt ash-shajarati.** *The woman is sitting under the tree.*)

You're sending an e-mail to a good friend. To complete it, select the appropriate forms of the participles from the word bank. You need to use all the different types of participles discussed in this chapter for this exercise.

مُتَأَسِّف (**muta'assif**)   مَوْلودة (**mawluuda**)   المُقَرَّر (**al-muqarrar**)

السّابِق (**as-saabiq**)   مُوافِق (**muwaafiq**)   مَسْروراً (**masruuran**)

مُؤَكَّد (**al-mu'akkad**)   باحِثاً (**baaHithan**)

0. _____ لَمْ أَدْخُلْ لِأَنَّ البابَ كانَ (**lam 'adkhul li'anna-l-baaba kaana**
_____)

A. لَمْ أَدْخُلْ لِأَنَّ البابَ كانَ مَقْفولاً. (**lam 'adkhul li'anna-l-baaba kaana <u>maqfuulan</u>.**
I didn't enter because the door was <u>locked</u>.)

```
┌─────────────────────────────────────────────────────────┐
│ ✉ New Message                                            │
├─────────────────────────────────────────────────────────┤
│  ✉      ✂      ▢      ▢      ↶    │  abc✔               │
│ Send   Cut   Copy   Paste  Undo   │  Check              │
├─────────────────────────────────────────────────────────┤
```

يا صَديقي.

yaa Sadiiqii

9.   أنا _____ لأنّي لَمْ أُرسِلْ لَكَ أخباري.

'ana _____ li'anni lam 'arsil laka 'akhbaarii.

10.   تَرَكْتُ شَقَّتي أمْس _____عَن الكاتِبة المَشهورة بَيْت.

taraktu shaqqatii 'amsi _____ 3an bayti al-kaatibati al-mash-hurati.

11.   أنا كُنْتُ _____ جِدّاً جِدّاً لَمّا وَجَدْتُهُ أخيراً.

'ana kuntu _____ jiddan jiddan lammaa wajadtuhu 'akhiiran.

12.   أمّا هِيَ فَكانَتْ _____ في السَّنة ١٩٣٧. ألَّفَتْ كُتُباً رائِعةً عَن التَّربِية.

'amma hiya fa-kaanat _____ fii-s-sanati 1936. 'allafat kutuban raa'i3atan 3an at-tarbiyati.

13.   مِن _____ أيْضاً أنّها غَيَّرَت نِظامَ التَّعليم في بَلَدِها.

min _____ 'ayDan 'annahaa ghayyarat niDHaama at-ta3liimi fii baladihaa.

14.   عَلِمْتُ أنّها تَعَرَّفَتْ عَلى الرَّئيس_____وَهِيَ كانَت ساكِنَةً في أمْرِكا.

3alimtu 'annaha ta3arrafat 3alaa-r-ra'iisi _____ wa-hiya kaanat saakinatan fii 'amriika.

15.   والآنَ أنا _____ مَعَكَ أنّها مُهِمّةٌ جِدّاً.

wal'aana 'ana _____ ma3aka 'annaha muhimmatun jiddan.

16.   مِن _____ أنّي سَأرْجِعُ يَوْمَ الخَميس فَأتَّصِلُ بِكَ بَعْدَ ذلِكَ إنْ شاء الله.

min _____ 'anni sa'arji3u yawma-l-khamiisi, fa-'attaSilu bika ba3da dhaalika 'in shaa'a allah.

```
└─────────────────────────────────────────────────────────┘
```

Answer Key

1 Active (*drinking*): شـارب (shaarib); شـاربة (shaariba); شـاربونَ (shaaribuuna); شـاربات (shaaribaat)

Passive (*drunk*): مَشْـروب (mashruub); مَشْـروبة (mashruuba); مَشْـروبونَ (mashruubuuna); مَشْـروبات (mashruubaat)

2 Active (*knowing*): عـالِم (3aalim); عـالِمة (3aalima); عـالِمونَ (3aalimuuna); عـالِمات (3aalimaat)

Passive (*known*): مَعْـلوم (ma3luum); مَعْـلومة (ma3luuma); مَعْـلومونَ (ma3luumuuna); مَعْـلومات (ma3luumaat)

3 Active (*exiting*): خـارج (khaarij); خـارجة (khaarija); خـارجونَ (khaarijuuna); خـارجات (khaarijaat)

Passive (*exited*): مَخْـروج (makhruuj); مَخْـروجة (makhruuja); مَخْـروجونَ (makhruujuuna); مَخْـروجات (makruujaat)

4 Active (*leaving*): تـارك (taarik); تـاركة (taarika); تـاركونَ (taarikuuna); تـاركات (taarikaat)

Passive (*left*): مَتْـروك (matruuk); مَتْـروكة (matruuka); مَتْـروكونَ (matruukuuna); مَتْـروكات (matruukaat)

5 Active (*searching*): بـاحِث (baaHith); بـاحِثة (baaHitha); بـاحِثونَ (baaHithuuna); بـاحِثات (baaHithaat)

Passive (*searched*): مَبْـحوث (mabHuuth); مَبْـحوثة (mabHuutha); مَبْـحوثونَ (mabHuthuuna); مَبْـحوثات (mabHuuthaat)

6 Active (*arriving*): واصِل (waaSil); واصِلة (waaSila); واصِلونَ (waaSiluuna); واصِلات (waaSilaat)

Passive (*arrived*): مَوْصول (mawSuul); مَوْصولة (mawSuula); مَوْصولونَ (mawSuuluuna); مَوْصولات (mawSuulaat)

7 Active (*writing*): كـاتِب (kaatib); كـاتِبة (kaatiba); كـاتِبونَ (kaatibuuna); كـاتِبات (kaatibaat)

Passive (*written*): مَكْـتوب (maktuub); مَكْـتوبة (maktuuba); مَكْـتوبونَ (maktuubuuna); مَكْـتوبات (maktuubaat)

8 Active (*connecting*): رابِط (raaTib); رابِطة (raaTiba); رابِطونَ (raaTibuuna); رابِطات (raaTibaat)

Passive (*connected*): مَرْبوط (marbuuT); مَرْبوطة (marbuuTa); مَرْبوطونَ (marbuuTuuna); مَرْبوطات (marbuuTaat)

9. مُتَأسّف (**muta'assif**; *sorry*)

My friend,

I'm sorry that I haven't sent you my news.

10. باحِثاً (**baaHithan**; *searching*)

I left my apartment yesterday looking for the famous author's house.

11. مَسْرُوراً (**masruuran**; *happy*)

I was very, very happy when I finally found it.

12. مَوْلودةً (**mawluuda**; *born*)

She was born in 1936. She composed wonderful books on education.

13. مُؤكّد (**al-mu'akkad**; *certain*)

She also certainly changed the system of education in her country.

14. السّابِق (**as-saabiq**; *former*)

I learned that she made the acquaintance of the former president when she was living in America.

15. مُوافِق (**muwaafiq**; *agreeing*)

So now I agree with you that she is very interesting.

16. المُقَرّر (**al-muqarrar**; *decided*)

It's been decided that I will return on Thursday. So I will give you a call after that, God willing.

Part V
The Part of Tens

In this part . . .

No *For Dummies* book is complete without the Part of Tens. In this book's Part of Tens, you get chapters on the ten common mistakes to avoid and the ten ways to further hone your ever-increasing Arabic skills.

Chapter 19

Ten Mistakes to Avoid in Arabic

I hope you've made a lot of mistakes in Arabic. Because that means you've tried to use your Arabic, no matter how much of a beginner you may yet be. That said, I'm sure you'd like to know how to avoid some of the most common mistakes English speakers tend to make when producing Arabic either in speech or in written form. Knowledge is the power to ever improve your use of Arabic. So in this chapter, I compile the ten most common mistakes you should be careful to avoid.

Using Incorrect Word Order

Both English and Modern Standard Arabic are *word order languages.* What's that, you ask? It's a language in which action is indicated by where the subject appears relative to the verb. Consider, for instance, this sentence: *The cat ate the mouse.* You know the cat did the action because subjects come before the verb in English. But, in fact, English and Modern Standard Arabic are two languages that don't use the same word order at all! The only common point between them is that the object of a verb comes after the verb. But if you adjust your English grammar instincts in just a few ways, you can improve your Arabic.

The following are some pointers to keep your Arabic word order in line:

✔ **Put your verb first, and then state your subject.** For example:

يُحِبُّ أَحْمَدُ أُمَّهُ.

(**yuHibbu** 'aHmadu 'ummahu. *Ahmad loves his mother.*)

✔ **Make sure your adjective is placed after the noun it describes.** Your English instinct is to talk about your *new car.* Instead, rave about:

سَيّارَتُكَ الجَديدَة

(**sayyaaratuka al-jadiida;** literally *your car the new*)

✔ **Place any adverbs at the end of your sentence.** For example:

سَنُسافِرُ إلى مِصر غَداً.

(**sanusaafiru 'ilaa miSr ghadan.** *We will travel tomorrow to Egypt.*)

To explore word order and verbs in more detail, see Chapter 2. For more information on the use of adjectives and adverbs, go to Chapter 6.

Writing in the Wrong Mood

If you use the wrong mood when writing Arabic, everyone will still understand what you mean. But they'll also, of course, understand that you don't know how to use the right mood! One way around the problem, especially when you're just starting out, is to drop off all the final vowels from your verbs. Putting the wrong vowel on a verb is worse than no vowel at all. But when you want to distinguish yourself, lock in your knowledge of the formation and use of the Arabic verb moods. You'll be sure to stand out. (See Chapter 13 for more on the many moods of Modern Standard Arabic.)

Adding Colloquialisms to Your Writing

It's good to know some colloquial Arabic, especially if you're going to be spending any significant time in an Arabic-speaking country. But Arabs are proud of their formal language, which they call Modern Standard Arabic. So learn some colloquialisms to use with new friends in speech, but keep them completely out of your writing.

 While I'm on the topic of colloquial speech, I want to give you a word of warning about slang. You've probably seen books for sale that promise to tell you all the "naughty" language your teacher never taught you. But don't fall for it. No one will be impressed if you use the Arabic equivalent of profanity. Instead, stand out as an accomplished writer of Modern Standard Arabic and keep it clean.

Translating Word for Word

Translating word for word is an understandable habit when you're attempting composition in a new language. And you can even learn the use of important vocabulary just by trying to look up words that you think you need. But do remember that languages convey meaning in different ways.

Languages like Spanish and Italian are related enough that a word-for-word-translation from one to the other would probably be accurate most of the time. English and Arabic, however, are completely unrelated. As a result, what English uses a word to convey, Arabic may accomplish through a particular form of the verb. And Arabic may have one word where English has two.

 The only way to get out of the bad habit of translating word for word is just to get a lot of Arabic practice under your belt. As you immerse yourself in the sentence structures and cadences of your new language, you'll develop a sense of how to express yourself in Arabic without thinking through English first.

Overusing Pronouns

English has lost the verb endings that its distant cousins like Russian and Spanish still maintain. As a result, in English, you have to use pronouns to convey who's doing the action of a verb. Arabic, on the other hand, puts prefixes and suffixes on the verb to tell your reader or listener who's being described as performing the action of the verb.

But Arabic pronouns are used in some instances. For example, they can be used to express emphasis. Take a look at this sentence:

هَلْ أَنْتَ تُريدُ أَنْ تَذْهَبَ أَيْضاً؟

(**hal 'anta turiidu 'an tadh-haba 'ayDan?** *Do you want to go as well?*)

The pronoun also can be used as the *copula* (a word that links the subject and predicate in a sentence). When used in this way, the pronoun stands in place of the absent present tense verb *to be,* as in this sentence:

أَمّا الرَّجُلُ هُناكَ فَهُوَ صَديقي.

(**'ammaa ar-rajulu hunaaka fa-huwa Sadiiqii.** *The man over there is my friend.*)

But in most sentences with a verb, you can leave the pronoun out all together, such as with the second verb of this sentence (English usage still requires the use of the pronoun, but the Arabic can go without):

تَرَكَ مُحَمَّدُ أَمْس لكِنْ سَيَرْجِعُ غَداً إِنْ شاءَ الله.

(**taraka muHammadu 'amsi laakin sa-yarji3u ghadan 'in shaa'a 'allah.**
Muhammad left yesterday, but he will return tomorrow, God willing.)

I underlined the second verb to show you the lack of the pronoun there. Refer to Chapters 2 and 8 for more details on Arabic pronouns.

Forgetting to Coordinate Gender

One of my students recently had a difficult time with the concept that in Arabic the word for table, طاولة (**Taawila**), is feminine. She wanted to know what made the table feminine. The answer is that nothing made the table feminine. It just is. But knowing the gender of a noun is crucial if you want to describe the noun with an adjective or make it the subject of a verb. After all, Arabic practices gender coordination with those parts of speech.

My advice is to go ahead and play it pretty loose at first. As long as you're putting your adjective right after the noun and putting your subject right after the verb, you'll be understood even if you make gender mistakes. The mistakes will correct themselves when you have encountered enough cases of the right answer.

Using the Incorrect Case

Knowing when to use the nominative, accusative, and genitive case endings in Arabic can take a lot of practice. But don't worry! There are exercises in this book that can help you get a handle on how they work (see Chapter 4).

If you're uncertain about what case ending you should use, just leave the final syllable vowel-less. The formal final vowels of Modern Standard Arabic are ordinarily not pronounced at all in media sources anyway. So, if you don't fill out the final vowels, no one will suspect that you did it because you were unsure of them. But also go ahead and develop a sense for when the cases are correct and add them in so that you can stand out as an accomplished Arabic speaker and writer.

Spelling Words Improperly

Some of the consonants in Arabic are close in pronunciation to others. As a result, nonnative speakers and writers sometimes forget over time whether, for instance, a word has a ح (**Haa'**) versus a خ (**khaa'**) or a س (**siin**) versus a ص (**Saad**). (But I've seen plenty of misspelled words written by native Arabic speakers and writers as well.) If you're ever in doubt, reach for your dictionary to be sure of the correct spelling. You'll not only deepen your knowledge, but you'll keep your writing as pure as possible.

Ignoring Idiomatic Uses of Prepositions

Prepositions are notoriously idiomatic in any language. I recently used the idiom *plugging away* in a conversation with my Romanian-American wife. She speaks excellent English, but she had to ask me what exactly was being *plugged* and how anything could be plugged *away.* When I told her that the idiom means to be *persistent in an action,* she rolled her eyes and replied, "And you say Romanian is difficult!"

When you look in the dictionaries of this book, you'll notice that two different prepositions can mean *with.* Two different prepositions can both mean *to* as well. And another preposition can mean both *in* and *at,* depending on the context. I explain in the dictionaries the distinctions between these prepositions.

Make sure that when you learn a preposition you don't just memorize a simple English equivalent. The precise usage is an important part of the prepositions. You can review prepositions in Chapter 12.

Making Words Plural That Shouldn't Be

There are two important cases when your English instinct will suggest the use of plural but Arabic actually would use singular. If you use the singular in these cases, you'll prevent a common mistake. Here are the two cases to watch for:

- ✔ As you know, verbs should come before the subject in an Arabic sentence. When the subject is plural, you use a singular verb (even though many people may be doing the action). Any verbs that follow the plural subject are plural. Here's an example of this grammatical construction:

    خَرَجَ الرِّجالُ مِنَ البَيْت وَدَخَلوا المَدْرَسَة.

    (**kharaja** [sing. verb] **ar-rijaalu** [plural noun] **mina-l-bayti wa-dakhaluu** [plural verb] **al-madrasata.** *The men left the house and entered the school.*)

- ✔ When you have to create the plural of several inanimate objects, you always use feminine singular adjectives to describe them. Here's an example of what I mean:

    البُيوتُ في تِلْكَ المِنْطَقَةِ جَميلَةٌ.

    (**al-buyuutu** [plural noun] **fii tilkaa-l-minTaqati jamiilatun** [singular adjective]. *The houses in that area are beautiful.*)

Chapter 20

Ten Ways to Fine-Tune Your Arabic Skills

You've already demonstrated that you intend to do whatever necessary to improve your Arabic skills. After all, you've bought this book, haven't you? In this chapter, I share ten tips for how to best apply yourself to your exploration of the beautiful and important Arabic language.

Master the Alphabet Early

A language and its writing system aren't identical. A person can be illiterate and still be a native speaker of a language. The same goes for Arabic. I know plenty of native speakers of colloquial dialects who can't read and write the language much at all. But your progress in Modern Standard Arabic really does depend strongly on your developing the ability to function comfortably in the Arabic script.

The transliteration in this book is a tool to help you master the reading and writing of Arabic by comparing the transliteration to what you think you're reading in the Arabic script. The faster you learn the alphabet and how to both read it and write in it, the quicker you'll be able to start taking advantage of a world of other resources, such as online news in Arabic.

Learn Singular and Plural Nouns Together

Because the majority of Arabic nouns have irregular plurals that can't really be predicted from the form of the singular, you're really wasting your time by learning a singular noun by itself. After all, you're just as likely to refer to a specific number of books as you are to just one. So from the very start, learn the plural of any new noun you encounter. The dictionaries in this book include the plural of every noun included.

Build Your Vocabulary

Mastering grammatical constructions and the forms of irregular verbs is crucial business on your journey to being a competent writer and speaker of Arabic. But, let's face it; if you don't know the word in Arabic for *clock,* you're going to have a hard time talking about one! (By the way, the Arabic word for *clock* is ساعة [**saa3a**].)

Here are a few ways to boost your vocabulary:

✔ Spend some time speaking casually with friends or loved ones. Have a notebook handy, and every time someone uses a basic word you don't know in Arabic, write it down. Later, look up those words in a good English-Arabic dictionary and commit them to memory. Then you can practice forming sentences in which you need that new vocabulary item.

✔ Read large amounts of Arabic without worrying about understanding every word. Over time you'll pick up words that keep reappearing based on the context in which you encounter them.

Explore Arab Culture

Go online (or to the library) and begin exploring the world of Arab culture, whether it be the rich literary tradition, the impressive scientific achievements, or the cinema. Knowing more about the culture behind the language that you're learning helps you better understand the language because basic cultural concepts often come up in writing and speech.

As an example, knowing the importance of the month of رَمَضان (**ramaDaan;** *Ramadan*) will provide you with an abundance of phrases and vocabulary that appear yearly in Arabic language media. (Ramadan is the month during which Muslims observe a total fast during daylight hours.) Knowing more about the culture behind Arabic can also give you an appreciation of the global importance of the language you're learning (and thus inspire you to work hard to experience it more deeply).

One last point on culture: Don't forget to frequent an Arab restaurant — if one is near you. Personally, I adore the dish ورق عِنب (**waraq 3inab;** *stuffed grape leaves*). Order it and tell them I sent you. You won't regret it.

Memorize Proverbs and Passages

There's great value in memorizing some select Arabic proverbs. If you happen to pull them out at an apropos time, your Arab friends will be endlessly impressed. But besides wowing your friends, proverbs also can be good tools for learning vocabulary in context.

Here are a few proverbs to get you started:

فَتِّشْ عَن الجار قَبْلَ الدّار. (**fattish 3ani-l-jaar qabla-d-daar.** *Search out the neighbor before the house.*) In other words, your neighbors can make your life miserable, no matter how nice your house is.

مَنْ سَكَتَ سَلِمَ. (**man sakata salima.** *He who is silent is safe.*) So, if you don't speak rashly, you won't regret your words later.

الإِنْسانُ يُدَبِّرُ وأَللّه يُقَدِّرُ. (**al-'insaanu yudabbiru wa-'allahu yuqaddiru.** *Humans plan, and God preordains.*) (Essentially, this is the Arabic equivalent of the notion that if you want to make God laugh, tell *him* your plans.

No matter what your personal religious tradition is, memorizing key texts, such as the الفاتحة (**faatiHa**), the opening **Surah** (chapter) of the Qur'an, or the Lord's Prayer in Arabic will also ground you in some important vocabulary and convey your appreciation for Arab culture.

Be Brave and Use Any Arabic You Can

You'll continuously encounter Arabs who simply can't believe that you have learned even a little Arabic. As a result, everyone you encounter will be extraordinarily generous of you for your efforts. No matter what mistakes you make, you'll be praised with the words, "You speak it better than me!" (Even though you'll know better.)

The upshot of all this is that you can (and should) just relax and use whatever Arabic you have. It's a win-win situation for you. No matter what comes out of your mouth, you're a hero. And the effort of trying to produce Arabic will help you get even better.

Being brave is also good advice for working your way through this book. Don't labor too much over any one item in the practices. What's the worst that could happen? That you find out you were wrong? I wish I had a nickel for every time I tried to produce language and was wrong! When you don't get something right, just review it another day and your mistake will have been well worth making.

Practice Regularly

You've heard it said that Rome wasn't built in a day. And no one has ever learned everything there was to know about a language in a day either. You've likely seen books and programs promising that with their product you could speak Arabic in one week. Don't bother buying them. Unless you're a linguistic genius (and I'm certainly not), the book or program won't help you accomplish that goal.

Much more important is the regular study of Arabic. Ten minutes a day is better than 90 minutes once a week. To acquire a language, you need to regularly train your brain to think in the words and grammatical patterns of your target language. Obviously I suggest that you study more than ten minutes a day. But, whatever you do, do it regularly.

Consult a Variety of Resources

This book is a tool (and a good one at that!). There's a lot of Arabic for you to master between these covers. But you can supplement this book with other sources of the language. For instance, you can read and listen to Arabic news online at a variety of sites.

I recommend the BBC (news.bbc.co.uk/hi/arabic/news), where you can find news stories translated into Arabic as well as audio of the main stories of the day. The good thing about the BBC is that you can also click on the English page. There you can read the English source of the story and learn the English equivalents for any words you need without looking them up in the dictionary.

Another valuable pursuit is finding a few songs in Arabic and listening to them regularly. Combining music and language is not only aesthetically pleasing, but it's also helpful in learning.

Discover How You Learn Best

Personally, I'm a visual learner. I can't hear a word spoken and learn it in any credible way. I need to see the word written, in Arabic, in order to acquire it as a vocabulary item that I can then use myself when the situation demands it. But you, my dear reader, are not me. You may very well be an auditory learner. And no one is right or wrong when it comes to learning. You just need to discover how you, personally, learn a foreign language best.

If you're an auditory learner, you should make tapes of yourself reading the sentences and practices from this book. Burn it onto a CD and listen to it in your car. Download news from the Internet and do the same. If, on the other hand, you're like me, write out the exercises in your own hand and study them that way. You may even be a learner of a totally different sort. Try a number of different things. Try crazy things! Success can't be judged by anyone. Whatever helps you learn a language is what you need to focus on. Go find it!

Start All Over

Are you reading this chapter after working your way through the entire book? If so, let me congratulate you. But whether you have finished your exploration of *Intermediate Arabic For Dummies* or have just begun it, there's value in starting all over in your Arabic language study. Every now and then I break out my first-year books in a language that I work in and start from scratch. The basics of a language make up 70 percent of it all. There's no way to minimize the importance of deepening your mastery of 70 percent of Arabic (or any other language you want to function in).

Part VI
Appendixes

The 5th Wave   By Rich Tennant

"I have to remember that Arabic is read the way it's written—right to left. I once read an Arabic recipe left to right and made a cup of rice, a pound of ground lamb, and a jar of greens out of a plate of stuffed grape leaves."

In this part . . .

Do you need to quickly refresh your memory about one of the ten Arabic verb forms? This part has a chart for you to consult. And if there's an Arabic word on the tip of your tongue, but you just can't seem to recall it (and you need it to complete the exercises or talk to your friend or co-worker), this part helps you out with bilingual dictionaries.

Appendix A

Verb Chart

ooks on Romance languages, such as Italian, could include many charts showing you examples of the verbs — regular and irregular — in a reasonably-sized appendix. For Arabic, however, verb weakness issues would require dozens of pages to comprehensively show it all. So it's all in this book, in the chapters touching on verbs, commands, participles, and verbal nouns.

But I wanted to give you a one-page chart that you can consult whenever you need to see the big picture of the ten forms. This one-page chart can be helpful whenever you want to see at a glance all the parts of speech for the forms lined up with each other. You'll also find that it's easier to memorize when you see the parts of speech this way.

In Table A-1, I give you the third person singular forms of the past and present tense, the verbal noun, and the masculine singular active and passive participles of all ten verb forms. This chart uses the root فعل (f-3-l; *to do/make*). Using **f-3-l** as a dummy root to display the various verb forms is a common convention in Arabic books, even though the root doesn't actually occur in all these forms.

There's no singular word pattern used for the verbal noun in Form I. When no form appears, it means that the verb form doesn't exist.

Table A-1			Overview of the Arabic Verb		
Form	**Past**	**Present**	**Verbal Noun**	**Active Participle**	**Passive Participle**
I	فَعَلَ (fa3ala)	يَفْعَلُ (yaf3alu)	variable	فاعِل (faa3il)	مَفْعول (maf3uul)
II	فَعَّلَ (fa33ala)	يُفَعِّلُ (yufa33ilu)	تَفْعيل (taf3iil)	مُفَعِّل (mufa33il)	مُفَعَّل (mufa33al)
III	فاعَلَ (faa3ala)	يُفاعِلُ (yufaa3alu)	مُفاعَلَة (mufaa3ala)	مُفاعِل (mufaa3il)	مُفاعَل (mufaa3al)
IV	أَفْعَلَ ('af3ala)	يُفْعِلُ (yuf3ilu)	إفْعال ('if3aal)	مُفْعِل (muf3il)	مُفْعَل (muf3al)
V	تَفَعَّلَ (tafa33ala)	يَتَفَعَّلُ (yata-fa33alu)	تَفَعُّل (tafa33ul)	مُتَفَعِّل (mutafa33il)	مُتَفَعَّل (mutafa33al)
VI	تَفاعَلَ (tafaa3ala)	يَتَفاعَلُ (yata-faa3alu)	تَفاعُل (tafaa3ul)	مُتَفاعِل (muta-faa3il)	مُتَفاعَل (mutafaa3al)

(continued)

Table A-1 *(continued)*

Form	Past	Present	Verbal Noun	Active Participle	Passive Participle
VII	اِنْفَعَلَ (infa3ala)	يَنْفَعِلُ (yanfa3ilu)	اِنْفِعال (infi3aal)	مُنْفَعِل (munfa3il)	rare
VIII	اِفْتَعَلَ (ifta3ala)	يَفْتَعِلُ (yafta3ilu)	اِفْتِعال (ifti3aal)	مُفْتَعِل (mufta3il)	مُفْتَعَل (mufta3al)
IX	اِفْعَلَّ (if3alla)	يَفْعَلُّ (yaf3allu)	اِفْعِلال (if3ilaal)	مُفْعَلّ (muf3all)	rare
X	اِسْتَفْعَلَ (istaf3ala)	يَسْتَفْعِلُ (yastaf3ilu)	اِسْتِفْعال (istif3aal)	مُسْتَفْعِل (mustaf3il)	مُسْتَفْعَل (mustaf3al)

Appendix B
English-Arabic Dictionary

In this appendix, I provide some of the Arabic vocabulary used in this book, arranged alphabetically by the English translation, for your use in completing the practices or learning valuable new words. I provide you with the past and present tenses of all Arabic verbs (in that order). I also provide you with the singular of every noun and adjective as well as the plural (except where the plural is regularly formed, such as the sound plurals). To discover more about plural formation, go to Chapter 5. To search out the formation of adjectives, flip to Chapter 6.

to be able: اِسْتَطاعَ (istaTaa3a) / يَسْتَطيعُ (yastaTii3u)

about/concerning/for/away from: عَن (3an)

address: عُنْوان (3unwaan) / عَناوين (3anaawiin)

after: بَعْدَ (ba3da)

agreeing: مُوافِق (muwaafiq)

airport: مَطار (maTaar) / مَطارات (maTaaraat)

all/each/every: كُلّ (kull)

also/too: أَيْضاً (’ayDan)

ambassador: سَفير (safiir) / سُفَراء (sufaraa’)

America: أَمْريكا (’amriikaa)

and (prefixed to next word): وَ (wa-)

and so/and then (prefixed to next word): فَ (fa-)

angry: غَضْبان (ghaDbaan)

to announce: أَعْلَنَ (’a3lana) / يُعْلِنُ (yu3linu)

announcer: مُذيع (mudhii3)

to answer: أَجابَ (’ajaaba) / يُجيبُ (yujiibu)

answer: جَواب (jawaab) / أَجْوِبة (’ajwiba)

apartment: شَقّة (shaqqa) / شُقَق (shuqaq)

apples: تُفّاح (tuffaaH)

Arab/Arabic: عَرَبيّ (3arabii)

army: جَيْش (jaysh) / جُيوش (juyuush)

to arrive: وَصَلَ (waSala) / يَصِلُ (yaSilu)

article: مَقال (maqaal) / مَقالات (maqaalaat)

as for . . . : أَمّا...فَ (’ammaa . . . fa-)

to ask: سَأَلَ (sa’ala) / يَسْأَلُ (yas’alu)

assistant/helper: مُساعِد (musaa3id)

to be (was): كانَ (kaana) / يَكونُ (yakuunu)

beach: شاطِئ (shaaTi’) / شَواطِئ (shawaaTi’)

beautiful/handsome: جَميل (jamiil)

beauty: جَمال (jamaal)

because (+ possessive suffix): لأَنَّ (li’anna)

to become: أَصْبَحَ (’aSbaHa) / يُصْبِحُ (yuSbiHu)

before: قَبْلَ (qabla)

between: بَيْنَ (bayna)

to believe, think: اِعْتَقَدَ (i3taqada) / يَعْتَقِدُ (ya3taqidu)

beverage/drink: شَراب (sharaab) / أَشْرِبة ('ashriba)

big/large: كَبير (kabiir) / كِبار (kibaar)

black: سَوْداء (sawdaa') / أَسْوَد ('aswad)

blue: أَزْرَق ('azraq)

book: كِتاب (kitaab) / كُتُب (kutub)

born: مَوْلُود (mawluud)

to bother: أَزْعَجَ ('az3aja) / يُزْعِجُ (yuz3iju)

box: عُلْبة (3ulba) / عُلَب (3ulab)

boy/child: وَلَد (walad) / أَوْلاد ('awlaad)

branch: فَرْع (far3) / فُروع (furuu3)

breakfast: فَطور (faTuur)

to bring: أَحْضَرَ ('aHDara) / يُحْضِرُ (yuHDiru)

busy: مَشْغول (mashghuul)

but (with following accusative or possessive suffix): لكِنّ (laakinna)

but: لكِن (laakin)

to buy: اِشْتَرى (ishtaraa) / يَشْتَري (yashtarii)

to call (with **bi-**): اِتَّصَلَ (ittaSala) / يَتَّصِلُ (yattaSilu)

candidate: مُرَشَّح (murashshakh)

car: سَيّارة (sayyaara)

card: بَطاقة (baTaaqa) / بَطاقات (baTaaqaat)

cat: قِطّة (qiTTa) / قِطّ (qiTT)

to celebrate: اِحْتَفَلَ (iHtafala) / يَحْتَفِلُ (yaHtafilu)

certain: مُتَأَكِّد (muta'akkid)

it is certain that: مِنَ المُؤَكَّد أَنْ (min al-mu'akkad 'an)

to change: غَيَّرَ (ghayyara) / يُغَيِّرُ (yughayyiru)

choice: اِخْتِيار ('ikhtiyaar) / إخْتِيارات ('ikhtiyaaraat)

city: مَدينة (madiina) / مُدُن (mudun)

class: صَفّ (Saff) / صُفوف (Sufuuf)

clean: نَظيف (naDHiif) / نُظَفاء (nuDHafaa')

clinic: عِيادة (3iyaada)

coffee: قَهْوة (qahwa)

college: كُلِّية (kulliya)

color: لَوْن (lawn) / أَلْوان ('alwaan)

to come: حَضَرَ (HaDara) / يَحْضُرُ (yaHDuru)

company: شَرِكة (sharika)

to complete: أَكْمَلَ ('akmala) / يُكْمِلُ (yukmilu)

to compose: أَلَّفَ ('allafa) / يُؤَلِّفُ (yu'allifu)

composer: مُؤَلِّف (mu'allif)

computer: حاسوب (Haasub) / حَواسيب (Hawaasiib)

to consider: اِعْتَبَرَ (i3tabara) / يَعْتَبِرُ (ya3tabiru)

contract: عَقْد (3aqd) / عُقود (3uquud)

cook: طَبّاخ (Tabbaakh)

country: بَلَد (balad) / بِلاد (bilaad)

courage: شَجاعة (shajaa3a)

crate/box: صُنْدوق (Sunduuq) / صَناديق (Sanaadiiq)

cup: فِنْجان (finjaan) / فَناجين (fanaajiin)

dark: مُظْلِم (muDHlim)

daughter: بِنْت (bint) / بَنات (banaat)

day: يَوْم (yawm) / أَيّام ('ayyaam)

death: مَوْت (mawt)

it is decided that: مِنَ المُقَرَّر أَنْ (min al-muqarrar 'an) to deny: نَفـى (nafaa) / يَنْفـي (yanfii)

department/section: قِسْـم (qism) / أقْسـام ('aqsaam)

to describe: وَصَفَ (waSafa) / يَصِفُ (yaSifu)

details: تَفاصيـل (tafaaSiil)

director: مُدير (mudiir)

to do/make: فَعَلَ (fa3ala) / يَفْعَلُ (yaf3alu)

doctor/physician: طَبيـب (Tabiib) / أطِبّة ('aTibba)

dog: كَلْـب (kalb) / كِلاب (kilaab)

door: باب (baab) / أبْواب ('abwaab)

to doubt (with bi-): تَشَـكَّـك (tashakkak) / يَتَشَـكَّـكُ (yatashakkaku)

to drink: شَـرِبَ (shariba) / يَشْـرَبُ (yashrabu)

drinking (verbal noun): شُـرْب (shurb)

to earn: اكْـتَـسَـبَ (iktasaba) / يَكُـتَـسِـبُ (yaktasibu)

to eat: أكَلَ ('akala) / يَأكُلُ (ya'kulu)

eating (verbal noun): أكْل ('akl)

editor: مُحَـرِّر (muHarrir)

education: تَرْبيـة (tarbiya)

egg: بَيْضة (bayDa)

to elect: انْتَـخَبَ (intakhaba) / يَنْتَـخِبُ (yantakhibu)

employee: مُوظَّف (muwaDHDHaf)

engine: مُحَـرِّك (muHarrik)

enough: كِفايـة (kifaaya)

to enter: دَخَـلَ (dakhala) / يَدْخُلُ (yadkhulu)

to examine: تَفَـحَّـصَ (tafaHHaSa) / يَتَفَـحَّـصُ (yatafaHHaSu)

excellent: مُمْتـاز (mumtaaz)

expensive: غالـي (ghaalii)

experience: خِبْـرة (khibra) / خِبَـرات (khibaraat)

to explain: شَـرَحَ (sharaHa) / يَشْـرَحُ (yashraHu)

falafel: فَلافِل (falaafil)

famous: مَشْـهور (mash-huur)

father: أب ('ab) / آباء ('aabaa')

final/last: أخيـر ('akhiir)

finally: أخيـراً ('akhiiran)

to find: وَجَـدَ (wajada) / يَجِدُ (yajidu)

fine/good: جَيِّد (jayyid)

to fire: طَـرَدَ (Tarada) / يَطْـرُدُ (yaTrudu)

fire: نار (naar) / نيـران (niiraan)

first: أوّلاً ('awwalan)

food: طَـعام (Ta3aam) / أطْـعِمة ('aT3ima)

for/since: لِمُـدّة (li-mudda)

to found: أسَّـسَ ('assasa) / يُؤَسِّـسُ (yu'assisu)

friend: صَديـق (Sadiiq) / أصْدِقاء ('aSdiqaa')

from time to time: مِن حيـن إلى حيـن (min Hiinin 'ilaa Hiinin)

from/than: مِنْ (min)

garment/clothes: مَلْبَـس (malbas) / مَلابِس (malaabis)

to get to know (with 3alaa): تَعَـرَّفَ (ta3arrafa) / يَتَعَـرَّفُ (yata3arrafu)

to get (+ 3alaa): حَـصَلَ (HaSala) / يَحْـصُلُ (yaHSulu)

gift/present: هَـدية (hadiya) / هَـدايا (hadaayaa)

girlfriend: حَبيبة (Habiiba)

to give: أعْـطى ('a3Taa) / يُعْـطي (yu3Tii)

to go: ذَهَـبَ (dhahaba) / يَذْهَـبُ (yadh-habu)

God willing: إنْ شاء ألله ('in shaa'a allah)

going (verbal noun): ذَهاب (**dhahaab**)

grandfather: جَدّ (**jadd**) / جُدود (**juduud**)

grandmother: جَدّة (**jadda**) / جَدّات (**jaddaat**)

grilled fish: سَمَك مَشْوي (**samak mashwii**)

to happen: حَدَثَ (**Hadatha**) / يَحْدُثُ (**yaHduthu**)

happy: مَسْرور (**masruur**)

to have (+ possessive suffix)/*at*: عِنْدَ (**3inda**)

he: هُوَ (**huwa**)

to hear: سَمِعَ (**sami3a**) / يَسْمَعُ (**yasma3u**)

heart: قَلْب (**qalb**) / قُلوب (**quluub**)

to help: ساعَدَ (**saa3ada**) / يُساعِدُ (**yusaa3idu**)

here: هُنا (**hunaa**)

hospital: مُسْتَشْفى (**mustashfaa**) / مُسْتَشْفَيات (**mustashfayaat**)

house: بَيْت (**bayt**) / بُيوت (**buyuut**)

hungry: جائِع (**jaa'i3**)

husband: زَوْج (**zawj**) / أَزْواج (**'azwaaj**)

I: أَنا (**'anaa**)

if (condition contrary to fact): لَوْ (**law**)

if: إذا (**'idhaa**)

if: إنْ (**'in**)

immediately: فَوْراً (**fawran**)

importance: أَهَمّية (**'ahammiya**)

important/interesting: مُهِمّ (**muhimm**)

to improve: حَسَّنَ (**Hassana**) / يُحَسِّنُ (**yuHassinu**)

in order to/that: لِكَيْ (**likay**)

in order to/until: حَتّى (**Hattaa**)

in/at: في (**fii**)

to insert: أَدْخَلَ (**'adkhala**) / يُدْخِلُ (**yudkhilu**)

instruction: تَعْليم (**ta3liim**)

intelligent: ذَكيّ (**dhakii**) / أَذْكِياء (**'adhkiyaa'**)

jewel: جَوْهَر (**jawhar**) / جَواهِر (**jawaahir**)

job: وَظيفة (**waDHiifa**) / وَظائِف (**waDHaa'if**)

Jordan: الأُرْدن (**al-'urdun**)

journey/trip: رِحْلة (**riHla**) / رِحْلات (**riHalaat**)

juice: عَصير (**3aSiir**)

to kiss: قَبَّلَ (**qabbala**) / يُقَبِّلُ (**yuqabbilu**)

kitchen: مَطْبَخ (**maTbakh**) / مَطابِخ (**maTaabikh**)

to know: عَرَفَ (**3arafa**) / يَعْرِفُ (**ya3rifu**)

language: لُغة (**lugha**)

last/past: ماضي (**maaDii**)

lazy: كَسْلان (**kaslaan**)

to lead to: أَدّى (**'addaa**) / يُؤَدّي (**yu'addii**)

to learn: تَعَلَّمَ (**ta3allama**) / يَتَعَلَّمُ (**yata3allamu**)

to know/learn: عَلِمَ (**3alima**) / يَعْلَمُ (**ya3lamu**)

to leave: تَرَكَ (**taraka**) / يَتْرُكُ (**yatruku**)

Lebanon: لُبْنان (**lubnaan**)

lecture: مُحاضَرة (**muHaaDara**)

letter: رِسالة (**risaala**) / رَسائِل (**rasaa'il**)

library: مَكْتَبة (**maktaba**) / مَكاتِب (**makaatib**)

like/similar (with following genitive or possessive suffix): مِثْلَ (**mithla**)

to like (literally *to please*): أَعْجَبَ (**'a3jaba**) / يُعْجِبُ (**yu3jibu**)

little/few: قَليل (**qaliil**) / أَقِلّاء (**'aqillaa'**)

to live (*inhabit*): يَسْكُنُ (sakana) سَكَنَ (yaskunu)

living: ساكِن (saakin)

to look for: يَبْحَثُ (baHatha) بَحَثَ (yabHathu)

to lose: أضاعَ (’aDaa3a) يُضيعُ (yuDii3u)

to love: أَحَبَّ (’aHabba) يُحِبُّ (yuHibbu)

magazine: مَجَلّة (majalla)

man: رِجال (rijaal) رَجُل (rajul)

to get married: يَتَزوّجُ (tazawwaja) تَزَوَّجَ (yatazawwaju)

meal: أكْلة (’akla)

to meet (+ bi-): يَلْتَقي (iltaqaa) اِلْتَقى (yaltaqii)

memories: ذِكْرَيات (dhikrayaat)

money: أمْوال (maal) مال (’amwaal)

much/a lot: كِثار (kathiir) كَثير (kithaar)

near: قَريب (qariib)

to be necessary: يَجِبُ (wajaba) وَجَبَ (yajibu)

need/necessity: حاجة (Haaja)

negotiation: مُفاوَضة (mufaawaDa)

never: أَبَداً (’abadan)

new: جُدُد (jadiid) جَديد (judud)

news: أخْبار (khabar) خَبَر (’akhbaar)

nice: لِطاف (laTiif) لَطيف (liTaaf)

night: لَيْلات (layla) لَيْلة (laylaat)

no/not (+ jussive to form past tense negative): لَمْ (lam)

no/not: لا (laa)

not (with following past tense): ما (maa)

notebook: دَفاتِر (daftar) دَفْتَر (dafaatir)

to notice: يُلاحِظُ (laaHaDHa) لاحَظَ (yulaaHiDHu)

now: الآنَ (al’aana)

office: مَكاتِب (maktab) مَكْتَب (makaatib)

old: قُدَماء (qadiim) قَديم (qudamaa’)

on/upon/above/at: عَلى (3alaa)

only/alone: وَحيد (waHiid)

only: فَقَط (faqaT)

to open: يَفْتَحُ (fataHa) فَتَحَ (yaftaHu)

opening/inaugural: اِفْتِتاح (iftitaaH)

opinion: آراء (ra’y) رَأْي (’aaraa’)

opportunity/chance: فُرَص (furSa) فُرْصة (furaS)

optimistic: مُتَفائِل (mutafaa’il)

or (within a question): أَمْ (’am)

or (within a statement): أَوْ (’aw)

other (M and F): أُخْرى (’aakhar) آخَر (’ukhraa)

to oversee: يُشْرِفُ (’ashrafa) أشْرَفَ (yushrifu)

package: طُرود (Tard) طَرْد (Turuud)

page: صَفْحة (SafHa)

paper: وَرَق (waraq)

park/garden: حَدائِق (Hadiiqa) حَديقة (Hadaa’iq)

pen: أقْلام (qalam) قَلَم (’aqlaam)

perhaps/possibly/maybe/probably: رُبَّما (rubbamaa)

person: إنْسان (’insaan)

person: أشْخاص (shakhS) شَخْص (’ashkhaaS)

place: أماكِن (makaan) مَكان (’amaakin)

plate: صُحون (SaHn) صَحْن (SuHuun)

to be possible: يُمْكِنُ (’amkana) أمْكَنَ (yumkinu)

to praise: يَمْدَحُ (madaHa) مَدَحَ (yamdaHu)

preferable/favorite: مُفَضَّل (mufaDDal)

to prepare: حَضَّر (HaDDara) / يُحَضِّرُ (yuHaDDiru)

president: رَئيس (ra'iis) / رُؤَساء (ru'asaa')

previous/earlier: سابِق (saabiq)

to print: طَبَعَ (Taba3a) / يَطْبَعُ (yaTba3u)

prize/award: جائزة (jaa'iza) / جَوائز (jawaa'iz)

problem: مُشْكِلة (mushkila) / مَشاكِل (mashaakil)

products: مُنْتَجات (muntajaat)

professor: أُسْتاذ ('ustaadh) / أَساتِذة ('asaatidha)

program: بَرْنامَج (barnaamaj) / بَرامِج (baraamij)

proposal: إقْتِراح ('iqtiraaH) / إقْتِراحات ('iqtiraaHaat)

to publish: أَصْدَرَ ('aSdara) / يُصْدِرُ (yuSdiru)

Qatar: قَطَر (qaTar)

question: سُؤال (su'aal) / أَسْئِلة ('as'ila)

radio: راديو (raadyuu)

to read: قَرَأَ (qara'a) / يَقْرَأُ (yaqra'u)

ready/prepared: مُسْتَعِدّ (musta3idd)

really: فِعْلاً (fi3lan)

refrigerator: ثَلّاجة (thallaaja)

to remember: ذَكَرَ (dhakara) / يَذْكُرُ (yadhkuru)

reporter: صُحُفيّ (SuHufii)

restaurant: مَطْعَم (maT3am) / مَطاعِم (maTaa3im)

to return: رَجَعَ (raja3a) / يَرْجِعُ (yarji3u)

rich: غَنِي (ghanii) / أَغْنِياء ('aghniyaa')

to rise (with following **bi** + verbal noun, to undertake): قامَ (qaama) / يَقومُ (yaquumu)

room: غُرْفة (ghurfa) / غُرَف (ghuraf)

rumor: إشاعة ('ishaa3a)

same (with following genitive): نَفْس (nafs)

to save: أَنْقَذَ ('anqadha) / يُنْقِذُ (yunqidhu)

to say: قالَ (qaala) / يَقولُ (yaquulu)

scared: خائِف (khaa'if)

school: مَدْرَسة (madrasa) / مَدارِس (madaaris)

sea: بَحْر (baHr) / بِحار (biHaar)

search (verbal noun): بَحْث (baHth)

season/semester/chapter: فَصْل (faSl) / فُصول (fuSuul)

see you later: إلى اللِّقاء ('ilaa-l-liqaa')

to see: رَأى (ra'aa) / يَرى (yaraa)

to sell: باعَ (baa3a) / يَبيعُ (yabii3u)

senator/sheikh: شَيْخ (shaykh) / شُيوخ (shuyuukh)

to send: أَرْسَلَ ('arsala) / يُرْسِلُ (yursilu)

she: هِيَ (hiya)

shirt: قَميص (qamiiS) / قُمْصان (qumSaan)

to shoot: أَطْلَقَ ('aTlaqa) / يُطْلِقُ (yuTliqu)

sick: مَريض (mariiD) / مَرْضى (marDaa)

to sign (with **bi**-): وَقَّعَ (waqqa3a) / يُوَقِّعُ (yuwaqqi3u)

sincere(ly): مُخْلِص (mukhliS)

singer: مُغَنّي (mughannii)

sister: أُخْت ('ukht) / أَخَوات ('akhawaat)

to sleep: نامَ (naama) / يَنامُ (yanaamu)

sleep: نَوْم (nawm)

small: صَغير (Saghiir) / صِغار (Sighaar)

solution: حَلّ (Hall) / حُلول (Huluul)

sometimes: أَحْياناً ('aHyaanan)

soon: قَريباً (qariiban)

sorry: مُتَأَسِّف (muta'assif)

specialty/specialization: تَخَصُّص (takhaSSus)

stadium/playground: مَلْعَب (mal3ab) / مَلاعِب (malaa'ib)

star: نَجْمة (najma) / نَجَمات (najamaat)

to start: بَدَأَ (bada'a) / يَبْدَأُ (yabda'u)

station: مَحَطّة (maHaTTa)

still/yet (auxiliary): ما يَزالُ (maa yazaalu)

storeroom/stockroom: مَخْزَن (makhzan) / مَخازِن (makhaazin)

story: قِصّة (qiSSa) / قِصَص (qiSaS)

student: طالِب (Taalib) / طُلّاب (Tullaab)

study (verbal noun): دِراسة (diraasa)

to study: دَرَسَ (darasa) / يَدْرُسُ (yadrusu)

stuffed grape leaves: وَرَق عِنَب (waraq 3inab)

subject/issue: مَوْضوع (mawDuu3) / مواضيع (mawaaDii3)

to submit/to greet: سَلَّمَ (sallama) / يُسَلِّمُ (yusallimu)

success: نَجاح (najaaH)

suitcase/bag: حَقيبة (Haqiiba) / حَقائب (Haqaa'ib)

summer: صَيْف (Sayf) / أَصْياف ('aSyaaf)

Syria: سورية (suuriya)

system: نِظام (niDHaam) / أَنْظِمة ('anDHima)

table: طاوِلة (Taawila)

tall/long: طَويل (Tawiil) / طِوال (Tiwaal)

tasty/delicious: لَذيذ (ladhiidh) / لِذاذ (lidhaadh)

to teach: دَرَّسَ (darrasa) / يُدَرِّسُ (yudarrisu)

teacher: مُدَرِّس (mudarris)

telegram: بَرْقِية (barqiya)

telephone: هاتِف (haatif) / هَواتِف (hawaatif)

to tell: أَخْبَرَ ('akhbara) / يُخْبِرُ (yukhbiru)

to test: اِمْتَحَنَ (imtaHana) / يَمْتَحِنُ (yamtaHinu)

test/examination: اِمْتِحان (imtiHaan) / اِمْتِحانات (imtiHaanaat)

thanks: شُكْراً (shukran)

that (FS): تِلْكَ (tilka)

that (MS): ذلِكَ (dhaalika)

that (with following accusative or possessive suffix): أَنَّ ('anna)

that: أَنْ ('an)

there is not: لَيْسَ (laysa)

there: هُناكَ (hunaaka)

they: هُم (hum)

thing: شَيْء (shay') / أَشْياء ('ashyaa')

to think (with bi-): فَكَّرَ (fakkara) / يُفَكِّرُ (yufakkiru)

thirsty: عَطْشان (3aTshaan)

this (FS): هذِو (haadhihi)

this (MS): هذا (haadhaa)

Thursday: الخَميس (al-khamiis)

time: حين (Hiin) / أَحْيان ('aHyaan)

time: وَقْت (waqt) / أَوْقات ('awqaat)

tired: تَعْبان (ta3baan)

to (with following genitive or possessive suffix): لِ (li-)

to/into: إلى ('ilaa)

today: اليَوْم (al-yawm)

together: مَعاً (ma3an)

tomorrow: غَداً (ghadan)

transportation: نَقْل (naql)

tree: شَجَرة (shajara)

truck: شاحنة (shaaHina)

to try: حاوَلَ (Haawala) / يُحاوِلُ (yuHaawilu)

to turn red: إِحْمَرَّ (iHmarra) / يَحْمَرُّ (yaHmaru)

typing: ضارِباً (Daariban)

to understand: فَهِمَ (fahima) / يَفْهَمُ (yafhamu)

university: جامِعة (jaami3a)

useful: مُفيد (mufiid)

very: جِدّاً (jiddan)

village: قَرْية (qarya) / قُرَىً (quran)

to visit: زارَ (zaara) / يَزورُ (yazuuru)

visit: زيارة (ziyaara)

vote/voice: صَوْت (Sawt) / أَصْوات ('aSwaat)

to wake up: إِسْتَيْقَظَ (istayqaDHa) / يَسْتَيْقِظُ (yastayqiDHu)

to walk: مَشى (mashaa) / يَمْشي (yamshii)

to want: أَرادَ ('araada) / يُريدُ (yuriidu)

water: ماء (maa') / مياه (miyaah)

we: نَحْنُ (naHnu)

to wear: لَبِسَ (labisa) / يَلْبَسُ (yalbasu)

weather: جَوّ (jaww) / أَجْواء ('ajwaa')

week: أُسْبوع ('usbuu3) / أسابيع ('asaabii3)

when: عِنْدَما (3indamaa)

when: لَمّا (lammaa)

which: مِمّا (mimmaa)

who/which/that (FS): الَّتي (allatii)

who/which/that (MS): الَّذي (alladhii)

who: مَنْ (man)

why: لِماذا (limaadhaa)

wife: زَوْجة (zawja)

to win: فازَ (faaza) / يَفوزُ (yafuuzu)

with: مَعَ (ma3a)

without (with following genitive or possessive suffix): بدون (bi-duun)

woman: إِمْرَأة (imra'a) / نِساء (nisaa')

wonderful: رائِع (raa'i3)

word: كَلِمة (kalima)

to work: عَمِلَ (3amila) / يَعْمَلُ (ya3malu)

work: عَمَل (3amal)

worker: عامِل (3aamil) / عُمّال (3ummaal)

to worry: أَقْلَقَ ('aqlaqa) / يُقْلِقُ (yuqliqu)

to write: كَتَبَ (kataba) / يَكْتُبُ (yaktubu)

writer: كاتِب (kaatib) / كُتّاب (kuttaab)

year: سَنة (sana) / سَنَوات (sanawaat)

yesterday: أَمْس ('amsi)

you (FS): أَنْتِ ('anti)

you (MP): أَنْتُم ('antum)

you (MS): أَنْتَ ('anta)

young woman: فَتاة (fataah) / فَتَيات (fatayaat)

Appendix C

Arabic-English Dictionary

1n this appendix, I provide some of the Arabic vocabulary used in this book. It's arranged alphabetically by the English transliteration, for your use in completing the practices or learning valuable new words. I provide you with the past and present tenses of all Arabic verbs (in that order). I also provide you with the singular of every noun and adjective as well as the plural (except where the plural is regularly formed, such as the sound plurals). To discover more about plural formation, go to Chapter 5. To search out the formation of adjectives, flip to Chapter 6.

Note: Other larger dictionaries you buy may organize the words by root, but I want you to be able to quickly find a word based on the form you actually have in your practice exercise. So I arranged this dictionary alphabetically by the order of the letters in the Arabic alphabet. You can find a list of those letters in order on the Cheat Sheet at the front of the book.

أَب ('ab) / آباء ('aabaa'): *father*

أَبَداً ('abadan): *never*

أَجابَ ('ajaaba) / يُجيبُ (yujiibu): *to answer*

أَحَبَّ ('aHabba) / يُحِبُّ (yuHibbu): *to love*

أَحْضَرَ ('aHDara) / يُحْضِرُ (yuHDiru): *to bring*

أَحْياناً ('aHyaanan): *sometimes*

آخَر ('aakhar) / أُخْرى ('ukhraa): *other* (M and F)

أَخْبَرَ ('akhbara) / يُخْبِرُ (yukhbiru): *to tell*

أَخير ('akhiir): *final/last*

أَخيراً ('akhiiran): *finally*

أَدّى ('addaa) / يُؤَدّي (yu'addii): *to lead to*

أَدْخَلَ ('adkhala) / يُدْخِلُ (yudkhilu): *to insert*

أَرادَ ('araada) / يُريدُ (yuriidu): *to want*

أَرْسَلَ ('arsala) / يُرْسِلُ (yursilu): *to send*

أَزْعَجَ ('az3aja) / يُزْعِجُ (yuz3iju): *to bother*

أَزْرَق ('azraq): *blue*

أَسَّسَ ('assasa) / يُؤَسِّسُ (yu'assisu): *to found*

أَسْوَد ('aswad) / سَوْداء (sawdaa'): *black*

أَصْبَحَ ('aSbaHa) / يُصْبِحُ (yuSbiHu): *to become*

أَصْدَرَ ('aSdara) / يُصْدِرُ (yuSdiru): *to publish*

أَضاعَ ('aDaa3a) / يُضيعُ (yuDii3u): *to lose*

أَطْلَقَ ('aTlaqa) / يُطْلِقُ (yuTliqu): *to shoot*

أَشْرَفَ ('ashrafa) / يُشْرِفُ (yushrifu): *to oversee*

أَعْجَبَ ('a3jaba) / يُعْجِبُ (yu3jibu): *to like* (literally *to please*)

أَعْطى ('a3Taa) / يُعْطي (yu3Tii): *to give*

أَعْلَنَ ('a3lana) / يُعْلِنُ (yu3linu): *to announce*

أَقْلَقَ ('aqlaqa) / يُقْلِقُ (yuqliqu): *to worry*

أَكَلَ ('akala) / يَأْكُلُ (ya'kulu): *to eat*

أَكْل ('akl): *eating* (verbal noun)

أَكْلة ('akla): *meal*

أَكْمَلَ ('akmala) / يُكْمِلُ (yukmilu): *to complete*

الآنَ (al'aana): *now*

الَّتي (allatii): *who/which/that* (FS)

الَّذي (alladhii): *who/which/that* (MS)

أَلَّفَ ('allafa) / يُؤَلِّفَ (yu'allifu): *to compose*

اليَوْم (al-yawm): *today*

أَمْ ('am): *or* (within a question)

أَمْكَنَ ('amkana) / يُمْكِنُ (yumkinu): *to be possible*

أَمّا...فَ ('ammaa . . . fa-): *as for . . .*

أَمْريكا ('amriikaa): *America*

أَمْس ('amsi): *yesterday*

أَنْ ('an): *that*

أَنَّ ('anna): *that* (with following accusative or possessive suffix)

أَنا ('anaa): *I*

أَنْقَذَ ('anqadha) / يُنْقِذُ (yunqidhu): *to save*

أَنْتَ ('anta): *you* (MS)

أَنْتِ ('anti): *you* (FS)

أَنْتُم ('antum): *you* (MP)

أَهَمِّية ('ahammiya): *importance*

أَوْ ('aw): *or* (within a statement)

أَوَّلاً ('awwalan): *first*

أَيْضاً ('ayDan): *also*

اتَّصَلَ (ittaSala) / يَتَّصِلُ (yattaSilu): *to call* (with **bi-**)

إذا ('idhaa): *if*

اِحْتَفَلَ (iHtafala) / يَحْتَفِلُ (yaHtafilu): *to celebrate*

اِحْمَرَّ (iHmarra) / يَحْمَرُّ (yaHmaru): *to turn red*

إخْتِيار / إخْتِيارات ('ikhtiyaar) / ('ikhtiyaaraat): *choice*

اِسْتَطاعَ (istaTaa3a) / يَسْتَطيعُ (yastaTii3u): *to be able*

اِسْتَيْقَظَ (istayqaDHa) / يَسْتَيْقَظُ (yastayqiDHu): *to wake up*

إشاعة ('ishaa3a): *rumor*

اِشْتَرى (ishtaraa) / يَشْتَري (yashtarii): *to buy*

اِعْتَبَرَ (i3tabara) / يَعْتَبِرُ (ya3tabiru): *to consider*

اِعْتَقَدَ (i3taqada) / يَعْتَقِدُ (ya3taqidu): *to believe, think*

اِفْتِتاح (iftitaaH): *opening/inaugural*

إقْتِراح / إقْتِراحات (iqtiraaH) / ('iqtiraaHaat): *proposal*

اِكْتَسَبَ (iktasaba) / يَكْتَسِبُ (yaktasibu): *to earn*

إلى ('ilaa): *to/into*

إلى اللِّقاء ('ilaa-l-liqaa'): *see you later*

اِلْتَقى (iltaqaa) / يَلْتَقي (yaltaqii): *to meet* (+ **bi-**)

اِمْتَحَنَ (imtaHana) / يَمْتَحِنُ (yamtaHinu): *to test*

اِمْتِحان / اِمْتِحانات (imtiHaan) / (imtiHaanaat): *test/examination*

اِمْرَأة (imra'a) / نِساء (nisaa'): *woman*

إنْ ('in): *if*

إنْ شاءَ اللّه ('in shaa'a allah): *God willing*

إنْسان ('insaan): *person*

اِنْتَخَبَ (intakhaba) / يَنْتَخِبُ (yantakhibu): *to elect*

أُخْت / أَخَوات ('ukht) / ('akhawaat): *sister*

أُسْبوع / أَسابيع ('usbuu3) / ('asaabii3): *week*

أُسْتاذ / أَساتِذة ('ustaadh / 'asaatidha): *professor*

الأُرْدُن (al-'urdun): *Jordan*

باب / أَبْواب (baab / 'abwaab): *door*

باعَ / يَبيعُ (baa3a / yabii3u): *to sell*

بَدَأَ / يَبْدَأُ (bada'a / yabda'u): *to start*

بَحَثَ / يَبْحَثُ (baHatha / yabHathu): *to search for*

بَحْث (baHth): *search* (verbal noun)

بَحْر / بِحار (baHr / biHaar): *sea*

بَرْقِية (barqiya): *telegram*

بَرْنامَج / بَرامِج (barnaamaj / baraamij): *program*

بَطاقة / بَطاقات (baTaaqa / 'baTaaqaat): *card*

بَعْدَ (ba3da): *after*

بَلَد / بِلاد (balad / bilaad): *country*

بَيْت / بُيوت (bayt / buyuut): *house*

بَيْضة (bayDa): *egg*

بَيْنَ (bayna): *between*

بدون (bi-duun): *without* (with following genitive or possessive suffix)

بِنْت / بَنات (bint / banaat): *daughter*

تَخَصّص (takhaSSus): *specialty/specialization*

تَرَكَ / يَتْرُكُ (taraka / yatruku): *to leave*

تَرْبية (tarbiya): *education*

تَزَوَّجَ / يَتَزَوَّجُ (tazawwaja / yatazawwaju): *to get married*

تَشَكَّكَ / يَتَشَكَّكُ (tashakkak / yatashakkaku): *to doubt* (with **bi-**)

تَعْبان (ta3baan): *tired*

تَعَرَّفَ / يَتَعَرَّفُ (ta3arrafa / yata3arrafu): *get to know* (with **3alaa**)

تَعَلَّمَ / يَتَعَلَّمُ (ta3allama / yata3allamu): *to learn*

تَعْليم (ta3liim): *instruction*

تَفَحَّصَ / يَتَفَحَّصُ (tafaHHaSa / yatafaHHaSu): *to examine*

تُفّاح (tuffaaH): *apples*

تِلْكَ (tilka): *that* (FS)

ثَلّاجة (thallaaja): *refrigerator*

جائِع (jaa'i3): *hungry*

جائِزة / جَوائِز (jaa'iza / jawaa'iz): *prize/award*

جَدّ / جُدود (jadd / juduud): *grandfather*

جَدّة / جَدّات (jadda / jaddaat): *grandmother*

جَديد / جُدُد (jadiid / judud): *new*

جامِعة (jaami3a): *university*

جمال (jamaal): *beauty*

جَميل (jamiil): *beautiful/handsome*

جَواب / أَجْوِبة (jawaab / 'ajwiba): *answer*

جَوْهَر / جَواهِر (jawhar / jawaahir): *jewel*

جَوّ / أَجْواء (jaw / 'ajwaa'): *weather*

جَيْش / جُيوش (jaysh / juyuush): *army*

جَيِّد (jayyid): *fine/good*

جِدّاً (jiddan): *very*

حاجة (Haaja): *need/necessity*

حاسوب / حَواسيب (Haasub / Hawaasiib): *computer*

حاوَلَ / يُحاوِلُ (Haawala / yuHaawilu): *to try*

حَبيبة (Habiiba): *girlfriend*

حَتّى (Hattaa): *in order to/until*

حَدَثَ / يَحْدُثُ (Hadatha / yaHduthu): *to happen*

حَديقة / حَدائِق (Hadiiqa / Hadaa'iq): *park/garden*

حَسَّنَ / يُحَسِّنُ (Hassana / yuHassinu): *to improve*

حَصَلَ (HaSala) / يَحْصُلُ (yaHSulu): to get (+ 3alaa)

حَضَرَ (HaDara) / يَحْضُرُ (yaHDuru): to come

حَضَّرَ (HaDDara) / يُحَضِّرُ (yuHaDDiru): to prepare

حَقيبة (Haqiiba) / حَقائب (Haqaa'ib): suitcase/bag

حَلّ (Hall) / حُلول (Huluul): solution

حين (Hiin) / أَحْيان ('aHyaan): time

خائِف (khaa'if): scared

خَبَر (khabar) / أَخْبار ('akhbaar): news

الخَميس (al-khamiis): Thursday

خِبْرة (khibra) / خِبَرات (khibaraat): experience

دَخَلَ (dakhala) / يَدْخُلُ (yadkhulu): to enter

دَرَسَ (darasa) / يَدْرُسُ (yadrusu): to study

دَرَّسَ (darrasa) / يُدَرِّسُ (yudarrisu): to teach

دَفْتَر (daftar) / دَفاتِر (dafaatir): notebook

دِراسة (diraasa): study (verbal noun)

ذَكَرَ (dhakara) / يَذْكُرُ (yadhkuru): to remember

ذِكْرَيات (dhikrayaat): memories

ذَكيّ (dhakii) / أَذْكِياء ('adhkiyaa'): intelligent

ذلِكَ (dhaalika): that (MS)

ذَهاب (dhahaab): going (verbal noun)

ذَهَبَ (dhahaba) / يَذْهَبُ (yadh-habu): to go

رائِع (raa'i3): wonderful

راديو (raadyuu): radio

رَأى (ra'aa) / يَرى (yaraa): to see

رَئيس (ra'iis) / رُؤَساء (ru'asaa'): president

رَأي (ra'y) / آراء ('aaraa'): opinion

رَجَعَ (raja3a) / يَرْجِعُ (yarji3u): to return

رَجُل (rajul) / رِجال (rijaal): man

رِحْلة (riHla) / رِحَلات (riHalaat): journey/trip

رسالة (risaala) / رَسائِل (rasaa'il): letter

رُبَّما (rubbamaa): perhaps/possibly/maybe/probably

زارَ (zaara) / يَزورُ (yazuuru): to visit

زَوْج (zawj) / أَزْواج ('azwaaj): husband

زَوْجة (zawja): wife

زيارة (ziyaara): visit

سابِق (saabiq): previous/earlier

ساعَدَ (saa3ada) / يُساعِدُ (yusaa3idu): to help

ساكن (saakin): living

سَأَلَ (sa'ala) / يَسْأَلُ (yas'alu): ask

سَفير (safiir) / سُفَراء (sufaraa'): ambassador

سَكَنَ (sakana) / يَسْكُنُ (yaskunu): to live (inhabit)

سَلَّمَ (sallama) / يُسَلِّمُ (yusallimu): submit/to greet

سَمَك مَشْوي (samak mashwii): grilled fish

سَمِعَ (sami3a) / يَسْمَعُ (yasma3u): to hear

سَنة (sana) / سَنَوات (sanawaat): year

سَيّارة (sayyaara): car

سُؤال (su'aal) / أَسْئِلة ('as'ila): question

سورية (suuriya): Syria

شاطِئ (shaaTi') / شَواطِئ (shawaaTi'): beach

شاحِنة (shaaHina): truck

شَجَرة (**shajara**): *tree*

شَجاعة (**shajaa3a**): *courage*

شَخْص (**shakhS**) / أشْخاص (**'ashkhaaS**): *person*

شَراب (**sharaab**) / أشْرِبة (**'ashriba**): *beverage/drink*

شَرَح (**sharaHa**) / يَشْرَح (**yashraHu**): *to explain*

شَرِبَ (**shariba**) / يَشْرَب (**yashrabu**): *to drink*

شَرِكة (**sharika**): *company*

شَقّة (**shaqqa**) / شُقَق (**shuqaq**): *apartment*

شَيْء (**shay'**) / أشْياء (**'ashyaa'**): *thing*

شَيْخ (**shaykh**) / شُيوخ (**shuyuukh**): *senator/sheikh*

شُكْراً (**shukran**): *thanks*

شُرْب (**shurb**): *drinking* (verbal noun)

صَديق (**Sadiiq**) / أصْدِقاء (**'aSdiqaa'**): *friend*

صَحْن (**SaHn**) / صُحون (**SuHuun**): *plate*

صَغير (**Saghiir**) / صِغار (**Sighaar**): *small*

صَفّ (**Saff**) / صُفوف (**Sufuuf**): *class*

صَفْحة (**SafHa**): *page*

صَوْت (**Sawt**) / أصْوات (**'aSwaat**): *vote/voice*

صَيْف (**Sayf**) / أصْياف (**'aSyaaf**): *summer*

صُحُفيّ (**SuHufii**): *reporter*

صُنْدوق (**Sunduuq**) / صَناديق (**Sanaadiiq**): *crate/box*

ضارِباً (**Daariban**): *typing*

طالِب (**Taalib**) / طُلّاب (**Tullaab**): *student*

طاولة (**Taawila**): *table*

طَبّاخ (**Tabbaakh**): *cook*

طَبَعَ (**Taba3a**) / يَطْبَع (**yaTba3u**): *to print*

طَبيب (**Tabiib**) / أطِبّة (**'aTibba**): *doctor/physician*

طَرَدَ (**Tarada**) / يَطْرُد (**yaTrudu**): *to fire*

طَرْد (**Tard**) / طُرود (**Turuud**): *package*

طَعام (**Ta3aam**) / أطْعِمة (**'aT3ima**): *food*

طَويل (**Tawiil**) / طِوال (**Tiwaal**): *tall/long*

عامِل (**3aamil**) / عُمّال (**3ummaal**): *worker*

عَرَبيّ (**3arabii**): *Arab, Arabic*

عَرَفَ (**3arafa**) / يَعْرِف (**ya3rifu**): *to know*

عَصير (**3aSiir**): *juice*

عَطْشان (**3aTshaan**): *thirsty*

عَقْد (**3aqd**) / عُقود (**3uquud**): *contract*

عَلى (**3alaa**): *on/upon/above/at*

عَلِمَ (**3alima**) / يَعْلَم (**ya3lamu**): *to learn*

عَمَل (**3amal**): *work*

عَمِلَ (**3amila**) / يَعْمَل (**ya3malu**): *to work*

عَنْ (**3an**): *about/concerning/for/away from*

عِنْدَ (**3inda**): *to have* (+ possessive suffix)/*at*

عِنْدَما (**3indamaa**): *when*

عِيادة (**3iyaada**): *clinic*

عُلْبة (**3ulba**) / عُلَب (**3ulab**): *box*

عُنْوان (**3unwaan**) / عَناوين (**3anaawiin**): *address*

غالي (**ghaalii**): *expensive*

غَداً (**ghadan**): *tomorrow*

غَضْبان (**ghaDbaan**): *angry*

غَني (**ghanii**) / أغْنِياء (**'aghniyaa'**): *rich*

غَيَّرَ (**ghayyara**) / يُغَيِّر (**yughayyiru**): *to change*

غُرْفة (**ghurfa**) / غُرَف (**ghuraf**): *room*

فَ (**fa-**): *and so/and then* (prefixed to next word)

فازَ (faaza) / يَفوزُ (yafuuzu): *to win*

فَتاة (fataah) / فَتَيات (fatayaat): *young woman*

فَتَحَ (fataHa) / يَفْتَحُ (yaftaHu): *to open*

فَرْع (far3) / فُروع (furuu3): *branch*

فَصْل (faSl) / فُصول (fuSuul): *season/semester/chapter*

فَطور (faTuur): *breakfast*

فَعَلَ (fa3ala) / يَفْعَلُ (yaf3alu): *to do/make*

فَقَطْ (faqaT): *only*

فَوْراً (fawran): *immediately*

فَكَّرَ (fakkara) / يُفَكِّرُ (yufakkiru): *to think* (with **bi-**)

فَلافِل (falaafil): *falafel*

فَهِمَ (fahima) / يَفْهَمُ (yafhamu): *to understand*

فِعْلاً (fi3lan): *really*

في (fii): *in/at*

فِنْجان (finjaan) / فَناجين (fanaajiin): *cup*

فُرْصة (furSa) / فُرَص (furaS): *opportunity/chance*

قالَ (qaala) / يَقولُ (yaquulu): *to say*

قامَ (qaama) / يَقومُ (yaquumu): *to rise* (with following **bi** + verbal noun, *to undertake*)

قَبَّلَ (qabbala) / يُقَبِّلُ (yuqabbilu): *to kiss*

قَبْلَ (qabla): *before*

قَديم (qadiim) / قُدَماء (qudamaa'): *old*

قَرَأَ (qara'a) / يَقْرَأُ (yaqra'u): *to read*

قَريب (qariib): *near*

قَريباً (qariiban): *soon*

قَرْية (qarya) / قُرى (quran): *village*

قَطَر (qaTar): *Qatar*

قَلَم (qalam) / أَقْلام ('aqlaam): *pen*

قَلْب (qalb) / قُلوب (quluub): *heart*

قَليل (qaliil) / أَقِّلاء ('aqillaa'): *little/few*

قَميص (qamiiS) / قُمْصان (qumSaan): *shirt*

قَهْوة (qahwa): *coffee*

قِسْم (qism) / أَقْسام ('aqsaam): *department/section*

قِصّة (qiSSa) / قِصَص (qiSaS): *story*

قِطّ (qiTT) / قِطّة (qiTTa): *cat*

كاتِب (kaatib) / كُتّاب (kuttaab): *writer*

كانَ (kaana) / يَكونُ (yakuunu): *to be (was)*

كَبير (kabiir) / كِبار (kibaar): *big/large*

كَتَبَ (kataba) / يَكْتُبُ (yaktubu): *to write*

كَثير (kathiir) / كِثار (kithaar): *much/a lot*

كَسْلان (kaslaan): *lazy*

كَلْب (kalb) / كِلاب (kilaab): *dog*

كَلِمة (kalima): *word*

كِتاب (kitaab) / كُتُب (kutub): *book*

كِفاية (kifaaya): *enough*

كُلّ (kull): *all/each/every*

كُلِّية (kulliya): *college*

لَمْ (lam): *no/not* (+ jussive to form past tense negative)

يُلاحِظَ (laaHaDHa) / لاحَظَ (yulaaHiDHu): *to notice*

لكِنْ (laakin): *but*

لكِنَّ (laakinna): *but* (with following accusative or possessive suffix)

لَبِسَ (labisa) / يَلْبَسُ (yalbasu): *to wear*

لَذيذ (ladhiidh) / لِذاذ (lidhaadh): *tasty/delicious*

لَطيف (laTiif) / لِطاف (liTaaf): *nice*

لَمْ (lam): *no/not* (+ jussive to form past tense negative)

لَمّا (lammaa): *when*

لَوْ (law): *if* (condition contrary to fact)

لَوْن (lawn) / ألْوان ('alwaan): *color*

لَيْسَ (laysa): *there is not*

لَيْلة (layla) / لَيْلات (laylaat): *night*

لِ (li-): *to* (with following genitive or possessive suffix)

لأنَّ (li'anna): *because* (+ possessive suffix)

لِكَيْ (likay): *in order to/that*

لِماذا (limaadhaa): *why*

لِمُدّة (li-mudda): *for/since*

لُبْنان (lubnaan): *Lebanon*

لُغة (lugha): *language*

ما (maa): *not* (with following past tense)

ماء (maa') مياه (miyaah): *water*

ما يَزالُ (maa yazaalu): *still/yet* (auxiliary)

ماضي (maaDii): *last/past*

مال (maal) / أمْوال ('amwaal): *money*

مَجَلّة (majalla): *magazine*

مَحَطّة (maHaTTa): *station*

مَدَحَ (madaHa) / يَمْدَحُ (yamdaHu): *to praise*

مَدينة (madiina) / مُدُن (mudun): *city*

مَدْرَسة (madrasa) / مَدارِس (madaaris): *school*

مَريض (mariiD) / مَرْضى (marDaa): *sick*

مَسْرور (masruur): *happy*

مَشى (mashaa) / يَمْشي (yamshii): *to walk*

مَشْغول (mashghuul): *busy*

مَشْهور (mash-huur): *famous*

مَطار (maTaar) / مَطارات (maTaaraat): *airport*

مَطْبخ (maTbakh) / مَطابِخ (maTaabikh): *kitchen*

مَطْعَم (maT3am) / مَطاعِم (maTaa3im: *restaurant*

مَعَ (ma3a): *with*

مَعاً (ma3an): *together*

مَكان (makaan) / أماكِن ('amaakin): *place*

مَكْتَب (maktab) / مَكاتِب (makaatib): *office*

مَكْتَبة (maktaba) / مَكاتِب (makaatib): *library*

مَخْزَن (makhzan) / مَخازِن (makhaazin): *storeroom/stockroom*

مَلْبَس (malbas) / مَلابِس (malaabis): *garment/clothes*

مَلْعَب (mal3ab) / مَلاعِب (malaa'ib): *stadium/playground*

مَنْ (man): *who*

مَقال (maqaal) / مَقالات (maqaalaat): *article*

مَوْضوع (mawDuu3) / مَواضيع (mawaaDii3): *subject/issue*

مَوْلود (mawluud): *born*

مَوْت (mawt): *death*

مِثْلَ (mithla): *like/similar* (with following genitive or possessive suffix)

مِمّا (mimmaa): *which*

مِنْ (min): *from/than*

مِنَ المُؤَكَّد أنْ (min al-mu'akkad 'an): *it is certain that*

مِنَ المُقَرَّر أنْ (min al-muqarrar 'an): *it is decided that*

مِن حين إلى حين (min Hiinin 'ilaa Hiinin): *from time to time*

مُؤَلِّف (mu'allif): *composer*

مُتَأَسِّف (muta'assif): *sorry*

مُتَأكِّد (muta'akkid): *certain*

مُتَفائِل (mutafaa'il): *optimistic*

مُحَرِّك (**muHarrik**): *engine*

مُحَرِّر (**muHarrir**): *editor*

مُحاضَرة (**muHaaDara**): *lecture*

مُخْلِص (**mukhliS**): *sincere(ly)*

مُدَرِّس (**mudarris**): *teacher*

مُدير (**mudiir**): *director*

مُذيع (**mudhii3**): *announcer*

مُرَشَّخ (**murashshakh**): *candidate*

مُساعِد (**musaa3id**): *assistant/helper*

مُسْتَشْفَيات / مُسْتَشْفى (**mustashfaa** / **mustashfayaat**): *hospital*

مُسْتَعِدّ (**musta3idd**): *ready/prepared*

مَشاكِل / مُشْكِلة (**mushkila** / **mashaakil**): *problem*

مُظْلِم (**muDHlim**): *dark*

مُغَنّي (**mughannii**) *singer*

مُفاوَضة (**mufaawaDa**): *negotiation*

مُفَضَّل (**mufaDDal**): *preferable/favorite*

مُفيد (**mufiid**): *useful*

مُمْتاز (**mumtaaz**): *excellent*

مُنْتَجات (**muntajaat**): *products*

مُهِمّ (**muhimm**): *important/interesting*

مُوافِق (**muwaafiq**): *agreeing*

مُوَظَّف (**muwaDHDHaf**): *employee*

نيران / نار (**naar** / **niiraan**): *fire*

نامَ / يَنامُ (**naama** / **yanaamu**): *to sleep*

نَجاح (**najaaH**): *success*

نَحْنُ (**naHnu**): *we*

نَجَمات / نَجْمة (**najma** / **najamaat**): *star*

نَظَفاء / نَظيف (**naDHiif** / **nuDHafaa'**): *clean*

نَقْل (**naql**): *transportation*

نَفى / يَنْفي (**nafaa** / **yanfii**): *to deny*

نَفْس (**nafs**): *same (with following genitive)*

نَوْم (**nawm**): *sleep*

أَنْظِمة / نِظام (**niDHaam** / **'anDHima**): *system*

هذا (**haadhaa**): *this (MS)*

هذِه (**haadhihi**): *this (FS)*

هَواتِف / هاتِف (**haatif** / **hawaatif**): *telephone*

هَلْ (**hal**): *(particle introducing question)*

هَدايا / هَدية (**hadiya** / **hadaayaa**): *gift/present*

هُم (**hum**): *they*

هُنا (**hunaa**): *here*

هُناكَ (**hunaaka**): *there*

هُوَ (**huwa**): *he*

هِيَ (**hiya**): *she*

و (**wa-**): *and (prefixed to next word)*

وَجَبَ / يَجِبُ (**wajaba** / **yajibu**): *to be necessary*

وَجَدَ / يَجِدُ (**wajada** / **yajidu**): *find*

وَحيد (**waHiid**): *only/alone*

وَرَق (**waraq**): *paper*

وَرَق عِنَب (**waraq 3inab**): *stuffed grape leaves*

وَصَفَ / يَصِفُ (**waSafa** / **yaSifu**): *to describe*

وَصَلَ / يَصِلُ (**waSala** / **yaSilu**): *to arrive*

وَظائِف / وَظيفة (**waDHiifa** / **waDHaa'if**): *job*

أَوْقات / وَقْت (**waqt** / **'awqaat**): *time*

وَقَّعَ / يُوَقِّعُ (**waqqa3a** / **yuwaqqi3u**): *to sign (with **bi-**)*

أَوْلاد / وَلَد (**walad** / **'awlaad**): *boy/child*

أَيّام / يَوْم (**yawm** / **'ayyaam**): *day*

Index

• N •

• O •

• *Q* •

• *R* •

• *S* •

• Z •

BUSINESS, CAREERS & PERSONAL FINANCE

Accounting For Dummies, 4th Edition*
978-0-470-24600-9

Bookkeeping Workbook For Dummies†
978-0-470-16983-4

Commodities For Dummies
978-0-470-04928-0

Doing Business in China For Dummies
978-0-470-04929-7

E-Mail Marketing For Dummies
978-0-470-19087-6

Job Interviews For Dummies, 3rd Edition*†
978-0-470-17748-8

Personal Finance Workbook For Dummies*†
978-0-470-09933-9

Real Estate License Exams For Dummies
978-0-7645-7623-2

Six Sigma For Dummies
978-0-7645-6798-8

Small Business Kit For Dummies, 2nd Edition*†
978-0-7645-5984-6

Telephone Sales For Dummies
978-0-470-16836-3

BUSINESS PRODUCTIVITY & MICROSOFT OFFICE

Access 2007 For Dummies
978-0-470-03649-5

Excel 2007 For Dummies
978-0-470-03737-9

Office 2007 For Dummies
978-0-470-00923-9

Outlook 2007 For Dummies
978-0-470-03830-7

PowerPoint 2007 For Dummies
978-0-470-04059-1

Project 2007 For Dummies
978-0-470-03651-8

QuickBooks 2008 For Dummies
978-0-470-18470-7

Quicken 2008 For Dummies
978-0-470-17473-9

Salesforce.com For Dummies, 2nd Edition
978-0-470-04893-1

Word 2007 For Dummies
978-0-470-03658-7

EDUCATION, HISTORY, REFERENCE & TEST PREPARATION

African American History For Dummies
978-0-7645-5469-8

Algebra For Dummies
978-0-7645-5325-7

Algebra Workbook For Dummies
978-0-7645-8467-1

Art History For Dummies
978-0-470-09910-0

ASVAB For Dummies, 2nd Edition
978-0-470-10671-6

British Military History For Dummies
978-0-470-03213-8

Calculus For Dummies
978-0-7645-2498-1

Canadian History For Dummies, 2nd Edition
978-0-470-83656-9

Geometry Workbook For Dummies
978-0-471-79940-5

The SAT I For Dummies, 6th Edition
978-0-7645-7193-0

Series 7 Exam For Dummies
978-0-470-09932-2

World History For Dummies
978-0-7645-5242-7

FOOD, HOME, GARDEN, HOBBIES & HOME

Bridge For Dummies, 2nd Edition
978-0-471-92426-5

Coin Collecting For Dummies, 2nd Edition
978-0-470-22275-1

Cooking Basics For Dummies, 3rd Edition
978-0-7645-7206-7

Drawing For Dummies
978-0-7645-5476-6

Etiquette For Dummies, 2nd Edition
978-0-470-10672-3

Gardening Basics For Dummies*†
978-0-470-03749-2

Knitting Patterns For Dummies
978-0-470-04556-5

Living Gluten-Free For Dummies†
978-0-471-77383-2

Painting Do-It-Yourself For Dummies
978-0-470-17533-0

HEALTH, SELF HELP, PARENTING & PETS

Anger Management For Dummies
978-0-470-03715-7

Anxiety & Depression Workbook For Dummies
978-0-7645-9793-0

Dieting For Dummies, 2nd Edition
978-0-7645-4149-0

Dog Training For Dummies, 2nd Edition
978-0-7645-8418-3

Horseback Riding For Dummies
978-0-470-09719-9

Infertility For Dummies†
978-0-470-11518-3

Meditation For Dummies with CD-ROM, 2nd Edition
978-0-471-77774-8

Post-Traumatic Stress Disorder For Dummies
978-0-470-04922-8

Puppies For Dummies, 2nd Edition
978-0-470-03717-1

Thyroid For Dummies, 2nd Edition†
978-0-471-78755-6

Type 1 Diabetes For Dummies*†
978-0-470-17811-9

---

* Separate Canadian edition also available
† Separate U.K. edition also available

INTERNET & DIGITAL MEDIA

AdWords For Dummies
978-0-470-15252-2

Blogging For Dummies, 2nd Edition
978-0-470-23017-6

**Digital Photography All-in-One
Desk Reference For Dummies, 3rd Edition**
978-0-470-03743-0

**Digital Photography For Dummies,
5th Edition**
978-0-7645-9802-9

**Digital SLR Cameras & Photography
For Dummies, 2nd Edition**
978-0-470-14927-0

**eBay Business All-in-One Desk Reference
For Dummies**
978-0-7645-8438-1

eBay For Dummies, 5th Edition*
978-0-470-04529-9

eBay Listings That Sell For Dummies
978-0-471-78912-3

Facebook For Dummies
978-0-470-26273-3

The Internet For Dummies, 11th Edition
978-0-470-12174-0

**Investing Online For Dummies,
5th Edition**
978-0-7645-8456-5

iPod & iTunes For Dummies, 5th Edition
978-0-470-17474-6

MySpace For Dummies
978-0-470-09529-4

Podcasting For Dummies
978-0-471-74898-4

**Search Engine Optimization
For Dummies, 2nd Edition**
978-0-471-97998-2

Second Life For Dummies
978-0-470-18025-9

**Starting an eBay Business For Dummies,
3rd Edition†**
978-0-470-14924-9

GRAPHICS, DESIGN & WEB DEVELOPMENT

**Adobe Creative Suite 3 Design Premium
All-in-One Desk Reference For Dummies**
978-0-470-11724-8

**Adobe Web Suite CS3 All-in-One Desk
Reference For Dummies**
978-0-470-12099-6

AutoCAD 2008 For Dummies
978-0-470-11650-0

**Building a Web Site For Dummies,
3rd Edition**
978-0-470-14928-7

**Creating Web Pages All-in-One Desk
Reference For Dummies, 3rd Edition**
978-0-470-09629-1

**Creating Web Pages For Dummies,
8th Edition**
978-0-470-08030-6

Dreamweaver CS3 For Dummies
978-0-470-11490-2

Flash CS3 For Dummies
978-0-470-12100-9

Google SketchUp For Dummies
978-0-470-13744-4

InDesign CS3 For Dummies
978-0-470-11865-8

**Photoshop CS3 All-in-One
Desk Reference For Dummies**
978-0-470-11195-6

Photoshop CS3 For Dummies
978-0-470-11193-2

Photoshop Elements 5 For Dummies
978-0-470-09810-3

SolidWorks For Dummies
978-0-7645-9555-4

Visio 2007 For Dummies
978-0-470-08983-5

Web Design For Dummies, 2nd Edition
978-0-471-78117-2

Web Sites Do-It-Yourself For Dummies
978-0-470-16903-2

Web Stores Do-It-Yourself For Dummies
978-0-470-17443-2

LANGUAGES, RELIGION & SPIRITUALITY

Arabic For Dummies
978-0-471-77270-5

Chinese For Dummies, Audio Set
978-0-470-12766-7

French For Dummies
978-0-7645-5193-2

German For Dummies
978-0-7645-5195-6

Hebrew For Dummies
978-0-7645-5489-6

Ingles Para Dummies
978-0-7645-5427-8

Italian For Dummies, Audio Set
978-0-470-09586-7

Italian Verbs For Dummies
978-0-471-77389-4

Japanese For Dummies
978-0-7645-5429-2

Latin For Dummies
978-0-7645-5431-5

Portuguese For Dummies
978-0-471-78738-9

Russian For Dummies
978-0-471-78001-4

Spanish Phrases For Dummies
978-0-7645-7204-3

Spanish For Dummies
978-0-7645-5194-9

Spanish For Dummies, Audio Set
978-0-470-09585-0

The Bible For Dummies
978-0-7645-5296-0

Catholicism For Dummies
978-0-7645-5391-2

The Historical Jesus For Dummies
978-0-470-16785-4

Islam For Dummies
978-0-7645-5503-9

**Spirituality For Dummies,
2nd Edition**
978-0-470-19142-2

NETWORKING AND PROGRAMMING

ASP.NET 3.5 For Dummies
978-0-470-19592-5

C# 2008 For Dummies
978-0-470-19109-5

Hacking For Dummies, 2nd Edition
978-0-470-05235-8

Home Networking For Dummies, 4th Edition
978-0-470-11806-1

Java For Dummies, 4th Edition
978-0-470-08716-9

**Microsoft® SQL Server™ 2008 All-in-One
Desk Reference For Dummies**
978-0-470-17954-3

**Networking All-in-One Desk Reference
For Dummies, 2nd Edition**
978-0-7645-9939-2

**Networking For Dummies,
8th Edition**
978-0-470-05620-2

SharePoint 2007 For Dummies
978-0-470-09941-4

**Wireless Home Networking
For Dummies, 2nd Edition**
978-0-471-74940-0

OPERATING SYSTEMS & COMPUTER BASICS

Mac For Dummies, 5th Edition
978-0-7645-8458-9

Laptops For Dummies, 2nd Edition
978-0-470-05432-1

Linux For Dummies, 8th Edition
978-0-470-11649-4

MacBook For Dummies
978-0-470-04859-7

Mac OS X Leopard All-in-One Desk Reference For Dummies
978-0-470-05434-5

Mac OS X Leopard For Dummies
978-0-470-05433-8

Macs For Dummies, 9th Edition
978-0-470-04849-8

PCs For Dummies, 11th Edition
978-0-470-13728-4

Windows® Home Server For Dummies
978-0-470-18592-6

Windows Server 2008 For Dummies
978-0-470-18043-3

Windows Vista All-in-One Desk Reference For Dummies
978-0-471-74941-7

Windows Vista For Dummies
978-0-471-75421-3

Windows Vista Security For Dummies
978-0-470-11805-4

SPORTS, FITNESS & MUSIC

Coaching Hockey For Dummies
978-0-470-83685-9

Coaching Soccer For Dummies
978-0-471-77381-8

Fitness For Dummies, 3rd Edition
978-0-7645-7851-9

Football For Dummies, 3rd Edition
978-0-470-12536-6

GarageBand For Dummies
978-0-7645-7323-1

Golf For Dummies, 3rd Edition
978-0-471-76871-5

Guitar For Dummies, 2nd Edition
978-0-7645-9904-0

Home Recording For Musicians For Dummies, 2nd Edition
978-0-7645-8884-6

iPod & iTunes For Dummies, 5th Edition
978-0-470-17474-6

Music Theory For Dummies
978-0-7645-7838-0

Stretching For Dummies
978-0-470-06741-3

Get smart @ dummies.com®

- **Find a full list of Dummies titles**
- **Look into loads of FREE on-site articles**
- **Sign up for FREE eTips e-mailed to you weekly**
- **See what other products carry the Dummies name**
- **Shop directly from the Dummies bookstore**
- **Enter to win new prizes every month!**